Capturing

Jack the Ripper

NEIL R. A. BELL

AMBERLEY

First published 2014

Amberley Publishing
The Hill, Stroud
Gloucestershire, GL5 4EP

www.amberley-books.com

British Library Cataloguing in Publication Data.
A catalogue record for this book is available from the British Library.

ISBN 978-1-4456-2162-3 (hardback)
ISBN 978-1-4456-2168-5 (ebook)

Typesetting and Origination by Amberley Publishing.
Printed in the UK.

Contents

Foreword by M. W. Oldridge   5

Part One: The Establishment of the Police Force   7
1   I Beg to Report   9
2   The Birth of the Bobby   11
3   Recruitment   30
4   Police Stations and Section Houses   42
5   Blue Bottles   60
6   Tecs   93

Part Two: The Murders   109
7   Emma Smith, 4 April 1888   111
8   Martha Tabram, 7 August 1888   119
9   Mary Ann 'Polly' Nichols, 31 August 1888   128
10   Annie Chapman, 8 September 1888   141
11   Elisabeth Stride, 30 September 1888   154
12   Catherine Eddowes, 30 September 1888   171
13   Letters, Leaflets, Lusk and a Lull   188
14   Mary Jane Kelly, 9 November 1888   196
15   After the Canon, 1888–91   211

Notes   222
Acknowledgements   246
Index   249

Foreword by M. W. Oldridge

Jack the Ripper's awful innovations took place against a social canvas which made policing difficult at best. Late Victorian London was a miscegenation of stinking industry, radical politics, terrorism and – particularly, but not exclusively, in east London – appalling poverty. In fact, with the possible exception of terrorism, which targeted the more prestigious and symbolic locales further west, Whitechapel, Spitalfields, St George in the East and the other areas which were known – are known – collectively as the East End portrayed the capital's general social problems as if examined through a microscope. Intense want appeared all the more intense through the East End's unique lens; gruesome lifestyles seemed all the more gruesome; those who were on the margins of society disappeared into deep orbit, distant satellites of the global authority of the British Empire. Amid it all, serial murder broke out. If this was a phenomenon which was, strictly speaking, not unknown before widespread industrialisation, it was nonetheless one which only reached its unhappy maturity in post-industrial society.

The police were neither ready nor equipped to compete with the Ripper's audacity; they were unfamiliar with his strangely modern ways. Public scandals had affected popular confidence, and there was dissension within the upper ranks. Modernising trends met opaque organisational inertia head on. Journalists, especially those working for publications with overt political leanings, had their say, criticising, hinting at mismanagement. Jack the Ripper wrote – or so it was said – to a news agency, and managed his own publicity strategy; but the police were finding bloodhounds to be a technology beyond their ability to marshal.

In this book, Neil Bell considers the strengths and weaknesses of the attempts of London's twin police forces to capture Jack the Ripper. In addition, however, he takes us behind the scenes, into the offices of Scotland Yard and the cells at Commercial Street alike. We peek at the disagreements among London's most senior policemen, and we admire the honesty and decency of constables with – in more than a few cases – quite limited professional experience. We watch as strategies come and go, as efficiencies are wrung out, and as new protocols are forced to develop.

And we see the personal cost of policing; the mark that the job left on its practitioners and their families; the risks that were sometimes faced; the camaraderie and the stress; and, swirling around every lonely bobby on the beat with only his lantern for company, the night-side of nature in the den of the East End.

Jack the Ripper's notoriety left his victims and his pursuers frozen in aspic, remembered now though so many others are forgotten, immortalised by their association with the world's most famous, and yet most faceless, murderer. Here, we look more closely at the men who could not see their own prey clearly enough. Grope forwards in the enveloping darkness, and lift the beam to read ...

M. W. Oldridge
June 2014

PART ONE

The Establishment of the Police Force

1

I Beg to Report

Reviewing the literature on the subject of Jack the Ripper, both authors were struck that despite the plethora of books, nobody had approached the subject from the police viewpoint.[1]

Stewart P. Evans and Donald Rumbelow,
Scotland Yard Investigates (2006)

The quotation above, written by two former police constables with many years' service, who both hold a deserved position of esteem in the annals of historical true crime research and literature, draws attention to a key aspect of the Whitechapel Murder cases, and that of Jack the Ripper,[2] namely the minimal understanding by students on the subject of policing procedure and protocol during the period these crimes were occurring. Their work, *Scotland Yard Investigates*, is pivotal in that quest to comprehend the police investigative aspect of the Whitechapel murders, and therefore those of Jack the Ripper. While other books such as *Jack the Ripper Sourcebook*[3] and *The Complete History of Jack the* Ripper[4] both provide a supreme factual account of surviving police records held on the crimes, as well as excellent overviews of the whole case, there is no in-depth book which covers the day-to-day life of being a constable in Whitechapel during this specific period in the late Victorian era, when a serial killer walked the streets and alleyways of London's East End. It is my intention to shed some light on this life as a Victorian police constable during the height of these most infamous of crimes, in hopes that it grants us a better understanding not just of those police procedures and protocols, but also what it was like for the individual to police the most dangerous urban area in London, if not the world.

This book intends to provide an in-depth understanding of the police aspect during the period, and in particular in connection to the Whitechapel murders and those of 'Jack the Ripper'. It aims to comprehend how the police operated during this time, and why, and what exactly was required for a man to be a constable in H Division and the City of London Police in and around 1888. We shall be looking into the history of the City of

London and Metropolitan Police forces, how a Victorian man would apply to join the police, what training was undertaken, what equipment was used, what life was like in a police station and section house, what duties were carried out and what roles were taken on. We will also take a look at protocols and investigation methods of the Victorian police, taking a specific example from each of the Whitechapel Murder cases, and analysing it for better understanding, and well as revealing, for the first time, insights on police procedure directly connected to the Whitechapel Murder investigations.

So, let us view the most famous mystery of them all from a different angle – that of a Victorian policeman trying to capture Jack the Ripper.

Neil R. A. Bell
Leicestershire, June 2014

2

The Birth of the Bobby

I will first organise a force.

Sir Robert Peel, 1828

The Metropolitan Police Act (1829) and the City of London Police Act (1839) created two new organisations within the city and metropolis of London. Each was dedicated, on the one hand, to the apprehension of criminals and to their presentation before the judiciary; and, on the other, to the maintenance of public order and the peace. The structural and methodological principles that these new police forces established were soon to be adopted in numerous other cities around the world, and their basic infrastructure continues to influence policing today. To understand how these organisations came into being one must first examine the complexities of policing prior to 1829, and to do that we must go back some distance into history.

All successful communities across the globe, no matter how big or how ancient, have cherished order as a foundation stone. In small nomadic tribes and great civilisations alike, it is realised that, to thrive as a collective and as an individual within that collective, order and peace must ultimately prevail. Law and order within the British Isles really started to develop during the tribal Anglo-Saxon period. There was great turmoil not just between tribes but also within them. However, King Alfred of Wessex managed to unite a large number of tribes under a single code when he introduced the Doom Book,[1] the foundation to common law. While the king and his advisers drew up the laws of the land, law and order was predominantly maintained locally. Shire-reeves[2] were appointed and held personally responsible by the king's administrators for keeping the peace within their particular shire, holding the right of high justice and, if needs be, execution. They would hold regular court and preside over sittings, meting out fair judgement and punishment as they did so. Providing the physical presence of the law was the tythingman.[3] He was in command of a small group of men and reported to the shire-reeve. The men, known as tythings, patrolled the shire, maintaining the peace as they did so and bringing wrongdoers before the shire-reeve for judgement.

After the Norman invasion of the British Isles in 1066, William I took the throne, making a promise to his new kingdom that the laws of the land would remain as they were under previous kings. The basic tythingman system remained; however, there were certain areas within the kingdom in which the common law was disregarded, with local injustices taking its place. A reform of the tythingman system was required and, in 1195, King Richard I, choosing to address this very issue, decided that a few of his knights should be despatched across the land to enforce the common law and the king's peace. These keepers of the peace, or conservators of the peace as they were also known, were assigned to areas where court hearings were held and would pass judgement on criminals brought before them.[4]

In the Ordinance of 1252,[5] King Henry III formalised the role of the parish constable and decreed that each parish should maintain one or two constables. However, the Statute of Winchester, which was introduced under King Edward I in 1285, reformed the Ordinance of 1252 yet further, instigating the watch and ward systems and bringing increasing organisation to the judicial system. The powers and responsibilities of the parish constable were also clarified.

The Justices of the Peace Act (1361) modified the role of Richard I's conservators of the peace, excluding knights and replacing them with trusted, respected, law-abiding local citizens who would uphold order and the peace. The title of justice of the peace, which thereby came into being just over 650 years ago, is still with us today – nowadays, however, they are more typically referred to as magistrates. While the justices of the peace were to uphold the laws of the land, they were not expected to track down and apprehend criminals; this task remained with the community, the watchman and the constable. In particular, it was the community's responsibility to report all crimes to the watchman or constable. Watchmen were paid by townsfolk to protect them from undesirable strangers and criminals. They were also expected to apprehend felons and to present them to the constable, who would detain them before presenting them to the justice of the peace.

Constables were appointed by the justice of the peace and typically took on the duty for around a year. The justices of the peace chose only reliable, upstanding people for the role – often they selected property owners, who were thought to have just the right motive to be highly vigilant. Their own premises would, of course, be as vulnerable to prowling burglars as any others in the parish. On the other hand, the constable's job was unpaid and taken on in addition to one's own daily work, so the prospect of being summoned to fulfil this enforced duty was not an attractive one for most. Some well-to-do citizens summonsed to the role would actually hire a third party to undertake the constable's labours, and this was accepted as long as the duty was covered. In some areas, such as Westminster and the City of London, paid beadles were used to assist the constable if required.[6] The constable was expected to investigate and provide reports of crimes, felons and nuisances to the justices of the peace, as well as executing any warrants they issued. Essentially, the constable was the long arm of the justices of the peace, obtaining information and seizing criminals to enable justice to be administered.

Though predominantly defenceless, constables were permitted to carry truncheons; however, even these were more symbolic than practical. Decorated with a painted seal of authority and hung outside the belt, the truncheon functioned as a sign that its holder was authorised to conduct the duties of a constable. They were also hung outside constables' homes to show who dwelt inside; in this way, they were the forerunners to the iconic blue lamp of more recent years. At times of crisis, the justices of the peace had the power to recruit more constables, forming a sort of *posse comitatus*. During these periods, the justices of the peace also had the right to ensure that constables were armed to defend themselves and restore order. While the justice of the peace had legal authority, and was supported by the work of the constable, the onus to maintain order remained with the community. Any constable who was struggling to apprehend a criminal was entitled to expect the assistance of the public around him; in fact, it was expected that the public should be ready to join in with the 'Hue and Cry'[7] and aid a constable at any time. After all, he was one of their own.

The watchman can trace his origins way back to biblical times; however, it was the Ordinance of 1233 that formally created the official position of watchman[8] within England. The role was developed to protect urban settlements at night, especially the City of London, which had grown into an extremely important commercial trading point by this time. The main threat to a watchman was not from wrongdoers within but from external attack, so his primary duty was to patrol the city walls at night, ensuring that the 'undesired' remained outside. The City of London was split into small areas known as wards. The watchmen were paid by those living within the wards to patrol their streets between the City's extremes, from the River Thames to the south and along the City Wall and gates.[9] Armed with a staff, holding a lantern for light, their task was to watch for potential wrongdoers entering London after curfew with the intention to pillage and steal, among other things. However, the watchman also undertook a secondary role. Any crimes spotted by him, whether perpetrated by locals or visitors, were reported to the constable who, in turn, conducted his investigations and reported to the justice of the peace. Any criminals apprehended by the watchman would also be handed over to the constable for detention, and then presentation before the court.

In 1663, during the reign of King Charles II, the Act of Common Council saw the deployment of a thousand men in a special force of night watchmen; these watchmen soon acquired the nickname of 'Charlies', after the king, and it was this name which stuck with the watchmen from then on in. This force was chiefly made up of elderly men who were no match for the young 'ruffians' of the day. They were rarely effective and were open to corruption and bribery, and it wasn't unusual for the watchman to be in cahoots with the villain. They also got a reputation for being lazy, hiding in their watch-boxes[10] and playing cards rather than catching criminals.[11] Overall, the Charlie was a despised and ridiculed individual and not trusted at all. Along with the watchmen and constables, the City of London had an extra level of policing authority built into its civic structure, this being the city marshal. He came under the authority not of the justice of the peace but rather the aldermen[12] and ultimately the Lord Mayor of London himself. The city marshal's responsibilities included supervising policing within the City, hiring constables and supplementary constables as required for events such as fairs and parades, and maintaining records – to name but a few. It was a paid, uniformed role and came with authority, as the city marshal also had one under-marshal and six[13] men to assist him in his work.

One other early policing role played a pivotal and notorious part in the build-up to the creation of the police force. During the seventeenth century, crime was perceived to be rife. In fact, it was only slightly worse than previous periods; however, the newspapers acted as a catalyst which fuelled the public's panic. This fairly new medium filled its pages with dreadful news of lawlessness, of terrible robberies and horrific murders. It was clear the constables and watchmen were no match for the criminals and those with enterprising minds saw a gap in the policing market. Privateers offered their services to victims of crime, promising to track down the thieves and reclaim their stolen goods for some small recompense. The age of the thief taker was born; some were not the protectors of justice and property they portrayed themselves to be. Probably the best-known of all thief takers was Jonathan Wild.[14] The son of a carpenter, and himself a buckle maker by trade, Wild had dabbled in petty crime before finding a more substantial role as a receiver of stolen goods. The receiver was a person to whom thieves would take their stolen goods to sell. Once a payment was made, the receiver then did one of two things. Firstly, he would anonymously approach the original owners via correspondence, claiming that he had heard of their recent 'misfortune' and stating that he was a person of some prominence. He would also claim that he may be able to obtain and return the stolen goods for a small fee. If the original owner agreed, the receiver would return to his premises, wait a few days, and then return with the stolen items – much to the pleasure of the owner, who would then hand over payment. If the original owner declined, the receiver would simply sell the goods on. In 1714, one of London's most notorious receivers was Charles Hitchen, who also happened to be an under-marshal for the City of London, trying to apprehend the very criminals who worked for him.[15]

Meanwhile, the old men of the watch system were being overrun by the criminal underworld. They were seen as either comical figures – old, infirm and unfit for purpose – or as corrupt, devious characters open to bribery and always on the lookout to benefit themselves rather than the community. The elderly watchmen were often openly challenged or disregarded as powerless, while the palming of a coin to a more corrupt watchman could ensure that street beatings and robbery were conveniently missed. Such acts were extremely common and it wasn't unheard of for thieves to brandish weapons and just walk into people's homes, stealing items from under the noses of their occupiers. A series of Watch Acts passed through Parliament during the early to mid-1700s in an effort to improve the watch situation. One Act, passed in 1735, increased parish taxes in order to help swell the numbers of watchmen in Westminster, and to provide them with new equipment. The City of London followed suit for their wards, with the introduction of the 1737 Watchman and Beadles Regulation Act, which decreed that the number of watchmen required to maintain order was to be left to the discretion of the wards and precincts.[16] It also allowed for the wards to levy taxes as they deemed fit. While Westminster and City led the way, other parishes across the metropolis followed suit; however, not all had the wealth of Parliament hosts Westminster or the financial stronghold of the City of London. The poorer parishes could not squeeze the required funds to help pay for better equipment and more men, and thus they rode the downward spiral as their inhabitants tried to fight off the evils of corruption and wrongdoing, becoming notorious playgrounds for crime and criminals.

While all in power agreed that wholesale changes were necessary, they would neither fund nor drive them. Accordingly, these Acts altered the watch system, but only gradually. Thanks to this new taxation the watchmen were being paid a slightly better wage, which brought slightly better standards. No one during this period can be pointed out as a better example of the improvement in these policing standards than the chief magistrate for Westminster, the novelist Henry Fielding.[17] Fielding was an astute man who seemed to have his finger on the very pulse of the issue; he was appointed chief magistrate in 1748 and held office at Bow Street in London.[18] Soon he was joined by his equally astute young half-brother John, who was blind,[19] and between them they devised and implemented many radical ideas designed to tackle the crime issue within London. Partly funded by a government which had recognised that the issue of crime could no longer be ignored, Fielding formed his own crack team of thief takers in 1749 and assigned them to his magistrates' court. These men, all constables, were selected for their intelligence, reliability, good character and the fact they were considered irreproachable: they were the Untouchables of their period. This new body formed to tackle crime became known as Mr Fielding's People, and as the years passed they expanded into a policing unit feared throughout the criminal underworld of London. Though they never recognised the name themselves, seeing it as a derogatory term, the world's first organised policing force, the Bow Street Runners, had arrived.

The issue that the Bow Street force had throughout its existence was funding. There was little money in the government coffers, and they were sometimes the victims of their own success. Critics would seize on a reduced crime rate – the result of properly funded work – to argue for subsequent funding cuts, which risked a return to higher crime rates. As ever, their main source of income was the irregular payment of reward monies, which left the door open for the corrupt to approach and attempt to buy off the more financially vulnerable of Fielding's men.[20] The situation was compounded by an ingrained belief across the land that the policing of the people should be predominately conducted by the people and not the government. The watchmen, who were being paid by the populace, remained in post, and there was great resistance to any reform. This national mindset was very hard for the police reformers to shake and the battle was hard and constant. However, while the old policing system remained, Fielding had nonetheless achieved something with his Bow Street office. He had erased some of the old stigmas of inefficiency and instilled in the public a new respect for his men. And when Fielding died in 1754 it was only natural that his half-brother John would succeed him. John Fielding continued the good working practices which he and his half-brother had established in the early years of the Bow Street force, and the Blind Beak of Bow, as John was known, introduced radical new ideas to aid them in their work, such as the use of constables on horseback. In later years, their brightly coloured red waistcoats gave them the nickname of 'Robin Redbreasts'.[21] He also introduced a publication, *The Quarterly Pursuit*, the forerunner to *The Police Gazette*, which gave information on criminals and recent crimes, escapees and the wanted, and this improved and rationalised information-sharing systems. Meanwhile, the conflict between the rapid evolution of detection work in the Bow Street office and the slow evolution of preventive policing outside it remained obvious, although there were slight improvements to the latter. The year 1774 saw the Westminster Watch Act come into effect across London. While the Act permitted parishes to continue their control of their own watchmen, it laid down a standard rate of pay and basic duties for all watchmen to abide by, thus slightly alleviating corruption within the watch.

The seed of the next major moment in the policing history of Great Britain lay in events far across the Atlantic Ocean, in the American colonies, and it grew into a huge thorn in the side of the British government on the other side of that ocean. The American War of Independence in the years 1775–83 had drained the British Army of its men. In order to recruit rapidly, the Papist Act of 1778 removed the need for Catholics to take the religious oath when joining the Army, as well as redressing some of the anti-Catholic imbalances caused by the Popery Act of 1698.[22] Many Protestants, led by Lord George Gordon, the President of the Protestant Association, objected to this reform and organised protest marches throughout 1779 and 1780. On 2 June 1780, a mob of around 60,000 Protestants marched on Parliament, surrounding the Houses of Commons and Lords. Soon violence erupted; some Members of Parliament had their coaches attacked and some received blows themselves. The small numbers of constables in attendance were simply no match for the mob, and it was ordered that a small detachment of soldiers be sent for. With their arrival, peace was seemingly restored; during the evening, however, the rioting began again. Firstly the Chapel of the Sardinian ambassador was burnt down and the Bavarian Embassy in Soho was then ransacked and recklessly destroyed. For five days there were outbreaks of rioting across London. The Bow Street force made thirteen arrests but could not pin the ringleaders. Moorfields, a poor area of London in what is known today as Moorgate, was home to a large Irish Catholic community. That was set upon, with many homes destroyed. The prisons of Newgate and the Clink were also targeted, with some of the escaping prisoners never being recaptured, and even the Bow Street force itself had its offices burnt out. From Clerkenwell to Whitechapel, from Holborn and back to the Houses of Parliament, disorder reigned until, on 7 June, the Army stepped in to break the riots. Made up chiefly of Horse and Foot Guards, with support from the Honourable Artillery Company, West Surrey Queen's Royals and militias from the surrounding counties, they quashed the mobs. The result of the Army's introduction was 285 deaths, 200 wounded and 450 arrests, with thirty of the latter being executed. The Gordon Riots, as they became known, highlighted from a policing viewpoint just how ill-prepared for mass disturbances the authorities truly were.

The reliance on a military solution did not sit well with either the public or the government, and it was clear that an overhaul of the watch system was in order. In 1785, five years after the Gordon Riots, Prime Minister William Pitt's Solicitor General, Archibald MacDonald, tried to bring about this reform by introducing the London and Westminster Police Bill of 1785 to Parliament.[23] The Bill, hoping to capitalise on the public's ill feeling towards the perpetrators of crime in the wake of the riots, showed no mercy to the criminal classes; however, it also showed no mercy to the common, law-abiding man. It permitted constables to enter properties with little or no good reason, and, should the homeowner complain and lay his hand upon the constable, the latter had the power to instantly arrest them under the threat of several years' imprisonment or even transportation.[24] Although MacDonald suggested a year's trial of the Bill, it was withdrawn. However, it must be recognised as a precursor to the 1829 Metropolitan Police Act, as it proposed a policing amalgamation between the City of London, Westminster, the Borough of Southwark and other adjacent areas. This police force would have been split into nine smaller areas called divisions and, had it been passed, the Bill would have seen the City of London integrated into the area covered by the Metropolitan Police. Another precursor to the creation of the Metropolitan Police Force which occurred in 1785 was the introduction of the 'City wide Patrole'. These were a group of men who patrolled the City of London at night, keeping a specific eye on vagrants and the drunk and disorderly. These men were very much akin to the special constables or the community support officers of today. Their uniform was to become familiar forty-four years later as it comprised a blue coat and hat, the very colours which the new police were to adopt.

In 1792, seven new police office buildings, inspired by the successful Bow Street office, were built at Hatton Gardens, Worship Street, Lambeth Street, Whitechapel, Shadwell, Union Hall in Westminster and Great Marlborough Street. It was the birth of the modern interlocking station system across London which still survives until this day. Sitting within these buildings were three magistrates,[25] six constables and resident clerks, gaolers and housekeepers.[26] Though the need for an independent police force was recognised, this increase in buildings and numbers was more a reaction to the crime that was plaguing the period, mainly highway robbery, than to any outright proactive reorganisation and restructuring of a system which was fast becoming outdated.

The year 1798 saw the creation of what was technically the world's first organised police force, the Marine Police Force.[27] The Pool of London[28] was besieged with thieves taking cargo and goods worth an estimated £500,000 every year, predominantly from the West India Docks. It was a major concern and one which Seaman Captain John Harriott was determined to tackle. Harriot had worked for the army of the East India Company, joining them at the age of twenty-five and becoming a deputy judge advocate[29] before being invalided out with a gunshot wound. He had noted the amount of crime upon the vessels and warehouses of the Thames and felt the river's own police force would benefit the companies who traded there. So Harriott discussed this idea with his friend, the magistrate for Whitechapel, John Staples, and it was he who, in 1797, encouraged Harriott to draw up a plan for the policing of the Thames and to present it to the lord mayor, under whose jurisdiction the River Thames fell and within whose boundaries most of the shipping companies who suffered from this blight of crime were based. However, the lord mayor rejected his idea, so Harriott turned to the Home Secretary, the Duke of Portland, hoping that he would take it on.

Unbeknown to Harriott, who was still stewing in his frustration at the lack of interest in his proposal, Scottish magistrate Patrick Colquhoun[30] had also noted the same problem. Colquhoun was a successful businessman who had an eye for data and statistics. His *Treatise on the Police of the Metropolis* had been published in 1796.[31] Like Harriott, he also foresaw the benefits of a policed Thames and made a case for the creation of such a force to the West India Merchant Company. They agreed with his proposal and suggested that it be put forward to the government under their recommendation for approval. In the meantime, Whitechapel magistrate Staples got to hear about Colquhoun's plans and suggested to the latter that he speak to a man he knew who had proposed similar ideas, unsuccessfully, to the lord mayor. Colquhoun agreed, and he and Harriott met in early 1798 to discuss their ideas for the policing of the Thames. Colquhoun was so impressed by Harriott and his well thought-out plans that he offered an alliance, which Harriott accepted. The pair then acted on the West India Merchant Company's recommendation and lobbied the Member of Parliament for Midlothian, the then War Secretary Lord

Dundas.[32] Dundas agreed to take the idea to the Chancellor of the Exchequer, William Pitt the Younger,[33] who agreed to part-fund a year-long trial. Colquhoun and Harriott managed to persuade the West India Planters and Merchants Committee to provide the rest of the money; and so, with funding of £4,200, Harriott and Colquhoun hired fifty men to patrol the Thames and its bank, with Colquhoun acting as superintending magistrate and Harriott as residing magistrate. By the end of 1798, the Marine Police Office had been established.

Their task was initially a mammoth one, as the Port of London at that time held around 33,000 workers of which, Colquhoun claimed, a third were corrupt and working either for criminals or as criminals. However, the year-long trial showed that the Marine Force was a success. Colquhoun, a statistics and figures man, stated that his organisation had 'established their worth by saving £122,000 worth of cargo and by the rescuing of several lives'. The establishment and success of the Thames Police was a key step on the path to the establishment of the much bigger Metropolitan Police. While the Bow Street Office was highly organised on the magistrates' side, its success was sporadic, and the reliance on private funding for the constables had caused issues. Colquhoun had seen that the Thames constables received their wage from the force's bipartite funding, meaning that payment to these constables was steady. There was less need to 'turn a blind eye for a back hander', whereas, on occasion, the Bow Street constables had needed to 'supplement' their income in lean financial times. The Gordon Riots had highlighted the need for a specialist police force quite independent from the military, not only for maintaining order but for preventing and combating crime. The Colquhoun and Harriott template had shown this could be achieved; however, it was to be another thirty years before the final piece of the policing jigsaw was put into place.

In 1799, Colquhoun published his proposals on police reform entitled *The Report of the Select Committee of the House of Commons relative to the Establishment of a New police in the Metropolis*. The select committee was one of many to be set up over the coming years, with further committees meeting in 1812, 1818 and 1822 to discuss solutions to the growing crime epidemic. It was during this period that Great Britain was in the midst of revolution within its industry and its social history, and at the centre of it all was the capital, London. The revolution did not just alter manufacturing; it altered the lives of all living within that period. Farm machines operated by one or just a handful of men reduced the numbers of farm labourers within agriculture. Desperate for work, these now redundant men took their families from the countryside to the cities to find employment. While some were disappointed, resigning their families' fate to the workhouse,[34] homelessness and fragmentation, others found work in the dangerous factories which had grown like weeds in an unkempt garden, making thousands upon thousands of various manufactured items for a country whose clichéd empire never slept, never stopped. To support these factories and their workers a vast infrastructure was required. Trains and canals kept the flow of raw materials going to the factories, and then delivered finished goods to the ports for export. And who would build the new trains and narrow boats that carried these goods? Who would build the train tracks and dig the canals? Yes, even more men. And these men and their families needed to survive, so up sprouted substandard and swiftly constructed buildings to house them, and butchers and bakers and various shops and markets to feed them. So with the revolution came growth; the empire, in need of more raw materials, got bigger and, fed by these new materials, industry got bigger. The bigger the industry, the more men required to operate it; the cities swelled and with that massive influx inevitably came a massive increase in crime. Between the initial 1801 census and the 1811 census London's population had grown by 16.7 per cent, and over the same period crime had risen by 55 per cent.

Keeping this huge increase of crime in check were the lowly watchmen and constables. The policing system that had been creaking for many years was beginning to fall apart. It was now time for action.

The year 1828 saw yet another select committee set up by the then Home Secretary, Robert Peel,[35] under the encouragement of the prime minister, the Duke of Wellington. Peel had been in the role for six years and had sponsored the consolidation of over three hundred Acts of Parliament dealing with criminal offences into a more manageable four: the Criminal Statutes Repeal Act 1827 (7 & 8 Geo.4 c.27); the Larceny Act 1827 (7 & 8 Geo.4 c.29); the Malicious Injuries to Property Act 1827 (7 & 8 Geo.4 c.30); and the Offences against the Person Act 1828 (9 Geo.4 c.31). By introducing what where to be known as the Peel Acts,[36] Peel had simplified criminal law. The 1828 select committee hearing followed that legal reform by recommending a radical overhaul of the police system within London to government. In a letter to John Hobhouse,[37] Peel outlines his vision of a new police force by stating,

I have under my consideration at present very extensive changes in the Police of the metropolis.

You perhaps have read the Police Report of last Session. I am now employing Gregson in drawing up a Bill to give effect to the recommendations of the Report, so far as they concern the constitution of the nightly watch.

My plan is shortly this – to appoint some authority which shall take charge of the night police of the metropolis, connecting the force employed by night with the existing police establishments now under the Home Office and Bow Street; the authority which has charge of the police establishments, horse patrol, day patrol, night patrol, to act under the immediate superintendence of the Home Office, and in daily communication with it.

I propose that charge of the night police should be taken gradually. I mean that my system of police should be substituted for the parochial system, not per saltum, but by degrees.

I will first organise a force, which I will not call by the name of 'watchmen', which shall be sufficient to take charge of a district surrounding Charing

Cross, composed, we will say, of four or five parishes. It shall extend on the City side as far as Temple Bar and the boundary of the City on that side, having the river as far as Westminster Bridge as the limit on another side. When it is notified to the parishes that comprise this district that this force is ready to act, and prepared to take charge of the district, the functions of the parochial watch in each of the districts shall terminate, and no rates be thereafter leviable on that account.

In the same way, as a little experience shall enable us to manage a more numerous force of nightly police, I propose to signify to other parishes from time to time that the police will take charge of them. Their present watch will continue to act until such signification be made, and will cease when it is made.

Peel continues,

Now the out-parishes such places as Brentford, Twickenham Isleworth, Hounslow, and so forth – in all which the police at present is scandalous, will feel, and very justly, that if the new police system succeeds for London, it will injure them, by driving a fresh stock of thieves from the heart of the metropolis into the environs, and it will be a great object to me, as well as to them, to devise some mode of improving their police. If I undertook the immediate change my force would be too large, the machine would be too cumbrous and complicated to be well managed by one authority. How, therefore, shall I proceed to provide for these out-parishes?

My notion is to take power for the Secretary of State to consolidate parishes bordering on the metropolis into a district for police purposes, to appoint Commissioners of Police, two for instance, resident in each parish within the district, who shall have the general superintendence of the district police.[38]

The Bill Peel mentions in this letter presented to Parliament many of the recommendations of the 1828 select committee, stating that all the regular police offices within the London area were to be amalgamated and were to be funded mutually by the parishes and the Treasury, thus ensuring a steady income for the new organisation's employees and reducing corruption. The new force was answerable to the Home Secretary and not to the administrators of each parish, which caused dismay among the people of the parishes as they wished to control the very organisation they were paying for. However, Peel was not to have this force fragmented; he wanted a professionally run organisation, outside the influence of the parochial masters. Not included in this Bill was the City of London. The City resisted what was to become known as the Metropolitan Police Act, since it wished to keep its watchmen and city patrols. A struggle with the powers of the financial capital increased the risk of the Bill failing, and so Peel conceded that the square mile known as the City of London would be exempt from the Act, and would retain its own policing system. In return, he expected a favourable vote from the City's Members of Parliament. They reciprocated, and on 19 June 1829 the Metropolitan Police Act was passed by the Duke of Wellington's government.

Despite the passing of this Act, the Bow Street Office and the Marine Police remained in existence and outside the authority of the Metropolitan Police, whose initial jurisdiction lay across a section of central London of about seven miles from east to west and four miles from north to south, with Charing Cross at its centre. As he had stated in his letter to Hobhouse, Peel wanted two commissioners; so, on 29 August 1829, forty-six-year-old Waterloo and Peninsular War veteran Colonel Sir Charles Rowan and thirty-two-year-old barrister Richard Mayne were sworn in as justices of the peace[39] by Lord Chief William Alexander.[40] With his military experience, it was logical for Rowan to turn his attention to the organisation of the personnel side of the force, whereas Mayne focused his attention on the legal and regulatory aspects of this fledging organisation. By all accounts these two men worked extremely well together, becoming firm friends in the process.

The public viewed this new force with great suspicion, swiftly providing it with unforgiving labels such as 'Raw Lobsters'[41] and 'Blue Devils' to name but a few. The Duke of Portland presented a petition to Parliament signed by the inhabitants of Hackney against the new police;[42] this was one of many petitions created which opposed the new police force. There were many concerns. Some people had low expectations after their experience of the unsuitable watch system and parishes resented having to pay for a system over which they had no authority; there was even anxiety stemming from the robust and sometimes secretive methods used in the French police system. *La Sûreté Nationale*, as the French called their 1812 version of the police force, had been developed from Napoleon's Secret Political Police. It was synonymous with shadowy manipulations and investigations, operating an *agents provocateur* approach to entice criminal activity and therefore lure criminals to their fate. This was deeply frowned upon in England. Any sign of deceit, even for the greater good, was unpalatable and dishonourable in the extreme, and any militarisation of the new police was fiercely resisted. *The Westmoreland Gazette*, taking its lead from the London publication called *The Age*, summed up the public's concern when in its 'Spirit of Journal' column it wrote, 'We should not be surprised if, before a year or two – we should have all civil offices whatever filled by the sons of Mars.'[43]

So it would not have gone down too well with the people of London had they known that Peel had been in contact with the great French criminologist and creator of *La Sûreté*, Eugène François Vidocq,[44] in order to seek advice on the new police force. A former criminal himself, Vidocq was a poacher turned gamekeeper, having initially offered his services to the French authorities as an informer before soon becoming part of the French policing structure, taking the role of the initial chief of *La Sûreté*. Strict record keeping, ballistic investigations, surveillance and the use of materials for evidence-gathering (for example, using plaster of Paris to obtain footprints) are just a few examples of the innovative ideas Vidocq bought to modern policing. It was Vidocq who aided Peel in the selection of the building within which the new force was to be based. No. 4 Whitehall Place was a nondescript building buried in among the government buildings of Whitehall. The building backed onto Great Scotland Yard, and it was this name which soon became associated with the Metropolitan Police force and renowned throughout the world. On 26 September, the new force was paraded and sworn in on the grounds of Coram's Foundling Hospital in Bloomsbury.

A few days later, on 29 September 1829, the first 1,000 constables of the Metropolitan Police took to the streets of London, each issued with high-collared, swallow-tailed blue tunics with a truncheon pocket inside one of the swallow-tails, a leather collar called a stock (to protect against garrotting), a thick leather belt, high-cut Wellington boots, and a high beaver-skinned top hat referred to as a 'stovepipe', which protected against blows to the head. They were also given long wooden truncheons, barrel handcuffs and a rattle to alert for assistance.[45] The very first police constable assigned was William Atkinson, who did not last a day in his new job as he was found in a drunken stupor some four hours later and dismissed.[46] They received a weekly pay of twenty-one shillings, giving them the nickname of 'the Guinea a week men',[47] and their pay was funded by a special parish rate levied by the overseers of the poor. Their remit, like that of the police today, was the detection and prevention of crime. Peel established the *Nine Points of Policing*. These points, which are still followed to this day, are as follows:

The basic mission for which the police exist is to prevent crime and disorder.

The ability of the police to perform their duties is dependent upon public approval of police actions.

Police must secure the willing co-operation of the public in voluntary observance of the law to be able to secure and maintain the respect of the public.

The degree of co-operation of the public that can be secured diminishes proportionately to the necessity of the use of physical force.

Police seek and preserve public favour not by catering to public opinion but by constantly demonstrating absolute impartial service to the law.

Police use physical force to the extent necessary to secure observance of the law or to restore order only when the exercise of persuasion, advice and warning is found to be insufficient.

Police, at all times, should maintain a relationship with the public that gives reality to the historic tradition that the police are the public and the public are the police; the police being only members of the public who are paid to give full-time attention to duties which are incumbent on every citizen in the interests of community welfare and existence.

Police should always direct their action strictly towards their functions and never appear to usurp the powers of the judiciary.

The test of police efficiency is the absence of crime and disorder, not the visible evidence of police action in dealing with it.

Covering eighty-eight parishes, liberties and hamlets, exempting the City of London, the Met, as it was to become known, was split into three districts and then subdivided still further into divisions. As Peel had outlined in his vision, he staggered the Metropolitan Police's divisional roll-out and, over the next two years, more divisions were created, with some being altered. Accommodation for these new divisions mainly consisted of old watch houses[48] or unused shops and empty buildings. However, these were phased out over the following years as new, state-of-the-art, purpose-built buildings were erected across the metropolis. By May of 1830, the number of men in the Metropolitan force had swollen to 3,295, with 17 Superintendents, 68 Inspectors, 318 Sergeants and 2,892 Constables.[49]

The year 1839 saw yet another Metropolitan Police Act passed by Parliament. It expanded the Metropolitan's jurisdiction outwards to certain locations within fifteen miles of Charing Cross and saw it merge with the Bow Street Office and the Marine/Thames River Police, although the latter was allowed to operate with autonomy to a degree. The year 1842 saw the formation of the Detective Branch, with former Bow Street constable Nicholas Pearce becoming its new senior inspector,[50] and assisting Pearce was Inspector John Haynes, along with six sergeants: Stephen Thornton, William Gerrett, Frederick Shaw, Braddick, Charles Burgess Goff and Jonathan Whicher. By 1860, the Royal Dockyards had come under the Metropolitan Police's care, along with military bases such as Portsmouth, Chatham, Devonport, Pembroke and Woolwich.

The resistance of the City of London to become part of the Home Secretary's police force had caused some concern both within and without the City itself, the main fear being that criminals would gather within the City for shelter from 'Peel's bloody gang'. Two weeks after the inception of the Metropolitan Police, a City of London magistrate sat on a case of a disorderly woman. The magistrate questioned the watchman who brought her in, asking, 'Do you find any increase of bad characters on your beat?' The watchman smiled as he replied, 'Yes, I believes I do. The new Policemen drives 'em into the City,' to which the magistrate retorted, 'Then you should drive them back again!'[51]

The Member of Parliament for the City of London, Matthew Wood, had spent many years pushing for policing reform in the City. He wanted the city patrols to be merged with the watchmen, and in 1832 this wish was granted, as the two policing bodies in the City did in fact merge to form a new policing force called the London City Police.[52] The 1839 City of London Police Act reorganised the City force and ensured it was kept separate from the Metropolitan Police, as well as changing its name to the City of London Police. On 11 November 1839, Wood's close friend, founder of the *Sunday Times* and former Member of Parliament for Colchester and Southwark, Daniel Whittle Harvey, became the City of London's first police commissioner. While the City retained its marshal and under-marshal, their roles were now purely ceremonial.[53] They also retained their watchmen for a further twelve months as the new force established itself. However, in 1840, old Charles Rouse, the last of the Charlies, hung up his lantern for the final time. While some companies maintained their own private watchmen, the era of the parochial watchman patrolling the streets of London was over. Despite holding on to some familiar aspects of their old way of policing, the City's restructuring was heavily based on the Metropolitan Police's modern template, initially locating its headquarters at Guildhall prior to moving to Old Jewry.

Nigh on half a century since these fledgling forces came in to existence, London's full and complete policing structure was published in the period's most comprehensive guide on all matters concerning the metropolis, *Dickens's Dictionary of London 1888*. It listed the strength of force[54] for both the City of London and the Metropolitan forces, each division, as well as the divisional headquarters details, including the heads of those divisions. The 1888 list for the Metropolitan Police force, with its total strength of 14,106 men, was as follows:

Central Office (Metropolitan)
4 Whitechapel Place, S.W.
Commissioner: Colonel Sir Charles Warren, G.C.M.G.
Assist. Commissioners: Lieut-Col. R. L. O. Pearson, A. C. Bruce, Esq. and J. Monro, Esq. (replaced by Dr Robert Anderson 31 August 1888).
Legal Adviser: J. E. Davis, Esq.
Chief Constables: A. C. Howard, Esq., Lt-Col. Roberts, Lt-Col. B. Monsell, Major W. E. Gilbert, and A. F. Williamson, Esq. (Criminal Investigation Department).
Criminal Investigation Department: Superintendent John Shore.
Executive Branch & Common Lodging Houses Branch: Chief Inspector Charles H. Cutbush.
Public Carriage Branch: Chief Inspector Edward Ware.
Lost Property Office: Chief Inspector Beavis.
Chief Clerk: W. F. M. Staples, Esq.
Receiver for the Metropolitan Police District and Courts of the Metropolis: Alfred Richard Pennefather, Esq.
Chief Clerk: E. Mills, Esq.
Surgeon-in-Chief: A. O. Mackellar, Esq.
Acting Surveyor: J. Butler, Esq.
Engineer under Smoke Nuisance Abatement Acts: W. R. E. Coles, Esq.
Storekeeper: Mr J. Mole
Inspectors 43; Sergeants 63; Constables 120. Total 229.

A or Whitehall Division
King Street, Westminster.
Joseph Henry Dunlap, Supt, also Charles Fraser;
Inspectors 38; Sergeants 60; Constables 835. Total 935.

B or Chelsea Division
Walton Street, Brompton.
Chas. W. Sheppard, Supt;
Inspectors 22; Sergeants 52; Constables 560. Total 635.

C or St James's Division
Little Vine Street, Piccadilly.
William G. Hume, Supt;
Inspectors 17; Sergeants 37; Constables 386. Total 441.

D or Marylebone Division
Marylebone Lane.
George Draper, Supt;
Inspectors 23; Sergeants 40; Constables 467. Total 531.

E or Holborn Division
Bow Street.
Rich. W. Steggles, Supt;
Inspectors 17; Sergeants 50; Constables 447. Total 515.

F or Paddington Division
Paddington Green.
Philip Giles, Supt;
Inspectors 21; Sergeants 41; Constables 377. Total 440.

G or Finsbury Division
King's Cross Road.
Charles Hunt, Supt;
Inspectors 23; Sergeants 46; Constables 480. Total 550.

H or Whitechapel Division
Leman Street.
Thos. Arnold, Supt;
Inspectors 30; Sergeants 44; Constables 473. Total 548.

J or Bethnal Green Division
Bethnal Green Road.
James Keating, Supt;
Inspectors 38; Sergeants 56; Constables 522. Total 617.

K or Bow Division
Bow Road.
George Steed, Supt;
Inspectors 48; Sergeants 71; Constables 619. Total 739.

L or Lambeth Division
Lower Kennington Lane.
James Brannan, Supt;
Inspectors 22; Sergeants 35; Constables 346. Total 404.

M or Southwark Division
Blackman Street.
Denis Neylan, Supt;
Inspectors 28; Sergeants 43; Constables 429. Total 501.

N or Islington Division
Stoke Newington High Street.
William J. Sherlock, Supt;
Inspectors 37; Sergeants 66; Constables 536. Total 640.

P or Camberwell Division
High Street, Peckham.
Thomas Butt, Supt;
Inspectors 44; Sergeants 68; Constables 599. Total 712.

R or Greenwich Division
Blackheath Road, Greenwich.
Christopher McHugo, Supt;
Inspectors 38; Sergeants 71; Constables 476. Total 586.

S or Hampstead Division
Albany Street, Regent's Park.
William Harris, Supt;
Inspectors 42; Sergeants 80; Constables 613. Total 736.

T or Hammersmith Division
Broadway, Hammersmith.
Wm. Fisher, Supt;
Inspectors 52; Sergeants 75; Constables 623. Total 751.

V or Wandsworth Division
West Hill, Wandsworth.
David Saines, Supt;
Inspectors 36; Sergeants 59; Constables 561. Total 657.

W or Clapham Division
Brixton Road.
Stephen Lucas, Supt;
Inspectors 39; Sergeants 72; Constables 571. Total 683.

X or Kilburn Division
Carlton Terrace, Harrow Road.
Frederick Beard, Supt;
Inspectors 40; Sergeants 53; Constables 469. Total 563.

Y or Highgate Division
Kentish Town Road.
William J. Huntley, Supt;
Inspectors 46; Sergeants 73; Constables 480. Total 727.

Thames Division
Wapping, near the river.
George Skeats, Supt;
Inspectors 49; Sergeants 4; Constables 147. Total 201.

Woolwich Dockyard Division
Woolwich Arsenal.
Thomas E. Hindes, Supt;
Inspectors 8; Sergeants 25; Constables 140. Total 174.

Portsmouth Dockyard Division
Portsmouth.
Wm. Ventham, Supt;
Inspectors 8; Sergeants 29; Constables 128. Total 155.

Chatham Dockyard Division
Chatham.
Geo. Godfrey, Supt;
Inspectors 6; Sergeants 24; Constables 157. Total 188.

Pembroke Dockyard Division
No Superintendent.
Inspectors 2; Sergeants 4; Constables 28. Total 34.

Dickens also listed the City structure as follows:

The City Police Force comprises 1 Commissioner, 1 Chief Superintendent, 1 Superintendent, 14 Inspectors, 92 Sergeants, and 781 Constables.

Office (City of London)
26 Old Jewry, E.C.
Commissioner: Col. Sir James Fraser, K.C.B. (On leave)
Chief Supt: Major Henry Smith (Acting Commissioner)
Receiver: J. W. Carlyon-Hughes, Esq.
Chief Clerk: John Whatley, Esq.

And the City of London divisional police stations were as follows:

No. 1: Moor Lane
No. 2: Snow Hill
No. 3: Bridwell Place
No. 4: Cloak Lane
No. 5: Tower Street
No. 6: Bishopgate

Between them, the Metropolitan and the City of London police forces covered the largest city on the planet, and the most populated then ever seen. These fledgling establishments had to endure further change – and, it has to be admitted, scandal too – during subsequent years; however, their foundations had been firmly planted. Despite the public's caution, their reputation as formidable organisations against crime was surely being established. By early 1888, this reputation was second to no other force in the country; but by the end of that infamous year, it was in serious question.

All due to one man, who was bent on murder.

3

Recruitment

In 1877, the Metropolitan Police force endured a scandal which shook its very core and forced a reshaping of the Detective Branch into the organisation we know today as the Criminal Investigation Department – CID for short. The infamous Trial of the Detectives scandal, as it was to be known, highlighted that there was still a plague of corruption within the policing system which had never really been shaken off, despite Peel's vision and drive to do so. The scandal was revealed after wealthy Parisienne Madame De Goncourt lost £10,000, and was exposed to potentially losing a further £30,000, to two British conmen, Harry Benson and William Kurr, during a horse racing betting scam. Soon Scotland Yard became involved and tried to pursue the two men across Europe in order to arrest them. Superintendent Adolphus Williamson[1] sent one of his most trusted men, Chief Inspector Nathan Druscovich, to Amsterdam in order to bring back the already arrested Benson and hunt down the elusive Kurr. Druscovich, half-Moldavian and half-English, had originally joined the Met as a constable. Druscovich was multilingual, and, accordingly, was sometimes given special duties centred on his language.[2] During the World Exhibition of 1862, he took an unlikely step in his career, becoming a clerk working for the superintendent's office.[3] However, by 1865 Druscovich was employed fully by the Detective Branch as a detective constable second class.

The introduction of the Extradition Act in 1870 had highlighted the Met's need for translators, as they were increasingly dealing with foreigners in criminal and policing matters. Druscovich, with his practical language abilities, was a rare commodity. However, he was more than a translator. Druscovich gradually rose to the rank of detective inspector, and, as he set off in pursuit of Benson and Kurr, he had Williamson's utmost trust. Eventually Druscovich brought back Benson (albeit with some difficulty); Kurr, though, remained elusive. Three Scotland Yard men, detective sergeants Manton, Littlechild and Roots,[4] were then sent in pursuit of Kurr. Several times they prepared to pounce on their man, but over and over again Kurr vanished. Eventually, they managed to pick Kurr up in Edinburgh. The difficulties Scotland Yard had experienced in arresting these men began to raise suspicions, and rightly so. The reality, as told to Scotland Yard officials by Benson and Kurr themselves, was that one of the most respected inspectors at Scotland Yard, John Meiklejohn, was actually on the payroll of Kurr, and had been for the past four years. It seemed that every time the authorities were about to pounce, Meiklejohn tipped the fugitive men off in return for a substantial amount of money. Not only that, but the man sent to arrest Benson, Chief Inspector Druscovich, had in turn accepted monetary offers from the corrupt Meiklejohn in return for his cooperation. Chief Inspector William Palmer, Detective Chief Inspector George Clarke and Police Solicitor Edward Froggat were also implicated in these accusations and, at their trial on corruption charges, each of the five received a two-year sentence. This scandal implied that corruption was rife within certain quarters of the Metropolitan force and that a shakeup was required. The subsequent reorganisation of the prestigious Detective Branch into the Criminal Investigation Department in 1878 was designed restore the British public's confidence in the police force as well as weed out the misconduct which had now embarrassed the force.[5]

As a result of this fiasco, the press heavily criticised the police, and the cracks began to appear in Metropolitan Police Commissioner Henderson's leadership. Sir Edmund Henderson[6] had steered the force away from the strict regime envisioned by Peel and implemented by Mayne and Rowan. Life was more liberal under Henderson; a simple and maybe petty example is that the men were permitted to grow facial hair under his tenure, something previously prohibited by Mayne and Rowan. Henderson also extended voting rights to an organisation which had previously forbidden its members to partake in any political action at all, including election voting. Some of Henderson's introductions were very positive. He bought in schoolmaster sergeants to improve the literacy standards within the force, added another two hundred men to the Detective Branch and oversaw the creation of the valuable tool that was the Habitual Criminals Register.[7] These actions made Henderson a very popular commissioner within the force itself. Outside the force, however, Henderson was not so popular with a populace which was still struggling to come to terms with this new-model police, and which held the view that constables were bumbling comedians who should be treated with scorn and ridicule. In 1872 his men went on strike for the first time over pay and a reduction in pension payments. Henderson had warned his paymasters against such a reduction in pension; his advice, however, was not heeded, and the men walked. Henderson reluctantly dismissed the strike's ringleaders, but he soon reinstated the majority of them, and this prompted unwanted accusations that the force was lacking strong leadership, that it had no firm direction.

The Fenian bombing campaign of 1883 triggered similar criticisms, and the investigation into these crimes was left largely in the hands of Henderson's assistants James Monro[8] and Charles Howard Vincent,[9] and advisor Dr Robert Anderson.[10] The final straw was the Trafalgar Square riot of 1886, and it was here that Henderson's inefficiency was exposed. The riot, also known as Black Monday, goes under a slightly misleading sobriquet, as rioting did not actually happen in Trafalgar Square itself. Two rival organisations, the London United Workmen's Committee and H. F. Hyndman's Revolutionary Social Democratic Federation, held meetings in the square on the same day. These meetings passed quite peacefully. However, it was when the two organisations dispersed that trouble began. Rather than going home, the crowds headed towards Hyde Park for a further meeting. Buildings and clubs around the area had their windows smashed by mobs high on political and social fervour, causing great damage and costs. Two days later, businesses along Oxford Street heard news that another mob was making its way along the street and, as a precaution, boarded up their premises and closed. The mob, however, didn't arrive, and the blame for this false panic and subsequent loss of trade was laid squarely at Commissioner Henderson's door. He had little choice but to resign and left a force lacking in order, confidence, popular trust and efficiency. The authorities now needed a man who could drag the force back on track, instil some order; someone who could restore respect in the eyes of the authorities and, more importantly, the people. Therefore it was decided that the best man for the job should be a military man, and that man was Sir Charles Warren.

When he took on the role of commissioner to the Metropolitan Police Force in 1886, Sir Charles Warren seemed very much the man for the job. Born in 1840, by seventeen years of age Warren had a commission as a second lieutenant in the Royal Engineers, becoming a surveyor and gaining promotion to captain as a reward for his good work. Along with surveying work, Warren was also a subterranean archaeologist whose most noted discovery was 'Warren's Shaft', a series of tunnels under one of Jerusalem's most sacred of religious sites, Temple Mount. In 1882 Warren was chosen by the Admiralty to discover what had happened to the eminent Orientalist Professor Edward Henry Palmer, who had gone to Syria to influence Bedouin tribes for British favour at a time of complex conflict in the area. Sadly Warren discovered Palmer had been murdered, and subsequently recovered Palmer's remains, returning them to St Paul's Cathedral for burial. Two years later, as major-general, Warren found himself operating as Her Majesty's Special Commissioner on an expedition to Bechuanaland, South Africa.[11] The aim of the expedition was to assert British authority over the area and suppress the inter-tribal conflicts which were occurring. With 5,000 men under his command, Warren executed his task without one single loss of life and this resulted in him being appointed a Knight Grand Cross of St Michael and St George (GCMG) in 1885.[12]

Warren had inherited a force which was in quite some disarray. Six months after taking the appointment, he began to mould this force in his image, and, as far as Warren was concerned, that began with recruitment. On 23 August 1886 he issued an office regulation that Monsell

> will exercise a general supervision over the Candidate Dept and will bring to the notice of asst Commer [Col Pearson] any proposals he may have to make from time to time to facilitate awareness or enhance the efficiency of the Police Force.

Warren then went on to state that

> he [Monsell] will have immediate direction over the preparatory class and will pace them in drill etc, and will supervise the general drill instructions under the general of Colonel Pearson.[13]

The days of Henderson's laxity were over. Organisation and efficiency were the new watchwords, and for a new recruit that started from the day you joined.

Applicants to the Metropolitan Police force in late Victorian London were first required to write to the commissioner at 4 Whitehall Place.[14] Men from either a military or agricultural background were preferred; this was simply because it was thought these types of men would be used to the extreme physical hardship life as a working policeman brought. Men with good discipline were also favoured, as not only did they have to commit to the tasks a constable was expected to conduct without fail, but also they had to be beyond reproach, must not succumb to bribery and must keep a cool head in times of crisis and disorder. Additionally, they had to be between twenty-one and thirty-two years of age.[15] Men from outside London were also deemed physically fitter than their urban counterparts; due to his poor diet and environmental pollution, a city man was expected to experience poorer physical health and lower life expectancy. The regulation height of no less than five feet nine inches[16] was introduced because it was felt that a constable had to look physically intimidating, alleviating a lot of trouble before it began, and it was expected that a constable should be able to read and write fairly well, with a good knowledge of spelling and mathematics. Sailors were looked on favourably as well; however, they were often considered more suitable for the Police Fire Brigade due to their naval training with ropes, ladders and climbing.

Once the letter was received, an application form and a letter stating the conditions of service by which the applicant must abide was returned to the applicant, with an additional letter stating that at least two certificates of character were a requisite.[17] The application form itself consisted of several sheets. On the cover sheet were the applicants first, middle and surnames. As the applicant progressed through his training and career, this sheet was stamped with an admission date and leaving date, as well as a list of divisions he worked in. The next page was the declaration, a series of questions which the applicant had to complete truthfully and in his own writing. The various questions included name, trade or calling, age, height, eye colour, hair, complexion, marks on person (tattoos, scars, etc.) and the parish, nearest town and county in which the applicant was born. The declaration also asked whether the applicant was single, married or widowed; the number of children; the age of the youngest child (if applicable); whether the applicant had previously been in service in either the public service, the military, or with a railway company (and, if they had, the start date, the period of employment and with whom); and the name of the applicant's last employer and duration of last employment. A rather odd question that was asked was whether the applicant had been, or currently was, a member of a secret society, and, if so, what the name of that society was.

The second sheet outlined the conditions of service, and reads,[18]

THE APPLICANT WILL ONLY BE ADMITTED SUBJECT TO THE FOLLOWING CONDITIONS UNLESS THE COMMISSONER SHOULD FROM SPECIAL CIRCUMSTANCES THINK FIT TO DISPENSE WITH ANY OF THEM:-

A list of criteria :

He must not be under 21, nor over 32 years of age.

He must not be less than five feet nine inches in height without shoes.

He must not have more than 2 children.

He must not carry on any trade, nor will his wife be permitted to keep a shop.

He must read and write legibly.

He must produce satisfactory testimonials as to character.

He must be certified as physically fitted for the Service by the Surgeon of the Police Force.

He will be required to devote his whole time to the Police Service, to reside within the City of London, and conform rigidly to the provisions of the Act of Parliament under which he is appointed: and to the Rules, Regulations, and Orders of the Force, some of the most important of which are annexed for the Applicants information.[19]

For the misconduct of any kind, a Constable is liable to be dismissed with forfeiture of all pay due to him – to suspension without pay – to pecuniary penalties, not accompanied with suspension or dismissal, to the extent of one week's pay – to the reduction from one rank to any other rank – and, if convicted before a Magistrate of neglect or violation of his duty in his Office of Constable, to a fine of Ten Pounds, or imprisonment for one month with hard labour.

On appointment, the pay of Constable is Twenty-five Shillings per week, subject to certain deductions, during sickness, and for lodgings, &c.

Well conducted Constables are eligible, on discharge from the Service, for Superannuation allowance in accordance with the terms of the City Police Act, but they cannot, under any circumstances, CLAIM a superannuation allowance as a right.

At the end of the page came the Declaration

I HEARBY DECLARE that the answers made by me to the questions on the first page are in all respects full and truthful, and I FURTHER DECLARE that I have attentively read, and understand, the above conditions under which alone I can be appointed to the City of London Police Force, and I undertake, if I should so be appointed, to abide by them in every particular.

(Signature of Applicant) _____

(Residence) _____

Next was the witness declaration. This was completed by a high-ranking official, usually of superintendent ranking, who placed his signature at the bottom of the page.

The answers to the questions on the first page, and the above Declaration were filled in and signed by the applicant in my presence this_____

day of _____ 18___

Certificates of character were commonly obtained from either the applicant's previous or current employers, religious representatives such as vicars and rabbis, former teachers or any other person of good standing within the community, and were collated and attached with the application form. Great credence was put on these certificates, with each one being verified by the chief clerk of the force. If the applicant came from outside the London area, or presented a reference from elsewhere in the country, the force contacted the relevant local constabulary and asked them to verify the character certificate. Once this initial stage was completed, the application was assessed and passed; the candidate would be placed upon a list of those suitable candidates who would like to join the force. The list was a short one, and deliberately so. It was found that keeping a long list of candidates, for a long period of time, resulted in them finding employment elsewhere, and the force missing out on potentially good policemen; the turnaround from being accepted on the list to being taken on as a candidate was therefore only a matter of weeks. The successful few would have a letter issued to them, stating they were to attend either 26 Old Jewry[20] or Great Scotland Yard, Westminster, at their own trouble and expense, for the next phase of the process – Candidates' Day.

Tuesday was Candidates' Day in the Metropolitan Police,[21] when new recruits reported to either Scotland Yard or Wellington Barracks at ten o'clock sharp to meet the 'Police Maker', Chief Inspector George Rose. Rose had joined the Met in 1860, making a rapid rise to inspector before commencing his unique role within the preparatory class in 1865.[22] There he was to stay until his retirement in 1907, training approximately 60,000 men in that time. In fact, the majority of Metropolitan policemen who worked on the Jack the Ripper case in 1888 would have received the benefit of Rose's training and guidance in those first few formative weeks within the force. The recruits were sat in a room where Rose would tell each and every one of them the expectations which came with the job, and inform them of the terms and conditions of service.

The men were then escorted into the changing rooms, where they disrobed for the colloquial 'cough and drop', politely known as the physical examination. Clad in a long cloak to preserve their decency, the candidates would queue outside the room belonging to the police divisional surgeon-in-chief, Dr Alexander MacKellar.[23] McKellar would call the men in one by one, where he would ascertain height and weight, and rigorously check for ailments and deformities which may hinder the execution of duty. He would check that the feet were in good condition, as they were often the cause of physical failure among regular police constables, due to the hard and constant pounding nature of beat work. He would also conduct an eye test to ensure vision was suitable as observation was a key weapon in a policeman's armoury.

As the procession made its way through McKellar's office, those who had been medically examined re-dressed and prepared themselves for the final series of tests, covering the three 'R's: reading, writing and arithmetic. The men were asked individually to read various passages chosen at random, usually from the *Police Instruction Book* or Candidates' book, and then to take spelling and mathematic tests as a collective. Once these tests were completed, the men were thanked and told they could go home and await yet another letter to see if they had passed on to the next phase of the process – preparatory class.

Preparatory class for the Metropolitan Police was, on average, a two- to three-week period of extensive training based between Scotland Yard, Wellington Barracks and the candidates' section house attached to Kennington Lane station, where the candidates would eat, sleep and live.[24] It was the forerunner to basic police training held at Peel House and, more recently, Hendon.[25] The new recruit was paid during this training, albeit on a reduced rate compared to a regular constable, and he was considered to be on probation. The candidates, numbering anywhere between seventy and one hundred, were all kept under the watchful eye of Rose and his small team, which included the Kennington Lane section house sergeant, a drill sergeant and a constable.[26] At Wellington Barracks, the probationer undertook hours of marching referred to as drill work, where his stance and gait were assessed and corrected. It was, and still is, extremely important for a constable to look the part, to have an air of presence about him, so Rose ensured the slouch was removed and replaced by the strong, upright stance and purposeful walk.

Opened in 1833 for use by the Foot Guard Battalions in the British Army, and located not far from Buckingham Palace, Wellington Barracks was an ideal location to conduct drill work. The Metropolitan Police were permitted to conduct their exercises upon a part of the parade ground there and a purpose-built parade shed was installed for use during inclement weather. As well as drill work, the police also conducted various weapons training classes – chiefly training with cutlasses – at Wellington Barracks.

The use of cutlasses was strictly governed. In the early days of the force, all constables were trained in its use; however, they were forbidden to draw the weapon unless ordered to, or as a very last resort when lives were in danger. The drawing of this weapon at any other time could result in instant dismissal. New regulations introduced in 1885 stipulated that cutlasses were only issued to ten men in each division, mainly at senior level. As for firearms, the Bow Street force had flintlocks among their armoury, but Peel's new police avoided firearms as best they could. Upon the formation of the Metropolitan force, Commissioner Mayne did order fifty pairs of pistols; they were, however, very rarely used. A rethink was prompted in late 1867, when the Fenian bombing of Clerkenwell prison killed several people, injured many more, destroyed many buildings close by, and tore a hole in the side of the prison through which two convicted Fenian terrorists held at the prison, Richard Burke and Joseph Casey, hoped to escape. Mayne realised he needed more than mere cutlasses to combat this surge in Fenian activity, and responded by instigating official police firearms training, not at Wellington Barracks but at Wormwood Scrubs prison and the Museum of Fire Arms in Rye Lane, Peckham, directing that five constables from each division be trained in the use of revolvers.[27] In time, firearm training would become more extensive, and weapons such as revolvers and rifles were stored under lock and key at chief divisional stations, only to be used in emergency situations as stipulated by the local inspector: the Tottenham Outrages of 1909 and the Siege of Sidney Street in London's East End in 1911 are classic examples. However, the use of firearms as a mandatory piece of equipment for all constables to carry was, and still is, resisted by British police constabularies.

While the Army were quite happy for the police to use Wellington Barracks parade ground, one issue did arise during the early part of this relationship, and that was of the watering of the parade ground. The police watered the ground regularly, much to the annoyance of the army, who not only disliked the practice but also disliked having to pay a water bill. However, to avoid further tension, the man in charge of the Met purse strings, the receiver, agreed that the Met would foot the bill, and harmony was swiftly restored.[28]

Drill took up the majority of training. Warren wanted his men to be a manoeuvrable force, marching in procession on to and off from their beats, arranging themselves in swift order in times of emergencies, and to be ready and able to efficiently and rapidly distribute themselves as and where required. Warren felt that drill had been a neglected aspect of police training under Henderson's tenure, yet to him it was essential. Therefore Warren bought drill back with a vengeance and the timetable below shows that four hours per weekday were spent on drill (with another two hours fitted in on Saturdays):

9.00 a.m.	Parade
9.15 a.m. – 10.15 a.m.	Drill (rest fifteen minutes)

10.30 a.m. – 11.30 a.m.   Drill (go to dinner at 1 p.m.)
2.15 p.m. – 3.15 p.m.   Drill (rest fifteen minutes)
3.30 p.m. – 4.30 p.m.   Drill (dismiss)

Detective Inspector Edwin Woodhall, author of *Jack the Ripper or When London Walked in Terror* (1937), an account of the Jack the Ripper murders, recalls drill, stating that 'a squad of us would parade every morning at nine o'clock, drill and listen to instructions until twelve. Then came a two-hour interval for dinner and at two o'clock we paraded again until five'.[29] During the breaks in drill, the men would be asked questions from the *Instruction Book for Candidates and Constables*, a small book containing the basic information required for a new recruit, which had been issued to them upon entry to preparatory school.

However, it was not all gruelling marching. Recruits were given evenings off and permitted to stay out until 10.30 p.m., something which did not go down too well with the authorities, who felt Rose and his team should be a little stricter.[30] At Kennington Lane the men were awoken at 7.00 a.m. and breakfasted at 8.00 a.m., then they were either marched to Wellington Barracks for drill or to Scotland Yard for lectures. Some communication training was undertaken at the telegraph room at Kensington Lane, where the ABC system was taught to each candidate there,[31] while Chief Metropolitan Police Surgeon MacKellar provided basic first aid instruction, as well as elementary anatomy education, at Scotland Yard; his was one of five lectures given during this training period. MacKellar also provided one final service for the soon-to-be police constable, by jabbing them with a needle. The Vaccination Act (1873) made it compulsory for all in the United Kingdom to be vaccinated; however, it was also mandatory for all new police recruits to be re-vaccinated, as the conditions some of the men could encounter on the beat were unsanitary and rife with disease. During this period Rose and his team kept a close eye on these probationers, constantly advising them of the expectations upon a police constable. Any breach of discipline was ruthlessly dealt with by expulsion; however, if it was noted that a probationer was struggling despite showing lots of application and dedication, then encouragement, patience and guidance were the watchwords.

At the end of the probation period, the men would muster at Wellington Barracks for drill exercise, as they had done daily during the previous three weeks. However, this was different: this was the final proficiency drill, performed under the watchful gaze of one of the chief constables within the Metropolitan force. If the probationer was given his approval, they were ordered to appear at Scotland Yard the following Monday. Here they were marched in a processional file to stores, in order for them to collect their uniform, into which they changed. Then they were taken before the commissioner, or assistant commissioner, where the recruit would swear an oath, sign the oath book and be given a warrant number. This act was called the attestation. There were two oaths within the Metropolitan Force

– one for the divisions only, and the other connected to military bases and naval dockyards.

The divisional one read,

> I swear that I will well and truly to the best of my knowledge and ability act as a Constable for the Metropolitan Police district and within the Royal Palaces of Her Majesty Queen Victoria and ten miles thereof for preserving the peace and preventing robberies and other felonies and apprehending offenders against the peace and that I will well and truly execute such office of Constable and all powers and duties which I may be authorised or required to execute by virtue on an Act of Parliament passed in the tenth year of the reign of His Majesty King George the seventh for improving the police in and near the Metropolis or by virtue of an Act of Parliament passed in the third year of the reign of Her Majesty Queen Victoria for further improving the police in and near the Metropolis.
>
> So help me God.[32]

The military and naval dockyard constables oath read a little differently:

> I swear that I will well and truly act as a Constable for in Her Majesty's Naval Yards and the stations of the War Department and within 15 miles of such yards or stations for preserving the peace and preventing robberies and other felonies and apprehending offenders against the peace and that I will well and truly execute such office of Constable and all powers and duties which I may be authorised or required to execute by virtue on an Act of Parliament passed in the 23rd and 24th year of the reign of Her Majesty Queen Victoria for the employment of the Metropolitan Police force in Her Majesty's Yards and Military Stations.
>
> So help me God.

Once the attestation ritual was completed, the recruit could now call himself a police constable. All that was left was to assign the new constable to a division, to consolidate what he had already learnt, and further training in the day-to-day life as a bobby. This process of allocation could take up to a week, so in the meantime the men would return to Kensington Lane station and undertake duties there while awaiting their fate; however, most likely, the allocation was instantaneous. Once allocated to a division, they were initially taken on as a reserve constable[33] for a period of one week, this to adjust to their new surroundings. Once the week was up they moved on to the lowest classification for a constable, that of fourth class,[34] at a subdivision station[35] located within the divisional area. Some locations, such as Whitechapel, were keenly avoided by most due to their high criminal activity. However, some relished the challenge, and saw it as an ideal division for a young bobby to cut his teeth. Superintendent George Cornish, who joined H Division (Whitechapel) in 1895, described the area as 'the best in which to test the worth of a fledging constable'[36] and Chief Constable Frederick Porter Wensley, who started his career in Whitechapel in 1888, stated that it was the knowledge he gained during his early years in H Division which formed the foundations of his success in the police force.

The divisional register, a large, A3-sized ledger, held all the collar numbers, page by page, for each subdivision, and it was in this book that the newest constables' details were entered on the relevant page relating to his new collar number. Now officially part of the division, the new constable would attend the police courts over a period of two weeks, in order to observe how they work in relation to his role and to gain experience, supplementing the training undertaken in preparatory class. There he would observe as many cases as he could, taking notes if needs be and writing down questions to ask of his superiors upon his return to the station. The new recruit would also take an hour aside each day to study his book of rules and regulations. All new constables, both in the Metropolitan and City of London forces, were issued by the superintendent himself with a variation of this book which was designed to guide them through various situations which might occur. It was divided into parts, the first being a breakdown of duties for all divisional ranks within the force from superintendents and inspectors to sergeants and constables. The second part concentrated on instructions should a specific scenario occur, such as a house fire or coming across an unlicensed dog, for example. In addition to the instructions, and laid out at the back of the book, were the various Acts of Parliament which defined the police's authority in numerous situations, and laws of arrest.[37] This book stayed with the constable until the day he left; it was essentially his bible, and he would be constantly quizzed by his superiors as to its contents.

During this initial period as constables, the men also undertook various station duties (usually menial tasks such as swabbing out cells, sweeping yards and kit cleaning); however, this was mixed with more interesting tasks, performed under the watchful eye of a more experienced bobby. The force also provided the new constable with lodgings. If the constable was married, police-owned quarters within his division would be offered, if they were available; if not, lodgings as near to the division as possible would suffice.[38] The police authorities usually purchased buildings in rows, or close together in blocks, so that constables lived close to fellow constables; the men themselves preferred this, as it enhanced camaraderie. Another scheme connected to property was also in place by which the landlord of an empty dwelling could approach the police and request these premises be inhabited by a constable and his family rent-free, providing the house was in a fit condition and fully furnished. This meant that the landlord had secure police presence on his property, the constable and his family had somewhere to live, the police force did not have to purchase many properties (merely cover the fuel costs) and the area had a constable living in it.[39] By contrast, single men were assigned to a section house, in case of outbreaks of mass crime, such as rioting. In an era before telephones, it was easier to muster the men if they were already together rather than issue runners to each individual's home. However, housing a group of young men together brought its problems. It wasn't unheard of for arguments to break out and brawling was fairly common. Also, to break the monotony, boxing matches were organised (with money being wagered) as an alternative to the dull parlour games and cribbage, which the men were encouraged to undertake to ease the boredom.

Policing was often physically demanding and relentless, and nobody suffered more than the constable on the beat. A new recruit spent five hours per day on beat work. A seasoned constable would demonstrate how to prepare for a beat and how to present themselves at muster, and go through the ins and outs of what was expected during the beat, while again reiterating the rules and regulations.[40] Over a period of two weeks, it was expected that fresh constables would establish themselves on the beat, with the more seasoned old-timer taking a less and less active role. Eventually, the new recruit would take over his beat on his own, with the occasional monitoring of the beat sergeant. This was considered by the cynical 'old hands' to be the point when the new constables' training really began. Experienced bobbies would pass on their invaluable knowledge and experience, and share some home truths about life as a policeman. They would explain that friends, wary of being labelled as police informers, would shun them and their families. Those who used to be friendly and sociable (they would say) might start to cross streets to avoid them, succumbing to the fear of association, and of being referred to – probably the highest insult any East Ender could give to another – as a 'Coppers Nark'.[41] The new constable soon realised that he would never be anything but a policeman to anyone other than his closest family; sometimes even for close family members it was too much to have a son, brother or uncle as a bobby. It wasn't unheard of for a policeman to be ostracised by his own father as soon as the latter had discovered that his son had recruited into the force, such was the distain with which the common policeman was regarded by many working-class folk throughout Whitechapel and the East End. If the new recruit withstood the hard training and unsociable hours, and the change of perception among family and friends, and if he was willing to place himself in the most stressful and dangerous of situations while maintaining a cool, calm head, and if luck was on his side, he could rely on twenty-five years' worth of regular employment. However, as Messers Gilbert and Sullivan's song states, 'a policeman's lot is not a happy one.'

4

Police Stations and Section Houses

Its proper name is a home.

Police! (1889)

Peel's vision for the Metropolitan force was to start small and then expand, so a year later, on 10 February 1830 to be exact, four new divisions were created as part of that plan, and one of those new divisions was H, which covered the Whitechapel area. Along with H Division, G Division (Finsbury), K Division (Stepney) and L Division (Lambeth) also came into existence. Due to a restructuring of the divisions in 1880, H Division's boundary was altered; by 1888 the actual jurisdiction covered consisted of all the streets bounded by the Hackney Road in Bethnal Green to the north, then on to Warner Place, Squirries Street, White Street, Nottingham Street and to Baker's Row; from Baker's Row to the busy Whitechapel and Mile End Roads, as far east as Regent's Canal, and south to the River Thames; back west towards the Tower of London and the City of London boundary; north along Norton Folgate to Shoreditch High Street, and back on to Hackney Road. Initially there were two main watch houses this fledgling division, one of which was located in Lambeth Street,[1] between Cable Street and the Highway, and the other at Chapel Yard, Whitechurch Lane, in the grounds of Whitechapel church.[2] These were supported by secondary watch houses based at Denmark Street,[3] Wellclose Square and Bethnal Green Road. By 1888, a new police subdivision station building had cropped up in Commercial Street, Leman Street had been renovated and made the divisional headquarters, and two new subdivision stations had fallen under Whitechapel's responsibility, leaving H Division with four main operational buildings, which were:

Leman Street Police Station, 74–78 Leman Street, Divisional Headquarters

Located in the south-western part of H Division's jurisdiction, on converted shop premises,[4] Leman Street station was H Division's headquarters. Here the head of the division, Superintendent Thomas Arnold,[5] was based, along with Chief Inspector John West,[6] who acted as superintendent when Arnold was unavailable. Also centred at Leman Street was H Division's CID, headed by Local Inspector Edmund Reid[7] and supported by his team of detectives, though they were permitted use of the other subdivision stations if needs be.[8] Leman Street provided police presence for the London Docks and HM Customs if required, as well as constables for the Royal Mint,[9] and a few men to cover the Great Eastern Railway and London and Blackwall Railway lines and premises.

Arbour Square Police Station, Arbour Street East

Built in 1842, Arbour Square police court and station, in the Stepney area of east London, just off Commercial Road, initially came under the jurisdiction of K Division, Bow. Police orders of 15 May 1880 saw a change in the divisional boundaries of K and H Divisions, meaning Arbour Square became one of the four subdivision stations in H Division. This two-storey building held a section house with room for nineteen men, sergeants married quarters and stables at the rear.[10] In the May of 1888, Arbour Square subdivision station and police court was purchased from its owners, the Mercers' Company, by the Metropolitan force for a sum of £7,500.

Shadwell Police Station, 10–24 King David Lane

As with Arbour Square station, Shadwell police station was located in the eastern part of the division, albeit a little further south toward Cable Street, not far from the old Denmark Street watch house, which had been 'recommended as unfit for service in 1881'.[11] Like Arbour Square, Shadwell came under H Division's wing in 1880, transferring from K Division. Situated on the junction with Juniper Street, Shadwell station was the smallest of the four subdivision stations based in H Division.

Commercial Street Police Station, 160 Commercial Street

Commercial Street station was built on land bought by the then Metropolitan Police receiver, Maurice Drummond, in the May of 1874, and came under the first classification of police buildings; that is, one specially designed for police work.[12] Designed by the Metropolitan Police's building surveyor, Frederick H. Caiger, completed in 1875 by the architects the Lathey Brothers[13] and opened in the March of 1876, this purpose-built police station replaced the old watch house near St Mary's church, situated on the corner of Spital Square and Lamb Street. Administrative and policing matters were dealt with on the ground floors, with accommodation being provided on the upper floors, and other facilities in the basement. These purpose-built police stations had cropped up between 1850 and 1880, with a total of seventy-seven being erected in that period.[14] Out went the old watch houses and in came the new-style modern police stations, or subdivisions as they were officially referred to, which were designed to hold a significant force of men and process the administrative side of policing with greater efficiency; the majority of these new stations had section houses connected to them, thus ensuring a constant manning of the station at all times. They were far larger buildings and more advanced than their predecessors: rooms were built to cover almost every requirement of a good, functioning police unit, and Commercial Street police station, covering the northern part of H Division, was one of these new buildings.

A police station was more than a place to work: it was home, a small community within which all its occupants worked and rested. The external fascia of a police station was designed to look imposing and secure, and the public entrance most often had above or to the side of the door a blue lamp, indicating the building was indeed a police station.[15] The lintel above the main entrance of Commercial Street was, like many others, carved with the words *Dieu et mon droit* ('God and my right'), a reference to the motto of the British monarch and a nod to British justice, and under that motto stood one word … police.

Once through the public entrance, the first room entered is the lobby. Situated in this room, and most often facing the entrance so visitors could be greeted, would be a huge desk constantly manned by at least one constable, under the supervision of the duty inspector or sergeant, who may also be present. Here, enquiries would be made, assistance sought or a crime reported. Also in this room would be a line of chairs or benches for the public to use, if they were waiting to see a specific individual. Witnesses, pending interview, would also be kept in this area if required.

Probably the very first thing one would notice about the station was its odour. As with hospitals, police stations had a unique smell, as carbolic acid or other antiseptic cleaning materials were used to cleanse the station on a daily basis. This is understandable when you consider the types of persons often bought into a police station, from drunks to the homeless to the disease-ridden to those with minor wounds; the smells were overpowering. Also noticeable were the light fixings, powered by gas, but with a metal mesh frame instead of a glass shade for protection. The reason is simple: sharp, breakable or dangerous items could be used to assault a constable by an apprehended villain waiting to be admitted to the cells, therefore temptation was not put in the villains' way.

The lobby would be the only room in the station which most law-abiding members of the public ever saw. The rest would predominantly be seen by the constables, while a few locations would be seen by those held in custody. Situated next to the lobby of Commercial Street station stood a large room simply titled the reserve room – this held a small body of men who would essentially be on standby, in reserve, should any emergency situation arise within the division, or elsewhere in the Metropolitan or City area. Introduced in a police order dated 2 July 1870, these reserves would not be sitting idle, waiting for something to happen. They would be carrying out minor tasks, delivering messages, cleaning and maintaining the station, processing mundane paperwork and tending to prisoners. They would also step in to cover beat duties should a brother constable be taken ill or injured, as well as undertaking fixed point duty in cases of emergencies. As with any team, the role of the reserve men was essential and their importance must not be underestimated; they did, after all, hold the same authority as regular constables and were often thrown into unsavoury situations at a moment's notice. To supplement the reserve, unpaid volunteers, who were attested constables, and therefore had the same powers of arrest, were utilised. Sacrificing their own time for the benefit of the community, these special constables were an invaluable source of manpower despite often being scorned by their own community.

Located within the reserve room at Commercial Street was an office which seems to have initially functioned as both the inspectors' office and a charge room. The charge room would be where suspects were interviewed and, if warranted, criminal charges formally made against them and noted down by the duty inspector or sergeant for use in the legal process. This room would also be utilised for witness interviews, and, at other times, as a makeshift medical centre for treating injured persons. However, in the Metropolitan Police's 1881 report into conditions of police stations, it was stated that the charge room should be just that, a room where charges were made against a prisoner, and later plans of Commercial Street station show that a new inspectors' office was built into the reserve room, next to the lobby, freeing up the old inspectors' room to be used solely as a charge room. The inspectors' office would be used by the duty inspector, and from here he would conduct the day-to-day running of the subdivision. In the inspectors' store room, weaponry – most commonly rifles, pistols and cutlasses – was securely locked away. These items were only issued to men who were trained to use them, and only in emergencies as decided upon by a chief inspector or any rank above.

From the commissioner's office to the local divisions, teams of administrators helped their colleagues in public-facing positions to uphold the laws of the land and to ensure public safety. Each division had its own clerical staff to ensure that local budgets were monitored and to attend to other practical matters, such as the overseeing of outside contractors. At Scotland Yard, a clerical team of civil servants would undertake these tasks; however, within the divisions, a small team of constables performed this duty, overseen by what was known as a clerk sergeant. However, with regards H Division, these clerical duties would be undertaken by the reserve team, as records show that no clerk sergeant, or clerical team, was assigned them during this period.

The cells at some stations (like Bishopsgate station, belonging to the City of London force) were located away from the main building, and usually across the muster room or yard. However, at Commercial Street, six cells were included as part of the original main building complex, with five measuring six feet by nine feet, one cell measuring six feet by just under fifteen feet, and all running off a main cell corridor which led from the reserve room.[16] Befitting its status as an up-to-date police station, the cell block at Commercial Street had, running through the floor, walls and ceiling, specially designed flues, which carried warm air throughout the block, making the cells at Commercial Street quite comfortable; certainly more so than the old rat-infested cells of the early to mid-1800s. The older stations, such as Leman Street, had stoves situated in the cell passage, with the idea being that it heated the whole cell block. These arrangements were, however, grossly ineffective, and the cells nearest the stove would heat up to an uncomfortable temperature, while those located furthest away barely got warm.[17] The temperatures of the cells were of great importance, especially with regards to prisoners who were drunk. Because of the vasodilatory effect that alcohol has upon the body, people who are drunk tend to feel warm even though their body temperature has dropped. This, combined with the fact that alcohol inhibits the body's natural attempts to warm itself up, led to constant anxieties about the prospect of a drunk dying of hypothermia in a police cell, so particular attention was paid to drunken prisoners, and a half-hourly visit was made to the cells by the gaoler to ensure all was well. Police orders of December 1887 stated that one cell had to be fitted with a sloping wooden floor, to accommodate incapable drunks, who would be laid upon the floor instead of the bench. This was to avoid the possibility of the drunk falling from the bench on to the floor and causing themselves some harm, as well as reducing the possibility of the incapable drunk choking in their own vomit, as the discharge ran down the slope. Modern cells, like those at Commercial Street, would be lined inside with tiles which made the daily cleaning and disinfecting of these cells extremely easy; by contrast, brick-lined cells at older stations would be hard work and had to be limewashed every few months. Some cell floors were asphalted, and easily cleaned with a mop and bucket, whereas others were wooden and difficult to maintain – so much so that it was proposed that wooden removable floors be fitted, so that they could be lifted out and placed in the yard for a thorough cleansing.[18]

As the Commercial Street cells were situated on the Elder Street side of the station, with the cell passage running along the yard side, windows were not built into the cell walls themselves. Instead fixed skylights, well out of the reach of prisoners, were built solidly into the roof, which was sloped towards the yard, thus restricting the view of the roof from the public in Elder Street. In 1886, under the approval of Commissioner Warren, the cell block at Commercial Street was renovated and extended upwards, with the larger cell being reduced to match the size of the other cells on the ground level and an additional floor added on top of the block, consisting of three more cells and a large association cell, this to house small groups of people.

To combat the darkness into which the ground-floor cells were now plunged (since this new building covered the fixed skylights), large widows with impenetrable panes where built above the cell doors, which enabled light to come in from across the yard via the cell passage. At night, light was provided from the gas fixtures that lined the cell passage, which were wholly ineffective for those who were in the cells, as only a smattering of light would make the way through the solid metal cell door by way of the five small ventilation holes drilled into it. Built into the cell door was a spy hole, known as a Judas Hole, which had a fisheye lens so the prisoner could be observed fully without the need for a constable to enter the cell.

Responsibility for all prisoners held in custody at a police station fell to the custody sergeant, who would be assisted in some stations, especially those in the City of London, by the gaoler. According to the City of London orders and regulations book, 'all persons in custody, on a charge of a felony, is to be searched',[19] and major offences, such as murder, were considered to be felonies. The prisoner's clothing would be removed, wrapped in clean paper and sent to the divisional surgeon for analysis – most commonly, this consisted of a search for bloodstains[20] – and a spare set of clothing was issued to the prisoner in the meantime. Minor offences, such as drunkenness, were known as misdemeanours. Prisoners who had committed a misdemeanour were searched for items which were considered dangerous to the prisoner themselves (braces or an apron, for example, could be used to commit suicide), along with items which could be used as weapons against third parties.[21] Any items removed from prisoners were recorded in the prisoners' property book and securely stored away. Upon release, these items would be returned to the prisoner, who would inspect the items and, if everything was correct, countersign the book.[22]

Within the same City of London orders and regulations book, it was stated that 'prisoners are to be frequently visited while in custody, especially in cases of drunkenness or attempted suicide. Prisoners charged with the latter should be continuously watched; in the case of females, a woman must be employed for the purpose.'[23] These women were known as police matrons, a female assistant to the gaoler within the station, used to conduct searches and watch of female prisoners and children who had been bought into custody. A report into police matrons revealed that H Division only used them 'when necessity arises',[24] however four were based within the division in 1894, with one living 440 yards from Leman Street station, one living 500 yards away from Commercial Street station, one a mere 150 yards away from Arbour Square station, and one some 300 yards distance from Shadwell station.[25] The City Police, as reported in their 1891 order book for Bishopsgate Police Station had, at that date, a rate for the hiring of these matrons, namely a shilling for every hour below four hours. Anything over four hours resulted in an additional eight pence per hour.[26] However, the use of police matrons was sparse in 1888, with the task most commonly falling to the wife of a station sergeant.

As the police were not legally bound to use police matrons, and the Human Rights Act was many years away, subdivisions often waived this piece of guidance in the interests of controlling expenses. In the May of 1888, the matter of police matrons, or rather their lack of use, was to be the subject of public exchange between philanthropist Louisa Twining[27] and the then Home Secretary, Henry Matthews. The commissioners on the condition of police courts and cells had commented of Twining's open letter in the *Standard* newspaper, bemoaning the lack of police matrons in all police stations, by stating that

> in our opinion it is utterly wrong that women prisoners should have no women about them at the places of detention ... There ought to be at each court, a female officer to take charge, under the gaoler or constables, of the women, a provision which by law has to be made for women in custody in a prison ... Besides the male officer, or officers in charge of the prisoner, there should be a female officer in charge under him, of the female prisoners.[28]

Matthews's response, reported in the *Pall Mall Gazette*, was 'that the existing system worked well on the whole', to which the *Pall Mall Gazette*, undoubtedly as a jibe to Matthews's confirmed bachelorism, retorted that 'possibly, if he [Matthews] were a married man, he might be made to think otherwise'.[29]

Once a search had been conducted, the prisoner would be escorted to the cell, most usually by the gaoler or a reserve constable.[30] This was done to detach the prisoner from the arresting constable who had bought the prisoner into the station, thus removing the potential of a malicious assault against them. If the offence was deemed serious by the duty inspector or sergeant, and enough evidence obtained, the prisoner would be charged. The prisoner would be sat either in a charge room, or in a quiet office in the station, and the details of the charge would be read to them. The charge book would be filled out: the name, age, and address of the prisoner; the names of witnesses; the details of the arresting constable; the circumstances of the charge; the details of the magistrate who would be hearing the case. In some cases, charges were made and later dropped; details of these cases would be transferred and entered into yet another book, the refused charge book.

Those who seemed to be suffering from ill health or mental illness would be assessed by the divisional surgeon on his rounds, who would then recommend a course of action (for example, committal, or a placement in a local hospital or another suitable institution for medical treatment). The Metropolitan and City forces differed in their procedures for releasing of drunken persons. In general, the Metropolitan force waited until dawn to release them, providing they had enough cell room, ensuring they were capable prior to release. The City force, however, would assess the drunk person constantly, and if they deemed them sober, and able to look after themselves, they would release them on to the streets, no matter what time of day or night it was. This they did with Whitechapel murder victim Catherine Eddowes; it was a decision which sparked a lot of contentious debate at the time and has continued to be debated since.

Those charged with committing an offence were detained overnight before being escorted to the magistrates' court the following morning for their hearing. The 1889 police code stated that 'necessary refreshments for the prisoner may be purchased out of money taken from them, providing the charge against them does not relate to the money. The amount expended for refreshments must be entered in the prisoner's property book.' The code continues by saying that 'no beer or spirits whatever should be given to them, or admitted to the cells, but only tea or coffee, with such eatables as are usual'.[31] A City of London police order dated 1 September 1891 supports the police code's advice on the treatment of prisoners, ordering that 'the prisoner would be offered coffee, or cocoa if preferred, and some bread and butter; however there was to be a fee of four pence to be paid by the prisoner for this'.[32] Hot water and soap were, however, provided in the morning, free of charge. Prisoners in wet clothes were also offered the option of having their garments dried, provided that the station had the facility to do so. A spare set of clothing was loaned to the prisoner overnight; and the prisoner had some comfort, back in his own, dry clothing, when he was presented in front of the magistrate the next morning. For convenience, some modern cells were fitted with water closets, which were nothing more than chamber pots built into the end of one of two benches that lined the wall. These chamber pots were tended to by the duty officers, reserves or police matrons depending on the sex of the prisoner; however, at Commercial Street, separate lavatories and basins were installed on each floor, with the prisoner being escorted from their cell and back again.

The electronic telegraphy system in 1888 was the internet of its day, and was used to exchange thousands of messages, and other pieces of information, across many miles of land, sea and even continents; therefore all stations were fitted with a telegraph room. Initially used sparsely in the Britain, it was not until the Great Exhibition of 1851, where many telegraph instruments were exhibited, that the telegraphic boom really took off. The first telegraph line Scotland Yard had installed was between Whitehall and Queen Victoria's London residence of Buckingham Palace in the 1850s, and by 1888 a complete private network for the police had been installed connecting the central offices of both Scotland Yard and Old Jewry, along with all stations of the Metropolitan and City Police forces, as well as other provincial police constabularies. It must be mentioned that while the police operated on a private line, for obvious reasons, they did have the facility to use the country-wide General Post Office system in times of emergencies.[33]

Due to its simplicity, both the Metropolitan and City forces used the ABC telegraphy system devised by Charles Wheatstone in 1858, where the user simply pressed a button situated upon the communicator, next to a letter, to spell out a message. Once the message was complete, the user then turned a handle until the indicator hit the stop button and the handle ceased rotating, which meant the message had been sent. This ABC system obviated the need to hire expert users of Morse code, who were expensive; but, on the other hand, the ABC system was a more laborious and time-consuming system than Morse code. The police's chief use of the telegram was to relay messages and instructions from Central Office, with the supplementation of issued police orders being the main daily message; however, the main traffic of telegraphs flowed between subdivision stations within a division, and on matters such as requests for reserves, information on persons obtained or the urgent calling of a colleague to another station. In 1867, codes were introduced for each station across the Metropolitan force, with H Division codes as follows: Arbour Square was AR, Commercial Street was CS, Shadwell was SL and the Royal Mint, RM. Leman Street, as divisional headquarters, had the simple code of HD, for H Division.

The cascading of telegrams was strictly laid down in the police orders dated 5 June 1888, which instructed that any received messages from Central Office would initially be only distributed to the division headquarters from A (Whitehall) to J (Bethnal Green). Each of those divisions had a 'buddy', consisting of one from the remaining divisions, K (Bow) to Y (Kentish Town), and for H Division this was K (Bow). Therefore if H Division HQ at Leman Street received a message to be cascaded, they would forward it to the subdivision stations of Arbour Square,[34] Commercial Street, Royal Mint, as well as their 'buddy', K Division (Bow), who would then cascade to their own sub-division stations. H Division also had an additional responsibility, as they also had to notify the Thames River Police based in Wapping of any telegrams received from Scotland Yard.

Shadwell was the only subdivision station Leman Street had no direct telegram connection with; therefore any telegram messages for that station had to be sent via Arbour Square. As well as Scotland Yard, all division and subdivision stations, telegraph lines also ran to and from the private residences of the Commissioner and his assistants, the Home Office, the House of Commons, the Horse Guards, the Fire Brigade, the British, Natural History and South Kensington museums, the National Gallery, the General Post Office and the City of London Police, whose telegraph code was CP.[35]

A telephone system had been set up at Scotland Yard in 1881 for the public to contact the police with information about criminal activity; however, this was quickly disbanded due to the fact that most calls were deemed trivial and unimportant, though telephone lines were kept for Commissioner Warren, Assistant Commissioner Monro (later Anderson), Metropolitan Police Receiver Pennefather, Home Office men Murdoch and Ruggles-Brise, as well as Wellington Barracks, Horse Guards, the Fire Brigade and the British Museum. Despite the use of this new technology, the telegraph system remained the mainstay of communication for both the City and Metropolitan forces, and it was to play an interesting, if lesser-known, part in the Whitechapel murder investigations. This shall be expanded upon later.

It is worth noting that all messages issued by all police forces were deemed 'strictly confidential', whether issued via telephone, telegram or messenger.

The majority of police stations had an outdoor open area called the yard, and at Commercial Street it was located behind the main building, with a high wall encompassing the other two sides. Here, in summer months, the men would muster for inspection or conduct training, such as hand-to-hand combat; or to adopt the latest edict on how to utilise their kit; or to take exercise. However, one of the main uses of the yard was for drill.[36] Commissioner Warren deemed drill essential, as it was a way to quickly organise and manoeuvre a large body of men during emergencies, including mass disturbances. According to the 1889 publication *Police!*, Warren stated that 'during the years 1886 and 1887 the drill was almost entirely given up'.[37] For the majority of constables in the Metropolitan force at the time, drill was something a candidate constable did predominantly at Preparatory School, and then on occasion within the division or sub division station, especially when upcoming parades or special events were known to be occurring. Almost as soon as he was appointed, Warren began addressing this issue of lack of drill. He significantly upped the number of hours men were to undertake drill per year and, on 6 November 1886, he had a police order drafted within which it was decreed that 'superintendents and inspectors are required to make themselves capable of giving the necessary instructions in marching their respective divisions and subdivisions'.[38]

The yard at Commercial Street had two entrances, both on the Fleur de Lys Street side. One was for people and the other for carriages, and through the latter the horse-drawn police vans known as Black Marias[39] entered the yard to drop off suspects, and to collect newly charged prisoners for transportation to court. The yard also housed the ground-level latrines which were located next to the cell block. Some yards at other stations were too small to conduct drill exercises or self-defence training; however, some stations, mainly within the City of London force, such as Bishopsgate station, were designed with flat roofs, allowing for such activities to occur among the chimney pots of London town. A parade room, or muster room as the City of London Police called them, was often located in most stations, or underneath the yard in the case of Commercial Street. This room acted as a place to muster in inclement weather, as well as a place for briefings and training.

Bishopsgate No. 6 police station, belonging to the City of London force, was unique among stations as it held its own hospital for ill or injured constables. Costing £3,750 to build,[40] financed by the City force's own police surgeon at the time, George Borlais-Childs,[41] built in the finest Portland stone by Messers Myers & Sons and constructed next to and in conjunction with the police station and section house at Bishopsgate, the hospital, or infirmary as it was also known, held four wards capable of tending to fifty ill or injured City constables, free of charge to them, along with a permanent dispensary and a consulting room.[42] The hospital had a team of nurses directly overseen by a matron, with the divisional surgeon taking full responsibility for all within the hospital. Constables, most usually reserves, would be assigned to cover night porter duties, and were issued with a saxe blue uniform, saxe being a light-blue colour familiar in today's nursing uniforms, to distinguish themselves from those on policing duties.[43] Probably the most famous resident of Bishopsgate hospital was there in and around the early 1880s; this was a large, rotund tabby cat known as Big Chap. It seems Big Chap was not only the resident pet of Bishopsgate police station and hospital, but also an integral working member, as it was his duty to keep both locations free of rats and other vermin. So successful was Big Chap at capturing these rats that he grew to an astonishing twenty-one pounds and seven ounces;[44] however, the author suspects that this huge weight gain was most likely aided by a few treats handed to him by soft-hearted constables and nurses.[45]

At other police stations, sick rooms were provided or the inspector's office utilised, so men could be assessed by their divisional surgeon, or another doctor appointed to cover should they be away or elsewhere on duty. All Metropolitan constables on long-term sick leave would be examined by the chief divisional surgeon, MacKellar, at Scotland Yard, and he would then complete a certificate outlining the ailment and estimating either the date the patient was due back on duty, to possibly undertake some light tasks, or the date for a follow-up examination, and this form was kept by the Executive Branch at Scotland Yard. Those men with poor medical history would be assessed as to their suitability for the job and, if considered unfit for duty, would be dismissed from the force on medical grounds. This was quite common, and was sometimes due to the heavy physical demands the job placed upon the men – especially beat work. Metropolitan Commissioner Warren, in 1888, stated that his men were walking around twenty miles a night,[46] and considering that boots of the period consisted of wooden soles, with rubber soles not coming into great use until the early 1890s, it is easy to see why these men were often signed off with the divisional surgeon's callous and brutally honest 'Worn out' upon their discharge certificate. During the 1880s, the Metropolitan Police set up a panel to hear requests for early pensions from constables who had been injured on duty. From this point on, the panel typically consisted of various senior-ranking Scotland Yard officials.

The job remained, however, a potentially dangerous one. Over in the City, twenty years after he had attended the scene of Catherine Eddowes' murder in Mitre Square, Detective Constable Edward Marriott had himself been injured on duty, struck by a horse and van in Basingham Street. He was taken to Bishopsgate City police hospital and examined, and, although it was found he had suffered concussion and a grazed arm, he was discharged from hospital soon after. A year later, DC Marriott was found unconscious in Redcross Street by the beat constable, who promptly took him, with the aid of a fellow PC from a nearby beat, to St Bartholomew's Hospital, and it was here, after an examination by the house surgeon, that Marriott was diagnosed as having suffered an epileptic seizure. He was transferred again to Bishopsgate police hospital, where divisional surgeon Dr Frederick Gordon Brown conducted his assessment of Marriott, and agreed with the house surgeon's diagnosis, stating that 'this is a case of True Epilepsy & in my opinion it is a consequence of his injury on the 19 Nov 1908. I do not think he will be fit for duty in future & should be pensioned.'[47] Brown completed an 'unfit for further service' certificate on Marriott, stating, 'I have carefully examined the above named man [Marriott] and find him totally unfit for further service from infirmity of mind as specified above [epilepsy], and that such infirmity has not been caused by vice or intemperance.' With his honour thus upheld, Detective Constable Edward Marriott's twenty-three years in the City of London force ended, discharged with an annual pension of £74 5s 4d.[48]

Some constables on long-term sick leave were not paid, but they were eligible for aid from the Metropolitan & City Relief Fund. This fund was set up to help constables and their families in troubled times. A board of trustees sat every week to hear requests for financial assistance by any constable or family member. The reasons for – and results of – these requests were published in police orders; however, the names of the officers involved were protected, and only their rank and division were revealed. Like the orphanage fund, money was raised via charitable events, or by generous donations made by policemen of all ranks, from commissioner to constable, as well as by businesses and members of the public appreciative of the work conducted by the police force.

All large police stations within the Metropolitan and City of London forces held accommodation quarters, within which typically resided unmarried constables. The idea came from initial Joint Commissioner Rowan, who felt that having a large group of men constantly together in one location would aid policing should emergency situations arise, enabling the men to be swiftly summoned to duty. Rowan's idea stemmed from the Army's use of barracks, and he initially followed suit in naming the police's version, rather unimaginatively, 'Police Barracks'.[49] The use of the word 'barracks' had military connotations, something the authorities within government were keen to avoid, so the name was altered to 'Section House',[50] although it is still possible to find some press reports around 1888 containing the old term. It is worth noting that not all section houses were connected to subdivision stations. Some small, single-section houses were dotted around the division, residential and with neither an administrative nor policing component attached. In H Division, these single Section Houses were located in the old watch house at 18 Denmark Street and at 102 Mile End Road.[51]

Police!, written by former policeman Charles Tempest Clarkson and journalist J. Hall Richardson in 1889, holds an excellent passage on life in a section house. While it is predominantly about the training section house in Kennington Lane, the description holds for any police section house in the metropolis. Clarkson and Richardson sum up the importance of a section house in one telling line: 'The section house, nevertheless, is more of a lodging-house than a school. It is not a barrack. Its proper name is a "home".' This may be a slightly false representation; while not appalling, conditions in most section houses were described as poor, even in reports written as late as the 1930s. However, as with the Army, resident constables in a majority of section houses built a strong bond of camaraderie, and although disagreements were had, a great sense of fellowship more often than not prevailed.

As a rule, all constables who stayed in a Metropolitan Police section house were charged seven to eight shillings per week for board, with an extra shilling to cover laundry costs, while those who stayed at a City of London Police section house were charged six pence extra (City constables were on a slightly better rate of pay). The board cost fluctuated due to the numbers staying there – the more men in residence, the lower the board[52] – and for their money the men would have a bed, pillow, sheets and blankets. The man in charge was the section house sergeant. He controlled the section house budget, and was responsible for the purchasing of provisions, as well as arranging for equipment to be replaced when it was damaged. Every so often, four pence was taken from the boarders to cover the cost of items such as utensils.[53] The sergeant also set the section house rules and ensured that discipline was maintained. The duties performed by the section house sergeant varied from station to station, and were dependent on the size of section house and the number of men occupying the building; for example, at a sizeable location like A Division's (Whitehall) King Street, the section house was manned by the sergeant on a constant basis, whereas at the smaller Vine Street, C Division (St James), the sergeant was restricted to four hours per week[54] within the section house. Section house sergeants were also expected to step in and undertake regular police duties in times of short staffing or emergency. In some section houses, to aid the sergeant, women were hired as housekeepers, cooks and maids. These, along with the police matrons, were the only women permitted to work within the police until the introduction of female police constables in 1919. The housekeeper was the senior female in the section house, and worked closely with the sergeant to carry out his instructions. The maid maintained cleanliness, and the cook was in charge of ensuring that meals were cooked on time, and with the finest ingredients found with the budget allowed. Again, the sergeant would liaise with the cook on what groceries should be purchased, and volunteers, most usually one or two of the men, would help purchase and serve the food when required. However, it must be pointed out that not all section houses had female assistants, and in those buildings the men themselves would take on the various roles. These men, known as 'Caterers', would be elected on a monthly basis by their brother constables.

Probably the most well-used room in a section house was the canteen, also known as the mess room. It was here that the constables ate and socialised together. They contributed an initial shilling's subscription when joining the mess, and then made a weekly payment of a penny towards its costs, and strict rules and regulations ensured that each man knew what was expected of him. An example of such rules and regulations, in this case in relation to the City Of London Force, can be seen below.

Mess Rules & Regulations

The Commissioner, having sanctioned the establishment of Messes at the various Station Houses for the greater comfort of the resident Sergeant and Constables, directs that the following Rules + Regulations be observed throughout the force.

Establishment: The Messes on establishment will be provided with sufficient quantity of crockery, cutlery, table linen and other articles free of charge, but on the understanding that the same are to be kept up and maintained in serviceable condition at the expense of the members of the mess.

Members: All Sergeants + Constables resident in a Station House – as single men will belong to the Mess of that Station.

Entrance Subscriptions: Every Sergeant + Constable in joining a mess will be called upon to pay an entrance subscription of one shilling. No further subscription will be charged on transfer from one Division to another.

Weekly Subscriptions: Every member of a mess will pay a weekly subscription of not less than 1*d* or such higher rate as the members may consider necessary for that maintenance of the mess property.

Mess Committee: A Mess Committee of not less than three members, of whom the Caterer shall not be one, will be elected quarterly. They will audit all accounts weekly, engage the Mess Servants as required and be responsible generally for the management of the mess.

Caterer: The members of the mess will elect monthly a Caterer, who will take entire charge of the mess establishment under instructions from the Committee. He will purchase provisions, hand them to the cook, give instructions for the various meals and see that they are properly served at the appointed hour, furnish to the resident Sergeant on Friday morning of each week, an account of the sum required from each member to meet the weeks expenditure and submit to the resident Inspector on each Monday an account of all receipts and outlay together with all books and vouchers for audit by the Committee.

Resident Sergeant: The amount due from each member for messing will be collected by the Resident Sergeant and handed to the Caterer.

Allowance to Caterer: A sum not exceeding 1*s*/6*d* per week may be charged in the messing and paid to the Caterer as compensation for the wear and tear of plain clothes.

Duties of Housekeeper and Mess Cook: The Station Housekeeper will perform her duties hitherto. The mess Cook, however, will have entire charge of the kitchen, scullery for during the time she is engaged in her duties.

Canteen: The Commissioner approves of the establishment of Canteens for providing members with beer and sundries. The profits should be kept as low as possible and must be applied as the members of the mess desire. No wines or spirits are to be sold in or obtained throughout the canteen.

Breakfast was most commonly bread, butter, eggs and bacon with tea or coffee, and cooked by the men themselves. Dinner consisted of the obligatory 'meat and two veg', most usually being roast or boiled beef, potatoes and maybe carrots or any other boiled vegetable, and, if they were lucky, a pudding dessert. Tea, again, would be down to the men to arrange and was often lighter than dinner, following the pattern of breakfast. Supper was bread and cheese with, if the men preferred, either a light ale or lemonade bought for three pence a pint from the canteen. Meals were served at set times throughout the day, but, for those on duty, meals could be taken in the canteen once they had come off duty. The men were also permitted to keep small amounts of food for themselves. Three-quarters of a pound of butter was handed to the men each week, and they could purchase small loaves of bread from the provisions shop[55] for two pence. These items would be stored in a small personal locker belonging to the individual, and usually situated in rows along the coolest corridor in the building; however, the reality was that these food lockers, as they were called, were used to store combs, hair oil, blacking, books, pipes, and 'occasional specimens of every article'.[56]

In the communal atmosphere of the mess room, the men ate their food with their colleagues, or simply drank a mug of steaming hot tea or coffee, and out of this constant mingling of constables during these periods in the day the police philosophy of 'canteen culture' was born. Although the term 'canteen culture' is in reference to the mess room's successor, the station canteen, the ideology stems from the Victorian period. Matters ranging from procedure, legalities and promotion to moral, religious and social issues would be discussed in this room, with the majority of men expressing their opinions in what is commonly termed a straightforward, black-and-white style.[57] This expression of opinion and ideas was most often fuelled by a sense of duty and pride in their work, and therefore underpinned the camaraderie held within their section house and, more generally, the police force as a whole. To the public, however, this feature of police life smacked of arrogance, and it gave the police a reputation for insularity.

Entertainment was provided in numerous ways. For those who preferred a quiet evening reading, a well-stocked library, with books, illustrated newspapers and periodicals, was provided in nearly all section houses. The recreation room most commonly housed a dart board and a billiard table. Parlour games and cards were also a popular pastime for the off-duty policeman, and it was not uncommon for the odd friendly bout of boxing to be undertaken in a cleared mess room, which acted as a gym. In most section houses, the provisions shop or canteen also provided ale, supplied in quart cans or pitchers, but no spirits were permitted to be sold. It was felt that if drink was provided within the section house the men would not see the need to frequent public houses, but off-duty men were allowed, with senior permission, to leave the section house of an evening, so long as they were back on premises by midnight roll call. Any late returnees were reprimanded.

It was preferred that drinking would be undertaken within the section house, under the watchful eye of the section house sergeant, keeping any embarrassing incidents in-house, and out of the public gaze. Discipline was the cornerstone of any good functioning section house. Any breach of the rules would result in a severe reprimand–as serious as for any misdemeanour conducted on duty. However, on rare occasions, and as with any 'family', altercations did happen and disagreements were settled with a swift bout of 'fisticuffs' out of the view of the watchful sergeant's eye. In the August of 1888, H Division's PC 51 Paitt was demoted from Constable second class to third class for a year for an attempted assault on a fellow constable. He was also required to pay for the repairs to some gas fittings which were damaged during the same altercation. It would seem that, on this occasion, Paitt's disagreement with one of his brother officers did not escape the sergeant's attention.

If discipline was the cornerstone of the section house, then sporting activities were the safety valve. While subdivision section houses as such rarely formed clubs, the divisions did. Athletics, boxing and swimming thrived along with other traditional team sports such as cricket and rugby. Even the relatively new sport of association football, which formed its first professional league in 1888, was beginning to muscle in on the Victorian policeman's sporting life. Inter-divisional sports competitions were held, as well as competitions against other local teams and against other borough police forces from across the country. In the June of 1899, the City of London Police beat Reading Borough Police by thirty-seven runs in a charity cricket match held at Elm Park, Berkshire, the then home of Reading Football Club. Detective Constable Baxter Hunt made a score of thirty for London, and his teammate, the retired inspector George Izzard, added a rapid eleven to the City Force's total. In Reading's innings, the pair claimed three wickets between them, Hunt taking two and Izzard the other.[58] In 1888, these men had worked together in Mitre Square on the night of Catherine Eddowes's murder.

While both forces had strong sporting teams, there was one particular sport in which they both excelled: tug of war. The legacy of both the Metropolitan and City of London forces' tug of war teams was ultimately established during the 1908 Olympics in London, which saw a unique feat. The gold medal winners, representing Great Britain, were the City of London force. Silver medal winners, again representing Great Britain, were the City of Liverpool police force, and the bronze medal was claimed by the Metropolitan men of Stepney's K Division, eastern neighbours of Whitechapel's H Division, who were also representatives of Great Britain. All the medal winners were serving policemen, and the gold and bronze winners worked within the two forces which policed London. So strong was the City of London force at the sport that they won the silver medal at the 1912 Olympics in Stockholm, though it must be noted that they and Sweden, the eventual gold medal winners, were the only teams who entered the competition that year.

At Commercial Street station, the ablution room was located in the basement and actually consisted of two smaller rooms. In one, the bathroom, stood two roll-top deep baths; and in the other, a washroom, was a bench with deep tin or enamel basins slotted into the cut-out holes and duckboards to stand on, raising the men's feet off the cold and wet floor. A hot bath was a luxury in most stations, with the majority being cold or tepid at best. As the condition of the constables' feet were of concern to the divisional surgeons, plenty of footbaths were provided, and these were gratefully used. These footbaths were far warmer than the average bath, as the hot water from the stove in the mess room was transferred quickly and in relatively small quantities to portable basins.

The boiler room was also situated in the basement, and was the main consumer of coal, which was carefully monitored. Coal holes were dotted around the station as other fires were used in individual rooms, and deliveries of coal were made on a regular basis. The 1881 *Report on the Conditions of Metropolitan Police Stations* figured that a station the size of Commercial Street, which held somewhere between sixty to seventy-four men at any given time, would consume around 125 to 145 pounds[59] of coal just to cook one group meal per day,[60] and the importance of efficient fuel use was impressed upon the cooks. Next to one of those coal holes at Commercial Street was the boot room, where constables stored their footwear neatly in wall-to-wall racking. Next to the boot room was the lamp room, where a similar layout could be found. The scullery, where the cleaning of cooking pots and dirty utensils took place, was situated in the basement, towards Elder Street, but the kitchen and mess were located at the opposite end of the building, towards Fleur de Lys Street. This meant a long traipse from one side of the station to the other with dirty utensils, via the washrooms and the brushing room, where the men brushed dried mud and dust from their clothing and boots.

Along with the operational rooms at ground level, the recreation room sat facing the yard at the corner of Fleur de Lys Street; sandwiched between the recreation room and the main lobby were the library and the clothes room. In the clothes room were kept the main items of clothing, such as greatcoats, capes and helmets, and its location near to the main entrance was purely for convenience.

There were two sixteen-man dormitories at Commercial Street, in addition to two more for five men and another two for four men, found on the first and second floors; fifty slumbering constables could be accommodated in all. The dormitories were located toward the Fleur de Lys Street end of the station, away from the cell block. They were used by two sets of men, day relief[61] and night relief, with a few hours in between during which the beds were aired and the bedclothes changed; locating the men away from the noisy cells ensured they would have a little peace and quiet as they attempted to sleep.

Lockers were provided in the dormitories, usually next to the beds, within which the men kept personal belongings, such as grooming products, books, personal clothing, underwear or letters and keepsakes. Some stations had personal screens fitted between beds, thus giving the men some privacy. These thin panels of wood did not run from ceiling to floor, as they were stood upon wooden feet and could be manoeuvred. Also located on the first floor, towards the Elder Street end of the station, were the inspectors' married quarters, including two bedrooms, a kitchen, a pantry and a sitting room. The same layout could be found directly above, on the second floor, for married sergeants. In 1888, a modern police station such as Commercial Street was well equipped to deal with its duty to the public. At the same time, it accommodated a number of men in relative comfort; luxury, in fact, compared to their neighbours across the street, who struggled in small rooms occupied by many, with some even sharing their floor space with poultry and other animals.

While the section house would be regarded as home by many a young constable starting life in the police force, its true value was always in the occupants it contained. Tempest-Clarkson and Hall-Richardson, in their 1889 work *Police!*, permit A Division's Superintendent Dunlap to sum up the importance of the police section house not only as mere accommodation, a warm home and place to eat and rest, but also as a source of positive influence upon impressionable constables. Dunlap, undoubtedly referring to the 'canteen culture' mentioned earlier, stated that 'from personal experience I can assert that section-house life, with its strict arrangements, its great comfort, and the benefit of discussion, in which the older constables join, on topics of interest concerning the service, is invaluable in the formation of the young policeman's character'. Within the jurisdiction of Whitechapel's H Division, that character was to be severely tested on a daily basis.

5

Blue Bottles

I wish you to feel the importance of a steady constant endeavour by your vigilance to prevent crime as much as possible, and not by your negligence tempt persons to commit it; as you do you fail in attention to your duty.
An address on police duties by the Honourable Sir Harry Hawkins, one of Her Majesty's judges, in the 1899 police code

To give a full account of a life as a Victorian constable, a series of volumes and a very patient reader would be required as their duties were endless and, quite often, a juxtaposed mixture of the monotonous and complex. Therefore I intend to give the reader an idea of that life by pointing out the most common tasks undertaken, as well as to give an insight into other aspects which affected constables as they worked through this part of their policing career.

In his initial volume of *Life and Labour of the People* (1889), a study which ran to twenty-nine volumes in thirteen years, philanthropist Charles Booth[1] justified his analysis of the poverty in London's East End, including those areas covered by the jurisdiction of H Division, by explaining that 'east London lay hidden from view behind a curtain on which were painted terrible pictures: starving children, suffering women, overworked men; horrors of drunkenness and vice; monsters and demons of inhumanity; giants of disease and despair. Did these pictures truly represent what lay behind, or did they bear to the facts a relation similar to that which the pictures outside a booth at some country fair bear to the performance or show within?'[2] The conclusion sadly lay with the former rather than the latter. During the final stages of this study, one of Booth's team, George Duckworth,[3] undertook a series of 'Police Walks', where he was guided around the East End by various police officers, including those of H Division, taking notes on the numerous aspects which influenced the criminal classes, as well notes upon police work itself. These notes are, as Professor Victor Bailey states in his book *Charles Booth's Policemen*, arguably 'the most important compilations of testimony that we possess for the policing of Victorian London'.[4] Duckworth was escorted on these walks mainly by senior officers, at inspector level and above, and was shown the homes and hangouts of numerous villains and troublemakers who had caused the local police much trouble over the years; he was also given tutorials on the types of criminals who were in those areas, and how they conducted their 'business'.

In the midst of the Whitechapel murder scare, Whitechapel held a population of around 76,000. By contrast, the police had a strength of 548 men[5] with which to police what were the most densely populated and most infamous areas for criminality in the East End. The Old Nichol slum, sitting just inside H Division's northern boundary, was one of those areas where constables truly feared to tread their beats; however, it was Flower and Dean Street, which ran between Commercial Street and Brick Lane, where the word 'notorious' could be used without fear of contradiction. Here, along with neighbouring George Street and Thrawl Street, sat a plethora of lodging houses, some registered and some not, rife with the criminal classes. During the slum clearances of the 1880s and 1890s, which heralded improved buildings for the poor with the construction of the Rothschild and Lolesworth accommodations, some of the residents merely dispersed to lodging houses in other nearby areas, such as Sclater Street off Brick Lane, or Dorset Street, opposite Christ Church on Commercial Street which, in turn, had a reputation as 'the worst street in London'.[6] The borders of H Division contained many immigrants from differing religious and cultural backgrounds, and they understandably mixed within their own in small communities dotted around the region, as they sought comfort with those who understood them, those who would help them best in times of need. And while the majority of newcomers abided by the laws of their new land, some were wary of the police and kept their distance from them. To those who had escaped the pogroms of eastern Europe, the police were shadowy figures not to be trusted; they saw them as political spies, corrupt infiltrators of the state, who would cause harm to friends and family on the flimsiest of excuses.

For others, the police were the nearest they got to the establishment, figureheads of a brutal empire which had destroyed their way of life in their homelands, and oppressed their people. Irish Fenianism was at its height during the late Victorian period, and numerous bombing 'outrages' for the 'cause' had been committed within London throughout the 1870s and 1880s. The Great Famine in Ireland triggered mass emigration during the late 1840s and early 1850s, resulting in a rise in Irish immigrants to the United States, Canada and the United Kingdom. Irish communities cropped up throughout the East End during the mid-1800s, and while the majority sought a peaceful life, they viewed the police with contempt, as representatives of a British authority they despised. In areas such as Spitalfields, St George in the East and around the docks, lodged pockets of Irish cockneys, who, H Division's Inspector Joseph Reid[7] told Duckworth, would rather keep disputes between themselves than involve a policeman. 'They fight it out at home,' Reid claimed, with what seems to be some relief, 'and don't give us any trouble'.[8] However, Inspector Carter, who policed what were colloquially known as the 'Fenian barracks' located at the eastern extent of H Division's jurisdiction, begged to differ, claiming that 'three policemen were wounded here last week, this block sends more police to hospital than any other in London. Men are not human, they are wild beasts. You take a man or a woman, a rescue is always organised. They fling brick bats, iron, anything they can lay their hands on,' adding that 'a cry of police brings help from every house. The inhabitants hustle the police, they organise rescues; not the least bit of good anything less than six constables going down in case of a row if there is any prospect of having to haul off any one to the police station.'[9] There was a tight bond of dubious camaraderie within the criminal element of these communities, also confirmed by Booth, who reported, in relation to the area around Sclater Street, that a 'rough class of costers, thieves and prostitutes were a very sporting set who live as a happy family, and "whip round" to make up a purse for bail or for defence of any one in trouble'.[10] The avoidance of arrest, and subsequent detention, was, for the obvious reason that it reduced their capacity to operate, a strong drive for the majority of 'working' criminals, so much so that, according to former Whitechapel Constable Vedy, 'many a culprit in the old days got, and preferred – and even asked for – "a good hiding" to being locked up. It was rough justice, often not adequate, but it saved trouble.'[11]

During the Whitechapel murders, the Reverend Samuel Barnett,[12] whose church of St Jude's sat within a short distance of the murder sites, wrote to *The Times* highlighting his concerns about the community. He, along with his wife Henrietta, drew four points on matters which they considered important enough to be addressed, with point one being an issue concerning the police. The letter reads,

Sir,

   Whitechapel horrors will not be in vain if 'at last' the public conscience awakes to consider the life which these horrors reveal. The murders were, it may almost be said, bound to come; generation could not follow generation in lawless intercourse, children could not be familiarized with scenes of degradation, community in crime could not be the bond of society and the end of all be peace.

   Some of us who, during many years, have known the life of our neighbours do not think the murders to be the worst fact in our experience, and published evidence now gives material for forming a picture of daily or nightly life such as no one has imagined.

   It is for those who, like ourselves, have for years known these things to be ready with practical suggestions, and I would now put some forward as the best outcome of the thought of my wife and myself. Before doing so, it is necessary to remind the public that these criminal haunts are of limited extent. The greater part of Whitechapel is as orderly as any part of London, and the life of most of its inhabitants is more moral than that of many whose vices are hidden by greater wealth. Within the area of a quarter of a mile most of the evil may be found concentrated, and it ought not to be impossible to deal with it strongly and adequately. We would submit four practical suggestions: –

1. Efficient police supervision. In criminal haunts a license has been allowed which would not be endured in other quarters. Rows, fights, and thefts have been permitted, while the police have only been able to keep the main thoroughfares quiet for the passage of respectable people. The Home Office has never authorized the employment of a sufficient force to keep decent order inside the criminal quarters.

2. Adequate lighting and cleaning. It is no blame to our local authority that the back streets are gloomy and ill-cleaned. A penny rate here produces but a small sum, and the ratepayers are often poor. Without doubt, though, dark passages lend themselves to evil deeds. It would not be unwise, and it certainly would be a humane outlay, if some of the unproductive expenditure of the rich were used to make the streets of the poor as light and as clean as the streets of the City.

3. The removal of the slaughter-houses. At present animals are daily slaughtered in the midst of Whitechapel, the butchers with their blood stains are familiar among the street passengers, and sights are common which tend to brutalize ignorant natures. For the sake of both health and morals the slaughtering should be done outside the town.

4. The control of tenement houses by responsible landlords. At present there is lease under lease, and the acting landlord is probably one who encourages vice to pay his rent. Vice can afford to pay more than honesty, but its profits at last go to landlords. If rich men would come forward and buy up this bad property they might not secure great interest, but they would clear away evil not again to be suffered to accumulate. Such properties have been bought with results morally most satisfactory and economically not unsatisfactory. Some of that which remains might now be bought, some of the worst is at present in the market, and I should be glad, indeed, to hear of purchasers.

Far be it from any one to say that even such radical changes as these would do away with evil. When, however, such changes have been effected it will be more possible to develop character, and one by one lead the people to face their highest. Only personal service, the care of individual by individual, can be powerful to keep down evil, and only the knowledge of God is sufficient to give the individual faith to work and see little result of his work. For men and women who will give such service there is a crying demand.

I am, truly yours,
SAMUEL A. BARNETT.
St. Jude's Vicarage, Whitechapel, Sept. 18.[13]

Barnett's letter gives us a good insight into the area of Whitechapel during the murder scare, as well as concerns regarding policing. New recruits, with only a few weeks training, were thrust into this very environment and expected to cope without complaint.

The allocation of constables to a division was not a hit-or-miss affair. It was sometimes done with forethought and precision, with the constable's temperament and noted skillset taken into consideration. For example, A Division, based in Whitehall, had the task of policing the area around the Houses of Parliament and its Ministries, Buckingham Palace and the Royal Courts, as well as overseeing the protection of all those who worked and resided within them. They also had to oversee protection for foreign dignitaries from far and wide. Therefore, the most astute and tactful of candidates were chosen to fall into that division, whereas Whitechapel – which was acknowledged by many as the roughest district in London, with its docks teeming with newly arrived sailors looking for their ideal pleasure ride, criminals and prostitutes haunting its dark alleyways and courts to prey on the vulnerable, and the vulnerable themselves, who would do whatever it took to survive – required a more robust constable, a constable who could handle himself if needs be, one who could dish out a 'dewskitch'[14] if the situation arose, yet who had the wherewithal and insight to initially try and deal with that situation with the understanding of a man who knew exactly who and what he was dealing with. When it came to deciding which candidate went where, the old adage 'horses for courses' was never more apt. Despite their training at Scotland Yard, Kensington Lane and Wellington Barracks, their constant review of the Candidates and Instruction books, their use of the police code and the advice they received from their senior and more seasoned colleagues, the new recruit would always lack what was considered the main 'weapon' in tackling the criminal underworld, against which he was about to pit his courage and wits: local knowledge. Nothing can be as effective to a constable in the execution of his duties as local knowledge; it is something which would keep many out of a sticky situation, enabling him to conduct his duties peacefully, and helping him to gain the respect of colleagues and locals alike. It is this local knowledge which the new constables of Whitechapel had to learn, and learn fast.

After the new constables had gained local knowledge and experience, and after establishing themselves in their initial year in the Metropolitan force, they would be moved up the classification scale, so long as their behaviour and work was deemed suitable enough. Upon being assigned to a subdivisional station, the constable would initially be placed as a police constable fourth class on a wage of around twenty-four shillings per week plus his uniform allowance; also, if he was married with a family, and had his own abode, he would receive a lodging allowance as well. If the constable worked hard and maintained good discipline throughout the year, he would rise to police constable third class, and so on every year until he reached the first class, and with that rise in classification came a rise in pay, until he hit the maximum pay for a constable of £78 per annum.[15] However, it must be remembered that pension deductions were made out of that wage, and a weekly payment of tuppence would also be made to the widows and orphans fund, set up to support the wives and children of constables who had died on duty.[16] When the maximum pay scale had been achieved by the constable, he would, should his disciplinary record permit and the opportunities arise, be eligible for promotion to sergeant. As with all promotions, an examination had to be taken. If successful, the new sergeant could expect a wage of thirty-two shillings per week, rising to thirty-four shillings per week after two years, and on to thirty-eight shillings some three years after that.[17] Again, as with the constables, if the sergeant reached first class, and if circumstances allowed, he would be eligible for the inspector position, pending the passing of his inspector examinations. Inspectors, and sergeants also, had three classes, with the first-class inspectors earning around £187 per annum. Above the inspectors came the superintendents, with their annual wage of £300 rising by ten pounds every year until the maximum yearly salary of £475.[18] Reserves had an additional shilling and sixpence per week for the constable rank, three shillings per week for the sergeant rank and four shillings per week for the inspector rank,[19] due to the flexibility required in the execution of their duties. Constables were paid weekly, receiving their wage in what was called 'pay bowls', a small wooden bowl within which their wage was placed. The men would be marched on a 'pay parade', in rank and classification, past a table full of these bowls all with the same amount of wage in relation to said rank and classification, where they would take their wage from the bowl and be marked off on a wage list by a senior-ranked officer.

The City of London force's classifications of rank ran side by side with their colleagues in the Metropolitan force, though their pay was slightly higher in comparison. A City constable could expect to start on the fourth-class pay £1 5s 7d per week, rising to £1 12s 3d when he reached first class. Sergeants would start at £1 17s per week and could rise to £2; however, the station sergeant could expect a high rate of £2 11s. Inspectors began at £3 1s 6d and ended up on £3 11s 9d when they reached first-class level,[20] and a City Police divisional superintendent would initially bring home £357, £57 per year more than their H Division counterpart. The higher wage structure in the City force meant that they could attract a better standard of constable, but this also meant that the City Police were far stricter on whom they accepted as a candidate. It was found that those applying to be a policeman would first try to join the City of London force, with their higher wage, and if rejected, turn to the Metropolitan force in hopes that they would be accepted by them instead. It was also common for constables already in position in the Metropolitan force, or in other constabularies outside of London, to try and apply for the City force; such was the lure of the City's better wage structure.

Detectives on both forces worked with the same classifications, though the detectives received a slightly higher wage than their uniformed colleagues. This was due to the public image of their rank, the idea that detectives were the *crème de la crème*, a cut above most policemen; however, this led to understandable resentment from those in uniform, who felt, quite rightly, that their work was equally as important. This resentment was disdained by some in the Criminal Investigation Department, who felt it was nothing more than jealousy, whereas those in Central Office attempted to keep peace on both sides by praising their detective force, which was an act of good public relations as well as a deterrent to the criminal classes, while constantly reassuring the uniformed branch that they were held in the highest regard. The mentality of detective work required intelligent men who were capable of thinking and acting on their own initiative, and the extra pay acted as an inducement to attract that type of man to the detective side.

The classing of policemen encouraged both good performance and behaviour. Those who did well were guaranteed to move up the class and pay scale. However, it could also be a disciplinary tool. Poor performance or bad behaviour could see the constable remain at a given class and pay for another year. Those who were already on a higher scale could, should their discipline be poor enough, be reduced in classification. In fact, it was quite common to see a constable reduced from second to third class for a misdemeanour, or a series of misdemeanours for which warnings had not been heeded. And it was not unheard of for constables on first class to be dropped completely down the scale to third or, on rare occasions, fourth class for extreme misbehaviour. Once demoted, the constable would again have to work a year, with good behaviour, before being considered for a rise in classification. Promotion through the ranks was encouraged, and if a constable had achieved first-class status, and had kept that status for over a year, he was permitted to undertake his sergeants' examinations should he wish to do so. The same progressive philosophy applied to the other ranks.

All promotion examinations came under the responsibility of the Civil Service Commission, based in Westminster, as it was they who set the qualification standards.[21] If an eligible constable wished to be promoted to sergeant, he would have to undertake a two-part examination, the first of which consisted of reading and copying manuscript, writing, spelling, elementary English composition and arithmetic, which included monetary questions, as well as the standard addition, subtraction, multiplication and division. This part of the examination would be undertaken at a location within the Civil Service Commission. The second part would be carried out at Central Office, Scotland Yard, where the candidate would have to compile a report on a fictitious occurrence, such as an accident, or on a news report. A sergeant's examination paper for the inspectors' role was, understandably, a little more taxing, and he would also be queried on English and metric weights, measures and reduction, vulgar fractions, decimals and recurring decimals. As well as fielding those questions, the ambitious sergeant would also have to tackle technical questions regarding policing and law, and these questions were set by the police commissioner's office, and not the Civil Service Commission. Inspectors who wished to be promoted to chief inspector had an elementary English examination along with a technical test, again set by the police commissioner's office.[22]

The technical examination of chief inspectors wishing to become divisional superintendents consisted of matters relevant to their intended duties; for example, from figures provided, the candidate would be asked to prepare an estimate of the divisional pay, as well as strength of force[23] and any variations. He would also have to prepare a fictitious 'morning state' report, a report of all important matters and events of the previous night within the division, as well as a further report centred on specific police duties as outlined by the police commissioner's office.[24]

With regard to the Metropolitan force, all examinations were undertaken in front of a board that consisted of the head of the candidate department, Chief Constable Colonel Monsell, and a selection of up to four superintendents from any of the divisions.[25] As well as an examination paper, candidates were also required to answer eight verbal questions posed to them by the board. Each question was potentially worth thirty marks, with a 'very good' answer receiving that amount; twenty-five marks were given for a 'good' answer, twenty for 'very fair', fifteen for 'fair', ten for 'tolerable' and a nil mark for an 'indifferent' response.[26] The verbal questions varied, and were selected by the superintendents on matters ranging from the 'apprehension of ambassadors' servants and diplomatic privileges', to the 'apprehension and general treatment of prostitutes', and on to the more familiar work such as locating missing post office letters, presenting evidence, local bylaws and any other miscellaneous police duties.[27] Successful candidates would be transferred to a new division; potential authority and respect issues could manifest when a former colleague of the same rank became a superior officer. Those who were not appointed to higher posts after examination would remain in their post and, if a promotion opportunity arose again, and their record was good enough, they would be encouraged to reapply, and so the process would begin again.

Promotion depended heavily on conduct, as only good-quality constables would be deemed suitable even to be considered for advancement. The 1889 police code listed thirty common acts of misconduct for a constable to be aware of and avoid. These were:

Drunkenness
Drinking on duty
Taking off the armlet to obtain drink from a publican
Insubordination
Disobedience of direct orders
Infringement of General orders, and Regulations, and the Periodical orders [police orders] issued to the particular force, with which every constable of every force is bound to make himself acquainted, and to know thoroughly
Disrespect to a superior officer
Unnecessary interference
Using unnecessary violence to a prisoner
Incivility, or use of improper language

Giving information to any person concerning orders received, or the progress of a case, without authority

Conveying information, either directly or indirectly, which may delay the execution of a warrant or service of summons

Leaving fixed point or beat improperly, inattention on a fixed point, or not properly working a beat

Neglect of duty, in not taking prompt steps to secure the arrest of an offender

Neglect of duty, in not discovering doors and windows open at night, or the effecting of felonious entry

Neglecting to mark exposed places at night

Talking and gossiping on duty

Soliciting a gratuity

Accepting any gratuity without reporting it

Absence without leave, or malingering

Absence from section house and roll call

Quarrelling with comrades

Unpunctuality for parade

Slovenly dress and appearance

Bringing in, or taking, an improper charge

Taking any unusual step, or leaving the district, without authority

Neglecting to obtain necessary names, in a criminal case, or case of accident

Neglecting to assist persons injured or taken ill in the street

Incurring debts

Bringing discredit on the police force, or causing any injury to the public service in any way

This list of thirty acts of misconduct came with a list of eleven punishments, in descending order of strictness depending on the severity of the misconduct offence, and these were:

To be charged before a Magistrate (Police Acts), involving dismissal, in addition any imprisonment, with hard labour, which may be inflicted, and forfeiting all right to gratuity or pension

Dismissal

Suspension, forfeiting all pay and service while it continues

Reduction in rank

Reduction in class

Placing at foot of class

Fines extending from 1s, to several days pay, usually not more than five

Removal from the reserve or special duty

Forfeit of leave

Severe reprimand and caution

Caution[28]

The most common offences constables committed were connected to drink. This was somewhat aided by the bribery of the constables by local publicans, among whom it was common practice for pots of ale to be left on pub window sills, ready to be picked up and consumed by the passing beat constable; in exchange, the constable would testify to the publican's good conduct when the latter's licence was up for renewal at the magistrates' court. Some of the constables who were involved in the Whitechapel murders case – Constables Pearce and Long to name just two – received punishments connected to drink, with Long being dismissed from the force for being drunk on duty in 1889.[29] Another constable who, like Constable Long, was in the thick of the action on the fateful night when Catherine Eddowes was found murdered in Mitre Square, was her discoverer, City Police Constable 881 Edward Watkins. Watkins had a rather poor start to his police career when, barely a year after joining the police, in the August of 1872, he was fined 2s 6d for being caught having 'sexual intercourse with a woman whilst on his beat'.[30] Watkins followed up this extraordinary misdemeanour with two drink-related acts of misconduct, and one of neglect by not noticing a key left in a shop door during his beat. He received fines or reduction of class as punishments, and it should be noted that by 1888 Watkins's behaviour had improved dramatically, as he was to commit only one further misdemeanour, being found drinking in a public house in 1889, before his police career ended in 1896.[31] While chances were given, these were few, and a constable could not expect to survive more than one severe misdemeanour.

Alongside the punishment system, a reward system was also in place. A constable who produced exceptional work (apprehending a wanted person, for example, or stopping a runaway horse) could expect to be recommended for a reward by his superiors. These recommendations would be made to the magistrates' court, and they would, if in agreement, reward the constable any amount up to £3 out of the fund put aside for such things. Gratuities – gift items donated by the members of the public – were accepted only with the permission of the commissioner, and usually for acts of great bravery or vigilance, such as that conducted by Catherine Eddowes's gaoler City PC 968 George Hutt, who received a gold watch in the February of 1886 from Messers Saqui & Lawrence, a jewellery shop in Fleet Street, for capturing thieves upon their premises.

Constables resided in one of three places: within the subdivision station's section house with other constables; within a section house not connected to a subdivision station; or, if married with children, in rented accommodation. One may think that constables who took the latter option would escape the steely grip of their employers, but this wasn't the case. It was decreed that policemen and their families 'may not live in a slum',[32] with the most common residence for police in the poorest areas of London being accommodation in the Peabody dwellings, which made policemen the fourth-largest occupational group for this type of dwelling.[33] Married constables were expected to live within close walking distance of their subdivision stations, and in areas not deemed to be frequented by any of the criminal classes, and, in order to maintain a perceived high social standing within the community in which the constable resided, a constable's wife was not permitted to take on employment.

The police widows and orphans fund was one of Metropolitan Commissioner Henderson's finest achievements within the police force. Henderson, along with five superintendents, set the fund up in 1870, to support the wives and children of deceased constables. A group of performers, which initially consisted of constables from Cannon Row police station, A Division (Whitehall) headquarters, set themselves up as a troupe, calling themselves 'The Metropolitan Police Minstrels', and organised shows in their spare time to raise money for the fund.[34] An orphanage was established in Twickenham, London, and by 1871, the City of London Police had joined the fund, establishing it across both forces of the London area. By 1888 a police widow could be granted a £15 pension, and £2 10s was given to each child up to the age of fifteen; however, a sergeant's widow received £25 per annum with their children receiving £5 per year. President of the orphanage in 1888 was Metropolitan Police Commissioner Warren, with his City counterpart, Sir James Fraser, sitting as vice-president along with Colonel Pearson, Alexander Carmichael Bruce and James Monro. The orphanage closed in 1937, but the fund remains in existence to this day as the Metropolitan & City Police Orphans Fund.[35]

Other charitable events for the police were also held, and in the January of 1889 the City of London force held its annual Police Festival, where 1,000 of its men, with their wives and children, were invited to Cannon Street Hotel to continue the New Year festivities, something which City Superintendent Foster had been arranging since 1868. Also invited was the Director of the Bank of England, Alfred de Rothschild, who thanked the men of the City force for protecting the financial powerhouse that is the City of London by presenting each of them with a pipe and a half pound of smoking tobacco in a pouch, whether they were smokers or not, and to each child a toy.[36]

When the very first of Peel's men walked out onto the streets of London in 1829, the clothing they wore was specifically chosen. Peel wanted his men to hold an air of authority about them; however, he also wanted to steer away from the militaristic style of policing that was in effect across the Channel in France, or, at least, to go some way to alleviate the British public's fears of such an organisation. Before Peel's force, the Bow Street office had a uniform consisting of a blue swallow-tail frock coat with yellow buttons, blue trousers, black boots, white gloves, black stovepipe hat and a distinctive red waistcoat.[37] The new force's uniform was extremely similar to its Bow Street predecessor, a blue swallow-tailed frock coat with, initially, eight gilt buttons. The frock coat came with a four-inch leather stock collar, designed specifically to protect its wearer from the most common assault of the period, garrotting. Also, upon the high collar, metal numbers were attached so that the constable could be identified when required; this swiftly replaced the original idea of embroidered collar numbers. A tall, stovepipe-style hat made of beaver skin and reinforced with leather and cane side panels was also taken from the constables of Bow Street. Blue trousers were to be worn in the winter months, with white trousers for the summertime. A truncheon and rattle, to raise alarm, were carried within a specially designed pocket inside the tail of the frock coat. The distinctive red waistcoats were done away with as Peel feared people would connect the new force to the Army, whose uniform of the period was predominantly in that colour. This was pretty much the standard template police uniform, but by 1888 the design had slightly changed and the accessories altered. The stovepipe hats were withdrawn in 1864, all replaced completely by 1865 with the new 'Custodian'-style helmet supplied by Messrs Gilpin and Co., Army suppliers of Northumberland Street, just off the Strand, who had been providing the policemen of the Royal Dockyards with the same helmet since 1863. The swallow-tailed frock coat was also replaced by a tunic in 1865, which came midway between the waist and knee.[38] The white summer trousers were also dropped and the protective stock was reduced from four inches in height to two. The result was an instantly recognisable uniform which was to become iconic of British policemen throughout the world.[39]

The 'Custodian' style of helmet, which is instantly recognisable today, was inspired by the military helmets of the period, and a hybrid of the British Home Service Army helmet and the Prussian pickelhaube. In 1881 the Metropolitan force adopted a helmet constructed of six panels of cork, lined with leather on the headband and fine, dark-blue wool protection covering the outside, with what is commonly known as a 'Rose' or 'Boss' crowned design upon the top, perforated with five small holes for ventilation. A thin leather band ran above the peak line and a japanned, seven-pointed Brunswick star helmet plate upon the front. A garter sat within the Brunswick star, embossed with the words 'Metropolitan Police', and within that was the divisional letter – H if the constable was based in Whitechapel – which was placed above the constable's collar number for identification; above the Brunswick star sat the crown of Queen Victoria. William Jones, a military outfitter based in Regent Street, had taken over the helmet contract from Gilpin & Co. in 1886, and he provided the Metropolitan force with their helmets in 1888.

The City of London police again took a 'Custodian' style of helmet; however, they preferred the 'Coxcomb' or 'Comb'[40]-style crown, which meant the ventilation hole was brought forward to the front of the crown, above the forehead, and ran down the back, rather similar to a fireman's helmet. Instead of a Brunswick star and Victorian crown, their helmet plate had the City of London coat of arms in black and, in gold, the constable's collar number in the middle, finishing with a leather band around the peak, just as the Metropolitan force's helmet did.[41]

Both forces instructed that the chinstrap was to be worn at the point of the chin, not under, to avoid the helmet being pulled back over the head, resulting in the wearer being potentially asphyxiated, and they were also ordered not to tuck the chinstrap into the crown, thus rendering the helmet susceptible to being knocked easily off.[42] To position the peak, the constable was instructed to place the base knuckle of his thumb upon the tip of his nose, and then to pull the helmet forward until it touched the tip of said thumb. Initially these helmets were awkward to wear, with many constables complaining of headaches, but, over time, as the cork softened up, they shaped themselves to the wearer's head and became far more comfortable. The helmet's main function, clearly, was to protect the constable from blows to the head, deflecting them down and to the side, something the original stovepipe helmets failed to do.

In 1888, uniforms came in a Melton cloth, which was preferred for its hardwearing nature and warmth, though the latter was a problem during the warm summer months.[43] Although uniforms varied in style within each force (an inspector's tunic was heavily embroidered, for instance, whereas the rank-and-file constables' tunics were plain), there were more similarities than differences between the forces, and a conventional style was increasingly mapped out. Both forces wore a single-breasted frock pattern, with the Metropolitan force opting for eight silver white buttons down the front, each embossed with the words Metropolitan Police and Queen Victoria's crown,[44] with a further two buttons on rear, whereas the City of London force took on brass buttons embossed with their name, and the City's coat of arms, which gave their tunic buttons a distinctive yellow look.

Leather stocks were initially worn around the neck, under the tunic, due to the fact that the most common assault upon a police constable during the force's early years was garrotting. However, as time progressed, garrotting assaults dwindled, and by 1880 the stock was discontinued; however, a thin strip of leather was still sewn into the collar lining of the tunic, giving it a high, restrictive look. Inserted into the collar was the unique identification number, or 'flash', of that specific constable. Each constable's collar number began with his division's identification letter, H in the case of Whitechapel, and then a two- or three-digit number. It was expected that these collar numbers were kept clean and legible; however, the Victorian fashion for men during that specific period was the growing of copious amount of facial hair, and long beards could often cover the collar number. It is a surprise that this was permitted, although identification of the constable could be made due to the fact his helmet plate also holds the same number. Some divisional inspectors were happy to permit long beards to obscure collar numbers, whereas others would issue instructions for the beards to be trimmed. The introduction of whistles in 1885 brought a problem, in as much that the tunics of that period had no pockets for the whistles to sit in. To counter this, a small pocket made of suede was tailored into the tunic, on the inside, which accommodated the whistle and kept it clean.

Trousers were, again, made of Melton cloth, tailored with a truncheon pocket, worn with braces; a constable would be issued with a new pair around every six to seven months. As with all pieces of Metropolitan Police equipment, a standard stamp, the 'Broad Arrow' or 'Crow's foot' marking as it was sometimes called, was placed upon each item on receipt from the contractor, indicating that it had passed a War Department inspection and was fit for use.

Initially, ankle boots were provided to the police courtesy of the convict department. However, contractors were brought in by 1888 and it was they who provided a steady supply of boots in varying sizes. Constables were issued a pair of boots every six months, which were always opened in the presence of a sergeant, and any deficiencies with the boots would be reported to stores by the latter.[45] Each boot would be stamped with the division's identification letter and the words 'Metropolitan Police'. Waterproofing of boots would be ordered just prior to the winter months, meaning the men had to work dubbing, a wax-based product similar to shoe polish, into their boots to ensure they were water resistant.[46] The heavy-duty boots usually had wooden soles, giving the wearer's steps an unmistakeable clumping sound, and leading to the police receiving the generic nickname of 'Plod'.

Appointments are items of equipment issued to each beat constable and carried when he conducted his beat. These included a truncheon, whistle (Metropolitan Police only), a set of handcuffs with key, pencil and notebook and, for those on night relief, a bullseye lamp. These items were inspected by the section sergeant both prior to beat patrol and upon the return from beat patrol to ensure they were clean and not damaged in any way.

The early truncheons were used as much for identification as they were as a defensive weapon, and the tradition of decorating them was carried into the new police in 1829. The styles of decoration and shapes varied throughout the country, but the newly formed Metropolitan force adopted a twenty-inch-long truncheon made either of lancewood or male bamboo,[47] painted black, with the royal coat of arms painted above the gold initials 'M. P.' set on a red background, with the division painted underneath. When the City of London force came into existence it took on a similar style, but they used the City's coat of arms rather than the royal one. These were initially worn in a specially designed pocket set in the tail of the original swallow-tailed tunics; when the tunics were altered in 1864, a spring-loaded truncheon case was introduced, to be worn on the belt. A complete overhaul regarding the truncheon was undertaken in 1887, with the spring-loaded case removed and a specially designed pocket built being into the trouser to accommodate the truncheon. By this point the truncheon had been altered, with four different 'types' being used.[48] Type 1 was fifteen and a half inches in length, made of lancewood, and was to be used during mass disturbances. Type 2 was twelve and a half inches in length, made of cocuswood, which had replaced male bamboo, and was issued to all uniformed constables. Type 3 was twelve and a half inches in length, and was for the use of the River Police only. Type 4 was slightly shorter in length at eleven and a half inches, and was issued to detectives, plain-clothes constables and inspectors.

All of these truncheons had a leather strap affixed to the handle, so the user could wrap it around their wrist. In the event that the constable lost his grip, the truncheon would still be attached to the wrist via the strap, thus preventing a third party retrieving it and using it against the constable. Out went the elaborate decoration, and in came a simple gold Victoria crown embossing stamped into the black wood halfway down the shaft, sitting above the initials 'V. R.', which stood for Victoria Regina.

Instruction upon the use of these truncheons was strictly laid out in the police code, which stated that 'the use of the truncheon must not be resorted to, except in extreme cases, when all other attempts have failed, and the prisoner is likely to escape, or be rescued, through the constable being ill used or overpowered'.[49] Training was regularly undertaken regarding the correct use of a truncheon, with the legs and arms being the primary target for strikes, and the head only being the final resort. The truncheon was predominantly used for restraint. If the constable was aware of a potential confrontation, the rapid application of the truncheon to pressure points around the body, in conjunction with various holds, often ensured a swift and relatively peaceful incapacitation of the prisoner.[50]

Initially, weighted rattles, taken on from the old watchmen, were used to raise alarms. By the mid-1880s the Metropolitan force felt that, among the constant noise of a London in the midst of massive growth and ongoing industrialisation, these rattles were rapidly becoming ineffective, and a solution was sought to find something which would ensure a raised 'hue and cry' could be heard. The Metropolitan force had begun to use whistles at their divisions within the naval and military bases during the 1860s, as well as during events such as noisy public demonstrations, so, in 1883, they turned to whistle maker J. Hudson & Co. of Birmingham, to see if they could design an effective, mass-produced whistle which could be used on the busy London streets. Hudson came up with the 'MP1' the following year, better known by its engraved name, 'The Metropolitan', and during tests conducted outside Scotland Yard it was found to be heard 900 yards further than the rattle. The Met were impressed, and ordered some 7,000 of them, although they had to loan Hudson some money to get the first batch made.[51] The police order dated 10 February 1885 decreed that every constable on day patrol was to have a whistle, with the same instruction to constables on night patrol not, oddly enough, being issued until some two years later, on 25 June 1887.

Although the City of London police also used whistles for special operations, such as crowd disturbances and so on, they did not turn their attention to the constant use of whistles for their constables until a year after the Whitechapel murders, when, in a police order dated 21 May 1889, Acting Commissioner Smith asked for the opinions of his divisional inspectors by enquiring 'in detail, whether in favour of, or against the proposition and referring to any instances in which a whistle would, in their judgement, have proved more useful in obtaining ready assistance in cases of need than the rattle now carried'.[52] It is clear that the City force was intending to follow the Metropolitan's lead in issuing whistles to their beat constables, as the police order finishes with an instruction to the divisional inspectors that 'in forming their opinions, it will be essential of course to bear in mind the size of the beats at night and the proximity of the constables to each other'.[53] It would seem the City of London Police's divisional inspectors agreed to the use of whistles, as some of the constables of the City force were issued with new whistles on 9 January 1890, and with that issue came the instruction on how to wear their new appointment item: 'The whistles, some of which will be issued today,' it stated, 'are to be, when the great coat is not worn, affixed by the hook to the second button hole of the tunic from the top and the whistle itself passed in about the second button from the waist.'[54]

The use of whistles was strictly governed by senior ranks: 'If at any time, he [the constable] requires immediate assistance, and cannot in any other way obtain it, he must blow his whistle or spring his rattle; but this is to be done as seldom as possible, as such alarm often creates inconvenience by assembling a crowd. He will be required to report to the sergeant of his section every occasion for using his rattle or whistle.'[55]

Handcuffs were initially used to restrain prisoners when required, and were kept at subdivision stations, only being issued directly to constables during special duties or a special operation; however, they eventually became part of the appointments and were issued to beat constables for use if required. Though there were many styles of handcuff restraints, two were chiefly used above all others: the Figure of Eight, also known as the 'come alongs' or, later, as 'nippers'; and the standard Hiatt 104 model named the Darby, also known as 'D cuffs'.[56] The Figure of Eight cuffs were used chiefly for the transportation of prisoners, either through the station or to and from court, with the prisoner's wrist shackled in one loop, and with the other loop either shackled to the constable or held tightly in his grip. Due to their inflexibility, a simple twisting of these cuffs by the constable would apply enough pressure to enable him to manoeuvre the prisoner with ease. The Darby cuffs were chiefly used during special duties or out on the streets, with both of the prisoner's wrists being secured. Both styles of cuffs used a barrel lock which was undone by the means of a key. The police code outlined the necessity to use handcuffs, stating clearly that handcuffs should never be used except when the prisoner becomes violent or 'if the number of prisoners to be conveyed, or the special circumstances, renders such a precaution necessary to impede a rescue'.[57] The code also warned that improper use of handcuffs may result in the prisoner bringing 'an action [to] recover damages against the officer'.[58]

The only source of lighting a Victorian policeman had during the dark nights was supplied to him by the bullseye lamp. Issued to each constable and section sergeant on night duty,[59] the lamp consisted of a few parts: a sturdy outer shell with a cowling to let the heat and fumes out, adjustable handles to ease holding, and a belt clip that allowed the constable to hang the lamp off his belt and free up his hands. A leather guard was issued in

1885, and was worn on the belt to protect the uniform from burns and oil stains, which was a common issue. An inner shell housed the reservoir lamp, and this could be rotated within the outer shell, thus eliminating the light without the need to extinguish the lamp. The reservoir lamp held enough whale oil fuel to maintain the flame throughout the constable's beat[60] and upon it sat the wick which, when lit, could be adjusted, thus altering the intensity of the flame. Situated on the side of the outer shell was a thick, rounded, magnified glass bullseye lens through which the light of the reservoir lamp shone, giving a fairly bright light for the period. It was this lens that gave the lamp its name.

These lamps were a necessity for night beats. The lighting of the time was poor in comparison to the modern lighting of today, and in Whitechapel, when compared against the richer parishes to the west, street lighting was extremely inadequate at best. During the height of the Whitechapel murders in 1888, H Division's Chief Inspector West[61] took a *Daily News* reporter around the district; the outcome was this damning report, which is worth reading in full to get a good idea not only about the issue of street lighting within Whitechapel during the murder scare, but also about the area and its life.

STREET LIGHTING IN THE EAST END

'Resolved, that this Board regards with horror and alarm the several atrocious murders recently perpetrated within the district of Whitechapel and its vicinity, and calls upon Sir Charles Warren so to regulate and strengthen the police force in the neighbourhood as to guard against any repetition of such atrocities.'

'Go to,' adroitly replies Sir Charles Warren. 'Look to your lamps. The purlieus about Whitechapel are very imperfectly lighted, and the darkness is an important assistant to crime.' There can be no doubt in the mind of anybody who knows the purlieus of Whitechapel that the commissioner has fairly scored one against the Whitechapel District Board of Works. 'You are decidedly of opinion, then,' was a question addressed to Chief Inspector West, 'that if your division were generally better lighted it would tend materially to render many forms of crime more difficult and the capture of criminals more easy?' 'Most certainly,' was the ready rejoinder. 'Look even at this Commercial street. It has always appeared to me to be very insufficiently lighted – a broad and important thoroughfare like this. It is none too brilliant now. Lying just off it there are some of the lowest of lodging houses, and you can see how easy it must be for rough characters to snatch from the persons passing along and rush off into their dens in the darkness with very little chance of their being identified or followed. But wait until the few shops are closed, and the public house lights are put out, and see then how wretchedly the street is lighted, and what opportunities there are for all sorts of mischief to go on.'

Looking up this main thoroughfare it is impossible to deny that there is much force in what the officer says, and turning into the minor streets and lanes in the neighbourhood the opportunities afforded by the murky condition of the streets for the perpetration of crimes of violence are very apparent. Put out the public house lamps at twelve o'clock, and shut up one or two little shops, and you have – for instance, in Fleur de Lys street – a dismal little lane suggestive of almost anything bad. Obscure thoroughfares like Elder street, Quaker street, Blossom street are all of them open to the same criticism, and a very little exploration will convince anybody that that in most of them there are deeper depths of gloom, affording really startling facilities for vice and crime. 'Look here, sir,' said an anxious and despondent woman to the officer who was looking round one of these murky lanes last evening. 'We may all be murdered here any night. This doors open all night long. People may get down in the cellar or out in the back yard, or up the staircases, and none of us can prevent 'em.' The house passage widened out into a sort of washhouse, and behind this was a very nasty yard, all in utter darkness. The District Board of Works saw, and reasonably enough of course, that they cannot be held responsible for this. It is the landlord's affair. But as a matter of notorious fact, in all the poorer quarters of London, the landlords do not look to the security of their tenement passages and back yards, and cannot be made to do so. And it is a fact which certainly seems to afford a strong reason why at least the actual streets should be well lighted. In many cases, however, not only is the lighting of the streets very insufficient either for comfort or security, but yards for which the authorities are certainly responsible are entirely neglected. Take as an illustration of this Pope's Head court in Quaker Street. It opens from the street by a public passage, and the yard itself is in utter darkness. The lodgers in an adjacent public house have a way to it by a back gate. Seen at any rate by night it has the appearance of a place specially planned for deeds of crime and vice; and the unfortunate people who have to grope their way to their rooms through the dirt and darkness are loud in their complaints. 'Been here six years,' said a rough looking occupant of a room in the court, 'and never had no key, and never had the front door locked. Look at that staircase leading up to that place there – anybody may get up them, and do just what they like. I have begged the landlord to give us a lock on the door, and a key. But not he; he takes no notice of us, and don't care a curse whether we gets murdered or not.' The lighting and cleansing at least of this court seem to be the work of the District Board, and the circumstances under which this nasty little retreat was found – quite incidentally in the course of an inspection of the street – certainly suggested the probability that many others of a similar character might have been found by further search in the same neighbourhood. Some of the courts and streets inspected in this poor neighbourhood are very fairly lighted, but every here and there one was found in which apparently the greatest economy of lamp lighting had been practised, in consideration of the fact that the flaring lights of public houses sufficiently supplemented the street lamps up till midnight. After midnight, however, such streets are terribly gloomy. Let anyone go down Spital Street, for instance, after twelve o'clock at night and say whether throat cutting and 'snatching' and general vice are not suggested by the murky darkness of the locality. From there go on to Buxton street and thence into Code street – not only wretchedly lighted, but ankle deep in mud, by the way. Hanbury Street, which is itself for the most part very poorly lighted. In this street, it will be remembered, it has already been shown that large numbers of the houses are let out tenements, and the street doors and passages are open all night long. The terror of many of the people at the time that murder was found out in one of these houses was intense. Said one woman, 'There are unlocked cellars down under these houses, and the yards are all open, and we may any of us be murdered in our beds.' Last night as a small party of inspectors moved about the neighbourhood there were abundant indications that this terror had by no means subsided. Again and again appeal was made that something should be done for their greater safety, and the general anxiety and sense of insecurity must unquestionably have been greatly intensified by the unsatisfactory lighting in the streets. 'When this public house is shut up,' said the police inspector, 'how could I possibly make out anything going on a few yards off?' The lamps, it may be, are not too far apart, but they are feeble flickerings wholly behind the times.

Now it must not be supposed that we are singling out the Whitechapel district for especial censure. Much of the evil character of Whitechapel as a region of slums and filth and squalor is purely a matter of tradition. It may have been true of it a generation ago, but it is true no longer, as regards by far the greater part of the district at least. In lighting and cleansing and general management Whitechapel is at least on an equality with localities in the south and north, and even in many parts of the west. But there are 70,000 people here, and among them a police sergeant observed last night that he had in the district assigned to him no less than 6,000 residents in common lodging houses. Of course they will include a serious proportion of the criminal and cadger class, and lighting and patrolling that might be sufficient elsewhere may very well be wholly insufficient among a population like this. Having regard to the character of the population, Sir Charles Warren says unequivocally that the neighbourhood is imperfectly lighted, and that the darkness is an important assistant to crime. The District Board of Works will we understand shortly have the Commissioner's letter under consideration, and the reply they may be expected to make is that they do not increase their lamps for precisely the same reason that Sir Charles Warren does not increase the number of his men. Lamps, like policemen, cost money, and the lighting of Whitechapel cannot be rendered more brilliant without a serious addition to the rates. Roughly speaking, every street lamp represents a hundred pounds capitalised. That is to say, the annual maintenance of a lamp costs about the interest of £100, and altogether the lighting of the entire district costs in round figures £5,000 a year. It is a good round sum no doubt but if it is really true that an increase of light would tend decidedly to the suppression of crime it seems very probable that the addition of even another £5,000 and the doubling of the light would be a good investment. But a good deal less then this would effect a great improvement in the safety and comfort of thousands of people, and very much the same may be said of many other large districts of London. At no very distant date it may be science and public spirit may combine to banish darkness altogether. Science, indeed, is quite ready to undertake the business offhand, and to pour over any section of London such a blaze of light that slums and passages and back yards can no longer give shelter to deeds of darkness. But funds, alas, are not yet forthcoming. As yet we prefer to spend our money in providing plunder for thieves, and in maintaining them when we have caught them in spite of all the difficulties of darkness. No doubt we shall be wiser some day, but an intelligent comprehension of these matters is like the revolution of electric lighting – a matter of slow and gradual progress.[62]

At Commercial Street police station, bullseye lamps were stored in their own room, and it was here that the lamp trimmers would cut the wicks straight, thus ensuring a steady and even burn. The lamp trimmers, provided by the contractors Messers J. & C. Christie of Mansell Street,[63] would visit every station within the jurisdiction of the Metropolitan force on a daily basis, calling at H Division's headquarters Leman Street and Commercial Street police stations at 7.00 a.m., Shadwell at 9.45 a.m. and finally at Arbour Square at 11.30 a.m.[64] Along with wick trimming, lamps were refilled with oil and, if required, blacked for heat protection, as well as undergoing general maintenance.

These bullseye lamps were predominantly made and supplied by Hiatt & Co., based in Birmingham, although other manufacturers such as Camelinat, again of Birmingham, and Dolans of Vauxhall were also noted suppliers. One company, T. Joyce, appears as a Metropolitan force supplier of lamps for a time in 1871 and, reviewing their address of 43 Bishopsgate without, London, it would be logical to assume that Mr Joyce also supplied bullseye lamps to the City of London force as well, as their address is extremely close to the City's Bishopsgate police station.[65] However, it must be stressed that this is only the author's considered opinion.

All constables were issued with a pocketbook, also known as a notebook, within which he must write down, in pencil, information on enquiries made, or about to be made, names and addresses of persons to be summonsed, witness details, details of significant events such as accidents or crimes, and so on.[66] Times relating to these significant events were also to be noted; however, if these times were not known exactly then an approximation to the nearest five minutes was advised. Also held in these pocketbooks would be photos of missing persons and/or persons wanted, of whom the beat constable was expected to keep a lookout for while patrolling.

Other appointments were also essential to a working constable, and therefore deemed a requirement by the authorities in the police orders of 31 December 1887. Armlets, a strip of material with a buckle fastening, were introduced in 1830 simply to distinguish between an on-duty and off-duty constable, and were necessary due to the fact that, until 1869, constables had to wear their uniforms at all times, even when off duty.

Worn on the left arm to indicate they were on duty, and consisting of blue and white vertical stripes for the Metropolitan force, and red and white vertical stripes for the City of London force,[67] the armlets were worn around the cuff of the tunic or greatcoat sleeve. Sergeants initially wore their armlets upon the right arm; however, this had become unnecessary by 1888, as the rank identification marks, which were introduced in 1864, saw three chevrons placed upon the sergeant's sleeve, meaning that his rank was easily identifiable. Therefore, all policemen on duty wore the armlet on the left arm in 1888.

Greatcoats were of huge benefit during the cold winter months, double-breasted and heavy so as to combat the extreme weather. Oddly, the men were instructed to button up one side in one month, and switch to the other side the next month, presumably to ensure even wear. Each constable was issued with two greatcoats, and each coat was affixed with the constable's own collar number. Truncheon pockets were also tailored into the greatcoat.

Belts, each stamped with the divisional letter, were initially introduced solely to carry the cutlass. However, since these were not worn as items on their own after 1863, the two-and-a-half-inch-wide 'S' clasp, or snake belt, was introduced. Worn over the tunic, the belt had, in 1885, a strip of leather added to it, to protect it and the tunic from scorch marks left by the bullseye lamp, which was worn on the belt by constables on beat patrol. The right-hand side of the belt was actually thicker, so that the bullseye lamp could be slotted into position on the belt without fear of it coming off while walking.[68] Also attached to the belt was a cape carrier, a small metal loop through which a rolled-up cape could be inserted.

Capes came in differing styles and sizes: a heavy Melton wool cape, with finger loopholes, for the winter weather; and a lighter one for protection against rain showers. Constables were only permitted to wear them if the weather was either cold or very wet. Constables who were five feet and nine inches in height and above were given a twenty-seven-and-a-half-inch cape, and constables under that height were issued with a twenty-five-inch cape[69]. The 'vegetable leather' shower cape was initially used in 1860; however, it was soon found that the waterproofing cracked and peeled off, and from that time onwards an oilskin cape was the preferred option. As stated, the use of the cape was strictly monitored, due to the fact that it became a hindrance when tackling criminals, who would creep up behind a constable, and either flip the cape over his head to render him helpless before assaulting him, or grab the sides of the cape together to restrict the constable's arm movements before, again, assaulting him. Therefore constables would remove the cape when not in use, roll them up, and carry them in the metal loop, called a 'runner', attached to the belt on the left hip, which was provided for such a task. If the cape was wet, the constable would drop it off with some night watchman or pub landlord, so they could dry out, returning to pick the cape up prior to the end of his beat shift.

Gloves were initially part of the police uniform; however, in 1886, a police order confined the wearing of black worsted gloves to periods of extreme cold weather between 1 October and 31 May, and the wearing of white gloves to special occasions or when directing traffic. Leather gauntlets were supplied to each subdivisional station and were to be worn during the collection of stray dogs, which was the responsibility of the police, who would transfer the dogs to Battersea Dogs' Home, and all stray dogs collected in H Division were kept at Shadwell subdivision station, as it had a drinking trough for dogs. Rabies was still a very serious concern in 1888, despite Pasteur and Roux's vaccine having helped reduce fatalities, so gauntlets were a necessary precaution. Any dogs found to be suffering from rabies were swiftly dealt with, and the 1889 police code covers this, stating that 'dogs found by the police undoubtedly suffering from rabies should be killed with the truncheon or some other weapon as speedily and as painlessly as possible, the officer taking great care to avoid being bitten, or allow any of the saliva to touch him or his clothes'.[70]

Issued four times a day, at 9.30 a.m., 1.30 p.m., 6.30 p.m. and 10.30 p.m., police orders were the daily provision of information cascaded down through the ranks to all constables from the commissioners' offices in both Scotland Yard and Old Jewry, with the initial 9.30 a.m. report being known as 'morning state'. In them was held a wealth of orders and information, so much that it would be broken down into headed sections to include promotions, gratuities, resignations, dismissals, acts of bravery and so on. Police orders would also hold direct instructions to constables on numerous matters, be it relevant to them personally, such as medical inspections, mess regulations or clothing issues, or matters to be attended to in the course of duty, such as special duties or amendments in procedure,[71] and it wasn't unknown for updates to be telegraphed through to the various divisional headquarters for cascading. At subdivision stations, the orders would be referred to during the changeover of shifts, with pertinent information being read out to everyone present, and copies would be left in the reserve room and libraries, and anywhere else where they could be easily referred to by the constables and other ranks.

In addition to police orders was the 'Information', a list of people who were wanted for criminal acts, which contained names, descriptions, information about possible places they frequented and details of their crimes. It was expected of a constable to retain this information and keep a lookout for these wanted persons. A list of stolen items or goods, known as the 'Pawnbroker's list', was issued to pawnbrokers and second-hand goods dealers, and it held descriptions of items which had been stolen. Pawnbrokers were expected to be aware of such items and, if they came across anything which matched the description laid out on that list, they were to contact the nearest beat constable or police station.[72]

The year 1881 saw the first publication of a book which was to become the main written reference for all working policemen during the late Victorian era, as well as those whose work concerned police matters and law: the police code. Written by the father and then head of the modern Criminal Investigation Department, Sir Charles Howard Vincent, with a direct address to all police constables on how to conduct their duties legally by the notable judge Sir Henry Hawkins[73], the police code was issued to every constable, with copies kept in every subdivision station library, and by 1888 it was into its fifth edition. Arranged in alphabetical order for ease of use, and designed as the definitive reference book for all constables to use in moments when guidance was required, or points of law needed to be clarified, it was most commonly referred to as the policeman's bible.[74]

One of the most useful tools used to aid policing was the weekly publication the *Police Gazette*. Born out of Fielding's first Bow Street publication in 1772, *The Quarterly Pursuit*, this publication endured a number of curious name changes – it became *The Hue and Cry, and Police Gazette* in 1797, and then the *Police Gazette: or, the Hue and Cry* in 1828, before becoming the *Police Gazette* in 1839.[75] It held information on matters concerning wanted criminals, escapees, thieves, stolen property, absentees from the armed forces and so on. Descriptions of wanted persons would be circulated via this journal, including aliases, height, hair colour, eye colour, tattoos, and all manner of useful information which would aid in the capture of a wanted person, or the retrieval of stolen items. As the *Police Gazette* was circulated nationwide, other constabularies across the land would also receive this valuable information. As time progressed, the *Police Gazette*, under the stewardship of Howard Vincent, evolved into an effective mechanism for providing information far and wide, and therefore grew in content, resulting in an inevitable split into more manageable supplements. The regular weekly issue was maintained, with updates on recent crimes committed and requests for information issued by other constabularies, as well as details concerning convicts out on licence, and those under police supervision. A fortnightly supplement was published covering details on currently active criminals, which included some photographs, as well as those who had absconded from the armed forces.

On and Off Duty, a monthly journal first produced by the Christian Police Association in 1883, was also an extremely popular leisure magazine with the men, with 200,000 copies being distributed at one point,[76] and the *Police Review and Parade Gossip* was also to become a much-favoured journal, although it did not come into publication until 1892.

Special duties can cover a wide range of police work – anything which does not come under the everyday normal remit of policing. This includes attendance for providing protection at court, crowd control and accompanying dignitaries on visits. Constables could also effectively be 'hired' to either watch over warehouse premises or attend special events, for a fee. In 1888, if one wished to have police presence at a function or rally, then a written request would have to be made to the relevant divisional superintendent. If granted, it would cost the people organising the event anything between five and ten shillings – depending on the size of the event and the number of constables required – and each constable who undertook this particular kind of special duty did so voluntarily.[77] Other governmental departments could also 'hire' constables; the Royal Mint paid for constables from H Division's Leman Street, and an 1890 strength of men report gives a good indication of how many policemen, from across all ranks, were employed on special duties, with a total of 1,678 out of 15,264 men, including 1,423 constables, 197 sergeants, 54 inspectors and 4 superintendents undertaking this role.[78]

Police courts were essentially magistrates' courts attached to a police office, and due to their close proximity, these courts were handy for a new constable to attend and gain some court experience. The Metropolitan Police instruction book for candidates and constables states that 'a constable who has apprehended a person must attend the police court the next morning, clean and properly dressed, with his prisoner, and be quite ready when his case is called'.[79] When one considers the fact that night beat constables completed their duties at around 6 a.m., and as the police courts opened at 10 a.m. on average, it gave the constable little time for rest; however, it must be noted that some courts had set times for remand hearings: 11 a.m. for the Thames Magistrates' Court (Arbour Square) and noon for the Guildhall (City Police), for example[80].

The instruction booklet continues, 'On entering the witness-box he is to stand to attention, and pay all possible respect to the magistrate.' Once sworn in, the constable would give his name, collar number, division, the date and time when the significant event occurred, and then proceed to give his evidence, keeping to the truth, embellishing and omitting nothing. It was preferred that the constable relayed his testimony from memory; however, he was permitted to refer to his pocketbook if required. Once produced, the pocketbook became the court's property to view, as 'any writing referred to must be produced and shown to the adverse party, if he requires it, and such party may cross examine a witness thereupon'.[81]

To ensure a constant police presence in the community, shift patterns would be adopted, and these shifts were known as reliefs. Inspectors and sergeants would rotate with the reliefs, ensuring at least one of their ranks would constantly be undertaking the role of duty inspector or duty sergeant. The duty inspector had sole control of the subdivision station, and he would be aided by the duty sergeant. Once the duty inspector had completed his shift, he handed over responsibilities to the incoming duty inspector (likewise with duty sergeants). Upon handover, the duty inspector/sergeant would update his successor as to any matters which they needed to be aware of, sickness or leave of constables, prisoners held and for what offence, and so on. With regards to prisoners, gaolers would also brief their incoming counterpart regarding prisoner and arresting officer details, and once the incoming duty inspector had been updated, he, or the duty sergeant, would address the incoming relief constables. This rotation of reliefs ensured that the subdivision stations were constantly manned, and that there was always a police presence out on the streets monitoring order.

Fixed-point duty is often confused with fixed points. The latter, fixed points, is a term predominantly used within the force only, and was an agreed spot on a constable's beat where the section sergeant met with the constable and received information regarding any minor incidents or details, such as the moving on of certain sleeping persons from doorways, and unsecured shutter windows, and so forth. Most commonly, this location would be near a lamp, or some other brightly lit spot, just in case the section sergeant required some illumination to aid his note taking. Fixed-point duty, meanwhile, was a role specifically created in 1870 by the Metropolitan force, introducing to the streets of London what were known as fixed-point constables. As the name suggests, these constables were assigned to one particular spot, each at around 100 yards' distance, and they were not permitted to move any more than ten feet away from that spot.[82] These 'public fixed points', which would be advertised in the newspapers and upon the police station notice boards, would be dotted around the division and manned by a constable commonly between the hours of 9.00 p.m. and 1.00 a.m.; however, in H Division, there were a few fixed points which covered a 3.00 p.m. until 7.00 a.m. time slot. On occasions, fixed-point constables may be called away for special emergency duties by their superiors, leaving the point unmanned. If this occurred the beat constable would, upon seeing the empty point and knowing it should be manned, temporarily take on the role until a reserve arrived from the station to relieve him.

Should a member of the public require police assistance, or information, they could approach the fixed-point constable to obtain it, though it must be remembered that a constable could not leave this fixed position unless ordered to by his superior. In cases of emergency, the fixed-point constable would do one of two things: direct the member of the public to the nearest police station, fire station, hospital or another constable from whom they could get immediate assistance; or raise an alarm by blowing his whistle, to which the nearest constables would respond, arriving to render aid. If the fixed point was not manned, the public were instructed to gain police attention either by blowing a whistle, throwing a rattle, swinging a bell or shouting constantly, which would also gain the attention of nearby policemen, off duty or on.

The matter of fixed-point policing was often a hotly debated one, especially during the Whitechapel murders. Constables despised them as they were sedentary and boring; they also tended to be located near to notorious local trouble spots, and the public were frustrated at the fact that a constable on fixed-point duty was not permitted to render assistance in emergencies. Once Jack the Ripper victim Annie Chapman was discovered, witness Henry Holland found a fixed-point constable outside Spitalfields church, opposite the market, and was frustrated that, instead of following Holland a few hundred yards to the murder scene, the constable informed him to go to nearby Commercial Street police station to gain help. Ignoring the fixed-point constable's instructions, Holland returned to the scene, by which time another witness, Davis, who ironically enough went in the opposite direction to Holland, toward the police station, had managed bring the authorities' attention to the murder. So annoyed was Holland at the fixed-point constable for not moving from his position that he made a complaint at Commercial Street police station in the afternoon of the very same day. I am sure that he would have been informed that the constable, as frustrating as it was, adhered correctly to the instructions he was given.

Earlier in this chapter, an acknowledgement was made to the value of local knowledge, and nothing aids the obtaining of that local knowledge more than beat work. The City of London Police orders and regulations book for 1839–94 refers to constables and, specifically, their beat work. Section 3 states quite clearly that 'he [the constable] will be held responsible for security of life and property within his beat, and for the preservation of peace and general good order during the time he is on duty'. It was this accountability that helped shape a constable and feed his knowledge of the area he was responsible for. A vast amount of police work for constables in both H Division and the City of London (as with the majority of all constables across the country, in fact) consisted of walking the beat. This constant pounding of the hard pavements, in all weather, would last for around eight hours a day, which is why there was a preference for young, fit men to enrol. The physical demands were quite telling, with many men succumbing to the curse of the beat bobby, plantar calcaneal bursitis, more commonly known as policeman's heel; however, it was exposure to the elements which often resulted in bouts of bronchitis and other related illnesses, and accounted for the majority of sick leave undertaken during this period. Assaults were another common cause of sick leave for beat constables: H Division's Superintendent Arnold stated that, in 1889, 40 percent of his men had been assaulted, with half ending up on sick leave.[83] Therefore, to undertake the demands of the beat, the fitter, younger, and most often newly recruited constables would be assigned to beat roles, with the older hands taking a more clerical role back at the station, with many making the transition into a reserve role.

Working the beat, as the bobbies called it, was the physical patrol of a small area of streets within a section. Each division was subdivided, and each subdivision then was spilt into what were known as sections, small fractions of a division's jurisdiction. Each section came under the responsibility of a section sergeant, who would be in charge of, on average, around eight to twelve beat constables. Initially each beat route would have been walked with a beat wheel, a device designed to measure distances, and the exact length of the beat would be noted down along with the time taken to complete it, with all beats during a single relief being set at similar distances.[84] The route would be drawn in what was called a beat book, as well as being typed or written down. The beat would be given a number, and this number would be allocated to a constable. There would be numerous variations of these beats, but they would largely be grouped into two categories, day and night patrols, with two-thirds of the beat force undertaking night beat work and the remaining third responsible for day beat duty. A roster would be posted in each station showing the hours of work expected from each man, the times he was due on and off duty and, if pertinent, the beat to which he was allocated. The beats during the day were longer, usually taking around thirty minutes to walk; during the evening and early hours these beats were split in two, meaning the night-relief beat constables had fifteen minutes to cover a shorter distance. This obviously required more men, and hence the need for two-thirds of the beat force during the evenings and early mornings. The reason for the shortening of the beat during the evening hours was simple. The majority of crime occurred within this period, during the darkness of night, and a shortened beat meant a heavier police presence in the necessary areas.

Beat constables would operate on a shift pattern, taking eight months of night work and four months of day work per annum, the pattern being two months of night beats to a month of day beats. On the whole a beat was covered in three eight-hour patrols, which were early relief (6 a.m. until 2 p.m.), late relief (2 p.m. until 10 p.m.) and night relief (10 p.m. until 6 a.m.).[85]

Section sergeants were instructed to come on duty an hour prior to the relief time, in order to familiarise themselves with any special directives which may have come through from Central Office via the police orders, as well as to be briefed on anything relevant by the previous section sergeant. Constables were instructed to be at the police station at the hour ordered, and usually at least fifteen minutes before they were due to be assembled in the parade room by the section sergeant; at that moment they were considered to be on duty, with armlets in place. This was called mustering, and it was at this stage that the section sergeant would inspect the men to see that they were sober and fit for duty, as well as to ensure that their appointment items were correct and presentable. The section sergeant would then notify the constables as a collective of any special instructions – whether they were to keep an eye out for any missing persons, for example, or the reversing of the beat. Beat reversing was a ploy used to outwit any criminal who had been watching the beats closely and timing them. Due to the circular nature of beat work, it wasn't difficult for burglars, thieves, prostitutes and those with crime on their mind to estimate, quite accurately, what time the constables were due to appear at the intended scene of crime. The reversing of the beat, which meant the constable walked his route in the opposite direction, was a way of combating this issue. However, it was only effective for a short period, as the more intelligent criminal always stood back and watched the first few 'rounds' the constable did, and from that it was easy to figure a pattern.[86] To combat this, the beat constable would, if possible, slightly alter his beat by entering alleyways or courts from more than one entrance, and an article published in the *Daily News* during the 'October Lull'[87] emphasised the importance of altering the beats by initially quoting the police code:

'The method of working beats,' says the Police Code, 'must be frequently changed, and the police must be careful not to allow evil disposed persons to ascertain the system of working and the consequent hour of absence from a given spot ...' The caution against allowing the system of beat duty to be known refers, of course, simply to the way in which beats are patrolled. It is not always to be done in the same way. A man must go first in one direction and then in another, so as to avoid any regularity of time.[88]

Other instructions laid at muster included paying particular attention to vulnerable buildings such as jewellers, unmanned warehouses, railway arches, shops or recently burgled properties, as well as keeping a careful eye on suspicious persons.[89]

Once the men had been inspected, and orders issued, they were marched out in single file, with the section sergeant at the head of the column, to relieve their brother constables who were already on patrol.[90] As stated, the beats were numbered and allocated to a constable, with the constable at the end of the line undertaking No. 1 beat, which was traditionally the beat closest to the police station. When arriving at his starting point, the constable commencing his beat would peel away from the column and carry on his beat route, with the constable he was relieving joining on the end.[91] The section sergeant would then lead his men onto the starting point for No. 2 beat and the next man in line would peel off, with the relieved constable again tagging onto the end. Once the section sergeant had walked his men around his section, with those due to undertake beat work peeling off, he would then march the relieved beat constables back to the station and set them in rank and file. Here, just as he did before they were marched out to their beats, the sergeant would inspect the constables to make sure they were sober, as it was common for publicans to gain favour with constables by giving them free drinks, which some constables found hard to resist. The section sergeant would also ensure that the constables all still had their appointment items, and that they were in good working order. It was also at this stage that the constables would report back to the sergeant about any outstanding minor issues, such as unfastened coal holes or malfunctioning gas lamps,[92] which would be noted in the occurrence book.[93] Once all the men had reported back in, they would be marked off the beat register; this ensured that all the relieved men had returned to the station. When back at the station, the constable would complete reports on any relevant incident which occurred on his beat, such as arrests, broken windows, disturbances and so on. Other tasks were also conducted, such as dealing with their kit; taking wet greatcoats, tunics and capes to the dry room to dry them out, or to the washroom if soiled; and handing the bullseye lamps over to the lamp room where they were stored ready for the lamp contractor's man to refuel in the morning. Other general repairs were also carried out, and only then could the constable be considered off duty. It is no surprise to learn that, on average, a constable would endure a working week of between sixty and seventy hours.[94]

During the day beats, the constables walked at the curb side of the pavement so that they were visible to pedestrians and road users should their assistance be needed. Again, they were required to ensure that crime was not taking place, or about to take place, as well as ensuring, as best they could, the public's safety. The most common form of pavement accident during the period was tripping. The beat constable would make sure that shop owners did not clutter up walkways with goods or displays, and would move on any unlicensed costermongers or pitches set up to sell goods. He would also ensure that coal holes were sealed securely and that cellar doors to public houses were closed when not in use. During busy times on the pavement, he would also direct the public as he would traffic, making sure the left-hand rule of travel was employed and stopping pedestrians if needs be. Again, the *Daily News* outlined the responsibilities and conduct of a beat constable by stating that 'all persons are to be closely observed so to recognise any advertised for apprehension in the *Police Gazette* or Police Information, and if any such are met they are to be stopped and questioned. Policemen must not loiter or gossip; they must move smartly and not slouch or look slovenly; they must answer all questions with civility and good temper; they must act quietly and discreetly, not interfering unnecessarily, but when need arises, showing firmness and discretion. Above all, ladies, foreigners, and strangers should be treated with civility.'[95] A great emphasis was placed on a constable's ability to control his temper, and this was enforced right from the beginning, with one of the first publications a new recruit received, the *Instruction Booklet for Candidates and Constables*, stating that a 'perfect command of temper is indispensable. A man must not allow himself to be moved or excited by any language or threat, however violent; the cooler he keeps himself the more power he will have over his assailants.'[96]

The ability of a constable to control his temper would never be more valuable than around midnight, because around that time of night was chucking-out time from the public houses. During the week, depending on the jurisdiction, public houses opened at 5 a.m. in the City of London and the liberties thereof, or at 6 a.m. in the Metropolitan Police area. They closed at 12.30 a.m. in the City, and 11 p.m. in the Metropolitan area. Saturday openings differed from weekdays only within the City, when their public houses closed at midnight. Sunday openings were shorter, broken into two parts, and married with Bank Holidays and Christmas, with a 1 p.m. to 3 p.m. early opening, and a 6 p.m. to 11 p.m late opening in the City of London, and a 12.30 p.m. to 2.30 p.m. early, and a 6 p.m. to 10 p.m. late opening in the Metropolitan area.[97] Drunk and disorderly was the most common offence constables had to deal with while on night beat, with most drunks being quietly advised to move along, as there was no law at the time enabling constables to effect an arrest on a person merely for being drunk and incapable.[98] However, those who were causing a disturbance, and gathering a crowd, would be deemed disorderly, and therefore ran the risk of being arrested. The drunk would be taken to the cells for monitoring, and later their fate would be decided, with a charge depending on the severity of the crime. Some were allowed to leave with a warning, while recognised habitual offenders or those who committed assault or damage to property were charged, with the majority being summonsed to attend a hearing at a magistrates' court on a later date. This sometimes caused great inconvenience to the police, as on occasion the accused failed to turn up for his hearing, resulting in a constable having to apply for an arrest warrant for failure to attend court. It was yet another duty to perform.

The section sergeant, or inspectors on occasion, would hold regular random inspection patrols, visiting the constable on his beat to ensure he was conducting his work correctly; however, these inspections were never received with relish by the beat constable, as he knew that the section sergeant would be trying to catch him out on some misdemeanour or error.[99] Donald Rumbelow, renowned author on the Whitechapel and Houndsditch murders and former constable in the City of London Police force, once stated that, when conducting his beat, which included Mitre Square, the site of Catherine Eddowes's murder by Jack the Ripper, he would sometimes become aware that the section sergeant was close by. If he encountered a fellow bobby on an adjoining beat, he would rub the buttons on his tunic frantically as a code of warning to his brother PC, thus preparing him for the impending inquiry. The section sergeant would also meet his beat constable at a fixed point upon the beat constable's patrol, awaiting a small briefing from the constable to establish if anything of minor concern had occurred on the beat. If so, the sergeant would attend to the matter, or provide advice if required.

It was expected for the beat constable to 'make himself perfectly acquainted with all parts of his beat, and with the streets, thoroughfares, courts, and houses within it'.[100] Not only that but the constable also had to know every shop, public house and stable, as well as every person whose property came under his beat route, and there to aid him were the night watchmen. Night watchmen were hired by private companies to watch over their properties and all items within them, and the most common of night watchmen fell into two categories, warehouse and works, the latter most usually employed on road or building works. These men were akin to our modern security guards and kept a keen eye on their own premises, outbuildings and street works, as well as looking out for trouble in their vicinity. The beat constable would liaise with the night watchmen, most commonly during his tea break, on matters concerning the security of the immediate area; however, it was only natural for other subjects to be discussed and idle gossip traded. While many saw this as a neglect of duty, it was actively encouraged by the authorities – in moderation. It bred an atmosphere of trust between night watchmen and policemen which, in turn, cemented a bond of reliance and co-operation between the two. However, too much of this would have indeed been a neglect of duty, so it was a brave beat bobby who pushed his luck in abusing this arrangement in the face of a patrolling section sergeant looking out for such misdemeanours. Premises which had no night watchmen were given particular attention, and it was common to find keys inadvertently left in locks, which would be seized by the constable for handing over after ensuring the premises were secure. If a beat constable came across unlocked doors, or open windows, he would notify his section sergeant who, in turn, would instruct a reserve constable to fetch the owner. Upon arrival, the owner would go through the premises, along with the constable, to make sure all was well and that the property was secure.

While on their night beat, the constables conducted an act known as 'marking', the placement of small detection devices upon premises which were deemed vulnerable. Items such as orange peel or tiny whalebone fragments were placed in the cracks of doors or shutters, and thin pieces of thread were hidden across thresholds. Once placed, the constable would inspect the items upon his return beat and would conduct a closer inspection of the premises if the items had been disturbed. To improve stealth, the shutters of their bullseye lamps were 'closed', meaning no light was shining despite the lamp being on, and they kept to the inside when patrolling (that is to say, to the building side of pavements), just to hide their approach to any criminals who may be operating on their patch. As well as reporting defunct gas lamps, night beat bobbies also ensured shutters and doors were secure, and if not would either report them to the beat sergeant when they met during a fixed-point meeting, upon which the sergeant could immediately send for the owners to make the property safe; or, if late in their beat, make a note and report it upon their return to the station, notifying the relief so they were aware of the situation.

A carry over from the old watchman days was the duty of 'knocking up'. Before the age of alarm clocks, constables on the beat were permitted to supplement their wages by waking people in time for them to go to work, and this was called 'knocking up'. Those who lived on the constable's beat would pay them weekly for this act, and the constable would note the location of the person and the time at which they wished to be woken. As stated, this task was permitted by the authorities; however, it must be stressed that it was only allowed if it did not impede the constable's policing duties of the prevention and detection of crime. This was to be an issue in the Mary Ann Nichols murder in the late August of 1888, when it was claimed that, despite being told by witness Charles Cross that a woman was found 'either dead or drunk' in Buck's Row, just off the Whitechapel Road, H Division's PC 55 Jonas Mizen carried on his 'knocking up' tasks instead of going to the scene to render his assistance.[101]

The Vagrancy Act of 1824 gave the beat constable powers to arrest all vagrant persons, beggars, unlicensed street vendors, prostitutes and so on, all of which were rife in Whitechapel; however, the more experienced of these knew exactly what they had to do to avoid such a thing. These vagrancy old hands knew that if they carried just a small amount of change upon their persons, a visible means of subsistence, they would avoid being labelled as destitute, resulting in the constable being unable to execute an arrest under said Vagrancy Act. The only option left to the constable was to move them on, and this they did, from park bench to park bench, shop doorway to shop doorway, though it must be admitted that many constables would rather this than have to effect an arrest. As the then superintendent of H Division, John Mulvaney, stated, the 'police dislike touching the class who do this because they are covered in vermin & won't come to the station without considerable handling. Result, they are left sleeping on the doorsteps.'[102] Those who were penniless could, if they wished to do so, apply for a stay in a casual ward, a short-term version of the workhouse, where the occupant would receive a meal and bed for the night, in return for some form of menial labour. The Metropolitan force were used as relieving officers by the authorities. Those who felt they had little option but to spend a night in the casual ward could apply at their local police station, and in return they would receive a card of admission which they handed over to the casual ward authorities upon arrival.[103]

Night refuges, sometimes known as night shelters, were set up throughout London by charitable organisations often connected to Christian charities, and at these refuges women could seek shelter for the night should they require it. As with the casual wards, admission to these could be obtained via the local police station. Other shelters catered for 'unfortunate women', a euphemism of the period for prostitutes, and one such refuge existed in Crispin Street, yards away from Dorset Street, which accommodated women any time of the day or night, and it was rumoured that this shelter was once used by one of Jack the Ripper's victims, Mary Jane Kelly. Another such shelter existed at Hanbury Street, as well as one near to Arbour Square Police Station, though this shelter accommodated women under the age of twenty only.[104]

Another power granted to constables under the Vagrancy Act came in the form of section 4, commonly known as 'Sus laws', and this was, as the term suggests, aimed at those suspected of committing a crime, and those who were about to, and most commonly affected reputed criminals and incorrigible rogues, those known to the police as habitual offenders.[105] This 'Sus law' gave the constable the power to stop, search and, if needs be, detain any person who was in possession of property which the constable deemed suspicious, and constables were also instructed to stop and make enquiries with people carrying suspect packages between sunset and sunrise.[106] All 'Sus law' searches were required to be noted, with details such as names and addresses written into the constable's pocketbook and then transferred into a ledger for such matters, the Stop book, upon the constable's return to the station. 'Sus law' searches must not be confused with stop-and-searches, which were conducted on persons upon whom a reasonable suspicion of illegal activity was placed by the constable.

On average, the beat constable stayed on his beat for a month, after which he was moved to another beat within the section. Over a period of around a year, he covered all of the beats within that section, and he would return to his original beat to start the cycle again. This was to avoid familiarity and the temptations of collusion, while ensuring that local knowledge remained.[107]

Some constables were happy with their lot, keeping to the same tasks and duties day in and day out throughout their entire twenty-five-year career, whereas others had an ambition to progress, an instinct to better themselves. For them, the choice was a simple one – a progression in uniform or in plain clothes? Those who felt comfortable in maintaining order, working with the community as part of a large group, often stayed in uniform, whereas those who both preferred the excitement of pursuing criminals within a small team and had the initiative to think for themselves in a logical, clinical manner often found themselves longing for a career in plain clothes, as a detective with the Criminal Investigation Department.

6

Tecs

Dear Boss,
You have not caught me yet you see, with all your cunning, with all your
'tecs', with all your blue bottles.

'Jack the Ripper' letter (25 July 1889)

Within the first ten years of the existence of the Metropolitan force, Joint Commissioner Mayne was already compiling a list of constables whom he considered to be extremely competent policemen – those he thought would excel as detectives. As an official detective branch did not exist in these early years, with the detection side of policing being predominantly undertaken by the Bow Street office, Mayne took on this assessment for the need of a specialised detection team as a personal project, with designs on making the police force more dynamic, and he performed this review with a degree of autonomy, out of sight of his paymasters, the Home Office. While Joint Commissioner Rowan was fully aware of Mayne's work on this aspect of policing, he did not agree that the formation of a specific detective team within the Metropolitan force was the way forward; however, by 1842 it seems Rowan had come around to his colleague's way of thinking, as he was a co-signatory on a memorandum he and Mayne had forwarded to Home Secretary Graham,[1] which suggested the formation of a detective branch within the Metropolitan force.[2] The principle was agreed, and on 15 August 1842 the Detective Branch was formed. Headed by former Bow Street 'Runner' Inspector Nicholas Pearce, deputised by Inspector John Haynes, and with six sergeants, it was based at Scotland Yard, and operated on an as-and-when-requested basis throughout all the divisions; this meant that if a murder took place in West Ham, K Division would send a request to Central Office for a detective to aid the investigation, and one would be immediately despatched to try to solve the crime. This arrangement was not restricted to the police divisions of the Metropolitan force. Provincial and borough constabularies, as well as others in authority, could also issue requests to Scotland Yard for detectives, with perhaps the most famous example of the period being the call for Detective Inspector

Jonathan Whicher, of Scotland Yard, by the local magistrate during the infamous Road Hill House murder case of 1860.

By the end of the 1860s, Henderson had taken over as commissioner. He wasted no time in restructuring the Detective Branch. While a detective presence was to remain at Central Office, Scotland Yard, Henderson decided that a localised, divisional detective force would be more effective across the metropolis. In 1870, therefore, the Detective Branch was increased in numbers with detectives attached to all the divisions throughout the Metropolitan area. Henderson was very proactive in his early years as commissioner. Not only did he rearrange the Detective Branch into more forceful localised teams, but he also formed specialist temporary teams designed to tackle specific forms of crimes, such as fraud or jewellery robberies. This was a format the Metropolitan force were to follow in later years with the creation of specialist teams, with the famous Flying Squad being the most obvious example.

However, by 1888, the Detective Branch had suffered some damaging setbacks. The Trial of the Detectives had exposed a high level of corruption within the sleuthing office, and a series of blunders prior to this exposé had also helped to reinforce the public's suspicion of incompetency in the police. The Harriet Buswell murder, which took place during the Christmas of 1872, was one of these cases: E Division's Superintendent Thomson was given the task of running Buswell's murderer to ground, only to arrest the wrong man on the basis of poor eyewitness testimony, damaging the police's reputation even further and exposing their detectives to ridicule. It was therefore decided, in 1878, that action was required in the form of a commissioned report, with the intention of improving matters within the Detective Branch. The then Home Secretary, Richard Assheton Cross, turned to a twenty-seven-year-old lawyer from Sussex, Charles Edward Howard Vincent, for assistance in this reassessment, and asked him to compile a report on the Parisian detective force. The intention of Howard Vincent's report was to help Cross see how detection was effectively carried out across the English Channel; Vincent had closely studied the Parisian police while he was at the School of Law in the University of Paris just a year previously, so Cross felt him the right man for the job. So impressed was Cross by Howard Vincent's final report and his knowledge of policing matters, especially the detective side, that he offered Howard Vincent the position as head of the new Criminal Investigation Department, which had risen, phoenix-like, out of the ashes of the now discarded Detective Branch.

Detectives, according to that 1878 commission report, were expected to be 'shrewd and sharp' and to display 'cool judgement' alongside being honest and steadfast,[3] and detectives at Scotland Yard had to be a 'more educated type of character'.[4] So Howard Vincent took to shaping this new department with those aims in mind; a higher wage was granted to induce the bright new men, which the commission report so craved, into the fold, though detective constables were largely recruited from the uniform branch, who in turn were recruited mainly from those with an agricultural or military background, which meant that the educational standards for detectives were, on the whole, rarely better than those for uniformed constables. However, a few years' service enabled the brighter constables to shine through and chances were given to those who showed promise. One facet Howard Vincent did not tweak was the divisional detective aspect of CID, with the reason confirmed by Metropolitan Police Commissioner Sir Charles Warren in an 1888 article in *Murray's Magazine*, in which he explained that this arrangement protected the working relationship between the detective and uniform men: 'The great aim of the present system is to keep up the most cordial relations between the uniform branch and detective service, consistence with efficiency in both branches.'[5]

Howard Vincent, who by now had turned to politics, summed up a detective's lot in Tempest Clarkson and Hall Richardson's 1889 work *Police!*, claiming,

There is probably no class of public servants who have so thankless a duty to perform as the detective police. They are habitually expected to accomplish impossibilities; although afforded by the law the most scanty and inadequate facilities, although working in the dark with their hands to a great extent tied, there is usually dissatisfaction if they cannot bring home an offence to its author. It is often easy to find out the author of an offence, but it is quite another matter to be able to prove the legal guilt of the delinquent by legal means. For this a considerable knowledge of criminal law and practice is required. The work is attractive in the eyes of the novel-readers, and it has beyond question its interests, but it is also attended with very considerable risk, for, with the most honest intentions in the world, a detective officer may find himself in very serious trouble. It is therefore not a matter of surprise that the difficulty of finding good men is very considerable. Without at least two or three years' experience of ordinary police duty they are valueless.[6]

Continuing, he explained the difficulties in training new detectives, highlighting that those two or three years in uniform were the best possible training a detective constable could obtain, saying that 'it is difficult to lay down hard and fast rules for the best training of the detective force, as the duties they are called upon to perform being exceedingly different in their character and scope, but I think the best general groundwork is to be found in the ordinary life of a constable in a large and busy town for two or three years, added to a theoretical study on the elementary principles of criminal law'.[7] Much training was consequently received by osmosis, and no formal detective training school existed until 1936; however, visits to the Metropolitan Police Crime Museum[8] were also undertaken, with the aim of educating a detective constable on what to look out for; and intensive in-house training was conducted by senior detectives within the early months of a fledgling detective constable's career.

There was a renewed emphasis on discipline, with detectives and uniformed constables subject to almost exactly the same punishments.

The only exception was that detectives could also face demotion into the uniform branch. In fact, this is what happened to H Division's Detective Sergeant New, who was demoted to a uniform constable first class in the early autumn of 1888 for assaulting a woman and destroying items of clothing she was carrying.[9] Recruitment for new detective constables was often done not directly from the public, but mainly from the uniform branch at constable level, as it was vital that a good basic level of both police knowledge and experience was in place before consideration for detective work could be given. It was rare for a uniformed constable to be considered for CID without some experience of work in plain clothes, and uniformed constables whose record and performance were exemplary would often be placed into plain clothes and seconded to the local CID for fixed periods. This act was twofold; it gave the uniformed constable an insight into detective work, which would aid his application to CID should the time arrive, and it also gave the local CID a boost in numbers when required, especially during a periods when a complex case would take the bulk of CID's attention (during the Whitechapel murders, for example). The tasks undertaken by plain-clothes men were basic duties at detective constable rank, such as supporting the beat constable by clearing prostitutes, drunks and vagrants from the streets and enquiring into illegal gambling, unlicensed hawking and so on, which gave the plain-clothes constable an opportunity to develop his observation and oral skills. Making enquiries of various kinds would also be a main duty: enquiring at another divisional station, making door-to-door enquiries, obtaining descriptions from witnesses, relaying information to and from other authorities, and so forth. Obtaining information was bread-and-butter detective work, and plain-clothes men gained experience and credibility with their detective officers in the process.[10]

The 1869 Habitual Criminals Act, and the following Prevention of Crime Act in 1871, gave the police, chiefly CID, powers to monitor those convicts who were most likely to reoffend. To aid with this monitoring, the Habitual Criminals Register was officially introduced, holding detailed information and photographs of thousands upon thousands of former offenders who had been convicted more than twice. This information was kept in numerous albums so one could search for a specific criminal under height, age, markings and tattoos or even eye colour. The register was kept at the Convict Supervision Office at Scotland Yard, where it was open for viewing by any policemen, prison warders, HM Customs, or any other person with authority between the hours of 10 a.m. and 5 p.m.[11]

In addition to the Habitual Criminals Register, there were remand parades. Prisoners who were on remand pending a trial hearing were sent to Holloway prison where, three times a week, they would be paraded in front of local CID representatives from numerous divisions. This allowed these CID men to identify any already captured criminals wanted for outstanding crimes within their jurisdiction, and avoided the need to wade through page upon page of the register. Habitual criminals soon became well known to experienced CID men, so much so that they could recognise them anywhere, and it is this recall which detectives to put to good effect during these parades. On top of the remand parades, local CID also conducted their own identification parades, with, according to East End Edwardian criminal Arthur Harding, local criminals being rounded up with impunity, from pubs, coffee houses or even their homes, and told to attend the identification parade in relation to whatever offence had occurred within a division. Harding himself recalls an occasion when two CID men entered his bedroom, ordered him to dress, and then marched him to Commercial Street police station, where he was told he wasn't there to be charged, but was required to take part in a number of parades 'to see if any witness could pick me out'.[12] They didn't, and Harding was allowed to leave.

Prisoners who had received custodial sentences from the courts could, through good behaviour, be released early from prison sentences; however, they were required to continue to report at their local police station every month for the duration of their original sentence, and they were strictly monitored by the local CID for fear they should reoffend. These men were officially known as supervisees or convict licence holders; however, they were more commonly referred to as 'ticket-of-leave men', as they were required to carry with them a ticket explaining their status at all times. Once released from prison, ticket-of-leave men had forty-eight hours to report either to the Convict Supervision Office based at Scotland Yard or to their local police station, as directed by the prison authorities. Then, as mentioned, they had to report to that station once every month between the hours of 9 a.m. and 9 p.m., where they were required to confirm that they were indeed staying at the address they gave, and, if they intend to move within the following month, the address of their next abode.[13] These men were known to the Convicts Supervision Office at Scotland Yard, who were set up to monitor ticket-of-leave men. Only detectives or plain-clothed men were permitted to speak to ticket-of-leave men outside of the station, so that no attention was drawn to them (unless, of course, they had committed a crime).

It was the responsibility of local CID to ensure that ticket-of-leave men were indeed staying at the claimed address, with Wheler Street, Gun Lane and Wilkes Street being the most well-known areas for them to lodge in H Division.[14] Local CID also had to ensure that these men were living by honest means, and though CID were not permitted to inform an employer that their new starter was an ex-convict, the reality was that, on occasion, if asked by said employer, a confirmation or denial was sometimes given.[15] Such monitoring was open to abuse by the local police, especially CID, with Harding calling the Prevention of Crimes Act 'fly paper', due to the fact that once you were caught it was extremely difficult to escape.[16] Harding felt that when a prisoner became a ticket-of-leave man, the former convict would be at the mercy of the police who could, if they wanted, make their life extremely difficult, creating trumped-up charges or spreading malicious rumours, unless certain favours, such as the transmission of criminal information, were granted. Harding also worried that ticket-of-leave men could be rearrested just to improve the crime figures. Inspector Morgan, of G Division Finsbury, did not share Harding's anxieties, claiming that 'it was very rare now that detectives got up imaginary burglaries etc. to gain kudos for themselves'; although he confessed that 'it was done and is still done sometimes'.[17]

The detectives of the two policing forces within London, the City of London and Metropolitan forces, liaised with each other on a daily basis, with memoranda and telegrams flowing between the two headquarters at Old Jewry and Scotland Yard. These contained requests for enquiries to be made in each other's jurisdiction, information obtained from informers, and so on. While there is no doubt that rivalry existed, with the City detectives taking a superior air over their Metropolitan counterparts, and the Metropolitan detectives treating the City force as an inexperienced, spoilt younger sibling, the reality was that when it came to cooperation, both were very forthcoming with their assistance. The police orders of 2 February 1888 clearly outlined the significance of cooperation, especially in relation to divisions which bounded the City, by decreeing that 'the attention of superintendents of divisions bordering on the City is especially directed to the importance of keeping up a good feeling between the police of their divisions, and that of the City, that the duty between the Metropolitan and City Police may be carried on with mutual goodwill, and with such cooperation as to effect the common object of the two services'. Eight months later, that order was to hold some weighty significance.

However, there were occasions when lack of communication led to some embarrassing incidents, such as the one involving City Detective Constable Robert Sagar,[18] where the two forces conducted observations on the same property. While this was a case of poor communication, this incident also gives us a wonderful insight into detective work and some of the actions they undertook, as well as a view on how the two forces cooperated. On 12 November 1883, Sagar, along with City Detective Sergeant Harry Webb and Detective Constable Davidson, were conducting observations on suspicious persons at a house in Nightingale Lane, which came under the Metropolitan Police jurisdiction of V Division Wandsworth, when Metropolitan Detective Inspector Shaw and another detective constable emerged from the neighbouring house, along with its owner, the Reverend Curtis. Shaw immediately recognised Webb and went across to him, and, after a brief exchange, the five detectives moved a little further down the lane, away from the house, to thrash out the confusing situation. Shaw updated Webb on the situation from their side, stating that the Metropolitan force had also received relevant information on the same suspicious persons; that the house had been watched since 5 November, for just over a week; and that he – Shaw – had been instructed to oversee this case personally by the head of the Metropolitan's CID at the time, Adolphus Williamson. Shaw also mentioned that there had been little action at the house during that previous week, other than the arrival of a private cab, which was promptly boarded by the suspicious persons and then moved off. Due to the fact that the detectives watching the house were on foot, they had little chance of following it. Shaw told Webb that he hoped Williamson would authorise the use of a horse-drawn cart in future, in case the cab should return.

Shaw then took Sergeant Webb to the rear garden of Reverend Curtis's house where, propped against the wall, there was a ladder. Webb climbed the ladder and saw that when he reached the top of the wall, he could see clearly into the suspicious persons' house; however, as he was doing so, a man appeared from that house and called out to Webb, 'What are you doing there? What do you want to see?' Fearing that he had blown his cover, and with it the whole observation operation, Webb immediately climbed down the ladder and made for the reverend's home, shutting the door once he and Inspector Shaw were inside. Meanwhile, the other detectives were continuing observations on the front of the house, when they saw a man and a woman leaving via the front door. City Detective Constable Davidson followed the couple, and they unknowingly led him to a house on Wilton Street in Brompton, information he was later to pass on to the Metropolitan force. In the meantime, Shaw and Webb retreated to Wandsworth Common police station, where they sat down and discussed the matter with Metropolitan Inspector Darling and Sergeant Mantle. Webb was informed that they had received 'special instructions' from Superintendent Digby, who wanted the matter cleared up swiftly. After clarifying just how involved the Metropolitan Police were in this case, Webb, along with Shaw, returned to Nightingale Lane, and both detective teams continued with their observations until 11.00 p.m., when the City detectives decided to leave. City Detective Sergeant Webb filed his report with his superiors the next day, and received it back with a note from City Police Commissioner Colonel Sir James Fraser himself. It simply read, 'Let the matter be now left with the Met police.'[19]

Clearly there had been a breakdown in communication. Ordinarily, the City force would issue notice to the relevant Metropolitan division that they intended to conduct some work in their jurisdiction, and this would avoid the confusion of two forces conducting observations in connection to the same case. However, once it had become clear the two were indeed working on the same lead, Metropolitan's Shaw, recognising that City's Webb still had a job to do, and that he had to report back to his inspectors, brought him fully up to speed with the situation on their side. This, coupled with City detective Davidson following the man and woman, shows each force respecting the other's position, and realising they had a responsibility to their duty; in this case, this common ground resulted in the ad hoc briefing and cooperation we see here. The geography of London is such that people freely crossed the boundary between the City and Metropolitan on a regular basis, and this includes criminals; therefore it was imperative that the two forces' detective departments recognised this fact, and worked together to reduce the criminal activity which spread across both the jurisdictions.

The City of London detectives' workload predominantly mirrored that of those in the Metropolitan force; however, due to their location within London's financial district, they also had to deal with complex cases connected to financial crime. Therefore the City force often required detective constables who were numerically sound and had a good understanding of the financial world and fraud. As they also undertook regular travels to all parts of the globe to make enquiries, the City of London Detective Department, as it was known, required men who could understand or speak a foreign language.

Immigration boomed during the latter part of the Victorian age, and with it came an influx of foreign criminals. To monitor this, Scotland Yard began to employ some multilingual detectives who were based at Central Office in Scotland Yard, and who could be seconded out to the divisions, to other constabularies around the country[20] or to various governmental departments as the need arose.[21] They would chiefly work on extradition cases, aid in translating documents written in foreign languages, assist with naturalisation papers and, like their City force counterparts, conduct enquires outside of Great Britain.[22] H Division, with its many nationalities and different languages, required constables who understood what was being spoken, especially when it came to the taking of statements. While there were a few constables who spoke various languages within the division, these men would be used mainly to eavesdrop on local criminal whisperings, with a view to obtaining useful information which may be of some use. However, when it came to taking statements, to maintain impartiality and integrity should a case go to court, independent interpreters were hired to assist the detectives, as well as to aid with translating when charging or when in court.

As with the constables, detectives were also briefed through morning state reports and police orders, as well as information and pawnbrokers lists. However, the detectives also had an additional report to go through, namely the 'morning report of crime', which, for H Division, would have been complied by Inspector Reid. This report held a list of outstanding crimes for which known suspects were sought for arrest and charging, along with specific CID information from Central Office – suggestions on investigatory techniques, and lists of reprimands and commendations tied solely to the detective side of policing.[23]

Some detectives had a specialist field (fraud, bank robberies, pickpockets and so on), and should any one of these occur within a division, these detectives would most often be sent for. Upon viewing the fraudulent document, or crime scene, or by interviewing the victim, they would be able to identify a potential suspect, and thus start on a line of enquiry which may lead to the culprit.[24]

In yet another connection to their brothers in uniform, detectives would, when not involved in an investigation, undertake patrol duty and walk a designated area within their jurisdiction, most often in pairs, in order to observe and apprehend criminals such as pickpockets or street gamblers. Again, like their constable counterparts, detectives also carried appointment items such as a notebook and pencil, with which they noted any occurrences, interviews and even their expenses; they also had truncheons (shorter than those given to constables) and their warrant card. Detectives would also conduct observation and surveillance work, or 'shadowing' as Warren's replacement as commissioner, Monro, liked to call it.[25] This sometimes required the use of disguises. These were generally not outlandish, and subtle differences in the combing of the hair, or the wearing of glasses or a different hat, would be trusted to make the difference. More extreme make-up would only be used if it was really necessary. Besides, due to the hours of drill work these detectives undertook when they joined the force as lowly uniformed constables, the more seasoned of criminals instantly knew a detective in disguise simply by the way he walked – the straight, upright gait was an immediate giveaway.

The discovery of a suspicious death in public triggered a course of events which were pivotal in the early days of an investigation, and depended heavily on the understanding and cooperation between the uniformed branch and CID. If a constable came across, or was called to, a dead body in the street, there was a procedure to which he had to adhere; his first action would be to send for either the divisional surgeon or the nearest doctor. As the divisional surgeon would most likely be some distance away, or committed to other duties, the constable would most often call the nearest doctor first, usually the one whose surgery or private home was on his beat. The constable would also send for the chief inspector of the nearest subdivision station within his division, which was commonly the one at which the constable himself was based.[26] While the constable was waiting for assistance to arrive, he would make a brief note of the names of witnesses and the appearance of the victim, noting what they were wearing, and finding blood spots if any were around, locating wounds, cuts and bruises, and taking any weapons into his possession. He would also ensure that any onlookers were kept back, so as not to contaminate the scene for CID.

Upon the arrival of the doctor, the constable would maintain the scene while the doctor conducted his initial medical examination. If the person was alive, the doctor would give instruction on what should be done so as to give the person the best possible chance of survival. However, if the person was dead, the doctor tried to assess cause and time of death, if they could, and note any injuries upon the body, body position, and so on. When the inspector arrived, he liaised with the doctor, and took note of any pertinent information: the possible time of death, the position of the body, injuries, the condition of the deceased's clothing, the possible type of weapon, and so on. He would also liaise with the first constable on the scene, asking if there was anything suspicious either at the scene or in the area, be it odd behaviour or people seen. If the constable called to the scene was not the constable upon whose beat the crime had occurred, the inspector would seek out and speak with the beat officer, and ask the same questions. Did he see anything or anyone suspicious on his beat? If so, where? What did they look like?

In these situations, the inspector was the link between the uniformed branch and CID, and while the uniform constables had a peripheral area to control, CID had the remit of investigating the actual scene of crime, ensuring that any clues were not destroyed. While it has been claimed in many books upon the subject of the Ripper murders that forensics science was in its infancy, and in comparison with today that is true, it must be noted that there did exist some methods of obtaining information which would aid both the investigation and potential prosecution. Perhaps the most common forensic clues available to the Victorian CID came in the form of footprints, made either in soft mud (from which casts were taken) or in blood, which would leave an initial trail and give the detectives a clue as to the direction in which the culprit had fled. Preservation was key and this is where, initially, the inspector's responsibilities lay. To use modern parlance, the inspector would 'manage' the scene of crime, assessing what was required with regard to the medical aspects of the case, giving orders for the victim's pockets to be searched, or having the body removed to the nearest mortuary for post-mortem, or notifying the divisional surgeon. He would also, if required, send a runner back to the station to obtain reserve support, and instruct immediate enquiries to be made in the vicinity.

Once all initial investigations of the scene had been completed, it was imperative that things got back to normal. With the body removed, and all residue of the crime cleared away as best it could be, the beat constable would resume his beat until relieved at changeover and, once relieved, he would return to his police station and write a report on what had occurred. The inspector would also compile a detailed 'special report' of the events, which would subsequently be reviewed by his superior, the superintendent, who would countersign it either with or without comment, before it was submitted to Scotland Yard for immediate review. This report would be the official document which handed responsibility of the case to CID and therefore triggered the investigation.

A police order dated 9 February 1888 laid out a directive on the compiling, issuing and updating of crime reports, and it is often quoted in many of the reports contained in the Whitechapel murder files. Reports were a necessity on many fronts, as they laid down factual information, showed the progress of the investigation, highlighted the evidence gathered and enabled senior officials to review and decide upon certain courses of action. All known crimes committed within a police division had a report written upon them, with the majority of these reports being placed into the category labelled 'morning reports'; these included minor acts of crime such as threatening behaviour, violence, theft and so on. These morning reports would be collated throughout the day, and despatched the following morning to Central Office at Scotland Yard, where they were reviewed by the chief constables and, if necessary, Central Office CID, the assistant commissioner and the commissioner, before being taken to storage. However, if the investigation into these crimes was ongoing, only copies of the reports would be issued to Central Office. The original documents would be filed within the division, in the correct order and correctly docketed. Follow-up reports regarding an investigation, known as 'further reports', were issued to Central Office every fourteen days unless the case was closed.

More serious crimes – such as murder, serious fraud, and so on – fell in the category of 'special reports'; as with morning reports, copies of special reports were also despatched to Central Office for reference.[27] The initial special report was meant to hold as much information on the case as was known at that moment in time. It was expected to contain the particulars of the crime (date, location, and name of victim if known), the names of witnesses, the full collar numbers, ranks and names of the policemen involved and details of any action undertaken. This initial special report would be compiled by a senior officer, and was most often built upon the reports and notebook information supplied to him by the constables already involved. Unlike the morning report, special reports were urgent and therefore despatched immediately to the Executive Branch at the Central Office, with copies also retained in the division. Special reports which required immediate action were all given a green label, and once the report was reviewed and possible action taken, and completed, the green label would be removed.

Further reports in connection to special reports were to be issued to Central Office as and when matters altered; however, the time between these updates was not to exceed seven days, instead of the standard fourteen as with the morning reports. Once a case had been closed, a final report was completed, giving full details of the outcome of the case. As stated, copies of all reports were retained at the division and filed with the same reference code and in the same manner as they were in Central Office, for ease of reference. All reports were deemed confidential and were not to be discussed with anyone outside of the police force unless specific permission was granted by a senior officer.

Along with drink, another vice which blighted constable and detective alike was gambling. Like many men in the East End, policemen bet on almost any contest going. Such was the concern the police authorities had with gambling – specifically, the worry that debt would be incurred – that it was listed as one of the major misdemeanours in the police code. Constables in debt would be prone to corruption, and consequently open to financial inducements, and to reduce the risk of impropriety any constable who became bankrupt was immediately dismissed from the force. Gambling was viewed by some policemen as a victimless crime, and, although the Lotteries and Gambling Act of 1857 and the subsequent Metropolitan Streets Act in 1867 severely restricted it to racecourses and the odd betting shop (very rare as obtaining a licence in the moralistic

Victorian era was extremely difficult), gambling was rife in the East End. Illegal betting was undertaken in the alleyways and courts, the nooks and crannies of Whitechapel, in public houses and working men's clubs, and, according to Superintendent Vedy, in Charles Booth's *Life and Labour*, the Jewish population in Whitechapel favoured this vice, stating that 'the only recreation of the Jew was betting'.[28] Despite the anxiety about gambling, some of the Jewish gambling dens were permitted to remain open. This was because these dens would be infiltrated by undercover detectives in disguise, either local or from Special Branch, with the specific design of obtaining from those who frequented such places information on what was the scourge of the period – socialist and anarchist activity.[29]

During the Whitechapel murders, many detectives worked incognito on the streets of Whitechapel, observing what acting City of London force commissioner Henry Smith called 'suspicious couples' (a euphemism for a prostitute and her client), as well as mingling with the locals in an attempt to glean any useful piece of information which may spark a line of enquiry. This, coupled with the fact that some detectives were drafted into H Division to aid with the work and to cover absences during the height of the Whitechapel murders, led to an incident of some embarrassment in the September of 1888. One detective, who was conducting observations in Great Pearl Street, a notorious hangout for prostitutes just off Commercial Street, noted a man and a woman talking to each other at two in the morning. As Annie Chapman had been found murdered just yards away from this spot only weeks previously, the detective was immediately concerned, and approached the man with some caution, questioning him as to his business. This did not go down too well with the man who, so it seems, became extremely 'unpleasant' at the line of enquiry, so much so that the detective made an immediate arrest, taking the prisoner to a nearby police station. Upon arrival at Commercial Street station, the arrested man promptly produced his warrant card, thus proving he was a fellow detective who was also conducting enquiries.[30] Incidents like this were understandable, given the influx of unknown constables and detectives. At least they were attributable to action being taken, rather than leads ignored.

Detectives knew that convincing evidence was required to achieve a successful prosecution, and in the 1880s one of the best ways to obtain that evidence was via observations and surveillance. Observation could be carried out by numerous detectives from different positions – in the street, in the public house, outside the workplace or home; anywhere where the detective could blend in. During these observations, detectives monitored how long they had been watching the suspect, the suspect's height and description, how far away they were, visibility, third-party details (if the suspect interacted with another person), what exactly was done – and anything else of a suspicious nature. This would be noted down in the pocketbook as soon as was realistically possible, and then compiled in a report to be viewed by the detective sergeant or detective inspector.

Surveillance, or shadowing (as the Victorian detectives liked to call it), was the following of a suspect on the move, and this could be quite difficult in a busy East End street. Surveillance could be done in many ways, with the most common being one where the suspect was followed by a detective, who, in turn, was followed by a colleague, in case the suspect stopped suddenly, or turned unexpectedly in a different direction. If this happened, the first detective could 'break off' his follow, thus avoiding being compromised, knowing the second detective, some distance back, could view the situation and pick up the suspect, and continue with the chase, with the first detective assuming the role of the second detective, rejoining the follow behind his colleague.

In some areas it was impossible for uniformed constables to effect an arrest without bringing unwanted attention to themselves, but a more subtle presence, mingling in plain clothes, meant that unpleasant confrontations could often be avoided. It was a simple case of the detective pair moving in on the wanted man, one either side, and making the arrest. The police code explains that 'the usual way of effecting an arrest is to touch the shoulder of the accused lightly, and, if in plain clothes, saying, "I am a police-officer, and I arrest you for (name of the offence)"',[31] quietly bundling them into a Hansom cab, and off to the police station before anyone close by batted an eyelid.[32] However, things did not always go quite as smoothly when making an arrest in H Division. In George Dilnot's *Scotland Yard: The methods and organisation of the Metropolitan Police*, published in 1915, an unnamed seasoned policeman recalled a time, as a raw detective some twenty years previous, when he tried to arrest a gang leader in Whitechapel: 'His friends had knives, and they threatened to "lay me out" if I touched him. I didn't know whether I was justified, but I drew my truncheon and swore I'd brain the first man who came near me. But I was in a cold sweat all the time. They didn't coddle us in those days.'[33]

To help know exactly what criminal act was taking place, or was about to take place, on their patch, detectives relied heavily on information received, in particular from regular informers. Many of these were pivotal to East End life; publicans, pawnbrokers, lodging house keepers, betting men and cab drivers saw all that passed before them, both good and bad.[34] The police code of 1889 laid out guidance when dealing with informers, reiterating their importance, stating that 'detectives must necessarily have informants, and be obliged to meet with them when and where they can. But it is very desirable that the public-house should be avoided as much as possible. Tap-room information is rarely worth much. Occasionally, perhaps, refreshment must be given to an informant, but when possible it is best to give money.'[35]

The simple reality of East End criminal and policing life had a little of the flavour of the 'live and let live' policies on the front line during First World War, insofar as the criminal fraternity and the policing authorities knew the other existed, what its aims were and what it required in order to achieve those aims. The use of informers, an unfortunate yet essential requirement, paved the way for acts of bribery, and could lead to corruption. A 'nark'[36] who was a lodging house keeper may have preferred to forsake his payment for something far more lucrative in the long run, such as the turning of a blind eye to the fact he was running a disorderly house ... and so the dance begins. East End petty thief Arthur Harding describes H Division's CID as regular receivers of bribes and favours, as 'villains',[37] and this paints a picture of a corrupt police force; however, that is true only up to a degree, because while there was a minority of policemen across the ranks who did indeed take payments freely from the criminal fraternity in order to look the other way, there were also ones who, in an attempt to capture the bigger fish, did what it took to achieve their goals.

The head of divisional CID in Whitechapel during 1888 was Local Inspector Edmund Reid, who joined H Division in August 1887. Reid's previous beat, Bethnal Green, just north of Whitechapel, was a similar environment to his new one, and therefore Reid had some experience in dealing with the people of the East End. This, coupled with his fourteen years of detective knowledge, meant that Reid was the ideal man to replace H Division's legendary local inspector Frederick G Abberline,[38] who had been transferred to A Division Whitehall before moving on to Central Office CID at Scotland Yard. Reid's move to H Division is interesting, and was tinged with a slight controversy which could have been the catalyst for this transfer: days prior to undertaking his new role, Reid was reprimanded by the then head of CID, James Munro. The nature of Reid's misdemeanour is unknown; however, Connell and Evans, in their excellent biography on Reid, *The Man Who Hunted Jack the Ripper*, correctly surmise that 'the offence must have been minor, as he [Reid] retained his rank and pay'.[39] Abberline was a well-known and respected policeman in Whitechapel, having worked in that division since 1873, so Reid's task – to fill Abberline's boots – was by no means an easy one. However, Reid's team would help him find his own groove. Detective Sergeant William Thick, whose brothers Morgan, Charles and George all became policemen also, was originally assigned to H Division when he joined the Metropolitan force in 1868 as a young constable, and, apart from a brief stint in 1872 at B Division Chelsea and eight years at P Division Camberwell, he spent the whole of his police life in Whitechapel.[40] Thick was known as a tenacious detective. Crippen's arrestor, Walter Dew, described him as 'a holy terror to the local lawbreakers',[41] and Thick, who had by this time retired from the force, was to be Jack London's refuge if required during the author's residence in the Whitechapel area while he researched for his work on the life of the East End poor, *The People of the Abyss*. London described Thick as 'shades of old sleuth and Sherlock Holmes',[42] whereas Frederick P. Wensley, a raw constable in 1888 and later to become a renowned and feared detective in H Division, flatteringly described Thick as 'one of the finest policemen I have ever known'.

To take just two of the most common crimes to fall under CID's remit, there were, in 1884, 331 known burglaries and 932 known housebreakings. Of those burglaries, only ninety-three ended in the conviction of the culprit, with fifty-eight being found guilty of housebreaking.[43] While some may see this as an example of police incompetence, the reality was that this small group of men were working in an age before the advancement of forensic science made detection easier – even before fingerprinting was performed as standard – and in a densely populated environment full of a complex mixture of many foreign cultures and languages, some resident and some transient. This made Whitechapel the perfect breeding ground for crime. The sheer number of people in that area, the lack of manpower and the reluctance of magistrates to convict meant that the containment of crime was often the only feasible option the police had. When you tie in those factors with the first rule of East End life – look after your own problems and never squeal to the rozzers – the dice were loaded comprehensively against the policemen of Whitechapel. So, when women were being found murdered in the streets of their jurisdiction during 1888, H Division's CID, who had a mass of crime to deal with already, had no idea what was to follow.

No one did.

PART TWO
The Murders

7

Emma Smith
4 April 1888

'Those women there,' said our guide, 'will sell themselves for thru'pence, or tu'pence, or a loaf of stale bread.'
Jack London, *The People of the Abyss*

The Whitechapel murder files contain the reports concerning the murders of eleven women from 1888 to 1891. Unfortunately the records are incomplete, with items lost, stolen or routinely purged over the years. However, thanks to the meticulous research of several experts in the field (and their generous sharing of their findings), we now have a reasonable insight not only into the crimes themselves but also into the period of British history in which the Ripper flourished. Although access to information has widened considerably since the advent of internet and social media, some understanding of this hard-won background is required in order to comprehend the often complex reasoning which lay behind official actions taken at the time. This is, perhaps, especially true of the police. While there are other books which delve into Jack the Ripper and the Whitechapel murders in great detail, we shall be looking more specifically at the policing aspect of each case, examining the procedures and pressures which moulded their activity. I shall start with the first murder noted in the Whitechapel murder files: that of Emma Elizabeth Smith, who did not initially come to the attention of the police until after her death.

Emma Smith was, and still is, an enigma.[1] The great Scotland Yard detective Walter Dew, who worked as a young Constable in H Division during that autumn of 1888, and who later found fame when he brought the infamous Dr Hawley Harvey Crippen to justice, stated of her that 'her past was a closed book even to her most intimate of friends. All she ever told anyone of herself was that she was a widow who more than ten years before had left her husband and broken away from all her early associations'.[2]

Dew is seemingly correct; despite extensive research, little of certainty is known of Smith's early life. *The Complete Jack the Ripper A–Z*, one of the main research tools on the subject, says that Smith was born in Margate,

Kent, married a soldier, gave birth to two children and that she was later widowed.[3] Like so many of her time, Smith had endured the hardships of working-class London life; in order to endure these hardships she had to be of strong character with an instinct to survive. By 1888, she had found herself living as a prostitute in one of the most notorious areas in London, if not Great Britain: Whitechapel. She had taken lodgings in George Street, one of a nest of mean streets which sat between the two main north–south thoroughfares of Brick Lane and Commercial Street, which included the fearful Flower and Dean Street, and Thrawl Street. This small area was full of cheap lodging houses, housing an estimated 6,000 people, and a single bed and the use of a communal kitchen would cost you 4*d* nightly, and a double bed 8*d* – and these were nigh on the luxurious ones.[4] The majority of single 'beds' for men were known as 'four-penny coffins', owing to their coffin-like design; they were typically all arranged in rows on the floor, with little floor space left between them. A cheaper option was the 'two-penny rope', as highlighted in Charles Dickens's *Pickwick Papers*, where two ropes ran across the length of the room, and hanging between these ropes were many strips of stretched coarse sacking, creating 'beds' upon which each lodger slept for the night. At the lowest end of the lodging house scale were the 'penny sit-ups', where one would sit side by side with many others on a hard, wooden pew, and there you tried to sleep as best you could, either upright or slumped against your foul-smelling neighbour.

These lodging houses had become a severe concern for the authorities – especially the mixed-sex establishments, as it had become clear that these premises were nothing shy of brothels. When the lodging houses became regulated in the mid-1800s, they were routinely inspected by the police as it was felt they were breeding grounds for immorality, illness and crime. However, this did not alleviate the lodging houses' poor reputations, and despite the regulations the area had more than its fair share of disreputable dosshouses. Policing these rookeries, as the locals called them, was a bind to the local bobbies. Each registered lodging house had to be inspected thoroughly, and each room measured, with a plaque placed outside stipulating the number of lodgers the building could legally hold.[5] Linen was required to be changed weekly and, on the whole, men were separated from women; however, in some of the larger lodging houses, quarters housing married couples also existed. Ledgers were kept by lodging house keepers, but the reliability of the information contained within them was dubious. The fact that the districts around the docks (such as Whitechapel, Spitalfields, St George in the East and so on) were teeming with visitors who had just arrived in London from various parts of the globe – as well and every point of the United Kingdom – meant that it was a boom time for lodging houses. Their sheer numbers made maintaining the regulation extremely difficult for the police and, in the confusion, unlicensed lodging houses operated quite freely and in great numbers also.[6]

In 1888 Charles C. B. Dickens, the son of the great author, produced a list of streets and roads upon which lodging houses existed in the tenth edition of his handbook *Dickens's Dictionary of London*. He also cited within which police division and parish these streets fell. H Division had by far the longest list of streets, and therefore lodging houses, beating E Division (Holborn) and G Division (Finsbury). Their area covered Flower and Dean Street, Dorset Street, Paternoster Row, Thrawl Street, Keate Street, Brick Lane, Princes Street, White's Row, Hanbury Street, George Street, Pearl Street, Wentworth Street, Heneage Street, Brushfield Street, Wheeler Street and Mount Street in the parish of Christchurch. Nicoll's Row, White Street and Church Street in the parish of Bethnal Green. Wellclose Square, Leman Street, Osborne Place, Well Street, Dock Street, Grace's Alley and Bull Street in the parish of Whitechapel. Boundary Street and Hare Alley in Shoreditch. Gun Street in the Old Artillery Ground. St George's Street, Ship Alley, Princess Square, Cable Street, North East Passage, Ratcliff Street, Pell Street to the south in St George's in the East. London Street, Stepney Causeway, Broad Street and Narrow Street in Ratcliff. High Street, Cable Street, King David's Lane and Baroda Place in Shadwell. Turner Street, Lucas Street, Commercial Road, Greenfield Street and Lady Lake's Grove in Mile End Old Town and finally East Smithfield, Upper Well Alley and St George's Street located in the parish of Wapping.

Those who could afford lodging houses were lucky. Some had no choice but to take themselves to what was locally known as the 'Spike', the workhouse. Those who had nothing other than the rags they called clothes to walk in, and had nowhere else to turn, turned to the workhouse in order to get a roof over their head for the night and a hot meal. It was a last resort, and there was a price to pay. Designed to deter people from relying on the workhouse for support by providing a deliberately harsh environment to live and work in, the workhouse offered food barely fit for human consumption and beds – often just springs on a frame and a straw mattress – came in exchange for hard menial labour. The final alternative was to sleep on the streets or in parks and churchyards or gardens, which was predominantly a young person's preference. One such church garden in the area – outside Christ Church, Spitalfields – became notorious for the sleeping homeless. Jack London,[7] the eminent American author, in his social expose of working-class life in the East End of London entitled *The People of the Abyss*, wrote of this spot, known locally as Itchy Park:

The shadow of Christ's Church falls across Spitalfields Garden, and in the shadow of Christ's Church, at three o'clock in the afternoon, I saw a sight which I never wish to see again. There are no flowers in this garden, which is smaller than my own rose garden at home. Grass only grows here, and it is surrounded by sharp-spiked iron fencing, as are all the parks of London town, so that homeless men and women may not come in at night and sleep upon it.

As we entered the garden, an old woman between fifty and sixty, passed us, striding with sturdy intention if somewhat rickety action, with two bulky bundles, covered with sacking, slung fore and aft upon her. She was a woman tramp, a houseless soul, too independent to drag her falling carcass through the workhouse door. Like the snail, she carries her home with her. In two sacking-covered bundles were her household goods, her wardrobe, linen, and dear feminine possessions.

We went up the narrow gravelled walk. On the benches on either side arrayed a mass of miserable and distorted humanity, the sight of which would have impelled Doré to more diabolical flights of fancy than he ever succeeded in achieving. It was a welter of rags and filth, of all manner of loathsome skin diseases, open sores, bruises, grossness, indecency, leering monstrosities and bestial faces. A chill, raw wind was blowing, and these creatures huddled there in their rags, sleeping for the most part, or trying to sleep. Here were a dozen women, ranging in age from twenty to seventy. Next a babe, possibly of nine months, lying asleep, flat on the hard bench, with neither pillow nor covering, nor with any one looking after it. Next half a dozen men, sleeping bolt upright or leaning against one another in their sleep. In one place a family group, a child asleep in its mother's arms, and the husband (or male mate) clumsily mending a dilapidated shoe. On another bench, a woman trimming the frayed strips of her rags with a knife, and another woman, with thread and needle, sewing up rents. Adjoining, a man holding a sleeping woman in his arms. Further on, a man, his clothes caked with gutter mud, asleep, with his head in the lap of a woman, not more than twenty-five years old, and also asleep.

It was this sleeping that puzzled me. Why were nine out of ten of them asleep or trying to sleep? But it was not till afterwards that I learned. It is a law of the powers that be that the homeless shall not sleep by night. On the pavement, by the portico of Christ's Church, where the stone pillars rise towards the sky in a stately row, were whole rows of men asleep or drowsing, and all too deep sunk in a torpor to rouse or be made curious by our intrusion.[8]

Emma Smith could afford lodgings and was therefore able to avoid Itchy Park, and, looked at in this way, she was one of the luckier ones in Whitechapel. However, that was about to change.

On 6 April 1888 the police of H Division were notified by the coroner's office that an inquest had been called into the death of a woman who had died in the London Hospital, on the main Whitechapel Road, and that the inquest was to be held the following day, at the very same hospital. Inquests into deaths are called if the death is unexplained or suspicious; as a crime had potentially been committed, it fell to Detective Inspector Edmund Reid to investigate. His report states,

Emma Elizabeth Smith, 18 George Street, Spitalfields. Son and daughter living in Finsbury Park area. She had lodged at the above address for about eighteen months, paying 4*d* per night for her bed. She was in the habit of leaving at about 6 or 7 p.m. and returning at all hours, usually drunk.

On the night of 2 April 1888, she was seen talking to a man dressed in dark clothes and white scarf [that is, at 12.15 a.m. on the 3rd].[9] She returned to her lodgings between 4 and 5 a.m. She had been assaulted and robbed in Osborne Street (near Cocoa factory) Messers. Taylor Bros. [At] London Hospital she was attended to by Mr George Haslip, House Surgeon. She died at 9 a.m. on the 4th. The inquest was held by coroner Wynne Baxter at the hospital.

The first the police knew of this attack was from the coroner's officer who reported in the usual manner on the sixth inst. that the inquest would be held on the seventh inst. Chief Inspector West attended. None of the PC's in the area had heard or seen anything at all, and the streets were said to be quiet at the time.

The offence had been committed on the pathway opposite No. 10 Brick Lane, about 300 yards from 18 George Street, and half a mile from the London Hospital to which deceased walked. She would have passed a number of PC's en route but none was informed of the incident or asked to render assistance.

The peritoneum was penetrated by a blunt instrument thrust up the woman's passage, and peritonitis had set in which caused death. She was 45 years, 5'2" high, complexion fair, hair light brown, scar on right temple. No description of men.

Edmund Reid
Inspr.[10]

After attending the inquest, Chief Inspector West[11] wrote an additional report on the information he had obtained, adding,

Her head was bruised, right ear torn, rupture of peritoneum. According to statements made by the deceased the motive was robbery.

Deceased could not describe the men who had ill-used her but said that there were three of them, and that she was attacked about 1.30 a.m. on the 3rd, while passing Whitechapel Church. Witnesses Mary Russell, deputy[12] at 18 George Street, Spitalfields; Annie Lee, Lodger (these two escorted her to London Hospital); George Haslip and Margaret Hames (lodger at the above address who was last to see her alive.)

Coroner further expressed his intention of forwarding the particulars of the case to the Public Prosecutor as being one requiring further investigation with respect of the person or persons who committed the crime.

Witnesses stated they didn't think it necessary to report the circumstances to the police. Whole of the police on duty deny all knowledge of the occurrence.

Inspector West
Enquiry to be taken up by Inspector Reid

During the early hours of 3 April 1888, sometime between 4 a.m. and 5 a.m., Emma Smith had returned to 18 George Street. She had been severely beaten and was exhausted. The deputy lodging house keeper,

Mary Russell, who was in the kitchen at the time with lodgers Margaret Hames[13] and Annie Lee, asked what had happened to her. Smith replied that she had been attacked by a group of men who had followed her from St Mary's church,[14] on the Whitechapel Road. According to Smith, the assault had occurred at 1.30 a.m. near Messrs Taylor Bros' Mustard and Cocoa Mill on the corner of Osborn Street, Wentworth Street and Brick Lane.[15] This meant it had taken Smith around three hours to make the relatively short journey of what was, to most, only a few minutes back to her lodgings; such was the extent of her injuries, and the apathy of any passers-by.

Russell, Hames and Lee were so concerned with Smith's condition that they ignored her plea not to seek assistance and decided to walk her to the London Hospital on Whitechapel Road, half a mile away.[16] Upon arrival Smith was seen by the house surgeon, George Haslip. He noted her condition and injuries, stating at the inquest that 'when the deceased was admitted to the hospital she had been drinking but was not intoxicated. She was bleeding from the head and ear, and had other injuries of a revolting nature.' He further explained that 'she was suffering from rupture of the peritoneum, which had been perforated by some blunt instrument used with great force'. Haslip also added that Smith had told him a little more about the details of her attack:

> The deceased told him [Haslip] that at half-past 1 that morning she was passing near Whitechapel Church when she noticed some men coming towards her. She crossed the road to avoid them, but they followed, assaulted her, took all the money she had, and then committed the outrage. She was unable to say what kind of instrument was used, nor could she describe her assailants, except that she said that one was a youth of nineteen.[17]

Emma Smith died of peritonitis on Wednesday morning, 4 April 1888.

Reid's initial report (together with its addendum, added by West) is the only police record we have, albeit in the form of notes taken by subsequent researchers. Despite this, the information it contains is quite telling, at least as regards the police's perspective on the case. Clearly they were taken by surprise by the news of this death. The fact that Reid went out of his way to explain that the notice from the coroner's office was received by them a day before the inquest, two days after Smith's death, is a clear indication that he felt the need to exonerate the police for those two days of inactivity. That, or Reid was trying to ascertain why the police had not heard about the matter far sooner. The loss of investigating time must have been a frustration to him, though it must be pointed out that the timeline was quite usual for the period. The coroner's office, headed by the coroner, would have had numerous officers, each covering either one or more parishes within the jurisdiction of that office and the county.[18] The appropriate period between death and hearing was one to five days, with the hearing usually taking place two to three days after the coroner had been notified of said death. When Smith had died, the hospital would have notified the relevant coroner's office, in this case Whitechapel. Technically this could have been undertaken by anyone, but the fact remains that the coroner and his office could not act unless they had been notified. Once notified, the coroner's officer would conduct his preliminary investigation, contacting all parties concerned. He would then complete a form, for the benefit of the coroner, requesting permission to hold an inquest, noting down the details of the death and the circumstances, and making a suggestion as to where the inquest should be held. This location was usually in close proximity to the body's current location as the coroner, or the officer, was legally required to take the jury to view it during the inquest hearing. In the case of Smith, the location of the inquest was the London Hospital, as it was at this location that her body was being held. During the completion of the form, the officer would sometimes also give his opinion on the witnesses he has spoken to, such as 'This person is of good character' or 'This person is a stranger to the parish', in order to assist the coroner during his review. If necessary he would also advise the coroner on various matters, such as removal of a body to a selected mortuary.

This form was then passed on to the coroner for his review. The inquest into Smith's death was the responsibility of Coroner Wynne Edwin Baxter.[19] He would assess all the information presented and determine if an inquest should take place, as well as deciding whether a post-mortem needed to be undertaken, which often was the case. Baxter would also decide on which witnesses would be required to attend, informing the parish officer of the names of these people. Baxter clearly agreed that an inquest should be undertaken in the case of Smith, on the date and at the location suggested, as he issued his warrant to the coroner's officer. With the warrant in hand, the officer now had the authority to issue summons to all parties cited by Baxter. This would have been done either by the officer themselves or by a representative, serving the summons personally. Summonsed witnesses were also known to collect their summons from the local police station.[20] The officer would also issue notices to the police, and clearly this occurred two days after Smith's death, on 6 April 1888, in the 'usual manner' as Reid stated in his report; this probably means it was done via the postal service.[21]

Inspector Reid would have approached constables whose beats covered the Whitechapel Road, Osborne Street and George Street area, to establish if anything had either been reported to them or if they had heard via the station or local grapevine,[22] in case West was required to provide such information at the inquest. While the local constables denied having seen or heard anything regarding this brutal assault, it must be noted that assaults were common within the area. To deal with such a matter takes time and, while those who remained true to their duty would see the task through, it must be admitted that some, unfortunately, would have turned a blind eye. However, Smith was ferociously and brutally assaulted and, though she was able to walk to the hospital (albeit aided), there was visible physical damage upon her. Such was the state of Smith that it is hard to believe a policeman would have let a clearly injured woman pass by without stopping the party to make enquiries, if only to cover himself, should it be required. Of course, it must also be pointed out that there was an air of distrust of policemen, especially in the East End. Matters were dealt with on a personal level rather than left for the police to meddle with, so it is quite feasible that Smith and her party ducked past a few bobbies on their darkened route to hospital, leaving the boys in blue completely unaware of what had happened on or near to their beats.

The inquest into Smith's death returned a verdict of 'wilful murder against some person, or persons, unknown', which was to become an all-too-common verdict over the following months. Smith's murder was viewed as an occupational hazard of the period, which is not to say the police shrugged it off; they were, of course, policing the most notorious district in London, and resources were stretched. With the main witness dead, and the locals either oblivious to the assault or clamming up, there would be little or no hope of catching Smith's attackers unless a reasonable lead unexpectedly came forward. Smith's case, like all murder cases with perpetrators still undetected, remained open, and it remains open to this day. Smith's statement to Doctor Haslip and her associates in the lodging house describes a chain of events at the end of which she was the victim of a vicious attack by a gang of youths, and not the fog-enshrouded, top-hatted monster of myth. At least on the twin grounds of geography and timing, however, the murder of Emma Smith dovetailed neatly with the murders of others whose cases would soon join hers in the Whitechapel murders file.

8

Martha Tabram
7 August 1888

He ain't here.

Pearly Poll

A few months after the death of Emma Smith, in the early August of 1888, Inspector Ernest Ellisdon of H Division filed a report into the death of a woman found upon the landing of a common lodging house in George Yard,[1] Whitechapel, three days before. Dated 10 August 1888, and starting with the traditional 'I beg to report', Ellisdon laid out the details by stating that

> at 4.50am, 7 inst, John Reeves of 37 George Yard Buildings, George Yard, Whitechapel, was coming down the stairs of above Buildings to go to work, when he saw a woman lying on the first floor landing. He called PC 226H Barrett[2] (on the beat) who found the woman in a pool of blood. – there was no blood on the stairs leading to the landing. PC sent for Dr Killeen, 68 Brick Lane, who attended and pronounced life extinct – there being 39 punctured wounds on the body; the police ambulance litter was procured, and the body removed to Whitechapel mortuary to await inquest.
>
> Description, age 37, length 5 ft 3, complexion and hair dark: dress, green skirt, brown petticoat, long black jacket, brown stockings, side spring boots, black bonnet – all old.
>
> A description was circulated in 116 Infn. 7.8.88 – and the body was photographed the same date, but up to present time it has not been identified.
>
> Two copies of the photograph attached.
> E Ellisdon Insp
> T Arnold Supd[3]

The photographs were of Martha Tabram, *née* White, born in 1849 across the River Thames in Southwark to a warehouseman and his wife; she had married furniture packer Henry Tabram when she was twenty and their union bore two boys, Frederick (b. 1871) and Charles (b. 1872). The marriage lasted only six years because, according to Henry, Martha's drinking habits were too much for him, so he left. Their relationship continued to be tempestuous. Henry paid maintenance to Martha, but reduced it when he found she was living with another man – another Henry, this one with the surname of Turner. Martha retaliated when, in 1879, she took out a warrant for her estranged husband's arrest.[4]

Martha's continued drinking also affected her new relationship, and, in July 1888, she and Turner suddenly moved out of their lodgings at Star Place, just off the Commercial Road. Martha ended up at 19 George Street, Spitalfields, near to where Emma Smith had lodged a few months before, and by August 1888 Martha seems to have gained a reputation for drinking in the company of men.

As inspector, it was Ellisdon's duty to notify the coroner's office and forward to them all information so far obtained. In contrast to the Smith case, the police were fully aware within minutes of the body being discovered that a murder had taken place. The man who initially drew their attention, John Saunders Reeves, was leaving his lodgings in George Yard Building at 4.45 a.m. to go to work as a waterside labourer when he came across a woman's body in the open landing.[5] The astute Reeves knew that the local beat constable, PC 226H Thomas Barrett, walked his beat close by and went to locate him, and before long Reeves had returned with PC Barrett who, upon seeing a woman in a pool of blood, realised a doctor was required. Constables were expected to know the locations of all the doctors' surgeries – and doctors' private homes – on their beat, just in case assistance was required. In this case the nearest doctor to the scene was Dr Timothy Killeen,[6] who had his surgery in 68 Brick Lane. PC Barrett had the power to accost a member of the public and give them instructions to assist him if no other constable was available to provide aid, and to ignore such a request for assistance from a constable was an offence. However, it is not clear whether PC Barrett did instruct a member of the public (if so, the most likely candidate is the discoverer of Tabram's body, Reeves) or whether he gained aid from a fellow constable on an adjoining beat. The latter case was clearly suggested by the *East London Advertiser* in their report of the inquest, dated 11 August 1888: 'He [Barrett] sent another constable for a doctor.' The *East London Observer*, in a similar report dated the same day, wrote that 'the body was not moved by me [Barrett] or Reeves before the doctor came', which implied that Reeves had remained in attendance while awaiting Killeen.[7]

This latter line from the *East London Observer* is telling on police procedure with regard the discovery of a body. The first action – obtaining medical assistance – was under way; the next action for PC Barrett to undertake while awaiting the doctor was to make a preliminary inspection of the scene before him, and in doing so he noted that 'there were no marks on the staircase. The body was not moved before the doctor arrived. Her hands were lying by her side, clenched up, and there was nothing in them. Her clothes were torn and completely disarranged, the bosom of the dress being torn away. She was in such a position as to lead him [Barrett] to infer that someone had been with her. Her clothes were thrown upwards.'[8]

Upon arrival, Killeen's first call of duty was to determine if the woman was alive or dead. If the former, he would have worked on keeping her alive while issuing instructions to the police and those at the scene with regard to transferring the patient swiftly to his surgery, or to the local hospital. Unfortunately, Tabram was declared dead at the scene. It now fell to Dr Killeen to conduct a cursory examination, as best he could in the gloom, to note the condition of the body, and any injuries which might have suggested cause and time of death. Once this act was concluded, it was up to the police to transfer the body to the nearest mortuary, which in this case was Whitechapel mortuary, just off Old Montague Street.

And so the investigation into this crime began. The task fell upon the Criminal Investigation Department – the detective ranks – within H Division. Inspector Ellisdon formally passed the case on to the divisional head of CID, Inspector Edmund Reid, who was still working with his team on the Emma Smith case. Reid himself attended this inquest, which was opened on 9 August 1888 by coroner Wynne Baxter's deputy, George Collier, at the Working Lads Institute,[9] the nearest available venue to the mortuary. One of the witnesses called was Dr Killeen, who recalled his version of events, and laid out the results of the post-mortem he had undertaken on the woman's body. The inquest reports into Tabram's death have not survived, so we have to rely on newspaper transcription. *The Times* for 10 August 1888 reports Killeen revealing that the victim had thirty-nine stab wounds to her body, and that 'she had been dead some three hours. Her age was about thirty-six and the body was very well nourished'. Killeen continued, 'The left lung was penetrated in five places, and the right lung was penetrated in two places. The heart, which was rather fatty, was penetrated in one place, and that would be sufficient to cause death. The liver was healthy, but was penetrated in five places, the spleen was penetrated in two places, and the stomach, which was perfectly healthy, was penetrated in six places.'

Killeen also stated that he 'did not think all the wounds were inflicted with the same instrument. The wounds generally might have been inflicted by a knife, but such an instrument could not have inflicted one of the wounds, which went through the chest-bone. His opinion was that one of the wounds was inflicted by some kind of dagger, and that all of them were caused during life.'[10]

The *East London Advertiser*, in its issue of 11 August 1888, added a little extra detail:

He [Killeen] had since made a post mortem examination, and on opening the head found there was an effusion of blood between the scalp and the bone. The brain was pale but healthy ... There was food in the process of digestion in the stomach. Dr. Keeling [*sic*] then described where the wounds had been made, and in answer to questions stated positively that there were no signs of there having been recent connexion. In his opinion the wounds were caused by a knife, or some such instrument, but there was a wound on the chest bone which could not have been caused by a knife. An ordinary penknife could have made most of the wounds, but the puncture in the chest must have been made with a sword bayonet or a dagger. The wounds, he was of the opinion, were inflicted during life, and it was impossible for them all to have been self-inflicted, though some of them might have been. Then in reply to questions from the coroner as to whether he could tell whether the wounds were made by a right or left-handed person, the doctor said one of the wounds might have been made by a left-handed man, but not the others.[11]

The mention of a sword bayonet in Killeen's statement was interesting. PC Barrett, who was the first police constable on the scene, walked his beat along George Yard, and he admitted to accosting a soldier – and then moving him on – some hours before being summons by Reeves. PC Barrett stated that he saw the soldier at approximately 2.00 a.m., on the corner of Wentworth Street and George Yard. He asked the soldier what he was doing loitering there, to which the soldier explained that he was waiting for his friend, who had gone with a woman into George Yard.[12] From the description the constable gave, the soldier appeared to be a private in the Grenadiers, who were then based relatively close by, at the Tower of London. This information, divulged by the constable, was known to Reid hours after the discovery of Tabram's body, and when Killeen mentioned the potential use of a sword bayonet or dagger in his post-mortem report, H Division CID knew they had a promising clue.

Reid pounced, organising a swift identity parade at the Tower on the very day of the murder. PC Barrett, who had told Reid that he 'should know the private again',[13] was ordered to attend. The parade was held in the guardroom at the Tower Barracks. Here, PC Barrett walked along a line of soldiers who had been held as prisoners for minor indiscretions which had occurred the day before.[14] The parade was a fruitless one, however; PC Barrett did not recognise any of the men as the soldier he had seen near George Yard, later stating that, as the prisoners were not dressed in uniform, he could not be certain. Reid then requested a full parade of all the Grenadiers who had been on leave on 6 August, and was informed that such a request needed a little preparation, as some of the privates had not returned from leave.

Reid and Barrett returned to the Tower the next day at 11.00 a.m. sharp the next morning. They situated themselves near to the sergeants' mess, waiting for the soldiers to assemble outside in the guardroom, when Reid said to the constable that he had 'to be careful as to his actions because many eyes were watching him and a great deal depended on his picking out the right man and no other'.[15] He then instructed PC Barrett to walk along the ranks of men and tap the shoulder of the man he felt he had seen at the entrance to George Yard. Once he had issued his instructions to PC Barrett, Reid retreated with the Army officers and waited for the constable to commence. Barrett walked along the ranks from left to right and when, according to Reid, he got to the centre, he stopped and looked at a private wearing some medals. The constable stepped forward, tapped the soldier on the shoulder and began to walk back to Reid. Reid strode forward and met Barrett, instructing the PC to take another look, as it was important he got this identification correct. So Barrett returned to the ranks; however, instead of picking out the same soldier, he went up to a second private some six or seven places away from the soldier he has selected before. He tapped this man on the shoulder and returned to a perplexed Reid. The detective inspector asked the obvious question: 'How did you come to pick out two men?' PC Barrett explained that the first man he picked out was wearing medals; however, the man he saw at the entrance to George Yard was not wearing any medals at all. An undoubtedly annoyed Reid ordered PC Barrett to stand away. This was not going to be as straightforward as Reid had hoped.

In the meantime, enquiries had been made by H Division CID officers Lee and Caunter, and they had located two witnesses claiming to have seen the deceased, who at that stage had not been formally identified, in the company of a soldier. Knowing that a parade was currently taking place at the Tower, and not wishing to cause further inconvenience by arranging yet another parade, Lee and Caunter arranged for the two witnesses to attend at the Tower, in hopes they could identify the soldier they claimed to have seen. The witnesses, Mrs Jane Gillbank and her daughter, failed to pick out anyone, and were later found to be mistaken, as the deceased they claimed to have seen was a certain Mrs Withers, who was found alive and well some days later.

With this, the parade was over. The two soldiers picked out by PC Barrett were marched into the orderly room while the others were dismissed. As soon as they entered the room, Barrett mentioned that he had made a mistake with the first identification, stating again that the man he saw wore no medals, so this first man was allowed to leave (surprisingly without any of his details being taken). The other soldier gave his name as Private John Leary. Reid then asked him if he could give an account of his movements on the night of 6 August and the early hours of the 7th. Leary gave a detailed recollection of where he went and with whom he had spent the time, citing a Private Law as his companion. Law was sent for, and he corroborated Leary's story almost word for word. While Leary and Law could not recall the names of any others they spent time with, Reid was satisfied to let Leary go. The fact PC Barrett pointed out two different men, within minutes of the other, must have played on Reid's mind; the constable cannot have been entirely certain of whom he saw. There is no record of Reid examining Leary's bayonet or uniform, although it would seem unusual for him not to have done this, given the circumstances of the murder and the post-mortem results. On the other hand, Reid may not have been aware of Dr Killeen's findings at this stage.

While in attendance at the Tower, Reid was made aware of one soldier who was currently absent without leave, a Corporal Benjamin. The inspector was present at Tower Barracks on the following day, 9 August, when Benjamin returned. Reid immediately seized his clothing and bayonet before asking the corporal to account for himself. Benjamin explained that he had been staying at his father's hotel in Kingston upon Thames for the whole period. Reid immediately sent for enquires to be made, and Benjamin's father confirmed his son's story. Benjamin's clothes and bayonet showed no traces of blood, and since there was no further reason to suspect him, he was allowed to leave.

As Reid was interrogating Benjamin, a 'masculine-looking woman' known locally as Pearly Poll entered Commercial Street police station and gave a statement. She gave her full name as Mary Ann Connelly, and she claimed to have spent time with the deceased prior to her death, stating that they were both in the company of soldiers for the evening. This claim drew a huge amount of interest from CID, especially when coupled with Killeen's and Barratt's evidence hinting at a military involvement. Though Tabram had still to be formally identified, Connelly was sure the woman in the photo was Martha. Reid set up yet another identification parade at Tower Barracks for the following day; however when 11.00 a.m. came on the day of 10 August, Connelly was nowhere to be seen. A rather annoyed and undoubtedly embarrassed Reid had to explain to the sergeant major that the witness had not turned up, and that the men should be dismissed.

Detective Sergeant Eli Caunter was given the task of tracking Connelly down and, two days later, he was successful in finding Pearly Poll. She was presented before Reid and promised to attend yet another Tower Barracks parade that Reid had organised for the following day. This time Connelly appeared and, according to her statement, she was looking for two soldiers, one a corporal and one a private, with whom she and Tabram had spent the majority of the evening prior to Martha's murder. The *East London Observer* takes up the story, reporting that

> Inspector Reid, accompanied by 'Pearly Poll', proceeded to the Tower on Monday afternoon, where she was confronted with every non-commissioned officer and private who had leave of absence at the time of the outrage. They were paraded at the back of the Tower, unseen by the public – of whom on Monday there was a large number frequenting the historic structure – and 'Pearly Poll' was asked, 'Can you see either of the men you saw with the woman now dead?' 'Pearly Poll,' in no way embarrassed, placed her arms akimbo, glanced at the men with the air of an inspecting officer, and shook her head. This indication of a negative was not sufficient. 'Can you identify anyone?' she was asked. 'Pearly Poll' explained, with a good deal of feminine emphasis, 'He ain't here.'[16]

Reid gives us a little more insight into Connelly's attempted identification of the soldiers in his summary report of the identity parades dated 24 September: Connelly, he wrote, stated that the men were not among the line-up, and had 'white bands around their caps'.[17] There had been a mistake. Grenadiers did not wear white bands around their caps; however, soldiers of the Coldstream Guards did. With that, Reid thanked the sergeant major for all his assistance and the men were dismissed.

Reid wasted no time in arranging yet another identity parade, this time with the Coldstream Guards at Wellington Barracks – the same barracks the guards shared with the Metropolitan Police – and all corporals and privates who were on leave on 6 August were in attendance. Again Connelly walked the ranks and this time picked out two soldiers, a corporal named George and a private named Skipper. The two were taken into a room in order for Reid to conduct his enquires. Skipper claimed instantly that he has been in the barracks on the night from 10.00 p.m. on 6 August. The regiment logbook was sent for and this proved that Skipper was telling the truth, so he was dismissed.[18] George claimed to have been with his wife in Hammersmith Road from 8.00 p.m. on the 6th until 6.00 a.m. the following day. Again, Reid sent for enquires to be made; like Skipper, George was being truthful, so the private was also dismissed.

The final line in Reid's summary report of 24 September 1888 is telling. His exasperation with his two witnesses, Barrett and Connelly, is clear, stating that: 'having both picked out the wrong men they could not be trusted again as their evidence would be worthless'.

In the midst of these identity parades, on 14 August, Martha Tabram was formally identified by her estranged husband Henry. He had learnt of a woman's death in the newspaper and, upon reading her description, he felt that she was his wife Martha. Mary Bousfield,[19] landlady of 4 Star Place, where Martha had recently lodged with Henry Turner, confirmed Henry Tabram's identification.

Knowing the name of the victim was, however, scant recompense for Reid's wasted efforts with the soldiers. The police codes of 1886 and 1889 contained identical passages respecting the identification of prisoners, and therefore tells us how the police were expected to operate in 1888. The code opens, 'It is of the utmost importance that the identification of a person who may be charged with a criminal offence should be conducted in the fairest possible manner.'

While those in attendance at the parades were not classed as prisoners, they were potential suspects. Reid was very aware of this part of the code, and its guidance on fairness, as he pointed out to PC Barrett that he (Barrett) had 'to be careful as to his actions because many eyes were watching him and a great deal depended on his picking out the right man and no other'. On a matter as serious as murder, there was no room for errors.

The code continues by stating that

a person detained on suspicion, and whose identity is in question, should be placed, with not less than five or six others, of as nearly as possible similar appearance as to age, clothes, and position in life. The suspected person may be asked if he is satisfied, and any reasonable request on his part should be acceded to. The witnesses should then be introduced, one at a time, and told to go up to the person recognised. They must not communicate with each other in any way; and after the persons are placed for identification, no police officer should hold any communication with a witness.

This particular part of the code concerns identity parades featuring detained persons, which was not the case with the set of parades conducted at the barracks. However, it would have been wise to have adhered to this part of the guidance, and on the whole Reid clearly did. While there was no specific suspect in the line-up, Reid stood back and let PC Barrett, and Connelly, walk along the ranks. There was no communication between Reid and the witnesses, Barrett and Connelly; and once they had begun the process, they, in turn, held no communication with their potential suspects either, simply tapping them on the shoulder and walking away. The only part of this guidance to which Reid does not strictly adhere to was that part concerning the suspected person, for obvious reasons – since there was no suspect in custody, no suspect could be placed in the line-up. However, had there been a suspect, he would have been permitted to stand where he wished within that line-up. He would have been permitted to alter his appearance to a degree, such as by adopting a different way of combing the hair; these changes, however, would have been noted by the police and could, potentially, be used as evidence should the suspect go to trial.

The final part in the code regarding identification parades concerns what is commonly known as 'confrontation', which is the face-to-face way of conducting an identification. The code covers this by stating, 'Identification by bringing a suspect alone into a room, or by showing him to a witness in a cell, is not a fair mode of identification, and is likely to lead to difficulties and mistakes.'

The inference is clear. The witness would, most likely, assume they are identifying the perpetrator of the crime; they are face to face with the person who committed the heinous act, they suspend all thoughts that the suspect is potentially innocent. Without other persons around to compare, it is human nature to assume the person standing in front of you committed the act. However, this is not always a reasonable assumption, and there may be other variables which militate against the value of confrontation if, for example, the suspect is a relation of the witness, or is known to him socially, or has particularly distinguishing features. By way of variation, this form of identification can also be covert, with the suspect placed in a room and spied upon by the witness, without the former's knowledge.

As stated in the police code, this form of identification commonly led to difficulties and errors, and this was to be the case later in the investigation, when an identification event took place in a seaside home in the early 1890s, which since has become a hotbed of debate within the field of the Whitechapel murders. The evidence points to a 'confrontation' identification parade. The witness was unknown; the suspect, it was suggested, was Jack the Ripper.

The inquest into the death of Martha Tabram concluded on 23 August

1888 with a verdict of 'wilful murder against some person or persons unknown'. Reid and his CID team continued to work on this case, as well as that of Emma Smith. One of Reid's CID colleagues was to say of the Tabram murder that 'no crime more brutal has ever been committed in the East-end'.[20] Though it wasn't known at the time, this murder would be superseded by two more, both within little more than week of each other, stretching H Division CID to breaking point.

9

Mary Ann 'Polly' Nichols
31 August 1888

I'll soon get my doss money.
Mary Ann 'Polly' Nichols to the deputy of her lodging house,
31 August 1888

Prostitution was not, and still is not, a direct offence; therefore, constables could not arrest anyone simply for being a prostitute, though the act of behaving in a 'riotous and indecent manner in a public place' did become an offence under the all-encompassing Vagrancy Act of 1824. This, coupled with the Metropolitan Police Act of 1829, which forbade prostitutes to loiter in public spaces and annoy local 'inhabitants and passengers'[1] by accosting them, gave constables powers to tackle the prostitution issue, although the matter wasn't so clear cut. In order for magistrates to convict, they required witnesses – people who either saw the prostitute act in such a manner or were even accosted by them – to stand in a court and testify. Obviously, in an age of seemingly high moral decency, a gentleman's appearance at court on such a matter came with a stigma, and so was avoided at all costs. It was rare for a witness to appear against a prostitute at court; however, if a constable observed the offence, he could appear as a witness, resulting in evidence being provided against the prostitute and the case making it to court. The issue was this: how reliable was the constable's testimony? It was this question which left magistrates reluctant to find prostitutes guilty solely on the constable's evidence alone.

This matter was one which raised serious moral and policing questions just prior to the Whitechapel murders, with the conduct of beat constables and how they dealt with females assumed to be prostitutes coming under serious and justified scrutiny. Elizabeth Cass, a dressmaker from Stockton, was arrested in Marylebone by D Division constable Bowden Endacott in London's West End. At Marlborough Street court, Endacott claimed to have observed Cass soliciting in Regent Street; however, as no witnesses were produced to support the constable's claim, the case was dismissed, although the magistrate clearly supported Endacott's instinct that Cass was a prostitute at work, as he warned her that if he saw her again he would

BULL'S EYE ON BOBBY.

MR. BULL (*takes Policeman's lantern*). "THANK YOU. I'LL JUST HAVE A LOOK ROUND MYSELF. STRIKES ME
THE PREMISES AIN'T AS CLEAN AS THEY MIGHT BE!"

1. *Punch*'s cartoon verdict on the Trial of the Detectives in 1877. (Courtesy of the
Evans/Skinner Archive)

Left: 2. Metropolitan Police Commissioner Sir Charles Warren in 1886. (© Neil Bell)

Right: 3. James Monro, the Metropolitan Police's assistant commissioner, in charge of CID at the beginning of 1888 before resigning his position in August. He replaced Sir Charles Warren as commissioner in late 1888. (© Neil Bell)

4. Great Scotland Yard, *c.* 1880s. (© MPHC)

5. A *Strand Magazine* photograph showing fresh Metropolitan Police candidates at Wellington Barracks in 1901. (From Hargrave Lee Adam's *The Police Encyclopedia*)

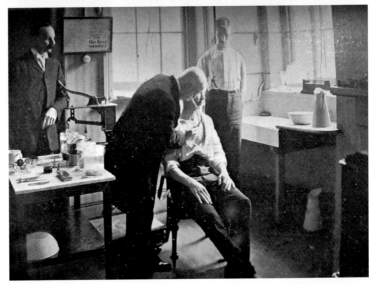

6. City of London Police divisional surgeon Dr F. G. Brown, who was involved in the Eddowes case, conducting a medical examination on a new City of London Police candidate around 1900. (From Hargrave Lee Adam's *The Police Encyclopedia*)

7. New recruits to the City of London Police undertaking self-defence training on top of Bishopsgate police station roof. (From Hargrave Lee Adam's *The Police Encyclopedia*)

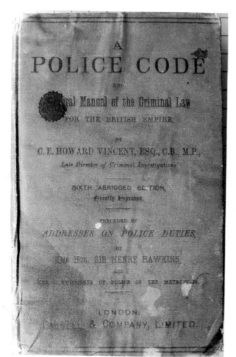

Left: 8. The front cover of Howard Vincent's 1889 edition of the police code. (© Neil Bell)

Right: 9. New Metropolitan Police recruits taking the oath in front of Inspector Rose. (From Hargrave Lee Adam's *The Police Encyclopedia*)

10. H Division (Whitechapel) Register entry for collar number 240H, showing Constable Ernest Thompson's name at the bottom. Thompson was to discover Whitechapel murder victim Frances Coles, in Swallow Gardens, just weeks after this entry. (© MPHC/Photograph Neil Bell)

11. The new frontage of H Division Headquarters at Leman Street police station, completed just after the Frances Coles murder in 1891. (© MPHC)

12. Arbour Square police station, on the right, c. 1900. (Courtesy Robert Clack)

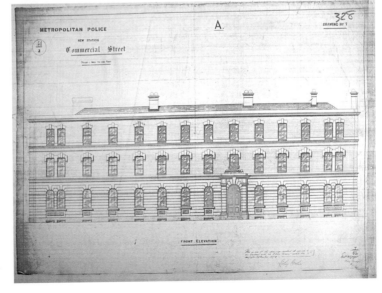

13. Commercial Street police station opened in 1876. Inspector Abberline and Inspector Reid had quarters here. (© LMA/Photograph Robert Clack)

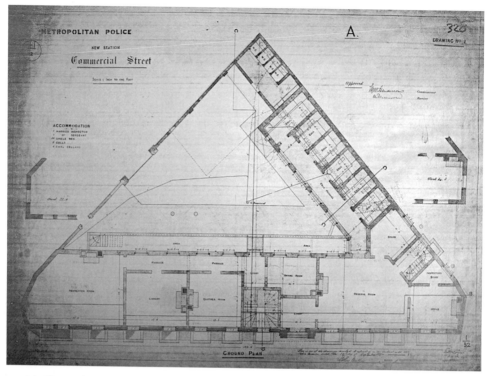

14. Plans of Commercial Street police station, showing the operational side at ground level. (© LMA/Photograph Robert Clack)

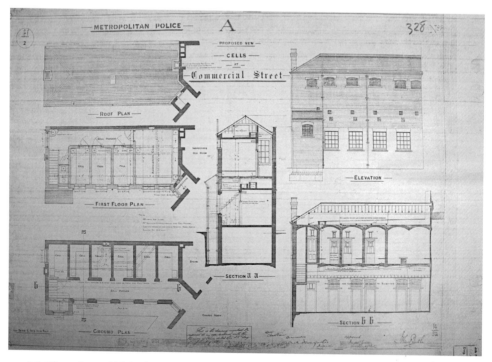

15. Plans from 1886 of Commercial Street police station showing the cell block. (© LMA/Photograph Robert Clack)

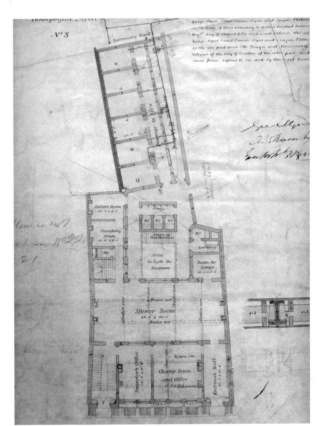

Right: 16. The ground-floor plan showing the operational side of the City of London police station at Bishopsgate. (© LMA/Photograph Neil Bell)

Below: 17. Drawing of Bishopsgate police station infirmary, as viewed from Rose Alley. (© LMA/ Photograph Neil Bell)

Elevation of Infirmary in Rose Alley

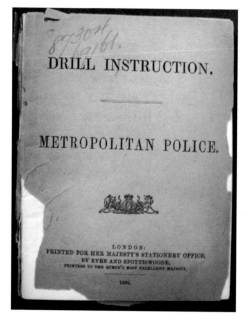
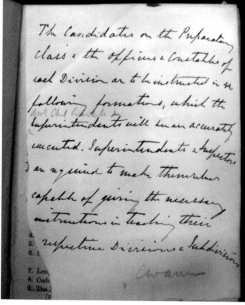

Left: 18. The cover of the 1888 *Metropolitan Police Drill Instruction Book.* (© NA/ Photograph Neil Bell)

Right: 19. Handwritten notes made by Metropolitan Police Commissioner Sir Charles Warren in the infantry's *Field Exercise & Evolutions* book he borrowed from the Metropolitan Police receiver. (© NA/Photograph Neil Bell)

III.

Words of Command.—1. Every command must be loud and distinctly pronounced, so as to be heard by all concerned.

2. Every command that consists of one word must be preceded by a caution; the caution, or cautionary part of a command, must be given slowly and distinctly; the last or executive part, which, in general, should consist of only one word or syllable, must be given sharply and quickly, as *Company—Halt   Half Right— Turn.* A pause of slow time will invariably be made between the caution, or cautionary part of a command, and the executive word.

3. The words given in the *Extension Motions* and *Balance Step* (Ss. 5, 11) must be given sharply, or slowly and smoothly, as the nature of the motion may require.

4. When the last word of a caution is the signal for any preparatory movement, it will be given as an executive word, and separated from the rest of the command by a pause of slow time; thus, *Right—Form.   Quick—March*, as though there were two separate commands, each with its caution and executive word.

5. When the men are in motion, executive words must be completed as they are commencing the pace which will bring them to the spot on which the command has to be executed. The cautionary part of the word must, therefore, be commenced accordingly.

6. Inspectors and sergeants should frequently be practised in giving words of command. It will be found a good plan to practice several officers together in giving words of command, first in succession, then

simultaneously; the time and pitch being first given by the instructor.

IV.

1. The superintendents are not to assemble the men for drill if the weather is unfavourable.

2. Drill is discontinued in winter and during very hot weather. The discontinuance or resumption of drill is directed by Commissioner in police orders.

3. A record is to be kept in divisions of the numbers of each rank attending each drill, and the dates and hours when the drill takes place.

4. A quarterly return of the numbers who attend drill is to be made to the Commissioner on the first of January, April, July, and October.

5. When drill is discontinued the men are occasionally to be put through their turnings and formation of fours when they parade for duty at stations.

6. Police are not to be required to attend drill if the distance from the stations to which they are attached to the drill ground exceeds two miles.

7. "Time off" is to be granted for attendance at drill as may be considered necessary by the superintendent, and at such times as is convenient, having due regard to the requirements of the duties.

8. Drill is invariably to be held on pay days and at the stations wherever this can be arranged.

9. Constables of long service or attached to exterior stations may, on the approval of the chief constable, be exempted from drill.

10. All ranks (except in dockyard divisions) prior to promotion to higher ranks are examined as to their proficiency in drill by an assistant chief constable, who certifies as to their qualifications in this respect.

20. Some of the rules outlined in the 1888 *Metropolitan Police Drill Instruction Book.* (© NA/Photograph Neil Bell)

The Candidates on the Preparatory Class and the Officers and Constables of each Division are to be instructed in the following formations, which the Assistant Chief Constable and Superintendents will see are accurately executed.

Superintendents and Inspectors are required to make themselves capable of giving the necessary instructions in teaching their respective Divisions and Sub-Divisions.

(Signed)　　CHARLES WARREN.

o 54572.　　　　　　　　　　　　　　　　　A 2

21. And the final, printed version of Warren's notes, as they appear in the 1888 *Metropolitan Police Drill Instruction Book*. (© NA/ Photograph Neil Bell)

From	To		Thence to								
	E Bow Street	Hunter Street									
		Vine Street (C)									
		King's Cross Road (G)									
	F Paddington	Notting Hill	Kensington, Notting Dale (X)	Hammersmith (T) Residence of A. C. Bruce, Esq. (Assistant Commissioner). Residence of Col. Roberts (Chief Constable)							
		Marylebone Lane (D)									
		Harrow Road (X)									
	G King's Cross Rd.	Old Street	Hoxton								
		Residence of Lieut.-Col. Monsell, Chief Constable									
		Bow Street (E)									
		Islington (N)									
		Albany Street (S)									
	H Leman Street	Commercial Street	Shadwell								
		Arbour Square									
		Royal Mint									
		Bow (K)									
		Wapping (TA)									
	J Bethnal Green	Hackney	Dalston, Stoke Newington (N), Leytonstone	Stoke Newington (N), Wanstead	Woodford	Loughton, Barkingside, Edmonton (N)	Epping (Essex Constabulary), Ilford (K).				
		Bow (K)									
		Stoke Newington (N)									

22. Police orders of 5 June 1888 showing the cascading of telegrams from Executive Branch to all subdivision stations, (© NA/Photograph Neil Bell)

Executive Branch, Commissioner's Office.

Left: 23. H Division's Mile End section house, as it looks today. Section houses had no operational function, and were solely used as accommodation for unmarried constables and sergeants. During emergencies, men were summoned to the house by the section house sergeant, who would stand at the door, and blow his whistle. (© Neil Bell)

Below left: 24. An example of an 1899 arithmetic examination paper for the rank of sergeant. (© NA/Photograph Neil Bell)

Below right: 25. Another example of an 1899 examination paper for the rank of sergeant, this time for reading and copying. (© NA/Photograph Neil Bell)

CITY OF LONDON POLICE.

Edward Watkins

No. ~~77~~, 944.

Joined the Force 25th May 1871,

Date	REPORT	AWARD	AUTHORITY
1872 Augt. 23rd	Having sexual intercourse with a woman on his beat;	Fined 3/6.	Actg Commissioner.
1873 Jany 1st	In a Public house while on duty	Reduced to 3rd Class of pay,	Commissioner.
-"- Feby 12th	Not discovering a key in a door on his beat.	Fined 3/-.	Commissioner.
1876 July 1st	In a Public house while on duty,	Reduced to 2nd Class of pay 3 months	Actg Commissioner.
1889 Oct. 11th	Drinking malt liquor while on duty,	Reprimanded and pointedly cautioned.	Commissioner.

26. City of London Constable Edward Watkins' disciplinary record. Note the entry for 23 August 1872. Watkins was later to discover the body of Catherine Eddowes in Mitre Square in 1888. (© LMA/Photograph Robert Clack)

27. An 1886 catalogue cover for William Jones & Company, providers of helmets to the Metropolitan Police. (Courtesy of James Traversh, Police Memorabilia Collectors Club)

28. Bulleye lamps. (© Neil Bell)

Left: 29. The pocketbook belonging to the head of the Whitechapel murders investigation, Chief Inspector Donald S. Swanson. (© Nevil Swanson & Adam Wood)

Right: 30. A beat wheel, used to measure out the distance of beats. (© MPHC/ Photograph Neil Bell)

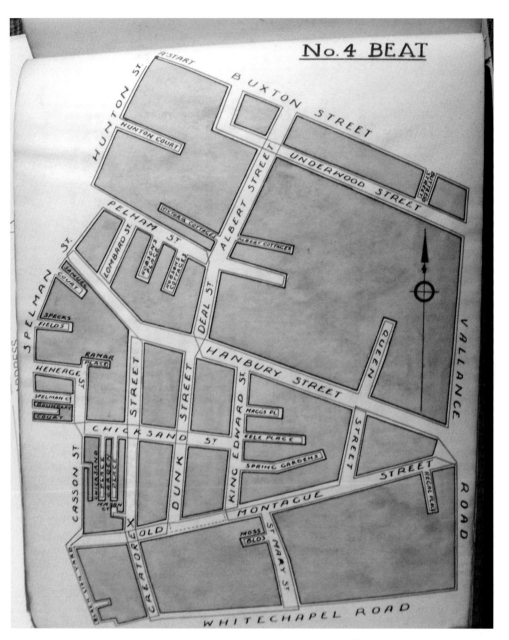

31. H Division beat book from the 1930s, showing the route of beat No. 4. (© MPHC/ Photograph Neil Bell)

Above: 32. City of London constables mustering for their night beats, possibly at Bishopsgate Police Station, *c.* 1900. (From Hargrave Lee Adam's *The Police Encyclopedia*)

52   POLICE CODE.

Convicts.—1. A convict is a person found guilty of a crime, and sentenced to penal servitude.

*2. During every such sentence a certain number of marks have to be earned by good conduct and industry. This can be done in about three-fourths of the total period of punishment in the case of men, two-thirds in the case of women. Every day, so many marks are awarded towards the total, and for misconduct and offences against prison discipline marks are forfeited, thus prolonging the period of actual detention.

3. Convicts who give information advancing the interests of justice, and especially with reference to receivers of stolen goods, and contemplated crime, are occasionally permitted by the Secretary of State to earn double marks; and so, while the period of release still depends on their behaviour, they can materially shorten their term of penal servitude.

4. A convict desiring to give information to the police, has only to signify his wish to the Governor, who communicates with the Chief Officer of the police force interested, and, under proper authority, two officers should be sent to take his statement, which must be treated as absolutely confidential.

***Convicts on License.** —* When convicts have earned the total required number of marks, they are released on license, and allowed their liberty so long as they conform to the subjoined conditions :—

Firstly.—That they report themselves where directed within forty-eight hours after liberation.

Secondly.—That they (women excepted), report themselves every month at the nearest Police Station to their place of abode, between the hours of Nine in the morning and Nine in the evening, on the day of the month named in the notice.

Thirdly.—That they reside—that is, sleep—at the address notified to the Police, in order that they may be at once found if required for any legal purpose.

Fourthly.—That they get their living by honest means, and regular employment.

Fifthly.—That if they change their address, or leave any Police District at all, they give notice of their removal at the Police Station at which they are reporting, and also at the nearest Police Station within forty-eight hours of arriving in any other Police District, in any part of the United Kingdom.

Sixthly.—That Convicts at liberty produce their Licenses when called upon to do so by a Police Officer.

Left: 33. The 1889 police code defining convicts, and outlining expectations of convicts on licence (aka ticket of leave men). (© Neil Bell)

34. A group photograph of H Division (Whitechapel) CID, taken at Leman Street in 1889, during the midst of the Whitechapel murders investigation. (© MPHC)

Left: 35. City of London Detective Department in 1888. On the back row, far left, is Detective Sergeant Harry Webb. (© Neil Bell)

Right: 36. H Division's local inspector Edmund Reid, on the right, with Sergeant William Thick on the left. (© MPHC/Photograph Neil Bell)

37. Common lodging house inspection sheet for H Division's 1889 visit to the Salvation Army lodging house in Whitechapel Road. (© NA/Photograph Neil Bell)

38. Entrance to George Yard Buildings in the 1960s, where, upon the first-floor landing, the body of Martha Tabram was found by resident John Sanders on 7 August 1888. The street junction is where Constable Barrett spoke to a soldier a short while before Martha Tabram's body was found. (© The Evans/Skinner Archive)

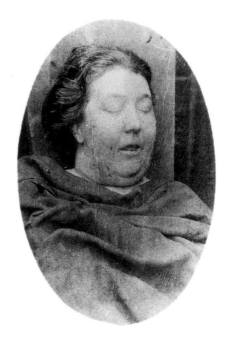

Left: 39. H Division's Detective Sergeant Eli Caunter, who tracked down the missing Pearly Poll during the investigation into Martha Tabram's murder. (© MPHC)

Right: 40. A typical mortuary photograph for the period, showing George Yard victim Martha Tabram. These photographs were taken purely for identification purposes, and not as evidence. (© The Evans/Skinner Archive)

41. A version of the Bischoffsheim handcart as used by the Metropolitan Force during the late Victorian period. (© Neil Bell)

42. This view, taken in 1961 from the spot where Mary Ann Nichols was found in Bucks Row, is looking west, from where Constable Neil approached the murder scene. (© Margaret Whitby-Green/Philip Hutchinson)

43. Taken from the same spot, this time in the opposite direction, east, towards Brady Street, from where Constable Thain approached after being signalled by Constable Neil. Witnesses Charles Cross and Paul also approached the murder scene from this direction. (© Margaret Whitby-Green/Philip Hutchinson)

Above left: 44. The mortuary photograph of Mary Ann Nichols, which would be issued to all constables making enquiries into her murder while her identity was being established. (© The Evans/Skinner Archive)

Above right: 45. The front of 29 Hanbury Street in the 1960s. The door upon the right was not in existence in 1888. The door upon the left leads to the passageway, and then on to the yard where Annie Chapman's body was found. (© The Evans/Skinner Archive)

Below left: 46. The 1961 view of the passageway of 29 Hanbury Street. John Davis climbed down the stairs upon the left, before going toward the yard seen through the doorway upon the right, where he discovered the body of Anne Chapman. (© Margaret Whitby-Green/Philip Hutchinson)

Below right: 47. The same passageway, this time looking toward Hanbury Street. Inspector Chandler secured this throughway, ensuring easy access for the police and medical men to the yard. (© Margaret Whitby-Green/Philip Hutchinson)

48. The yard of 29 Hanbury Street, where Annie Chapman's body was found. (© Margaret Whitby-Green/Philip Hutchinson)

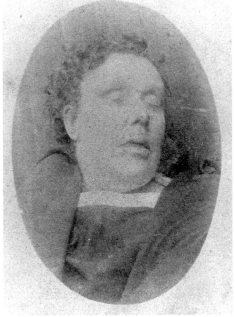

Left: 49. Albert Cadosch, who heard unusual noises emanating from the neighbouring yard of 29 Hanbury Street during the estimated time of Annie Chapman's murder. (Courtesy of Michele Heemskerk/Colin MacDonald)

Right: 50. The mortuary shot of Annie Chapman. As with Nichols, Chapman's photograph would be used to aid identification. (© The Evans/Skinner Archive)

Right: 51. Chief Inspector Donald S. Swanson, who was brought in to head the Whitechapel murders investigation just after the Annie Chapman murder. (Courtesy of the Swanson Family/Adam Wood)

Below: 52. H Division uniformed branch of Leman Street in around 1895. Some of the men here were involved in the Whitechapel murder and Jack the Ripper cases, especially that of Elisabeth Stride. (© MPHC)

53. The entrance to Dutfield's Yard around 1909. Note that the entrance did not have metallic gates in 1888. Also note the door and window on the far left, No. 44, from which Matthew Packer sold fruit on the night Stride was murdered in 1888. (© The Evans/Skinner Archive)

Above: 54. H Division Constable William Smith, whose beat included Berner Street. It was while on his beat that Constable Smith spotted Elisabeth Stride talking with a man close to the spot where she would be found murdered just some thirty minutes later. (© The Evans/Skinner Archive)

Right: 55. The mortuary photograph of Elisabeth Stride. (© The Evans/Skinner Archive)

INTERPRETATIONS & TRANSLATIONS.

NOTICE.

In all cases where the Prisoner or a Witness is a Foreigner, or is unable to speak English, the Constable having charge of the case is requested to notify Mr. Adolphus Herman Louis

(MESSRS. FLOWERDEW & CO.)

Official Interpreter to the Central Criminal Court.

HEAD OFFICES:
14, BELL YD., TEMPLE BAR.
CITY BRANCH:
11, POULTRY, E.C.,
LONDON.

TELEPHONE:
"900 HOLBORN."
TELEGRAPHIC ADDRESS:
"FLOWERDEW, LONDON."

56. An 1899 notice from Flowerdew & Co. solicitors, who specialised as interpreters and translators for the Metropolitan Police and courts. (© NA/ Neil Bell)

57. City of London police station at Bishopsgate. Catherine Eddowes would have been escorted through the right-hand doorway. (© LMA/ Neil Bell)

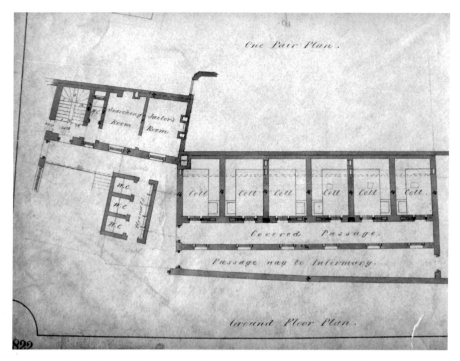

One Pair Plan.

Searching Room   Jailer's Room

m.c.

w.c.

Cell   Cell   Cell   Cell   Cell   Cell

Covered   Passage.

Passage way to Infirmary.

Ground Floor Plan.

822

58. The cell block of Bishopsgate police station, where Catherine Eddowes spent the night of 29 September 1888. (© LMA/Neil Bell)

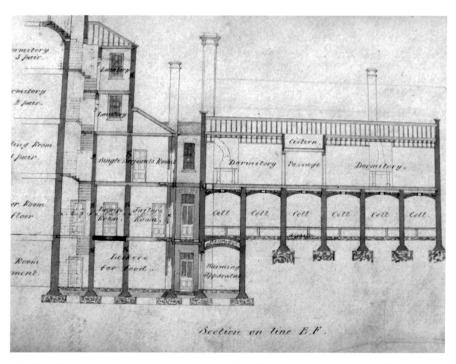

Dormitory 3 pair.

Dormitory 2 pair.

Lavatory

Lavatory

ing Room 1 pair.

Single Sergeants Room

Cistern

er Room floor.

Dormitory   Passage   Dormitory.

Lounge Room   Jailers Room.

Cell   Cell   Cell   Cell   Cell   Cell

Room ment?

Larders for food.

Warming Apparatus

Section on line E.F.

59. The side view of the block. Note the Jailers' Room, where Constable Hutt would spend most of his time while on duty, before doing his rounds of the cells to ensure all was well. (© LMA/Neil Bell)

60. City of London Constable 968 George Hutt, who was Catherine Eddowes' gaoler at Bishopsgate Police Station. (© Neil Bell)

Left: 61. Bishopsgate Police Station sergeant James Byfield. (© Neil Bell)

Right: 62. City of London Constable 964 James Harvey, whose beat took him almost in to Mitre Square. Constable Harvey was to assist Constable Watkins upon the discovery of Catherine Eddowes' body. (© The Evans/Skinner Archive)

Left: 63. A photograph of Mitre Square in the 1920s. Eddowes was found by City Constable 881 Edward Watkins under the window located upon the far left. (© The Evans/Skinner Archive)

Right: 64. City of London Police divisional surgeon Dr Frederick Gordon Brown in around 1909. Dr F. G. Brown viewed Catherine Eddowes' body in Mitre Square before conducting the post-mortem the following day. He was heavily involved in the Whitechapel murder cases. (© The Apothecaries Hall Society)

65. The only known photograph of wall writing connected to the Jack the Ripper murders. (Courtesy of CoLP museum. Photograph © Robert Clack)

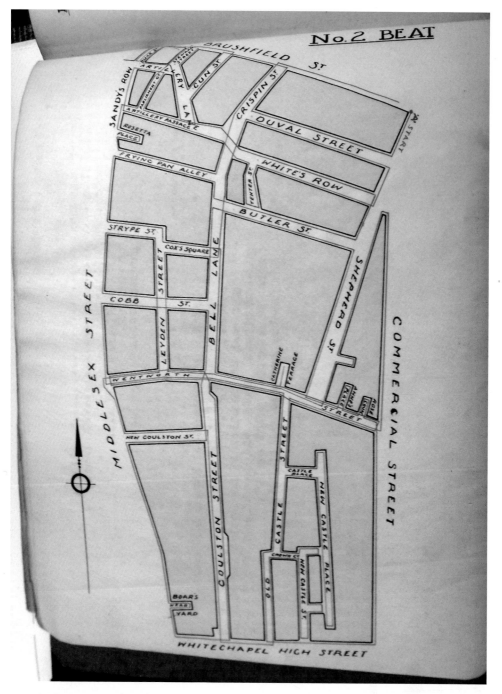

66. H Division's beat book from the 1930s, showing what could have been Constable Long's beat down Goulston Street. (Courtesy of MPHC. Photograph © Neil Bell)

67. City of London Police Sergeant 92 Herbert Jones, who collected some of Catherine Eddowes' belongings while attending the crime scene in Mitre Square. (© Neil Bell)

68. City of London uniformed men of Bishopsgate police station around 1887, with detectives sitting on the front row. Most of these constables were involved with the initial stages of the Catherine Eddowes murder investigation. (Courtesy of CoLP museum)

69. Mortuary photograph of Catherine Eddowes before post-mortem. Unlike the Metropolitan Police, the City of London force did not cover the Eddowes injuries. This is an indication the photograph was also part of evidence gathering, and not solely for identification, and therefore could be used in court if required. (© City of London Police Museum/Photograph Robert Clack)

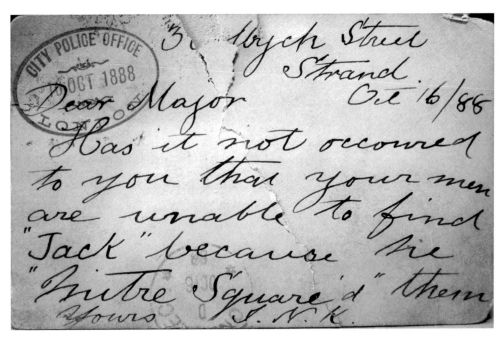

3 [...]lrych Street
Strand.
Oct 16/88
Dear Major
Has it not occurred
to you that your men
are unable to find
"Jack" because he
"Mitre Square'd" them
Yours J. N. K.

CITY POLICE OFFICE
OCT 1888
LONDON

70. Just one of the many letters and postcards received by the Metropolitan and City Police. Some claimed to be from the murderer, while others offered advice to the police. Some, such as this recently discovered postcard sent to the City of London Police in early October 1888, simply mocked their effort. (Courtesy of CoLP museum. Photograph © Robert Clack)

71. The police photograph showing room number 13 as viewed from Millers Court itself. The window upon the right, with its broken top-right pane, is the window Inspector Beck was asked to look through by witnesses Bowyer and McCarthy. (© The Evans/ Skinner Archive)

72. A police photograph of the inside of Mary Kelly's room, with her body upon her bed. It is the only photograph taken of the Whitechapel murders showing the victim in situ, and is thought to be the first crime-scene photograph to be taken in Great Britain. (© The Evans/Skinner Archive)

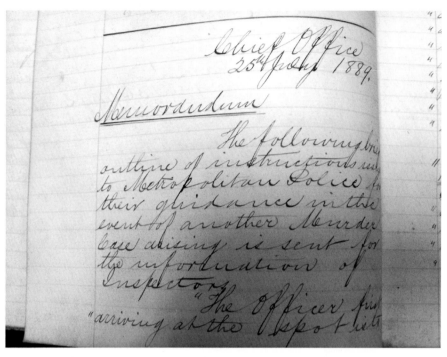

73. A City of London police order dated just days after Alice MacKenzie's murder in July, which outlined guidance on what should be done if any constable came across a body he felt was connected to the recent murders. (Courtesy of CoLP museum. Photograph © Neil Bell)

Left: 74. The City of London police order continued; note the telegram code 'Whitechapel Again!' (Courtesy of CoLP museum. Photograph © Neil Bell)

Middle: 75. Metropolitan Police Constable 240H Ernest Thompson, who came across a prone Frances Coles in Swallow Gardens on 13 February 1888. Thompson himself was to later die while on duty in 1900. (Courtesy of MPHC)

Right: 76. The City of London police order, dated the very day Frances Coles was found murdered, outlining the use of police whistles as a code, should another Whitechapel murder victim be found. (Courtesy of CoLP museum. Photograph © Neil Bell)

fine or imprison her. Cass's employer, Mrs Bowman, was so incensed at Cass's treatment that she wrote to the Home Secretary to highlight her concerns, and the matter was soon raised in the House of Commons by West Riding Member of Parliament H. J. Wilson and his Northwest Durham counterpart Llewellyn Atherley Jones. This resulted in public pressure being placed upon Metropolitan Police Commissioner Warren to suspend Endacott and conduct an inquiry, which eventually resulted in Endacott facing legal proceedings on a charge of perjury at the Old Bailey in October 1887. Endacott was found 'not guilty' and returned to duty, much to the annoyance of the press and the public.[2]

To compound matters, months after the Cass/Endacott incident, in the January of 1888, Police Constable Bloy of K (Bow) Division found a young woman drunk and disorderly at a house in the Tidal Basin, near to the banks of the River Thames. PC Bloy claimed that the woman, Annie Coverdale, was with 'several seafaring men, one of whom was naked to the skin', and that 'she was fighting and jeering at him'. During the trial, a desolate and distraught Coverdale flatly denied the accusations, and under cross-examination Constable Bloy was asked by Magistrate Baggallay if he previously knew Coverdale.

Bloy replied, 'Oh, yes, Sir; I have known her two or three years,' at which point Coverdale interjected. 'Sir,' she said, 'we have not been in Canning Town three years.'

The magistrate turned to the constable. 'How long have you known her?' he said, and warned Bloy against committing perjury by saying, 'Now, do be careful.'

Bloy responded, 'Well, I have known her twelve months, I am sure.'

Picking up on the discrepancy and uncertainty, the magistrate snorted, 'You said just now that you had known her for years. Have you seen her out at night before?' to which Bloy enthusiastically stated, 'Oh, yes, Sir.'

The magistrate asked, 'How long?'

Bloy replied, 'Every night, for the last three or four months, up to twelve and one in the morning, walking, about with sailors or seafaring men, different men.'

The defendant Coverdale again interjected – 'Sir, It is false, Sir (bursting into tears); it is false, Sir. I am not a girl of that sort. I am respectable, Sir. I have been in two respectable situations in Southampton, and have references in my possession, Sir. I have been asked to go back to my last situation. If I was such a girl as the constable says, I should not be asked to do that.' Here she handed over testimonials, which were perused by the magistrate. She further said that when the constable took her into custody he struck her, and when they passed her house she asked him to knock at the door and tell her father; but he refused, saying, 'You do not live there. I know your father well enough.'[3]

Despite her protestations, the case seemed hopeless against Annie Coverdale. One of Bloy's fellow constables supported his recollection of events by confirming that, in his opinion, Coverdale was drunk.

Coverdale's mother rallied to her daughter's aid, stating that Coverdale was a sober girl, and this was confirmed by two further witnesses. Then came forward the landlady of the house within which Coverdale and the men were found. In her testimony she claimed that she 'was the lady of the house where prisoner's [Coverdale's] young man had lodged', and that Constable Bloy ran into her house to arrest the young man for stealing, when really it was another man. She carried on, saying that Bloy 'was much excited, and treated the young woman very roughly'. Witness evidence, and the stumbling in his own testimony, began to lean toward the suggestion that Bloy had fabricated the story against Coverdale, leaving Magistrate Baggallay no choice but to throw the case out. Coverdale left the court with her mother, weeping uncontrollably due to the experience but a free woman. Metropolitan Commissioner Sir Charles Warren rallied around Constable Bloy, issuing a statement in the police orders declaring that he believed Bloy's testimony, and that the magistrate should not have thrown the case out against Coverdale. This declaration was an act of utter contempt of court; it was unprecedented by a commissioner, and it caused a furore in the House of Commons, so much so that Warren had little recourse but to back down, with full apology. These two incidents, where innocent women were arrested on false allegations, put the police in an extremely bad light. The press had a field day, with the *Pall Mall Gazette* first running with the headline 'The canonisation of St Bloy'[4] and then 'The whitewashing of St Bloy'[5]; and *Funny Folks,* in a sketch, depicted two kneeling constables in a stained-glass window, one with a mischievous grin upon his face and the other looking more sanctimonious, and between them Sir Charles Warren, under the words 'BOBBIES NEVER ERR!'.[6]

While these constables obviously acted abhorrently, there were understandable mitigating reasons, as the heavy responsibility of enforcing a moral shield around the public fell upon the police's shoulders, and this would have been understood by PC 97J John Neil, a thirty-six-year-old Irishman hailing from Macroom in County Cork, who, in the early hours of 31 August 1888, was walking his beat in the furthest reaches of his Bethnal Green Division, where it bordered with H Division. He worked his beat in an anti-clockwise direction, taking him past the London Hospital situated on the main thoroughfare of Whitechapel Road, where Emma Smith had died only a few months previously. Major roads were often used by prostitutes to pick up clients coming out of pubs and clubs, with one contemporary witness stating that the women who walked the Whitechapel Road were 'all sorts and sizes'.[7] Neil noted that the road was still busy with 'a number of women in that road, apparently on their way home',[8] a reference to prostitutes and an indication he was observing their activities. The time was around 3.45 a.m. as the constable walked along Whites Row, passed Thomas Street, and from there into the wide open space known as Great Eastern Square. Before him loomed the Board School, splitting the roadway into two thoroughfares, as it was at this point the road forked. To the right of the school stood the narrow Winthrop Street, and to its left the wider Buck's Row.[9] The constable walked the latter, heading towards Brady Street at the far end, crossing the bridge which ran over the railway line that led to Whitechapel underground station as he did so. Just after the bridge, on the north side of Buck's Row and to Neil's left, stood Essex Wharf, a narrow, three-floored building which ran back from Buck's Row;[10] however, Neil would have known that these premises were occupied by the building's manager Walter Purkiss, with his wife Mary Ann, their children and a servant, so there was no need to pay specific attention here. Opposite Essex Wharf, to Neil's right and on the south side of Buck's Row and also just after the bridge, stood the gated entrance to Mr Brown's stable yard and coach houses, and these were unoccupied at night, thus ensuring the constable's attention. As Neil looked towards this spot he noticed, in the gloom, a figure lying down on its back, and as he approached, with his bullseye lamp on and open, he could see the figure was a woman, lying parallel to the roadway. An initial look at her face indicated to Neil that this was serious, more than a mere drunk, as her eyes were open but there was no movement from her, and a closer inspection revealed to the constable that blood was oozing from a severe wound to her throat. He checked her arm, which was warm from the joint up, and noticed that her clothes had been disarranged.

As Neil was inspecting the woman, Constable 96J John Thain, also of Bethnal Green Division, had entered Brady Street from Whitechapel Road, and was heading north. He had just passed opposite the Winthrop Street junction, and was now crossing Buck's Row, looking down into the row as he walked his beat, when he noticed lamplight moving back and forth some way in the distance. Knowing instantly this was a signal from a brother constable, Thain made his way down the row towards the source of the light, Constable Neil, who pointed out the female figure before him. Procedure kicked in. Neil instructed Thain to notify the nearest doctor, Rees Ralph Llewellyn,[11] who was located at 152 Whitechapel Road, near to the junction with Brady Street, while Neil surveyed the scene best he could in the dark, noting that the woman's head was toward the east, toward Brady Street, and her feet facing the direction of the Board School; that the gated entrance was nine to ten feet high and was locked; that there was an absence of cartwheel tracks near the scene; that her left hand was up against the gates; that her bonnet had slipped off and was laying on her right side; that her eyes were open; and as he did this he was approached by another constable, 56H Jonas Mizen. Mizen came from the neighbouring Whitechapel Division, and his beat, like Neil's, brought him out to his jurisdiction's borders. The police code states that constables only had 'the authority to act within the jurisdiction they are sworn in'[12]; however, for Metropolitan constables the jurisdiction was the whole of the Metropolitan area, and while constables predominantly stuck to their own divisions and conducted their duties there, they could cross divisional boundaries either on a senior officer's order, or in emergency situations. As no senior orders were issued, Mizen must have been acting in an emergency situation, and as a woman's body had been found in the street with a serious throat wound, it was pretty clear the situation was indeed an emergency. The question is, how did Mizen know about this?

The answer lay in the fact that Constable Neil was not the first person to come across the body. Around five minutes earlier, Charles Cross,[13] a carman heading to work, had entered Buck's Row from Brady Street, and was just approaching Essex Wharf when, across the road, he saw 'something lying in front of the gateway like a tarpaulin'.[14] He wandered across to the middle of the road and saw it was a woman; however, due to the fact the street lighting was poor, he wasn't sure as to her condition, and it was at this stage that he noticed another man approaching, again from Brady Street. Robert Paul was also heading to work along Buck's Row, when he saw a man in front of him standing in the middle of the road. As he approached, the man moved back towards the pavement, and as Paul stepped into the roadway to pass, the man tapped Paul on the shoulder. It was Cross. 'Come and look at this woman here,'[15] he said to Paul, and the two men approached her.

Cross felt her hands, whereas Paul felt her hands and face. They both agreed these were cold, and Cross exclaimed, 'I believe she is dead.' Paul then, according to Cross, felt for a heartbeat, and tried to determine any breathing; however, he wasn't sure. The location was gloomy, and the men did not have the benefit of a lamp like Constable Neil, so they could not see the awful cut throat and the blood. Paul pulled down her skirts, to give her some decency, and as he did so he felt he noticed some slight movement. The men then agreed they would tell the first policeman they came across that there was a woman lying in Buck's Row, and the first constable they saw was PC 54H Mizen, who was on the corner of Baker's Row and Hanbury Street. They approached him, and Cross informed the constable that there was a woman in Buck's Row, 'lying down on the broad of her back'. He continued, 'She is either dead or drunk.'[16] Mizen disputed this recollection of events, stating that Cross merely said, 'You [Mizen] are wanted in Buck's Row,'[17] and it was claimed that Mizen continued with his 'knocking up' tasks before going to Buck's Row, an allegation he strongly denied.

In the meantime, Constable Neil had arrived on the scene, and was joined by Constable Thain, who had then been despatched to fetch the doctor. When Mizen arrived in Buck's Row he spoke with Neil, who instructed him to go to Bethnal Green subdivision station to fetch reinforcements and an ambulance. Ambulances in the Victorian period were mere handcarts, akin to modern gurneys, with the Bischoffsheim handcart being the one preferred by the Metropolitan Police.[18] Two large wheels sat on an axel around two-thirds of the way down the 'wooden stretcher', with a stand at the front; the ambulance also had an extendable oilcloth hood for use in poor weather, and three leather straps to hold down violent or drunk passengers. Ambulances were kept in small sheds at many of the subdivision stations, and were used predominantly for the transportation of drunks or injured persons to hospitals, and only on rare occasions for the bodies of the deceased. Situated just under the hood end of the cart was a small locker, which was equipped with a small first-aid kit. Ambulance classes were introduced in the Metropolitan force in the police orders dated 27 May 1887, and constable volunteers were trained in their use, and in first aid. The next class was due to be taken at Leman Street station, by H Division Surgeon Dr George Bagster Phillips, on 13 September 1888, a mere fortnight after this event.[19]

Mizen returned to Buck's Row with the ambulance and Sergeant J Henry Kirby, who was to state later that he had also been in a quiet Buck's Row only half an hour before Neil had found the woman – an indication that he was doing his rounds as section sergeant. It is at this stage that the situation broke away from the usual police procedure. Firstly, Constable Mizen and Sergeant Kirby arrived to find, along with Constable Thain and Dr Llewellyn, numerous people at the scene viewing the body, among them slaughtermen Henry Tompkins, James Mumford and, arriving after those two, Charles Bretton,[20] all working for horse slaughterers Messrs Harrison, Barber & Co., located just around the corner from the scene in Winthrop Street. Tompkins claimed to have been notified of the find by Constable Thain, who had popped in to collect his cape while on his way to fetch Dr Llewellyn (something Thain denied).[21] Walter Purkiss, the man who lived with his family opposite in Essex Wharf, also confirmed that people were milling around the body, stating that he was called up by the police at four o'clock and, upon opening the landing window to talk to them, noted two or three men along with three or four constables.[22] Emma Green, who lived in New Cottage, only a few feet away from where the body was found in the gateway of next door, testified that when she was roused by Sergeant Kirby at around 4 a.m., she opened and then looked out of her window and 'saw three or four constables and two or three other men'.[23] Patrick Mulshaw, a night watchman for the Whitechapel District Board of Works who was overseeing paving work in Winthrop Street and ensuring the materials were not being stolen, said he was spoken to by a man (maybe Bretton, who arrived at the body a little after his fellow slaughtermen), who said to him, 'Watchman, old man, I believe somebody is murdered down the street', so Mulshaw too went to take a look.[24] Here we have numerous people wandering around a crime scene, all viewing the body when they should have been held at a distance by the constables in attendance, thus avoiding potential contamination.

The second break from protocol was the instruction given out by Dr Llewellyn, who, upon inspecting the body, declared the woman deceased, and then ordered the constables present to 'move the woman to the mortuary; she is dead. I will make a further examination of her.'[25] This was not his order to give, and the most senior policeman at the scene, Sergeant Kirby, should have taken control of the situation and requested that the body stay in situ pending the arrival of the duty inspector. However, one can understand Llewellyn's reasoning; here he had a dead woman out in the open street, and a crowd gathering. There was nothing he could do with regards saving her life, and there was no more information he could obtain, other than the information he had already extracted while conducting his preliminary examinations, such as the observations she had not been dragged to the spot, that there was little evidence of a struggle, and that there was little blood pooling around her neck.[26] The duty inspector, John Spratling, was approximately a mile away in Hackney Road, Bethnal Green, when he was told of the discovery, and therefore did not arrive until sometime just after 4.30 a.m., so rather than leave a body out in the open, Llewellyn decided it should be removed. Therefore constables Thain, Mizen and Neil lifted the body on to the ambulance, again potentially contaminating the scene with their footprints, before Mizen and Neil, along with Sergeant Kirby, who had instructed Thain to wait for the inspector, took the body to the nearest mortuary, belonging to the Whitechapel Infirmary Workhouse, located in Eagle Place, just off Old Montague Street.

When Inspector Spratling did arrive in Buck's Row, he found Constable Thain, along with another unnamed constable, watching blood being washed away from the murder spot by Emma Green's son, James, who, according to Spratling, worked in Brown's Yard. Thain pointed to the spot where the body was found, and updated Spratling about the situation, informing him that the dead victim had been taken to the mortuary, at which point both men headed to Eagle Place. There they found the body, left outside, still on the ambulance, awaiting the arrival of the keys required to open the mortuary up. While waiting for the mortuary attendant, Robert Mann, to arrive, Spratling began to take note of her clothing and articles (including a broken mirror, piece of comb and a white handkerchief), and, upon Mann's arrival, continued to do so when the mortuary opened up and the body was transferred inside; however, when he lifted her skirts to record the undergarments, Spratling made a startling observation, so startling that, according to the *Evening News*, the inspector 'did not feel very well at the time, and the sight "turned him up"'.[27] Spratling had noticed that her abdomen had been opened up, with part of the intestines protruding. He sent again for Dr Llewellyn, and in his report, the first special report on this murder in the Whitechapel murder files, Spratling confirmed that

> Upon my arrival there [at the mortuary] and taking a description I found that she had been disembowelled, and at once sent to inform the Dr. of it; latter arrived quickly and on further examination stated that her throat had been cut from left to right, two distinct cuts being on the left side. The windpipe, gullet and spinal cord being cut through, a bruise apparently of a thumb being on the right lower jaw, also one on left cheek, the abdomen had been cut open from centre of bottom of ribs along right side, under pelvis to left of the stomach, there the wound was jagged, the omentium [*sic*], or coating of the stomach, was cut in several places, and two small stabs on private parts,

apparently done with a strong bladed knife, supposed to have been done by some left handed person, death being almost instantaneous.[28]

While still waiting for the recalled Dr Llewellyn, Spratling continued to take note of her description. Due to the sight of the abdominal injuries he had just witnessed, however, Spratling admitted that 'he did not make a very precise examination'.[29] The inspector reported,

> Description, age about 45, length 5 ft. 2. or 3, compx. dark, hair dark brown (turning grey), eyes brown, bruise on lower right jaw and left cheek, slight laceration of tongue, one tooth deficient front of upper jaw, two on left of lower d[itt]o; dress, brown ulster, 7 large brass buttons, (figure of female riding a horse an [a] man at side thereon), brown linsey frock grey woollen petticoat, flannel d[itt]o, white chest flannel, brown stays, white chemise, black ribbed woollen stockings, mans S.S. boots, cut on uppers, tips on heels, black straw bonnet, trimmed black velvet.[30]

By now J Division Detective Sergeant Patrick Enright had arrived at the mortuary, and the body was placed under his responsibility while Inspector Spratling and Constable Thain returned to Buck's Row to conduct enquiries. They spoke with Emma Green and Walter Purkiss, the two nearest people to the scene, with both informing the policemen that they had heard nothing which gave them the impression a murder had taken place so close by. Spratling also spoke with PC 81 GER, a railway constable assigned to the Great Eastern Railway Company, whose line the Buck's Row Bridge crossed, and who, despite being only fifty yards away from the scene, could only confirm what Green and Purkiss had stated.[31] Another J Division CID man, Detective Sergeant George Godley, had, by this stage, also arrived in Buck's Row to liaise with Spratling. The inspector decided to send Thain away to search the area and buildings near to where the body was found, while he and Godley conducted a search of railway stations and buildings belonging to the East London and District railways, and the railway embankments themselves, for a weapon or any clue whatsoever; they all drew a blank. At 6.45 a.m. the local inspector of J Division's CID, Joseph Helson,[32] was informed about the body found in Buck's Row, and he immediately went to the mortuary, arriving just as the victim was about to be undressed by attendant Mann and his assistant, James Hatfield. Helson watched the undressing, taking notes of the injuries the victim had received.[33]

Spratling, having taken some time out to recover, returned to the mortuary at noon to take a more precise inventory of the woman's clothing and belongings, which he found in a heap upon the mortuary yard floor.[34] Spratling fingered through them, and noted that 'the clothes consisted of a reddish-brown ulster, with seven large brass buttons. It was apparently an old garment, but a brown linsey dress looked new. There was a grey woollen petticoat and a flannel one belonging to the workhouse. Some pieces bearing the words "Lambeth Workhouse, P.R."[35] had been cut out by Inspector Helson with the object of identifying the deceased.'[36] The labels provided the first clue in the identification of the victim for J Division's CID, and the matron of Lambeth Workhouse was roused to appear at the mortuary in Whitechapel in hopes of putting a name to the face; however, this was to no avail, as she did not recognise her.

The police code addressed the issue of unidentified bodies, stating that 'if the body is not identified, it should be photographed prior to burial or post mortem examination, and dress nearly as possible as it was in life'.[37] Since the clothing had been discarded, the deceased's face was photographed with a sheet covering from the neck down, most likely just prior to the post-mortem which was conducted by Dr Llewellyn and his assistant, Mr Seccombe,[38] at noon on the Saturday. Though photography was quickly developing as a new and valuable resource for both the Metropolitan and City of London forces, in 1888 neither had an official photographic unit, instead using reliable private photographers. It wasn't until 1901 that such a specialist team was created, when the Metropolitan force set up photographic support to another new team in operation at crime scenes, the Fingerprint Bureau. The City of London Police lacked an official photographer until 1939, when they appointed a constable – and keen amateur photographer – named Arthur Cross to the role, giving him a room in the basement of Bishopsgate police station.[39] These private photographers were trusted individuals, as the information they obtained on glass plates, and what they themselves saw and heard at a crime scene, was strictly confidential. It seems the Metropolitan force preferred the services of one particular photographer to take the mortuary shots throughout the Whitechapel murders of 1888, from Martha Tabram onwards, namely Joseph Martin[40] of 11 Cannon Street Road, just off Commercial Road.[41]

Inspector Helson, in writing his obligatory further report seven days later, gave CID at Scotland Yard an update on the case. Re-emphasising the Lambeth connection and confirming identification, he wrote, 'I beg to report that the marks on the clothing led to the identification of the deceased as a woman who had been an inmate of Lambeth Workhouse on several occasions.'[42] Mary Ann Monk, a former inmate of Lambeth Workhouse, was taken to the mortuary by the police during the early evening of 31 August, to see if she could recognise the deceased woman. She could, and named her as a woman she last saw a few months previously: Mary Ann Nichols. According to Monk, she was also known as 'Polly' Nichols.[43] Monk explained that she and Nichols were at Lambeth Workhouse together during April and May 1888, and that Nichols left there on 12 May to take up a position in Rose Hill Road, Wandsworth, as a domestic for police clerk of works Samuel Cowdry and his wife, Sarah.[44] However, Nichols' new life did not pan out as maybe intended, as she absconded from the position some months later, stealing £3 10s, as well as some clothing.

Within hours of the murder, rumours were flying around Whitechapel that the dead woman was a resident of Willmott's lodging house at 18 Thrawl Street,[45] and one fellow lodger, Ellen Holland,[46] thought the body could have been a friend she knew as 'Polly'. Holland was taken to the mortuary and confirmed it was her; she then expanded a little on Polly herself, and her movements the night previous, just hours before she was found dead. Holland informed the police that, apart from Willmott's, she thought that Nichols also lodged at Cooney's lodging house at 55 Flower and Dean Street,[47] opening up another line of enquiry for H Division CID to conduct on behalf of J Division's detectives, and that she last saw Nichols hours before her death, at 2.30 a.m., just on the corner of Osborn Street and Whitechapel Road.[48] Holland testified that she spoke with a drunken Nichols at this spot; Nichols informed Holland that she had earned her doss money twice over that night, but had just drunk it all away at the Frying Pan public house, not far from where they were standing. She was off to earn some more. Holland tried to coax Nichols back to Willmott's lodging house, but Nichols flatly refused, leaving Holland behind as the last person we know to have seen her alive. The lodging houses became the investigation's focus of attention, and further enquiries made at Willmott's added a little more to Nichols's last known movements, as the lodging house deputy keeper there confirmed that they had thrown Nichols out of the lodging house kitchen just hours before her death. Following her visit to the Frying Pan public house, she did not have the four pence required for a bed. Nichols didn't seem to protest much, stating that she would soon earn enough money for her bed, pointing out her new 'jolly bonnet' as evidence in the process. This was to be found lying alongside her body by Constable Neil a few hours later.

Soon Nichols's name was in all the newspapers, and as a result, on 1 September, her father, Edward Walker, along with his grandson and Nichols's estranged husband, William, came forward and were promptly taken to the mortuary to make a formal identification. William had married nineteen-year-old Mary Ann at St Bride's church, just off Fleet Street, in 1864, and the couple had five surviving children, Edward John (1866), Percy George (1868), Alice Esther (1870), Eliza Sarah (1877) and Henry Alfred (1879).[49] The relationship ended bitterly, as, according to Mary Ann's father, William Nichols had a relationship with the nurse who looked after Mary Ann during her confinement with the fourth child, Eliza. This allegation was unverified, though it must be noted that William Nichols did not admit or deny the accusation of an affair by his father-in-law; he himself cited Mary Ann's issues with drink as the cause of the marriage breakdown. Whatever the reason, the split resulted in the eldest son, Edward, later choosing to stay with his grandfather in 1881,[50] with the other children taking residence with Mary Ann, releasing William Nichols to take on a new life with a new family, while paying maintenance to Mary Ann for their children. The main catalyst for Mary Ann's demise came in 1882, when she appealed to the courts against William's decision to stop paying her that maintenance, after he cited that she was living off immoral earnings. He successfully proved this to be the case, and the appeal was dropped. Then came six years of a declining spiral for Mary Ann, where she fell into a world of common lodging houses, workhouses, drink and prostitution. Her father argued with her over her drinking, and so ensued a period where they were in and out of contact. On 17 May 1888, during a period when they were in touch, Mary Ann had employment with the Cowdrys, and before she stole some of their clothing and money and ran away she wrote a letter to her father:

> I just write to say you will be glad to know that I am settled in my new place, and going all right up to now. My people went out yesterday, and have not returned, so I am left in charge. It is a grand place inside, with trees and gardens back and front. All has been newly done up. They are teetotalers and religious so I ought to get on. They are very nice people, and I have not too much to do. I hope you are all right and the boy has work.
> So good bye for the present.
> From yours truly,
> Polly
> Answer soon, please, and let me know how you are.[51]

As requested, the father did reply to his daughter's letter, but he never received a response. Walker, accompanied by his grandson, twenty-one-year-old Edward, arrived at the mortuary entrance on Saturday 1 September 1888, and was soon joined by his son-in-law, William Nichols, smartly dressed and carrying an umbrella.[52] The pair exchanged pleasantries, with Walker introducing Edward to his father for the first time in many years, causing Nichols to exclaim, 'Well, I really did not know him; he has grown so and altered.'[53] Father and son entered the mortuary, followed by Mary Ann's father, and together they confirmed the body was their estranged wife, mother, and daughter respectively.

The inquest into the death of Mary Ann Nichols, held at the Working Lads' Institute on Whitechapel Road, commenced the very day her body was identified by her family. Local Inspector Helson was present on behalf of the police, along with other J Division CID representatives Sergeants Enright and Godley. Central Office CID at Scotland Yard also sent Inspector Abberline to observe. The inquest continued on the Monday, and on to Tuesday, before being adjourned by Coroner Wynne Baxter for a fortnight, with an intended resumption date of 17 September 1888. During the midst of that first week after Nichols's murder, a Mr Tibbatts of Artillery Lane in Spitalfields wrote in to the *Daily News* venting his frustration at the police. It is worth placing his letter here in full, as it gives an insight, fairly or not, into local ill feeling toward the police at that precise moment in time. Mr Tibbatts wrote,

I contend, as an East End man, having business premises within a stone's throw of Whitechapel Church, that our police protection is shamefully adequate, and that the scenes that hourly and daily are enacted in this locality are a disgrace to our vaunted progress. I myself have witnessed street fights amounting almost to murder in the neighbourhood of Osborn Street, Fashion Street, &c., and never at any of these critical periods are the police to be found. Only within the last few days has a most disgraceful scene been enacted close to my own gates in Spitalfields, but then as ever the police were conspicuous by their absence, and such things are of common occurrence. It is quite time someone spoke out plainly. I have waited long enough, hoping that some of our representatives in the parish might take the matter up, but the time has arrived when I for one will no longer remain quiet. I only hope that this may be the means, with your valuable assistance, of calling attention to an altogether extraordinary condition of affairs.[54]

Meanwhile, those in the higher echelons of the Metropolitan force were, at this time, experiencing some struggles among themselves. Howard Vincent's successor as head of CID, James Monro, had been in conflict with Commissioner Warren, and this may be down to the fact that Monro had been favourite to take the commissionership when Henderson resigned, only to see Warren step into the role. Also, as head of CID, Monro was answerable directly to the Home Secretary, not Commissioner Warren; this meant that the detective side of the Metropolitan force was run almost entirely by Monro. There was little Warren could do about this situation and, to a man who felt that his remit was to remodel the entire Metropolitan Police force after Henderson's laid-back tenure, it was a great frustration that he could not have a direct impact upon CID. Therefore the pair clashed, and matters came to a head when Warren refused to accept Monro's choice of Melville Macnaghten as CID's new assistant chief constable.[55] Both men, probably calling each other's bluff, threatened to resign; however, it was Monro who blinked first, and placed his letter upon Home Secretary Matthews's table. Compromising best he could, as he then had a good relationship with Monro, Matthews accepted Monro's resignation, which came into effect the very day Nichols was found murdered in Buck's Row; however, he appointed Monro to the unauthorised role of 'Head of Detective Service' in Special Branch, which fell out of Warren's responsibility completely. Monro's successor in his CID position was his good friend Dr Robert Anderson, who had been Henderson's advisor when he was commissioner; Anderson, however, had taken sick leave on doctor's orders and was touring Europe, unable to take the post until his return.

Nichols's funeral took place at Ilford on 6 September 1888, with the *Evening Standard* reporting,

The mourners were Mr. Edward Walker, father of the deceased, and his grandson, together with two of the deceased's children. The procession proceeded along Baker's row and past the corner of Buck's row into the main road, where police were stationed every few yards. The houses in the neighbourhood had the blinds drawn, and much sympathy was expressed for the relatives.[56]

Baker's Row, at the junction of Old Montague Street and Hanbury Street, was the location where Constable Mizen had spoken with Charles Cross about a 'dead or drunk' woman in Buck's Row barely a week before. It was at the other end of Hanbury Street that, a day over a week after this *Evening Standard* report, another woman was found murdered in the yard of No. 29, a house occupied by seventeen people at that time. If the Buck's Row murder was the wake-up call, this Hanbury Street outrage was a call to action.

10

Annie Chapman
8 September 1888

*I am convinced that the Whitechapel Murder case is one which can be
successfully grappled with if systematically taken in hand.*
Sir Charles Warren, Metropolitan Police Commissioner,
15 September 1888

In the initial special report compiled by Divisional Inspector Joseph
Chandler, the body found in the yard of 29 Hanbury Street was named as
Annie Siffey.[1] It was around 6.02 a.m. on Saturday 8 September, daylight,
and Chandler was already on the corner of Hanbury Street when he
noticed a few men running in the direction of nearby Commercial Street
police station, which was located around the corner just yards away.
Chandler called them over. When he asked what the excitement was about,
one of the men replied, 'Another woman has been murdered.'[2] Chandler
immediately followed the men back along Hanbury Street to a run-down
three-storey house which lay on the northern side of the street, and in he
went through the passage which led to the back yard. The passage was
full of people; however, as he came out into the daylight of the yard, the
inspector noted that he was alone, save for the body of a woman lying on
her back at the base of the yard steps, to his left. Chandler knew she was
dead, and began taking notes for his report:

> Left arm resting on left breast, legs drawn up, abducted small intestine and
> flap of abdomen lying on right side, above right shoulder attached by a cord
> with the rest of the intestines inside body; two flaps of skin from lower part
> of the abdomen lying in large quantity of blood above left shoulder; throat
> cut deeply from left and back in a jagged manner right around throat.[3]

As with Constable Neil in Buck's Row, Chandler stuck to procedure.
He sent for H Division's surgeon, Dr George Bagster Phillips,[4] and an
ambulance from Commercial Street police station. Police reinforcements
had converged on No. 29 within minutes, and Chandler immediately put
them to work by instructing them to clear out the passageway to ensure

that Divisional Surgeon Phillips had access and space to work in, and posting a guard of constables at the front of the premises. While waiting for the doctor, he placed some canvas, handed to him by a member of the public who was originally standing in the passageway, over the body, and then took further notes in order to assist the CID investigation. Chandler saw that her head was turned to her right, that it was around two feet away from the wall of the house, and only six to nine inches away from the steps. He also noted six spots of blood upon the back wall of the house, about eighteen inches from the ground, above her head, ranging in size from a sixpenny piece to a point. The body ran parallel to what appeared to be a temporarily erected wooden fence dividing No. 29 from its neighbour, No. 27, and upon one of its wooden palings, again near to her head, were further blood marks about fourteen inches from the ground. The fence, despite its flimsy appearance, stood firm, and there were no signs it had been damaged by a clambering killer seeking to make his escape.[5] Chandler also noted that the yard was partially paved, a mixture of uneven stones and earth, and he saw no evidence that a struggle had taken place there.

Chandler then turned his attention to the occupants of the house, and initially the discoverer of the body, an elderly man by the name of John Davis. Davis stated he awoke at 6.45 a.m., a time he was certain of due to the chiming of nearby Spitalfields church. He partially dressed, deciding to carry his belt rather than wear it, and made his way down to the yard, undoubtedly to use the outside toilet situated there. As he stepped down the stairs, he noted the front door was open. This was not unusual as it was often left open all night, so Davis paid little heed as he arrived at the bottom of the stairs and turned left toward the back door. This was closed, which was also common as the door closed itself, so Davis pushed it open and passed through. It wasn't until he got to the bottom of the yard steps he noticed something to his left. It was a woman lying on her back, clothes all disarranged and with terrible injuries. Davis turned heel and headed back through the passage, out through the front door and into Hanbury Street, spotting two young men standing outside the open gates of Mr Bailey's packing case makers, at No. 23a. These men, James Kent and James Green, along with a passer-by, Henry Holland, followed Davis to the yard. Kent peered at the body from the top of the steps, seeing the same sight that Davis had seen some moments before: her face was smeared with blood, and he noted that her apron was thrown over her shoulder. The men left No. 29, and Davis headed straight to nearby Commercial Street police station; Holland accosted a constable on fixed-point duty near Spitalfields church and was most disgusted to be told that the constable could not leave his post and that he should direct himself to nearby Commercial Street police station; a shocked Kent disappeared to get himself some brandy, only to return later with a piece of canvas he was to hand to Chandler in order to cover the body. Green, who had gone with Kent, noted that there was a crowd of people hanging around outside No. 29 when Inspector Chandler arrived minutes later.

Along with Davis and his wife, some of the other occupants of the house were also interviewed. Sixty-six-year-old Amelia Richardson, who rented the entire ground floor, basement and yard, from which she ran her own packing case business, stated that she was informed of the murder by her fourteen-year-old grandson, Thomas, who was also living with her at No. 29; he had noticed the early-morning hustle and bustle in the passageway. Harriet Hardiman, sometimes known as Annie, sublet the ground-floor front and back rooms from Richardson, and from these she ran a cat meat shop. She shared a room with her son, sixteen-year-old William, and was awoken by the noise of Davis, Kent, Green and Holland as they came in to view the body.[6] Amelia Richardson later revealed the full list of occupants inside the house: along with those already mentioned, the elderly Mr Walker occupied the first-floor back room along with his son, whom Richardson described as inoffensive and 'weak minded'.[7] Sarah Wilcox, referred to as Cox in most reports, an old lady kept by Richardson as an act of charity, lived on the same third floor as Mr and Mrs Davis. Below the Davises slept Mr Robert Thompson, his wife and their adopted daughter, and joining them on the second floor was a cigar-making couple named Copsey.[8] All these people were in residence during the early hours of the 8th, apart from Robert Thompson, as he had left for his work in Brick Lane at 4 a.m., receiving a 'Good morning' as he did so from Mrs Richardson, who had been disturbed by his movements before returning to her slumber.[9]

Bagster Phillips arrived at the scene in Hanbury Street at around 6.30 a.m., and immediately proceeded to examine the victim. He noted,

> The head was about 6in in front of the level of the bottom step, and the feet were towards a shed at the end of the yard. The left arm was across the left breast, and the legs were drawn up, the feet resting on the ground, and the knees turned outwards. The face was swollen and turned on the right side, and the tongue protruded between the front teeth, but not beyond the lips; it was much swollen. The small intestines and other portions were lying on the right side of the body on the ground above the right shoulder, but attached. There was a large quantity of blood, with a part of the stomach above the left shoulder. I searched the yard and found a small piece of coarse muslin, a small-tooth comb, and a pocket-comb, in a paper case, near the railing. They had apparently been arranged there. I also discovered various other articles, which I handed to the police. The body was cold, except that there was a certain remaining heat, under the intestines, in the body. Stiffness of the limbs was not marked, but it was commencing. The throat was dissevered deeply. I noticed that the incision of the skin was jagged, and reached right round the neck. On the back wall of the house, between the steps and the palings, on the left side, about 18in from the ground, there were about six patches of blood, varying in size from a sixpenny piece to a small point, and on the wooden fence there were smears of blood, corresponding to where the head of the deceased laid, and immediately above the part where the blood had mainly flowed from the neck, which was well clotted.[10]

Prior to his search of the yard with Inspector Chandler, Dr Bagster Phillips ordered the body to be taken, under the guardianship of Police Sergeant 31H Edward Badham, to the same Whitechapel mortuary in which Nichols had laid only some hours previously. A full post-mortem was to be conducted here by Bagster Phillips later in the day, and he presented his finds at inquest on 13 September. During the inquest, Bagster Phillips saw an opportunity to draw attention to the dilapidated and poor state of the Whitechapel mortuary, which at best could only be described as a shed, stating that 'there were no adequate conveniences for a post-mortem examination; and at particular seasons of the year it was dangerous to the operator'.[11] *The Times'* transcription of the divisional surgeon's testimony relating to the post-mortem reads as follows:

The body had evidently been attended to since the removal to the mortuary, probably to be washed. He noticed the same protrusion of the tongue. There was a bruise over the right temple. On the upper eyelid there was a bruise, and there were two distinct bruises, each of the size of the top of a man's thumb, on the forepart of the top of the chest. The stiffness of the limbs was now well marked. There was a bruise over the middle part of the bone of the right hand. There was an old scar on the left of the frontal bone. The stiffness was more noticeable on the left side, especially in the fingers, which were partly closed. There was an abrasion over the ring finger, with distinct markings of a ring or rings. The throat had been severed as before described. The incisions into the skin indicated that they had been made from the left side of the neck. There were two distinct, clean cuts on the left side of the spine. They were parallel from each other and separated by about half an inch. The muscular structures appeared as though an attempt had been made to separate the bones of the neck. There were various other mutilations of the body, but he was of opinion that they occurred subsequent to the death of the woman, and to the large escape of blood from the division of the neck. At this point Dr. Phillips said that, as from these injuries he was satisfied as to the cause of death, he thought that he had better not go into further details of the mutilations, which could only be painful to the feelings of the jury and the public. The Coroner decided to allow that course to be adopted. Witness, continuing, said, – The cause of death was visible from the injuries he had described. From these appearances he was of opinion that the breathing was interfered with previous to death, and that death arose from syncope, or failure of the heart's action in consequence of loss of blood caused by the severance of the throat.

By the CORONER. – He should say that the instrument used at the throat and the abdomen was the same. It must have been a very sharp knife, with a thin, narrow blade, and must have been at least 6in. to 8in. in length, probably longer. He should say that the injuries could not have been inflicted by a bayonet or sword bayonet. They could have been done by such an instrument as a medical man used for post-mortem purposes, but the ordinary surgical cases might not contain such an instrument. Those used by slaughtermen, well ground down, might have caused them. He thought the knives used by those in the leather trade would not be long enough in the blade. There were indications of anatomical knowledge, which were only less indicated in consequence of haste. The whole of the body was not present, the absent portions being from the abdomen. The mode in which these portions were extracted showed some anatomical knowledge. He did not think these portions were lost in the transit of the body. He should say that the deceased had been dead at least two hours, and probably more, when he first saw her; but it was right to mention that it was a fairly cool morning, and that the body would be more apt to cool rapidly from its having lost a great quantity of blood. There was no evidence about the body of the woman of a struggle having taken place. He was positive that the deceased entered the yard alive. He made a practical search of the passage and the approach to the house and he saw no trace of blood. There was no blood on the apron, which had the appearance of not having been recently unfolded. He was shown some staining on the wall of No. 25. To the eye of a novice it looked like blood, but it was not so. The deceased was far advanced in disease of the lungs and membranes of the brain, but they had nothing to do with the cause of death. The stomach contained a little food, but there was not any sign of fluid. There was no appearance of the deceased having taken alcohol, but there were signs of great deprivation, and he should say she had been badly fed. He was convinced she had not taken any strong alcohol for some hours before her death. The injuries were certainly not self-inflicted. The bruises on the face were evidently recent, especially about the chin and the sides of the jaw, but the bruises in front of the chest and temple were of longer standing – probably of days. He was of opinion that the person who cut the deceased's throat took hold of her by the chin, and then commenced the incision from left to right. He thought it was highly probably that a person could call out, but with regard to an idea that she might have been gagged he could only point to the swollen face and protruding tongue, both of which were signs of suffocation. The handkerchief produced, together with the pocket, he separated from the rest of some articles said to be taken from the body of deceased at the Whitechapel mortuary, and not then in the custody of the mortuary keeper. A handkerchief was round the throat of the deceased when he saw her early in the morning. He should say it was not tied on after the throat was cut.[12]

The 'abrasion over the ring finger, with distinct markings of a ring or rings' was an interesting observation. An associate of the victim, Ted Stanley, stated that when he last saw her on 2 September, she was wearing two brass rings – one flat, one oval – on the same finger,[13] and as these were now missing the question was whether the victim had removed them, possibly for pawning, or whether they had been taken by the killer. Enquiries were made of all the pawnbrokers in the locale, and one assumes that these rings were added to the pawnbroker lists which were issued daily to all divisions for circulation. Lodging houses were searched by the police, and questions asked of their keepers and residents – had any bloodstained persons been noticed? Both these initial enquires at the pawnbrokers' and lodging houses drew a blank.

As noted, all special reports immediately winged their way to Central Office CID at Scotland Yard, and this gave Superintendent West, acting in the role as Arnold was still on leave, the opportunity to add a suggestion to the powers that be at the end of Inspector Chandler's report dated 8 September. As local inspector, and head of H Division's CID, Edmund Reid was also on leave; Divisional Inspector Chandler was placed into plain clothes[14] and took a lead in this new case along with detective sergeants Thick and Leach. West's suggestion was that Inspector Frederick Abberline, who was already providing Central Office CID assistance in the Nichols case, should be deputed to this enquiry also, to aid Chandler and, upon his return, Reid. Adolphus Williamson, head of CID, agreed and officially appointed Abberline to the case the very same day. Abberline therefore became the lynchpin between the murder of Nichols in J Division and the other murders which had occurred in H Division jurisdiction, including this new one in Hanbury Street.

Again, as per the established procedure, a description and photo was taken of the body at the mortuary, and issued to all stations for circulation. Meanwhile, enquires made at 29 Hanbury Street brought forth John Richardson, the son of resident Amelia Richardson. Mr Richardson lived in John Street, Spitalfields, and sometimes helped his mother out with her packing case business when he was not working as a porter at Spitalfields Market. He was in the habit of popping around to No. 29 as only a few months previously the cellar there, where he stored his tools, had been broken into, with two saws and two hammers being stolen; since then he ensured that the cellar was securely locked on his way to the market. It was 4.40 a.m. as he approached the house and, noting the front door was closed, unlatched it to walk through into the passage and toward the yard. Instead of entering the yard, he pushed the door open and stood upon the yard steps. Looking to his right, he could see the cellar doors were securely locked. However, rather than leave, Richardson decided to sit on the steps and cut some leather off his boots, as they had been causing him some discomfort. He was adamant at inquest that the body wasn't there at that time, and was certain that he would have seen it if it was.[15]

Another witness located near the scene was a lodger who lived at neighbouring No. 27, against whose fence the body was found. Albert Cadosch[16] was a twenty-eight-year-old husband and father from Finnis Street, Bethnal Green, but was staying at No. 27 to look after his ailing father.[17] Cadosch himself had also been ill, stating at inquest that he had just had an operation, with speculation that it was a urological affliction.[18] This may be the reason why he was on his way to use the outside toilet at around 5.15 a.m. when he heard a noise emanating from next door's yard. It was a voice exclaiming, 'No, no!' Some minutes later, as he returned to the house, he heard what he perceived to be a scuffle, then something fall against the fence on the other side.[19]

Another witness, Elizabeth Long,[20] brought confusion to Cadosch's testimony, as she stated she saw a man and a woman similar to the deceased standing near to the shutters of No. 29 at 5.30 a.m. as she walked from her home in Church Row, via Brick Lane, toward Spitalfields Market on Commercial Street.[21] This sighting occurred fifteen minutes after Cadosch's hearing of voices and 'scuffle'; however, at the inquest, Long was adamant about the time, as she had heard the chimes of the brewery clock located not far off. The man's back was toward her, the woman facing Long, and as she passed Long heard the man say to the woman, 'Will you?', to which the woman replied, 'Yes.' This sighting must have been brief, as Long continued her journey without taking a second glance at the couple; however, Long was sure that the woman she had seen in the mortuary was the one she witnessed that morning, and described the man, whose face she did not see, as a 'foreigner' (a euphemism at the time for a person with a Jewish appearance), over forty and only a little taller than the woman, and also as a 'shabby genteel'.[22] This description of Long's, the fact that she stated the man's ethnicity despite not seeing his face, and its discrepancies in timing with Cadosch's statement, are examples of just how difficult, and unreliable, witness testimony can be for detectives to analyse. This is an issue which crops up with many witnesses connected to the Whitechapel murders, including police constables.

H Division's Sergeant Lee, along with constables Barrett, Cooke, Hussey, Schmelzer, Sziemanowciz and White, all joined Inspector Chandler in plain clothes in order to help with conducting local enquires,[23] and it was these local enquiries which eventually brought forward witnesses from a frequent source of information for the police, the common lodging house. Timothy Donovan identified the deceased lying at the Whitechapel mortuary as one of his recent regulars, Annie Siffey, the name Inspector Chandler used for the victim in his initial special report. Donovan stated that he last saw her the evening before she was found dead, at around 7 p.m., when he let her stay in the kitchen of Crossingham's until 2 a.m.; then, according to Donovan, she told him that she had no money, saying, 'Don't let the bed; I will be back soon,'[24] before leaving. Another worker at Crossingham's, night watchman John Evans, watched her leave, noting that she entered the narrow passageway which ran alongside the lodging house called Little Paternoster Row, which led to Brushfield Street and Spitalfields Market. Evans also stated that the victim had been involved in a petty fight over a bar of soap some days previously, with a woman who was identified as Eliza Cooper, which would explain the old bruising seen on the victim's chest and temple by Dr Bagster Phillips during the post-mortem. However, it wasn't until a cleaner who worked predominantly for well-to-do Jewish families, Amelia Palmer, came forward that the victim's real name was revealed as Annie Chapman.[25]

Palmer had been a resident in Dorset Street for four years, and knew forty-seven-year-old Chapman well enough to give the police a brief outline of her past. Palmer knew Chapman had an estranged husband, stating the pair had lived apart for some years; however, she erroneously claimed that he was a veterinary surgeon named Frederick Chapman, when the reality was that he was a domestic head coachman named John who had died on Christmas Day 1886. Palmer also explained where the name 'Siffey' had come from, stating that once Annie had separated from John due to her drinking habit, she settled in Dorset Street with a man who made iron sieves, who went by the name of John Sivvey, often misheard as 'Siffey'.[26] She last saw Annie in Dorset Street at 5 a.m., just a few hours before Donovan saw her in Crossingham's. Palmer stated that during that meeting Chapman complained of feeling ill; however, later Chapman said to her, 'It's no use my giving way. I must pull myself together and go out and get some money, or I shall have no lodgings.'[27] Palmer was to give the CID two potential suspect leads: a man who went by the name of Harry the Hawker, and a man already mentioned named Ted Stanley.

Palmer alleged that Stanley was involved, albeit not directly, in Chapman's dispute with Eliza Cooper, and it was clear to the police that Cooper may have information of interest, so they sought her out. Cooper, thirty-nine years old, was a hawker, a street vendor who sold all manner of goods, and confirmed Evans and Palmer's account of a fight between Chapman and herself, explaining that Chapman had approached her to borrow some soap for Stanley. When Cooper asked for its return, Chapman, according to Cooper, flippantly stated that she would see her 'by and by'. The following day, Cooper saw Chapman in the kitchen of Crossingham's and again asked for the soap back. According to Cooper, Chapman threw down a halfpenny upon the kitchen table and told her to 'go and get a halfpennyworth of soap', which enraged Cooper. The pair quarrelled before parting, only to take up the quarrel again in the Britannia public house,[28] when Chapman lost her temper and struck Cooper across the face. Cooper responded by hitting Chapman in the left temple and on her chest, at which the older woman backed down.[29]

The 'items' mentioned by Bagster Phillips in his initial survey of the yard at 29 Hanbury Street refers to a portion of an envelope containing two pills. This find interested Inspector Chandler, who noted that a seal belonging to the Sussex Regiment was on the envelope's rear; on the front was a handwritten letter 'M', the Post Office stamp of 'London, 28 Aug.', and two letters, 'Sp', possibly the first two letters of 'Spitalfields'. This envelope may have been something of significance and required further investigation, and Abberline, sensing that a potential suspect may lie in connection to this clue, despatched Inspector Chandler to the Royal Sussex's regimental north camp, situated in Farnborough, on 14 September, without the commissioner's authority. Upon arrival at Farnborough, Chandler spoke to an adjutant by the name of Captain Young, who explained to Chandler that the envelope piece did indeed bear the regimental stamp, and the fact that it was posted at the local post office rather than in camp indicated that the person who posted it was either a soldier on leave or not a soldier at all. Further enquires made at camp with regards who could have posted a letter to Spitalfields drew a blank. Inspector Chandler left the camp and headed to Lynchford Road, where he proceeded to speak with the two postmasters of Farnborough post office, Messrs Summer and Thirkettle, who confirmed the envelope and letter would have been posted from there, but they could not say who posted it. They also confirmed that they had a large amount of these regimental letters and envelopes batched up and on sale to the public, meaning anyone from the locality could have posted the envelope.

The matter was cleared up the following day when William Stevens, a fellow lodger of Chapman's at Crossingham's, went into Commercial Street station and explained that he had observed Chapman pick up a piece of paper from the lodging house kitchen floor, and wrap two pills in it. This was undoubtedly the same piece of envelope found at the murder scene containing two pills, and the envelope could have been discarded at the kitchen by any one of many transient or regular people who had used that lodging house over the past few weeks.[30] The lead was now a dead one, but the matter of Inspector Chandler's authority to act in another's jurisdiction still had to be addressed, and so Abberline retroactively submitted this request to the Commissioner's Office at Scotland Yard.[31] Also issued for consideration were Inspector Chandler's incurred expenses. Chandler would have noted every expense he made during this investigation at Farnborough in his pocketbook. Every train journey taken, every meal eaten, and so on, would have been noted down, with tickets and receipts obtained; then, upon his return, these receipts would be issued to the senior officer, in this case Abberline, along with an expense sheet, for review. Any errors or discrepancies would be addressed prior to the claim's being forwarded to Central Office, where it would be processed and the officer reimbursed. For his trip to Farnborough, Inspector Chandler was given belated authority to act, and permission to be refunded a sum of eight shillings and eight pence by acting head of CID, Alexander Carmichael Bruce.[32]

Mrs Fiddymont, who ran the Prince Albert public house in Brushfield Street, not far from where Chapman was lodging, notified the police that during the morning on which Chapman was discovered, at 7 a.m., while Inspector Chandler and his men were making enquiries at 29 Hanbury Street, a man walked into her pub and ordered the cheapest drink, half a pint of 'four ale'.[33] The man's appearance drew Mrs Fiddymont's, and customer Mary Chappell's, attention: he had spots of blood on the back of his right hand, dried blood between his fingers and a streak of blood behind his right ear. The man quickly finished his drink and left, with Chappell choosing to follow this suspicious man. Shortly after leaving the pub, Chappell pointed out the man to another witness, Joseph Taylor, who continued the follow until he lost sight of the man near to the Jewish public house Dirty Dick's, opposite Liverpool Street railway station on Bishopsgate. With the Prince Albert pub located close to the murder scene, this account seems to have interested CID enough for some credence to be placed upon this story, and the witnesses were to be later used as a gauge when identifying potential suspects.

Many suspects quickly began to roll in. On 9 September 1888, just a day after Chapman's murder, a former publican in Hoxton, William Henry Pigott, walked into the Pope's Head public house in Gravesend, Kent, with what appeared some bloodstaining upon his person, and roused further suspicion by expressing, to anyone who would listen, his hatred of women. The landlady sent for the police, and Superintendent Berry, upon arrival, noted wounds upon his hands. Berry questioned Pigott intensively, and learned that, prior to going into the Pope's Head public house, he had actually stopped at Mrs Beitchteller's fish shop, leaving a parcel there.[34] Berry obtained the parcel, and found it to contain two shirts and a pair of stockings, with one of the shirts torn and stained, apparently with blood. When questioned further, Pigott admitted to being in Whitechapel just days before. While assisting a woman who has having a fit in Brick Lane, he said, he was bitten on the hand by her, hence the wound, which resulted in him striking her.

The police immediately connected Pigott with the bloodstained man seen by Mrs Fiddymont and company in the Prince Albert, and Abberline decided to go to Gravesend personally and to escort Pigott back to London, in order for the latter to attend an identification parade. The parade was attended by Fiddymont, Chappell and Taylor, and only Chappell pointed Pigott out as the bloodstained man they saw in the Price Albert; however, she was later to retract her identification. During this period, Pigott was showing signs of mental instability, and, since the three Prince Albert witnesses had failed to comprehensively identify him as the bloodstained man, Pigott was sent to the Whitechapel Infirmary Workhouse on 10 September 1888 by H Division CID man Detective Sergeant Leach, where he was treated for delirium tremens until his release on 9 October 1888.[35]

While Abberline and H Division CID were investigating Pigott, J Division's investigation into the death of Mary Ann Nichols gave up another potential lead. A name had cropped up in Inspector Helson's follow-up report, which was written the day before Chapman was murdered: the sinister sobriquet of 'Leather Apron', whose real name, according to Helson's report, was Jack Pizer.[36] Renowned and much-respected researcher Debra Arif has found that the name of 'Leather Apron' had begun to creep into press reports during early September 1888, as early as the day after the Nichols murder, with the *Sheffield and Rotherham Independent* citing information given to a reporter by a prostitute that

> the woman in a position similar to that of the deceased alleged that there is a man who goes by the name of the 'Leather Apron' who has more than once attacked unfortunate and defenceless women. His dodge is, it is asserted, to get them in to a house on the pretence of offering them money. He then takes whatever little they have and 'half kills' them in addition.[37]

News began to spread of this 'Leather Apron', and Helson, confirming the *Sheffield and Rotherham Independent*'s report, stated that this man was in the habit of 'ill-using prostitutes in this, and other parts of the metropolis'. H Division's experienced Sergeant Thick claimed to be fully aware of this 'Leather Apron', and apparently knew that this name was connected to Pizer, and therefore Helson was happy for this old-hand detective from the adjoining division to take up this particular lead. Despite a long delay in locating Pizer (due to the fact that he had gone to ground as he was aware of the press speculation concerning him), Thick managed to trace the thirty-eight-year-old cobbler to his brother's house, where he had been shielded by his family. Having already established his innocence to the police by providing two corroborated alibis, and after attending yet another identification parade during which the Prince Albert witnesses all failed to point out him out, Pizer made his innocence inescapably public when he was allowed to appear in front of the coroner at the Chapman inquest and explain all. This had the effect of ending the press speculation, and lifted the pressure placed upon the police to apprehend this monster known as 'Leather Apron'.

Divisional Inspector John Styles of Holloway subdivision station, which sat in the Metropolitan's Y Division Highgate, issued a telegram to acting superintendent John West of H Division at Leman Street, who actually received it at 4 p.m. precisely, while he was sitting in at Chapman's inquest on 12 September 1888. West passed it on to Abberline for action, and he issued it to an already busy Detective Sergeant Thick.[38] The telegram informed H Division that attention had been drawn by two Doctors, Cowan and Crabbe, to a butcher who had been acting suspiciously in recent days. The medics informed Inspector Styles that they had, in turn, been approached by this man's landlord, Mr George Tyler of 60 Milford Road, Holloway. The suspect's name was Joseph Isenschmid,[39] and Tyler had informed the doctors that he was in the habit of leaving his lodgings and returning at odd times, and that he feared that Isenschmid was involved in the recent Whitechapel murders.

Inspector Styles decided to investigate, taking Inspector Rose and Detective Sergeant Sealy of Y Division CID with him to 60 Milford Road, and there he spoke with the landlord, Mr Tyler. Tyler again reiterated what he had stated to Cowan and Crabbe, and gave a little background on how he met Isenschmid in Hornsey Road on 5 September, and how Isenschmid asked if he had any accommodation at which he could lodge. Tyler also gave an account of the odd hours this man kept, and explained that Isenschmid had recently left his wife, who lived in Duncombe Road, Holloway. Inspector Styles then made the short trip to speak with Isenschmid's estranged wife, Mary, who claimed she had seen her husband for the first time in two months only a few days ago, on 9 September, when he turned up at Duncombe Road to collect some clothing. She also notified the inspector that Isenschmid was in the habit of carrying knives upon his person; however, this was not as sinister as it sounded, as many working men carried knives with them (especially butchers, and Isenschmid was one by trade). What was worrying was how Mary also explained that

Isenschmid was suffering from mental illness, had violent tendencies, and how she was so afraid of him that she managed to obtain an order for him to be detained at a lunatic asylum.[40] Inspector Styles was immediately concerned and suspicious of Isenschmid, so much so he ordered PC 376Y Cracknell to keep a passing observation on the house in Milford Road, instructing the constable to immediately detain Isenschmid if he should see him there, and bring him directly to the station at once; Styles also ordered the same observations to be kept on the former marital home in Duncombe Road. Inspector Styles signed off his report by stating that, at the time of writing, no description of Isenschmid was to hand, and hinted that further enquiries should be made by CID.

Isenschmid was eventually detained as a parochial lunatic at 6.50 a.m. on 12 September, hours before Inspector Styles's telegram was received by H Division, and, after a brief stay at the police station in Holloway, he was ushered off to Fairfield Road Infirmary Asylum in Bow, via Islington Workhouse.[41] As stated, the man selected for the task of making these further enquiries into Isenschmid was Detective Sergeant Thick, and he, after making enquiries at Milford Road and in the neighbourhood Isenschmid frequented, moved on to the Fairfield Road asylum, and interviewed the medical superintendent there, Dr William Mickle. Mickle explained to Thick that Isenschmid had informed the doctor that the 'girls at Holloway had called him "Leather Apron"',[42] and that Isenschmid had assumed it was they who had informed the police. Thick managed to examine Isenschmid's clothing, but could not find anything incriminating, such as blood marks, upon them; despite this, he seized these items on behalf of the police.[43]

Abberline wished to conduct yet another identification parade, or rather arrange a viewing at the asylum, using the very same witnesses from the Prince Albert public house whom they had used during the Pigott and Pizer parades.[44] Isenschmid's doctor, Mickle, informed the inspector that this could not be done immediately, as his patient was in such poor health; however, Abberline was eager, as Isenschmid's physical description was very similar to the one given by those at the Prince Albert pub. The frustration the police were experiencing at this stage with this suspect is clear, although J Division's Local Inspector Helson, who was working jointly with H Division on this matter, showed a little patience when he stated that Dr Mickle has 'at my request promised that in his conversations with the man [Isenschmid] daily, he will obtain from him as much information as possible, as to his recent movements, and let me know the result (in confidence) if I call on him from time to time'.[45]

The three men mentioned, Pigott, Pizer and Isenschmid, were mere drops in the suspect ocean, to which we could add the names of McKenna, Ludwig, Puckridge, Sanders and many more; these names flooded the CID departments of both H and J divisions in the immediate aftermath of these two murders in just over a week. Pizer was cleared of suspicion early on in September, and Pigott and Isenschmid were absolved of any murderous responsibility when other murders in the series occurred during their detention. These men, along with many others, had to be investigated, which meant resources had to be pooled. Uniformed men from across the ranks were redirected into plain clothes to assist the detectives with their enquiries, and to offset this drain on the uniformed men, reserves were drawn in to H Division from other Metropolitan divisions. It was due to this flood of information – received not just at local level, but across the Metropolitan Police area – that Commissioner Charles Warren made a significant operational decision just a week after the murder of Annie Chapman. He decided that a reliable and experienced detective was required to oversee the investigation, to act a focal point through which all information passed through, so he turned to a man who was described by one of his contemporaries as 'one of the best class of officers',[46] Chief Inspector Donald S. Swanson.

Therefore, on 15 September 1888, Warren issued an instruction to be cascaded to Carmichael Bruce, who was covering Assistant Commissioner Anderson's sick absence, stating,

> I therefore feel the utmost importance to be attached to putting the whole Central Office work in this case in the hands of one man who will have nothing else to concern himself with. Neither you or I or Mr. Williamson can do this. I therefore put it in the hands of Chief Inspr. Swanson who must be acquainted with every detail. I look upon him for the time being as the eyes & ears of the Commr.

'In this particular case,' Warren continued, 'I give him whole responsibility.'[47]

The retention of Abberline within the ranks of H Division, with his experience and knowledge of Whitechapel and the area, coupled with introduction of Swanson, one of Scotland Yard's finest detectives, to lead and coordinate the investigation, was a clear sign from Warren that the Metropolitan force intended to capture the murderer, and capture him swiftly. Along with these intentions, Warren also had utmost confidence in the method of orderly police investigation, which he made clear in his instruction on the appointment of Swanson, writing, 'I am convinced that the Whitechapel murder case is one which can be successfully grappled with if systematically taken in hand.' While Warren obviously bought into this ideology, this methodical process, his words showed a lack of understanding of policing procedure and, maybe more significantly, a lack of understanding of the people of the East End, and what it took to police and investigate in that area of London.

And watching at a distance were the City of London force, who, in the course of their observation, had stepped up the vigilance during their patrols on the Whitechapel border of City and Metropolitan jurisdictions. It was a wise move on their part, albeit to no avail as one night late in September 1888 saw two murders, both within an hour of each other, which brought panic not only to an already jittery Metropolitan force but also to the City of London force, who had yet to experience this terror from the East End.

11

Elisabeth Stride
30 September 1888

She looked as if she had been laid quietly down.
Police Constable Henry Lamb 252H, 2 October 1888

The escalation of these murders was mirrored by the press in their reporting. Initially, few column inches were dedicated to the Emma Smith attack; however, many more lines were written in connection to the Martha Tabram murder, while the murder of Mary Nichols brought an explosion of coverage. This fuelling of the East Ender's concern seemingly reached a peak during Chapman's murder, and sensational headlines such as 'Horror upon horror, Whitechapel is panic stricken at another fiendish crime'[1] and 'Another Whitechapel Murder, a woman horribly mutilated, body found in back yard',[2] reeled off by the tabloid and radical press (the newspapers of choice in a working-class area populated by many anarchistic and socialist supporters) were not exactly aiding the constables of H Division, who were trying to maintain a calmness in the area. Questions were already being asked of the police, not just by these newspapers but by the locals of Whitechapel and Spitalfields, especially the tradesmen, who feared that the murderer was now beginning to affect their livelihoods, as evening trade in the neighbourhood rapidly diminished. The consensus among the regular population in the very area where the murders were occurring was, at that particular moment in time, that Whitechapel and its environs had no choice but to protect its people, and its businesses, by itself. *The Star*, a popular paper in the area, shared those views by reporting that there was 'one large Vigilance and Patrol Committee at work in the haunted districts. But one is not enough. If there is any public spirit in the East-end, there will be twenty such bodies formed before as many hours have passed.' The paragraph concluded, rather ominously for those reading it, 'Whitechapel, then, is practically defenceless. It must defend itself.'[3]

Vigilance groups and societies were not new in Victorian society. The *Penny Illustrated News*, dated 12 November 1870, gives an example of one of many committees, this example being for the Islington area of London:

LYNCH LAW IN ISLINGTON – Finding that the powers of the police are insufficient to check the rowdyism that has long been prevalent in Upper-street, Islington, on Sunday nights, a party of about twenty inhabitants, armed with canes, sallied out on the evening of the 6th and belaboured the roughs with so good an effect that the people returning from church were, to their agreeable surprise, allowed to walk home unmolested. The roughs were utterly astonished and beaten off by the unexpected attack, while the police were delighted with the vigorous display of civil force. A similar patrol is to be made on Sunday evening next. This vigorous action has apparently at length aroused Colonel Henderson, who has issued orders to his subordinates to adopt energetic measures for the preservation of the peace.

It was only natural that the residents of Whitechapel and Spitalfields eventually did the same. In fact, a vigilance committee had already been set up in the aftermath of the Tabram murder. In an open letter to many newspapers, written on 10 September 1888, Mr Thomas Hancock Nunn, the secretary of the St Jude's District Vigilance Committee, the committee referred to in *The Star* as 'one large vigilance and patrol committee', and based just a stone's throw from the Martha Tabram crime scene, explained his organisation's mission and its intentions to work closely with the police:

Although it is hardly true to say that the inhabitants of Whitechapel are in a state of panic, yet no doubt excitement does exist, and the committee which I represent think that the present moment is advantageous for turning the feeling which has been aroused into action. They hope, therefore, that your kindness in publishing this letter may lead others to take steps to do what private citizens can do better the state of our streets. A few days after the murder of the woman in George-yard, last month, a meeting of about 70 men, residing in the buildings in the immediate neighbourhood, was held, and after a discussion a committee of twelve was appointed to act as watchers, whose duties should be to observe the state of certain streets, chiefly between the hours of 11 and 1, and not only to try to support the action of the Police, when necessity arises, but also take careful note of disorderly houses and causes of disturbance. This committee has since met once a week to receive reports, which are carefully preserved and to decide on future plans. It must not be supposed that we have in any way attempted to supplant the regularly constituted authorities, or that we are concerned merely with particular outrages or their perpetrators. But it does not need a long residence in this district to convince anyone that many of the social conditions of the neighbourhood distinctly favour the commission of such crimes as those which have lately startled London. The Police, whom we have found courteous and ready to allow us to work with them, must remain practically powerless as long as the apathy of the neighbourhood tolerates the scandalous scenes of daily and nightly occurrence. We have at present no definite suggestion, but we feel strongly that until the deeply rooted causes of these evils are known and attacked, the action of police courts, School

Boards, and philanthropic institutions can do little to stamp out the disorder and crime which disgrace our city. The space which our committee is covering is very small, and must needs to be to secure efficiency, and as there is, at least, equal need for such district committees, for the better regulation of our streets elsewhere, we wish to suggest to those who feel as we do that steps should be taken in this direction without loss of time. If some communication could be set up between these committees, when constituted, our powers would be strengthened, and our opportunities improved.

The St Jude's men split themselves into pairs, and patrolled the streets in a similar vein to the beat constables; they even had men stationed at fixed points, and all carried sticks (for protection), lamps and whistles. As Mr Nunn stated, these patrols were set up to aid the police and to provide constables with information, not to undertake their duties, so regular liaisons with a police representative were organised and undertaken; however, not all the police were in support of these vigilance committees, and one, named as a 'police official with a long experience of street work' in the *Irish Times*, gave his personal opinion on vigilantes, stating,

It won't last a month. They'll get little help – at lest no more help than anyone else – from our chaps: and if they get interfering with respectable people our men will 'run them in' as a caution for future behaviour. With regard to the roughs, well all I can say is 'they will have a high old time of it' and to the benefit of our men. They can, to use their own words, 'smell a fly copper' – i.e. plain clothes man; and when they get hold of an 'amateur' or two, God help the amateurs! Kicking a regular policeman is a pleasure at any time not lightly to be spoken of, but the chances of 'booting' the head or ribs of an amateur 'slop' will afford a new and indescribable pleasure, and one to be indulged in on every possible occasion. These 'vigilants' will be looked upon as 'coppers noses' or 'coppers narks' – i.e. police informers – and to use the roughs own words, 'a copper' is bad enough, but his nark!' – well, kill him, and that is about what he will get, or something very near it. They have forgotten one thing in their outfit, and that is an 'ambulance' – that will be wanted oftener than truncheons. At least I think so.[4]

Following on from the St Jude's request for more vigilance committees, handbills were printed and handed out on 11 September 1888 in connection to a new vigilance organisation, The Whitechapel Vigilance Committee. The notice read,

IMPORTANT NOTICE. – To the Tradesmen, Ratepayer, and Inhabitants Generally, of Whitechapel and District. – Finding that in spite of Murders being committed in our midst, and that the Murderer or Murderers are still at large, we the undersigned have formed ourselves into a Committee, and intend offering a substantial REWARD to anyone, Citizen, or otherwise, who shall give such information that will bring the Murderer or Murderers to

Justice. A committee of Gentlemen has already been formed to carry out the above object, and will meet every evening at nine o'clock, at Mr J. Aarons', the 'Crown', 74 Mile End Road, corner of Jubilee Street, and will be pleased to receive the assistance of the residents of the District.'

Secretary Joseph Aarons, the landlord of the pub mentioned in the handbill, the Crown, also explained that their intentions were to assist the police, claiming that 'he wished it to be distinctly understood that the Committee was in no way antagonistic to the police authorities, who were doing their best, as he believed they always did, to bring the culprits to justice'.[5] Aarons had joined forces with other businessmen and locals, including actor Charles Reeves,[6] who once lived in Thomas Street, the very street Constable Neil walked past before stumbling upon Mary Nichols's body. Reeves's daughter, Ada, also attended the Board School located mere feet away from where Nichols was murdered, and recalled her mother's fear during the nights her father was on patrol, looking for the killer 'while only armed with a whistle and a stick as protection'.[7] Local Mile End builder and decorator George Lusk was this committee's chairman and president, and, due to his high profile, was to become an inadvertent player in the episode known as the Double Event.

The Jew in London, a contemporary study of the Jewish population in the East End of London, contains a series of maps drawn by Charles Booth's cartographer, George Arkell, and sets out the boundary of what was known as 'the Jewish East End',[8] defining it as the land between the City of London to the west, as far as the London Hospital to the east, and from Buxton Street, Mile End New Town, in the north, to the southern Cable Street in St George in the East. Within this area sat four distinct Jewish districts, one between Houndsditch, Commercial Street and Whitechapel High Street; another between Old Montague Street, Commercial Street and Hanbury Street; one more located behind Leman Street station between Great Alie and Great Prescot Streets; and finally, in the south-east of this area, the streets between Backchurch Lane and Cannon Street Road, including a small side street which ran south off Commercial Road named Berner Street.

Berner Street belonged in the parish of St George in the East, ran from Commercial Road south as far as Ellen Street, and had junctions with Sander and Fairclough streets. It was a mainly residential street, and, as with Buck's Row, a newly built Board School sat at the junction with Fairclough Street. Situated on the same junction, though on the opposite side to the Board School, was a beer shop known as Nelson's, and next to that and moving north were two small cottages, Nos 42 and 44, from which an elderly man named Matthew Packer sold fruit from an open window. Next to these cottages was the gated, unlit opening to a narrow court and yard in which, upon the south side, next to the back yard of No. 44 Berner Street, more cottages existed; to the north side sat the International Working Men's Educational Club.[9] The court opened out at its western end into a wider yard, within which stood an old workshop and some stables; these stables once were used by a van and cart builder, Arthur Dutfield, before his move to Pinchin Street in 1886. Despite the fact that he no longer utilised them, his name was still painted upon the main gates and used as a reference, with the yard being colloquially known as Dutfield's Yard.

Henry Lamb, thirty-six years old, was a Londoner born in Paddington,[10] and he had joined the Metropolitan Police in April 1875 after a brief stint as a labourer, a job he had found himself in upon leaving the Army.[11] He had resided with his wife, an East End girl named Sarah, and their three daughters, Sarah, Alice, Florence, and two sons, Henry and baby Edwin, in Rutland Street, Mile End New Town, since 1878 or 1879.[12] At five feet seven inches in height, he was one of the smallest constables in the police force. Lamb was given the collar number 252H when he joined H Division. He was working his beat on the south side of Commercial Road around 1.00 a.m. on 30 September, and pacing along with fellow constable 426H William Ayliffe,[13] who had just finished his fixed-point duty not far away on the Commercial Road, at Grove Street junction, and was on his way back to Leman Street station when two men came rushing straight toward the constables from the direction of Berner Street. One of these men, Morris Eagle, had spent most of his evening chairing a meeting on 'why Jews should be socialists' at the International Working Men's Educational Club in Berner Street,[14] a club frequented mostly by Russian and Polish social democrats and anarchists. Eagle exclaimed to Constable Lamb, 'Come on! There has been another murder!'

'Where?' asked Lamb, and, taking the constables to the corner of Berner Street, Eagle pointed down the street to where, in the dark distance, Lamb could make out the movement of a number of people.[15] The constables immediately made their way down Berner Street toward the small crowd, which had assembled around the gateway of Dutfield's Yard; breaking his way through, Constable Lamb saw something dark just inside the gated entrance, on his right-hand side. Opening his bullseye lamp, he noted the figure of a woman lying upon her left side, with her head inches from the wall of the club. He could also see that her throat had been cut. As with any such finds, Constable Lamb instructed Constable Ayliffe to immediately fetch a doctor, and instructed Eagle to make his way to Leman Street station and to inform the duty inspector immediately of the situation. While waiting for medical and police aid to arrive, Constable Lamb took stock of the situation, noting that a sizable crowd had begun to gather in the yard. As he was inspecting the body, he ordered the crowd to get back, out of fear they would get possibly incriminating blood marks upon themselves. Against protocol, and during his inspection of the woman, Lamb blew his whistle for assistance. He also felt her face, which was slightly warm, and, recalling his first-aid training, he felt her wrist for a pulse but could not find one. He then noted her position, lying upon her left side, her right arm across her breast, clothing undisturbed. To Lamb she looked as if 'she had been laid quietly down'.[16]

Constable 452H, William Smith, was the beat constable for the Berner Street area, a beat which took around twenty-five to thirty minutes to complete. Starting at the northern end of Gower's Walk, he walked east along Commercial Road to Christian Street, south along Christian Street to Fairclough Street, east again on Fairclough Street as far as Grove Street, before doubling back on himself toward Backchurch Lane, then north on to Commercial Road, west to Gower's Walk, before starting the beat all over again. Constable Smith also covered the interior streets of Sander Street, Batty Street and the northern section of Berner Street, and it was just a little after 1.00 a.m. when he entered Berner Street from Fairclough Street and saw the commotion outside the yard entrance and club. He went straight over to the yard and saw that Constable Lamb was on the scene. Once he had viewed the body, noting the cut on her throat, Constable Smith left Berner Street and headed straight to Leman Street station to fetch the ambulance.

Constable Lamb then instructed the yard gates to be closed, and continued to take charge until the arrival of a superior officer. He ordered one of the first assisting constables to guard the gates, which had a smaller wicket door set into them, and not to let any person without authority into or out of the yard. Lamb then entered the club and, after corralling into the main clubroom what he thought were around fifteen to twenty members of the public who had remained behind after attending Eagle's talk, he turned his lamp upon them, checking their hands and clothing for any blood marks. He then examined every room on the premises, and behind the stage, for anything suspicious. More constables began to arrive to secure the scene, and Lamb moved back outside into the yard, and to the small cottages opposite, where he did an initial exterior search, including the outside water closets, before rousing the tenants, who were all in bed. Lamb, in an attempt to keep the obviously concerned occupiers of the cottages in a calm state, explained to them when they answered his knock that 'nothing much' was the matter, before continuing with his enquiries.[17] Once they were completed, he conducted a thorough search of the yard, which was enclosed by high-walled buildings, peering into dustbins and rummaging through a dungheap as he did so.

In the meantime, Constable Ayliffe had arrived at the nearest doctors' surgery, Blackwell and Kay, at 100 Commercial Road, which sat just a street away at the main road's junction with Batty Street. Dr Frederick William Blackwell's assistant, Edward Johnson, who was also resident in the house, answered the door and, after relaying the news of a possible murder in Berner Street to Dr Blackwell, who was to join him there later, Johnson dressed and returned to the yard with Constable Ayliffe. Johnson noted a handful of people, including policemen, in the darkness of the yard entrance and, to the right, a body of a woman. With the aid of a bullseye lamp provided by a constable, Johnson performed a cursory examination of the body, observing that the throat wound 'appeared to have stopped bleeding'. Undoing the top button of her dress to assess how warm she was, but knowing that life was already extinct, there was little he could do pending Dr Blackwell's arrival.[18] Soon Dr Blackwell did arrive, noting the time as 1.16 a.m. as he did so, and, like his assistant Johnson, Blackwell also noted the position of the body, and the injury, writing,

> The deceased was lying on her left side obliquely across the passage, her face looking towards the right wall. Her legs were drawn up; her feet close against the wall of the right side of the passage. Her head was resting beyond the carriage-wheel rut, the neck lying over the rut. Her feet were three yards from the gateway. Her dress was unfastened at the neck. The neck and chest were quite warm, as were also the legs, and the face was slightly warm. The hands were cold. The right hand was open and on the chest, and was smeared with blood. The left hand, lying on the ground, was partially closed, and contained a small packet of cachous wrapped in tissue paper.[19] There were no rings, nor marks of rings, on her hands. The appearance of the face was quite placid. The mouth was slightly open. The deceased had round her neck a check silk scarf, the bow of which was turned to the left and pulled very tight. In the neck there was a long incision which exactly corresponded with the lower border of the scarf. The border was slightly frayed, as if by a sharp knife. The incision in the neck commenced on the left side, 2 inches below the angle of the jaw, and almost in a direct line with it, nearly severing the vessels on that side, cutting the windpipe completely in two, and terminating on the opposite side 1 inch below the angle of the right jaw, but without severing the vessels on that side. I could not ascertain whether the bloody hand had been moved. The blood was running down the gutter into the drain in the opposite direction from the feet. There was about 1lb of clotted blood close by the body, and a stream all the way from there to the back door of the club.[20]

Blackwell, in answer to questions put by the coroner during the inquest, stated that there was only a small amount of blood splattering around the body, and this had been trodden in. No blood marks were upon the wall, but he admitted that it was very dark, and that he had conducted his examination of the scene with a bullseye lamp. Blackwell also examined the clothes, finding no blood marks on them, and noted that the victim's bonnet was lying on the ground a few inches from her head. He also noted that her dress was unbuttoned at the top; however, this was due to Johnson's actions when he conducted his examination. Blackwell also confirmed at inquest that the injuries were impossible to inflict upon oneself; that she had been dead, in his estimation, for twenty minutes to half an hour before he had arrived; that her clothes were not wet with rain; and that the victim would have bled to death comparatively slowly on account of vessels on one side only of the neck being cut, and the artery not completely severed. He also confirmed that, due to her throat injury, there was no possibility of the victim crying out, and that he felt that her attacker had pulled her back by the silk scarf around her neck at the time;

once he let go, the free hand was placed upon the victim's nose and mouth, with the knife hand making the instantaneous and deadly cut across her throat, slightly cutting the scarf as he did so.[21]

H Division's surgeon, Dr Bagster Phillips, was also awoken, and after making the trip from his residence at Spital Square to Leman Street station he then went straight to Berner Street, where he saw Chief Inspector John West (who was now back in his usual role, as Superintendent Arnold had returned from leave) and Inspector Charles Pinhorn.[22] At 1.25 a.m., while Dr Bagster Phillips was conducting his own examinations, Local Inspector Edmund Reid, another who had just returned from leave, received a telegram at the inspector's quarters at Commercial Street station; he too made his way directly to the scene in Berner Street.[23] Once there, Reid noted that Superintendent Arnold had joined West and Pinhorn at the scene, monitoring the searches, establishing the course of events regarding the discovery of the body and organising initial house enquiries at some houses within Berner Street. Once the yard had been searched, those kept in the clubroom were allowed out into the yard where their names and addresses were taken, their hands and clothing inspected again and their pockets turned out. Each person – according to Reid, there were twenty-eight of them – was individually inspected and spoken to, and once they had accounted for themselves they were instructed to leave.[24] The cottages were then visited for a second time, and a more robust search undertaken, with the locked loft of one of the cottages being forced open only for nothing of significance to be found inside.

Enquiries established the situation prior to constables Lamb and Ayliffe's arrival, and clarified that a jewellery hawker, and steward of the club, Louis Diemshitz,[25] was the discoverer of the deceased. Diemshitz was returning on his horse and cart from a day selling his goods at a market in Crystal Palace, and the time was just after 1.00 a.m. as he turned his horse and cart into Dutfield's Yard. The animal shied significantly to the left and stalled. Peering down and to his right, Diemshitz could see something upon the ground; he tried to prod it with his whip, before hopping down off the cart to take a closer look. He struck a match to gain better light, and before the wind extinguished it he saw that it was a woman. He went into the club via its side entrance, passing the body as he did so, to find assistance. Club members, who had remained to socialise after Eagle's discussion, came out with Diemshitz, who had managed to light a candle by this stage, and he took them to the spot where the body lay, just feet inside the yard entrance. Blood could be seen oozing from an area around the woman's neck and trickling along the gutter, which ran parallel to the club wall, an indication that the assault was very recent. Diemshitz, along with a number of other men, including Morris Eagle, left the yard to raise the alarm, and they ran out in all directions. Diemshitz travelled south with another man, then along Fairclough Street toward Grove Street, shouting 'Police!' as loudly as he could, before returning, bringing a passer-by, Edward Spooner, back to the scene with him.[26] Meanwhile, Eagle had travelled north along Berner

Street and into Commercial Road. He may have been aware of Constable Ayliffe being on fixed-point duty at the junction with Grove Street as he headed in that direction, and came across the constable with another, Lamb, who then took charge of the scene.

Enquires also revealed that the ground floor of the two-storey workshop at the far end of the yard was used by Hindley sack manufacturers, with the upper floor unused. Also located in the yard, in a ground-floor backroom attached to the club, was the printing office for a weekly radical paper printed in Hebrew, *Der Arbeter Fraint* (*The Worker's Friend*). Here, its editor, Philip Krantz, worked from around 9 p.m. until he was told of the murder at around 1.00 a.m.; he stated that he saw and heard nothing unusual.[27] At 4.30 a.m., the body was taken to the mortuary located in the churchyard at St George in the East, near Cannon Street Road, while Local Inspector Reid made his way over to the home of coroner Wynne Baxter, at 170 Stoke Newington Church Street, to verbally inform Baxter of the atrocity before returning to the yard for one final and futile search in daylight.[28] At around 5.30 a.m., Reid instructed Constable Collins to wash the remains of blood away from the murder spot.

Once he had conducted his search, Reid made his way over to St George in the East, and specifically to the mortuary there, to take a description of the body. He estimated the age of the victim to be around forty-two; she was five feet two inches in height, with a pale complexion and dark-brown hair. Upon lifting an eyelid, he noted that her eyes were light grey, and an inspection inside her mouth revealed that she had lost her upper front teeth.[29] The description was circulated to all stations via telegraph and later, as with the other victims, a photograph was taken. Metropolitan constable Walter Stride recognised the woman in the photograph as the wife of his now-deceased uncle, John, and once he had seen the body in the mortuary he confirmed her identify as Elisabeth Stride.[30] Stride, who was forty-four years old at the time of her death, came to London from Stora Tumlehed, a tiny coastal village just north of Gothenburg in Sweden,[31] in February 1866, after a brief spell living in Gothenburg itself. In March 1865, she had been registered as a prostitute by the Swedish police; however, she had been removed from the register by November.[32] Three years after her arrival in London, Elisabeth married and settled down with a man named John Stride, and the couple ran a coffee shop business. However, by 1879 John was extremely ill, and cracks in the marriage began to show, resulting in the couple separating around 1881. As with Nichols and Chapman before her, Stride entered into the world of the common lodging house, scraping an existence as best she could, and serving a sentence of hard labour in 1884 for being found drunk, disorderly and soliciting. In early 1888 she was living with her boyfriend of three years, Michael Kidney. Her drinking had continued and she had received multiple charges for drunk and disorderly. By September 1888 she had split with Kidney, and she was on her own by the time of her murder, seemingly having fallen back on a life of prostitution just to exist.

Later in the day, Abberline instructed Detective Sergeant Stephen White, along with Detective Constable Charles Dolden, to conduct further enquiries in the Berner Street area, knocking on doors and speaking to the residents there. At 9.00 a.m. they called at 44 Berner Street, which was located only a door away from the murder site, and which was the home of the aforementioned Matthew Packer, his wife and two lodgers, Sarah Harris and Harry Douglas.[33] White, taking out his pocketbook as he did so, asked the elderly fruiterer what time he closed his shop the previous night. According to White, Packer stated that he had shut at 12.30 a.m., though this was later amended to 11.30 p.m. in White's report,[34] and Packer went on to state he 'saw no one standing about nor did I see anyone go up the yard. I never saw anything suspicious or heard the slightest noise.'[35] One can imagine Detective White's confusion when, in the *Evening News* dated 4 October, he read the headline 'MATTHEW PACKER'S STORY: INTERVIEW WITH THE MAN WHO SPOKE TO THE MURDERER'. Inspector Moore, who had been seconded to H Division CID from Central Office in order to assist, noted the headline, and immediately instructed Detective White to establish exactly what Packer had seen.

When White arrived at 44 Berner Street, he was informed by Mrs Packer that two detectives had already called for her husband, and that they had taken him to the mortuary. White went directly to the mortuary, and saw Packer there with another man. White asked why he was at the mortuary, to which Packer replied that 'this detective asked me to go to see if I could identify the woman', further explaining that he believed her to be a woman who had bought some grapes from him at midnight.[36] A second man joined the group, and Detective White asked them for their authority to act, at which point one of the men produced a card, but refused to let White hold it. The men were actually private detectives, J. H. Batchelor and Charles Le Grand,[37] who had been hired by the Whitechapel Vigilance Committee to oversee the organisation of their patrols, and to conduct investigations. White had no power to interfere in Packer's business; he was a free man, and was therefore free to make his own decisions as long as they abided by the law, so White had no choice but to let Packer leave with them. Batchelor and Le Grand eventually took Packer to Scotland Yard to see Commissioner Warren, and to make a new statement; however, it is highly unlikely that Warren himself took it, with the task most likely being delegated to a detective at Central Office. The statement was summarised by Carmichael Bruce, who was still standing in as head of CID in Anderson's absence. Carmichael Bruce wrote,

Matthew Packer keeps a shop in Berner St. has a few grapes in window, black & white.

On Sat night about 11pm a young man from 25–30 – about 5.7 with long black coat buttoned up – soft felt hat, kind of Yankee hat rather broad shoulders – rather quick in speaking, rough voice. I sold him 1/2 pound black grapes 3d. A woman came up with him from Back Church end (the lower end of street) She was dressed in black frock & jacket, fur round bottom of jacket with black crape bonnet, she was playing with a flower like a geranium white outside and red inside. I identify the woman at the St.George's mortuary as the one I saw that night.

.They passed by as though they were going up Com Road, but instead of going up they crossed to the other side of the road to the Board School, & were there for about 1/2 an hour till I shd. say 11.30. talking to one another. I then shut up my shutters.

Before they passed over opposite to my shop, they waited near to the club for a few minutes apparently listening to the music.

I saw no more of them after I shut up my shutters. I put the man down as a young clerk.

He had a frock coat on – no gloves

He was about 1 1/2 inch or 2 or 3 inches – a little higher than she was.[38]

Packer's second statement made at Scotland Yard was dubious, especially since he had initially stated that he could not recall any person. He was now claiming that he had served a man and a woman, identifying the woman as Stride, and that he watched their movements, albeit briefly. He also mentioned to White at the mortuary that he served the couple at midnight, yet in his later statement that time had altered to 11.30 p.m., and the fact that Packer started to embellish his story in various newspaper reports over the following days did little for his integrity. Should the case have reached court, a decent defence barrister could easily have dissected his story. It was this lack of faith in Packer's new account which, ultimately, was the most likely reason why H Division CID backed away from him.

Other witnesses came forward and claimed to have seen Stride during the course of the evening of 29 September, and the early hours of the 30th. Elizabeth Tanner, the deputy at 52 Flower and Dean Street, where Stride was recently lodging, last saw her at 6.30 p.m., as did Charles Preston, a barber who also lodged at 52 Flower and Dean Street. He stated that he last saw her in the kitchen at around 6 or 7 p.m.; another witness, Catherine Lane, saw Stride in the lodging house kitchen just a little after Tanner and Preston.[39] William Marshall, a labourer who lived at 64 Berner Street, claimed that he saw a woman matching Stride's description talking to a man who was 'decently dressed'[40] opposite No. 68, between Boyd and Fairclough Streets;[41] however, one witness was particularly significant. Constable Smith had walked his beat along the same path around thirty minutes before he came upon a crowd gathering around a woman's body in Berner Street, and at approximately 12.30 a.m. he had spotted a man and a woman opposite the yard gate, across the street and a little further north. Constable Smith made note of the couple, as the natural assumption would be that they were a prostitute and her client, and considering that Whitechapel Road and Commercial Road were frequented by prostitutes[42] this assumption would have been justified; however, maybe the recent Cass/Endacott scandal was on his mind, as it is seems Smith did not make an attempt to investigate this situation and chose to move on. He did take note of the couple's description, and instantly recognised the deceased Stride as the woman he had seen just half an hour before her body was discovered. The man she was with, according to Constable Smith, was around five feet seven inches in height, twenty-eight years of age, with a small, dark moustache, a dark, hard, felted deerstalker hat and dark clothes.[43] Constable Smith also noted that the man was carrying a newspaper parcel in his hand, about eighteen inches in length, and between six to eight inches wide.

Due to the timing and location of this sighting, Constable Smith's viewing of this couple was significant to H Division CID, and the man's description was not only telegrammed to all stations but was also permitted to be released to the press by Commissioner Warren.[44] The police code clearly defines the police perspective on the release of information to the newspapers, with two paragraphs covering both instruction and rationale:

Police must not on any account give any information whatever to gentlemen connected with the press relative to matters within the police knowledge, or relative to duties to be performed or orders received, or communicate in any manner, either directly or indirectly, with editors or reporters of newspapers on any matter with the public service, without express and special authority.

The slightest deviation from this rule may completely frustrate the ends of justice, and defeat the endeavour of superior officers to advance the welfare of the public service. Individual merit will be invariably recognised in due course, but officers, who without authority give publicity to discoveries, or the progress of a case, tending to produce sensation and alarm, show themselves wholly unworthy of their posts.[45]

The police orders dated 2 February 1888, just a few months before the Whitechapel murders began, re-emphasised that information was to be released to the press only with permission, and pressed the need for the police to be guarded when relaying said information. They also added a warning, stating that 'the Superintendent of the Executive Branch[46] is to search all newspapers, cut out, and submit to the commissioner any extracts bearing upon the Metropolitan Police, or the conduct of any individuals within it'.[47]

While Constable Smith's sighting was noteworthy, so much so that it was released to the public, there was another which seemed even more significant – an assault on a woman, at the murder scene, ten minutes after Constable Smith had seen his couple, had also been witnessed. Israel Schwartz, twenty-two years old, a Hungarian by birth and almost certainly Jewish, presented himself at Leman Street station during the evening of 30 September. His original statement is missing from the files, but Chief Inspector Swanson paraphrased it in his overall summary report dated 19 October 1888:

12.45 a.m. 30th. Israel Schwartz of 22 Helen [*sic*] Street, Backchurch Lane, stated that at that hour on turning into Berner St. from Commercial Road

& had got as far as the gateway where the murder was committed, he saw a man stop & speak to a woman, who was standing in the gateway. The man tried to pull the woman into the street, but he turned her round & threw her down on the footway & and the woman screamed three times, but not very loudly. On crossing to the opposite side of the street, he saw a second man standing lighting his pipe. The man who threw the woman down called out, apparently to the man on the opposite side of the road, 'Lipski'[48] & then Schwartz walked away, but finding that he was followed by the second man, he ran as far as the railway arch, but the man did not follow so far.

Schwartz cannot say whether the two men were together or known to each other. Upon being taken to the mortuary Schwartz identified the body as that of the woman he had seen & he thus describes the first man who threw the woman down: age, about 30, ht. 5 ft 5 in. comp. Fair, hair. dark, small brown moustache, full face, broad shouldered, dress. dark jacket and trousers, black cap with peak, had nothing in his hands.

Second man: age, 35; ht., 5 ft 11in; comp., fresh; hair, light brown; dress, dark overcoat, old black hard felt hat, wide brim; had a clay pipe in his hand.[49]

It is interesting to note that Schwartz stated that the first man had nothing in his hands. Clearly, this was in response to a question put to him by H Division CID in relation to Constable Smith's sighting of the man with Stride only minutes previously. Again, as with Smith, Schwartz's description of the first man was telegraphed to all stations; unlike Smith's, however, it was not released to the press.[50] Despite this, *The Star*, in a news report published the following day, made the police's circumspection immaterial, as they printed Schwartz's tale, in thrilling detail, under the sub-headline 'Information which may be important':[51]

Information which may be important was given to the Leman Street police late yesterday afternoon by a Hungarian concerning this murder. This foreigner was well dressed, and had the appearance of being in the theatrical line. He could not speak a word of English, but came to the police-station accompanied by a friend, who acted as an interpreter. He gave his name and address, but the police have not disclosed them. A *Star* man, however, got wind of his call, and ran him to earth in Backchurch-lane. The reporter's Hungarian was quite as imperfect as the foreigner's English, but an interpreter was at hand, and the man's story was retold just as he had given it to the police. It is, in fact, to the effect that he saw the whole thing.

It seems that he had gone out for the day, and his wife had expected to move, during his absence, from their lodgings in Berner-street to others in Backchurch-lane. When he came homewards about a quarter before one he first walked down Berner-street to see if his wife had moved. As he turned the corner from Commercial-road he noticed some distance in front of him a man walking as if partially intoxicated. He walked on behind him, and presently he noticed a woman standing in the entrance to the alley way where the body was afterwards found. The half-tipsy man halted and spoke to her.

The Hungarian saw him put his hand on her shoulder and push her back into the passage, but, feeling rather timid of getting mixed up in quarrels, he crossed to the other side of the street. Before he had gone many yards, however, he heard the sound of a quarrel, and turned back to learn what was the matter, but just as he stepped from the kerb.

A second man came out of the doorway of the public-house a few doors off, and shouting out some sort of warning to the man who was with the woman, rushed forward as if to attack the intruder. The Hungarian states positively that he saw a knife in this second man's hand, but he waited to see no more. He fled incontinently, to his new lodgings.

He described the man with the woman as about 30 years of age, rather stoutly built, and wearing a brown moustache. He was dressed respectably in dark clothes and felt hat. The man who came at him with a knife he also describes, but not in detail. He says he was taller than the other, but not so stout, and that his moustaches were red. Both men seem to belong to the same grade of society. The police have arrested one man answering the description the Hungarian furnishes. This prisoner has not been charged, but is held for inquiries to be made. The truth of the man's statement is not wholly accepted.[52]

How the *Star* reporter initially obtained Schwartz's information is unclear – maybe a bribe to a constable based at Leman Street paid off. However, the fact he did not speak English is interesting. The use of interpreters by the police depended on the situation, with the taking of statements usually facilitated by a constable within the division who spoke the required language, or by a friend of the witness who was prepared to assist, with a constable writing the statement down. In the case of Schwartz, the latter occurred (according to *The Star*'s report). But even in an area with so many differing languages and dialects, finding translators within the division, and even within the police force as a whole, could sometimes be difficult.[53] As late as 1903, there were no Yiddish-speaking constables in H Division, and the then Metropolitan Police Commissioner, Edward Henry,[54] put in a special request to his paymasters at the Home Office for some of his constables to be taught Yiddish, as they could only pick up the odd word here and there, and certainly could not decipher the handbills and posters created mainly by the Jewish socialist and anarchist societies and clubs.[55]

Professional translators would be hired for a fee, especially when translation on an important case at court was required, but they could be costly. Superintendent Arnold's successor in H Division, Mulvaney, reported that his division spent a little over £48 for the fiscal year 1899/1900 – around £2,700 in today's money – on 190 cases where interpreters were required between Leman Street and Commercial Street stations.[56] On the other side, interpreters were frustrated by the police's contempt for them, as they were often called via telegram then dismissed without use, resulting in a waste not only of their time, but also of the public's money, as a call-out fee would be charged. The matter came to the Metropolitan force's attention in 1895, when a professional German interpreter used by D Division Marylebone, Mr James Steiner, was called out only to be sent home by Duty Sergeant King, who then went on to conduct the translation himself, claiming the expenses for doing so as well.[57] However, no real action regarding interpreters was undertaken until 1899, when Chief Inspector Donald S. Swanson compiled a report into the use of interpreters at police courts. The police courts had the use of their own official interpreting company, and, at the courts' suggestion, and citing the desirability of ensuring continuity in cases, Swanson recommended the same company for use by the Metropolitan force. The company in question, Flowerdew & Co.,[58] promptly had a sign made up and posted in every Metropolitan police station announcing their appointment.

As the investigation into the murder of Stride continued, Metropolitan Commissioner Warren came under heavy pressure to ensure the culprit was captured. It seemed everyone had the solution, even the Whitechapel Metropolitan Board of Works, the forerunner to local government, which wrote to Warren on 2 October 1888 with their recommendations on how to prevent further murders. To add even more insult, the covering letter to Warren was also issued for publication in *The Times*:

Office of the Board of Works, Whitechapel District, 15, Great Alie Street, Whitechapel, Oct. 2.

Sir,
At a meeting of the Board of Works for the Whitechapel District a resolution was passed, of which the following is a copy:

'That this Board regards with horror and alarm the several atrocious murders recently perpetrated within the district of Whitechapel and its vicinity and calls upon Sir Charles Warren so to regulate and strengthen the police force in the neighbourhood as to guard against any repetition of such atrocities.'

And by direction of the Board the copy resolution is forwarded to you in the hope that it will receive your favourable consideration.

I am, &c.,
ALFRED TURNER, Clerk.[59]

We are not party to what recommendations the board made to Warren, but we obtain an idea in Warren's extensive, and clear, reply, which highlighted the fact that regular policing of the metropolis had to be maintained, despite the issues which the police were facing at the time. He also emphasised the point that the murders had raised social questions which the community as a whole would need to address, including the board themselves:

Sir, – In reply to a letter of the 2nd inst. from the Clerk of the Board of Works for the Whitechapel District transmitting a resolution of the Board with regard to the recent atrocious murders perpetrated in and about Whitechapel, I have to point out that the carrying out of your proposals as to regulating and strengthening the police force in your district cannot possibly do more than guard or take precautions against any repetition of such atrocities so long as the victims actually, but unwittingly, connive at their own destruction.

Statistics show that London, in comparison to its population, is the safest city in the world to live in. The prevention of murder directly cannot be effected by any strength of the police force; but it is reduced and brought to a minimum by rendering it most difficult to escape detection. In the particular class of murder now confronting us, however, the unfortunate victims appear to take the murderer to some retired spot and to place themselves in such a position that they can be slaughtered without a sound being heard; the murder, therefore, takes place without any clue to the criminal being left.

I have to request and call upon your Board, as popular representatives, to do all in your power to dissuade the unfortunate women about Whitechapel from going into lonely places in the dark with any persons – whether acquaintances or strangers.

I have also to point out that the purlieus about Whitechapel are most imperfectly lighted, and that darkness is an important assistant to crime.

I can assure you, for the information of your Board, that every nerve has been strained to detect the criminal or criminals, and to render more difficult further atrocities.

You will agree with me that it not desirable that I should enter into particulars as to what the police are doing in the matter. It is most important for good results that our proceedings should not be published, and the very fact you may be unaware of what the Detective Department is doing is only the stronger proof that it is doing its work with secrecy and efficiency.

A large force of police has been drafted into the Whitechapel district to assist those already there to the full extent necessary to meet the requirements; but I have to observe that the Metropolitan police have not large reserves doing nothing and ready to meet emergencies, but every man has his duty assigned to him; and I can only strengthen the Whitechapel district by drawing men from duty in other parts of the metropolis.

You will be aware that the whole of the police work of the metropolis has to be done as usual while this extra work is going on, and that at such a time as this extra precautions have to be taken to prevent the commission of other classes of crime being facilitated through the attention of the police being diverted to one special place or object.

I trust your Board will assist the police by persuading the inhabitants to give them every information in their power concerning any suspicious characters in the various dwellings, for which object 10,000 handbills, a copy of which I enclose, have been distributed.

I have read the reported proceedings of your meeting, and I regret to see that the greatest misconceptions appear to have arisen in the public mind as to the recent action in the administration of the police. I beg you will dismiss from your minds, as utterly fallacious, the numerous anonymous statements as to the recent changes stated to have been made in the police force, of a character not conducive to efficiency.

It is stated that the Rev. Daniel Greatorex announced to you that one great cause of police inefficiency was a new system of police whereby constables were constantly changed from one district to another, keeping the ignorant of their beats. I have seen this statement made frequently in the newspapers lately, but it entirely without fountain. The system at present in use has existed for the last 20 years, and constables are seldom or never drafted from their districts except for promotion or from some particular cause.

Notwithstanding the many good reasons why constables should be changed on their beats, I have considered the reasons on the other side to be more cogent, and have felt that they should be thoroughly acquainted with the districts in which they serve.

And with regard to the Detective Department – a department relative to which reticence is always most desirable – I may say that a short time ago I made arrangements which still further reduced the necessity for transferring officers from districts which they knew thoroughly.

I have to call attention to the statement of one of your members that in consequence of the change in the condition of Whitechapel in recent years a thorough revision of the police arrangements is necessary, and I shall be very glad to ascertain from you what changes your Board consider advisable; and I may assure you that your proposals will receive from me every consideration.
I am, Sir, your obedient servant,
CHARLES WARREN.[60]

Commissioner Warren poured available constables into Whitechapel from other divisions, enabling others to be freed up to conduct house-to-house enquiries and to issue handbills: these were examples of the 'particular causes' that he had mentioned in his letter. However, one of the bobbies drafted into Whitechapel from A Division Whitehall prior to 30 September was already deeply involved in the Whitechapel murder case. At 2.50 a.m. on that same day, while many constables from H Division were busy searching a yard in Berner Street, Constable Alfred Long, 254A, came across a bloodstained piece of apron in the entrance of some dwellings in Wentworth Street, and feared that another victim that night was to be found nearby. Constable Long walked a beat which closely matched H Division's boundary with the City of London force, and though he had heard rumours of one murder, he knew for certain that another had been committed – not on his patch, but in the City. Less than an hour after Elisabeth Stride had been found in Dutfield's Yard, a woman's body was discovered in the darkest corner of Mitre Square by a City constable – and the apron piece Constable Long found belonged to her, meaning that the killer had moved west and out of Whitechapel, into the City of London, killing and moving back again within just forty-five minutes.

12

Catherine Eddowes
30 September 1888

All right, good night old cock.
Catherine Eddowes to City of London Constable 968 George Hutt,
30 September 1888

Louis Robinson, a former coachman with the mail-order business of Messrs Copestake, Hughes, Crompton & Co. and now City of London Constable 931, was working his beat in Aldgate High Street on the evening of 29 September 1888. He noted that a crowd had gathered around the shopfront at No. 29, just a few doors down from the Bull's Head inn.[1] Fighting his way through, he saw, in the midst of the group, lying against the shutters, a very drunk and incapable middle-aged female. He asked the crowd if anyone knew who she was, or where she lived, and upon receiving no answer he turned toward her and tried to get her to her feet, which he managed to do, only to see her slump down sideways to the floor again.[2] While pondering how he was to get this drunk back to the police station at Bishopsgate, fellow City Constable 959 George Simmons[3] arrived on the scene and gave his assistance. The two constables then proceeded to walk her, one assumes with great difficulty, back the considerable distance to Bishopsgate police station, arriving there at around 8.45 p.m., where the on-duty station sergeant, James Byfield,[4] booked the drunk in. Byfield asked her name and received a reply of 'Nothing', so he instructed that she be taken to the cells in order for her to sober up. Later, hopefully, she would be clearheaded enough to answer his questions.[5]

Changeover time for constables at Bishopsgate police station was 9.45 p.m., and so it was at this time that responsibility for the prisoners fell to Constable 968 George Henry Hutt, a gaoler at that station.[6] Hutt visited the cells every half-hour, and though she was asleep when he first conducted his rounds, he could, at 12.15 a.m., hear that she was awake and singing to herself. On his next tour, at around 12.30 a.m., she asked him when she was going to be let out, to which Hutt replied, 'When you are capable of taking care of yourself.' Her response was that she was already capable.[7] Finally, at 12.55 a.m., Hutt, under the direction of

Station Sergeant Byfield, released her from the cells; she asked Hutt the time as they made the walk back to the charge room, and Hutt responded that it was 'too late for you to get any more drink'. However, she was persistent. 'Well, what time is it?' she asked again. 'Just on one,' Hutt replied. 'I shall get a damned fine hiding when I get home,' she said. Hutt retorted, maybe with tongue in cheek, 'And serve you right – you have no right to get drunk.'[8] Hutt walked her in to the charge room, to the desk manned by his station sergeant, Byfield. Here she was asked her name, and she said that she was called Mary Ann Kelly, and gave her address as 6 Fashion Street, Spitalfields.[9] Byfield decided not to charge her, and deemed her sober enough to look after herself, so he ordered Hutt to escort her off the station premises.[10] When the pair made their way to the door which led to the entrance hall, Hutt opened it for her. 'This way, Missus,' he said, and he watched her shuffle along the long hall toward the outer door. 'Please pull it to,' requested Hutt, to which she cheerily replied, 'All right, good night old cock.'[11] Hutt noted that she turned left, towards Houndsditch; however, he wasn't to know that he would see her again, in a few hours' time, laid out at a mortuary in Golden Lane.

City of London Constable 881, Edward Watkins, a constable with seventeen years' experience, was working beat No. 8[12] on the eastern side of the City of London, near Whitechapel, during the early hours of 30 September 1888.[13] He had started this beat at 10 p.m., and it was now around 1.45 a.m.; it had been some forty-five minutes since Elisabeth Stride's body had been discovered in Berner Street, only a ten- to fifteen-minute walk away from where Constable Watkins was now located, which was a small thoroughfare off Aldgate called Mitre Street. Mitre Street was narrow, a mixture of fruit shops with dwellings above them on its south-west and north-east sides and warehouses on the south-east side. Constable Watkins had just passed the premises of sailcloth maker Andrew Lowson at number 40,[14] with Copeland & Co. Oil and Provision Merchants on the opposite side, and was now heading north-west, past the empty cottages and former coffee rooms on his right-hand side, towards Mr Tayler's picture-frame maker's shop.[15] Tayler's shop was the last before a carriageway which opened out upon the right of Mitre Street, leading to a small, gloomy open space known as Mitre Square, with its looming warehouses. Taking a swift look up and down Mitre Street, Watkins walked into the square, undoubtedly checking that Mr Tayler's shop door was secure first, and turned right. He was heading towards the rear of the empty cottages, and Heydemann & Co.'s storage yard, which was located in the darkest corner of the square; to combat this darkness, Watkins had his lamp open, giving himself some light to work with. He knew that just near the gate of Heydemann's was a coal hole which required inspection, so he turned his lamp toward the ground, only to find, with her head upon that coal hole, the severely mutilated body of a woman. 'The stomach was ripped up,' he was later to say at the inquest, adding, 'She was lying in a pool of blood.'[16]

City constables had no whistles with which to raise an alarm; however,

Watkins knew that a night watchman was working nearby, at one of the large warehouses of Kearley & Tonge Wholesale Grocers, a company whose premises dominated Mitre Square, so he ran over and pushed open the already ajar warehouse door. Ex-Metropolitan police constable George Morris[17] was the night watchman for Kearley & Tonge; he was sweeping the stairs, having just opened the main door a little, when Constable Watkins arrived in a state of some agitation. After explaining the sight he had just seen, Watkins waited for Morris to fetch his lamp before the pair made the short distance back to the body. Upon seeing the terrible sight before them, Morris, taking his whistle from his pocket, left Mitre Square via Mitre Street, and headed towards Aldgate, blowing the whistle repeatedly, where he met City Constable 964 James Harvey.[18] Harvey had, just minutes previously, walked down Church Passage (which connected Mitre Square with Duke Street), and had gone as far as the square before turning on his heels and doubling back, as his beat required. He saw nothing then to raise his suspicions, so he must have been very surprised to hear Morris explain that a woman's body had been found 'ripped up in Mitre Square',[19] literally yards from where the constable had stood not so long ago. Harvey noticed, on the opposite side of the road, fellow City Constable 814 Frederick Holland.[20] 'Come with me!' yelled Harvey to Holland, and the pair, along with Morris, ran to the scene.

Meanwhile, Constable Watkins was taking in the sight before him, noting the bloodied finger marks upon the victim's chemise, and the filthy state of her clothing, which was cut open and pushed up, above her waist. She was lying on her back. Her exposed stomach had been opened, with her bowels protruding and, like the other victims, her throat cut; Watkins noted that, unlike the previous victims, her face had been horrifically mutilated. Once Morris arrived with constables Harvey and Holland, Watkins instructed Holland to send for the nearest doctor, Dr George Sequeira[21] of 34 Jewry Street. As Holland was rousing Dr Sequeira, news of the murder in Mitre Square was reaching the City Police's nearest subdivisional station to the scene, Bishopsgate police station. Inspector Edward Collard[22] was on duty as the station inspector[23] at around 1.55 a.m. when he heard the news. He immediately telegraphed to the City Police headquarters at Old Jewry, despatched a constable to fetch the City Police's divisional surgeon, Dr Frederick Gordon Brown[24] from Finsbury Circus, and set off to the square himself to take charge of the scene.[25] Upon arrival, Inspector Collard noted that Dr Sequeira had already arrived, and had declared the woman deceased, noting that 'where the murder was committed was probably the darkest part of the square, but there was sufficient light to enable the miscreant to perpetrate the deed'.[26]

Collard then proceeded to manage the scene, closing off from the public the three entrances into Mitre Square, from Mitre Street, St James's Passage and Church Passage, in readiness for the City of London Police's version of CID, the Detective Department; however, they had already been on the scene prior to Collard's arrival, and were now on the lookout for the miscreant.

In his main report, dated 27 October 1888, the head of City's Detective Department, James McWilliam, explained that City Police Commissioner Colonel Sir James Fraser had, as early as August 1888, flooded No. 6 Bishopsgate subdivision, the closest station to Whitechapel, with extra constables in response to the murders across the jurisdictional boundary in the Whitechapel area, and ordered his men to keep 'close observation on all Prostitutes frequenting public-houses and walking the streets'.[27] City Detective Constable Daniel Halse was carrying out this instruction, conducting patrols with a small team of detectives around the Aldgate area; just prior to 2.00 a.m., he, Detective Sergeant Robert Outram and Detective Edward Marriott got wind of a murder. They were outside St Botolph's church, located on the corner of Aldgate High Street and Houndsditch, and the crime had been committed merely a minute's walk away in Mitre Square. The three detectives ran over to the square, where Halse had one of the constables already at the scene turn their lamp upon the body. It was clear to him that a murder had taken place, and that it was recent, so Halse gave the order for the detectives to fan out and search the immediate area, stopping every man seen and examining them. Halse himself headed across the jurisdiction boundary towards Whitechapel, which he was permitted to do if circumstances required. He crossed the Middlesex Street boundary which separated the two forces, and found himself on Wentworth Street when he came across two men who, when he stopped them, gave a 'satisfactory account of themselves'.[28] He then headed south, into Goulston Street, at around 2.20 a.m. and, seeing nothing of further significance, headed back to Mitre Square, where he liaised with Inspector Collard who had, by that time, arrived on the scene. In Goulston Street, Metropolitan Constable 254A Alfred Long, who had been drafted in to support H Division from A Division Whitehall, was conducting his beat, tramping along the street at around 2.20 a.m. as well; Long did not see Halse, and Halse did not report seeing Long, but since Halse was approximating his timings it is possible he was a few minutes out in his estimation.

I have viewed H Division's beat books for the 1930s, the oldest surviving records so far located, and Long's possible beat, No. 2 in this book, shows that Goulston Street was not covered in one continuous sweep in the 1930s, but rather broken into three sections, each section covered separately and at different times. If the 1930s beat book holds as 1888, the first section would have begun with Long entering Goulston Street from Wentworth Street, moving south along the east side of Goulston Street as far as Whitechapel High Street. Here he would turn west along the High Street to Middlesex Street, and travel north on Middlesex Street to New Goulston Street. New Goulston Street would be where the second section began, as he would turn east along this street, and walk back to Goulston Street. Once at the Goulston Street junction, he would head north, along the west side of Goulston Street to Bell Lane. At this point he would have explored the many streets and courts around Bell Lane before finding himself back on Wentworth Street, heading toward Castle Alley. Long would move south along Castle Alley, then west once he had arrived at the Whitechapel High Street junction. He would then enter Goulston Street for a third time, this time from its southern entrance, and walk north, on its western side, as far as New Goulston Street, into which he would turn west and walk toward Middlesex Street, and then on to continue his beat, which would take around thirty minutes to complete. Long's beat, if similar to the 1930s beat, would have been extremely complex to patrol, but it must be noted that the landscape had altered a little by the 1930s, and we must not presume that this beat record mirrors the one trod by Constable Long. The most telling aspect of the 1930s beat book is that Goulston Street was not actually covered in one sweep; therefore, it may give us an insight into how Goulston Street was patrolled at this crucial time. It may not have been walked at once, but rather tackled in three parts.

Back in Mitre Square, as Halse was walking down Goulston Street, City of London divisional surgeon Dr Frederick Gordon Brown had arrived at the scene to conduct his examinations of the deceased in the presence of Dr Sequeira. Notes taken of Brown's testimony by coroner Samuel Langham at the inquest describe the scene:

> The body was on its back, the head turned to left shoulder. The arms by the side of the body as if they had fallen there. Both palms upwards, the fingers slightly bent. Left leg extended in a line with the body, the abdomen was exposed. Right leg bent at the thigh and knee.
>
> The throat cut across.
>
> The intestines were drawn out to a large extent and placed over the right shoulder – they were smeared over with some feculent matter. A piece of about two feet was quite detached from the body and placed between the body and the left arm, apparently by design. The lobe and auricle of the right ear was cut obliquely through.
>
> There was a quantity of clotted blood on the pavement on the left side of the neck round the shoulder and upper part of arm, and fluid blood-coloured serum which had flowed under the neck to the right shoulder, the pavement sloping in that direction.
>
> Body was quite warm. No death stiffening had taken place. She must have been dead most likely within, the half hour. We looked for superficial bruises and saw none. No blood on the skin of the abdomen or secretion of any kind on the thighs. No spurting of blood on the bricks or pavement around. No marks of blood below the middle of the body. Several buttons were found in the clotted blood after the body was removed. There was no blood on the front of the clothes. There were no traces of recent connection. When the body arrived at Golden Lane [mortuary] some of the blood was dispersed through the removal of the body to the mortuary. The clothes were taken off carefully from the body. A piece of deceased's ear dropped from the clothing.

Prior to the removal of the body to the mortuary, City Police Sergeant 92 Herbert Jones had located, upon the deceased's left-hand side, three small black buttons, a metal thimble[29] and a small mustard tin which contained two pawn tickets, which raised hopes of a lead on the victim's identification. Inspector Collard instructed that the backs of the empty cottages be searched for forced entry or any signs of footmarks; however, no evidence was found, so Collard widened the search to the immediate neighbourhood before the arrival of the head of CID for the City Police, James McWilliam, along with Detective Sergeant Downes. McWilliam, prior to leaving headquarters at Old Jewry for Bishopsgate police station and going from there to Mitre Square, was briefed about the find in the square by Bishopsgate station sergeant George Izzard at Old Jewry, and so telegraphed Scotland Yard to inform the Metropolitan force of the City Police's news of a fresh murder. As McWilliam entered the square he was greeted by Inspector Collard, along with acting City Police Commissioner Major Henry Smith,[30] Superintendent Alfred Foster and a number of City detectives already at the scene.[31] McWilliam instructed the detectives to start searching the streets around Mitre Square for anything suspicious, and to make enquiries at nearby lodging houses. In fact, the only tangible clue the killer had left to date was shortly discovered in Goulston Street, where Constable Long was conducting his beat, and so the focus of the investigation temporarily moved from Mitre Square to a small doorway in Whitechapel.

At 2.50 a.m. Constable Long had returned to Goulston Street on his beat round, and he had stopped at the entrance to 108–119 Wentworth Model Dwellings, located on the north-eastern corner of the street. The dwellings were newly built, and as he crossed over the short gantry which bridged the recess wells in front of the dwellings he noted a dirty rag deposited in the entrance. Constable Long had heard of a murder in the City, so one could imagine his concern when he noted that the rag was dotted and soaked with blood and other matter. Thinking that another murder had taken place in that building, Long drew open his bullseye lamp from the floor, passing the beam upwards along the wall as he searched for further bloodstains. He found none. However, he did find something which caused debate almost from the moment it was discovered. Chalked on the black fascia were the words, 'The Juwes are the men that will not be blamed for nothing.'[32] Long conducted a search of the staircase, climbing six or seven flights in the process, looking for anything to rouse his interest. He found nothing, so he returned to ground level where he obtained the assistance of Constable 190H Willie Bettles, whom he instructed to guard the dwellings entrance and to maintain observations on any person entering or leaving, before he himself departed for his subdivision station at Commercial Street to report his find.[33]

The rag actually belonged to the victim; it was a piece torn away from her apron, and was later matched up with her clothing at Golden Lane mortuary. The only reasonable solution as to how it made its way from Mitre Square to Goulston Street was that, in all probability, it was transported by the murderer, and it therefore gave the police an indication of the killer's movements in the time between the murder at around 1.45 a.m. and Long's discovery at 2.50 a.m. This small dwelling entrance suddenly became significant to both the Metropolitan Police and the City of London Police alike. When the City Police got wind of the apron find, detectives Halse and Baxter Hunt were sent to Leman Street police station, and then headed to Goulston Street. Once they had viewed the writing upon the fascia, Halse maintained the City force's presence by remaining at the scene; Hunt returned to Mitre Square to update their superior, McWilliam, who ordered that the chalked wall writing must be photographed. Hunt returned with the message, and it would seem that this was in the process of being organised as the pair, with the permission of the Metropolitan force, began to interview every tenant in that block, without any positive result.[34]

Life in Whitechapel was, albeit slowly, beginning to stir that morning and daylight was now just starting to break. Soon Jewish vendors, who had market pitches in and around Wentworth and Goulston Streets, would start to rise and make their way to Cox's Square, a place where they stored their goods and provisions, and Goulston Street would be full of pedestrian traffic. This concerned the Metropolitan force, as they were fearful that, if the writing should be seen, the words could cause some riotous angst toward the Jewish population inside the dwelling and maybe beyond. Jews had already been the recipients of anti-Semitic assaults, largely courtesy of the negative Leather Apron news coverage during the period of the Chapman murder. One particular reader of the *Evening News* sent in a letter to the editor on 10 September, just days after Annie Chapman was found murdered, and, published under the headline, 'Slaughtering the Jews', it read,

Sir,

With reference to the above heading, on Saturday, evening last, I found it difficult to traverse the streets in the vicinity of the Whitechapel, without observing in almost every thoroughfare, knots of persons (consisting of men, women and children), and overhearing their slanderous and insulting remarks towards the Jews, who occasionally passed by. With justice to my countrymen, I mention that the foul epithets was made use of by people of the most ignorant and dangerous class, promoted by the information they had casually obtained that a man known as 'Leather Apron' had a Jewish appearance, and was wanted for the recent Whitechapel murders. Even were it the case that the actual perpetrator belonged to the Hebrew class, is it not cowardly and unjust that in the extreme to calumniate a sect for the sins of one? Spotless indeed would be the flock entirely minus of black sheep. The Jew predominates in the neighbourhood where I am and have been residing for years, but notwithstanding the crimes committed by the members of our so-called Christian race average at least 99 per cent, in excess of those imputed by the Jews. Therefore if there were base enough to take a mean advantage of this knowledge, and impugn and molest every respectable Christian pedestrian they chanced to meet, no doubt riot and disorder would

be the result daily. 'Hard words break no bones,' but often they lead to that end. The Jew is certainly no coward when on the defensive and if such conduct as I personally witnessed on Saturday last is not suppressed, the consequences may be serious indeed. My knowledge of the Jews impresses me with the belief that they are a persevering, thrifty and generous race. Clannish they may be, and it is a pity there is not more of such brotherly feeling existing among Christians; again, seldom have I seen a subscription list opened for the benefit of a deserving Christian that has not been contributed to by the Jews. Those who forget themselves so far as to insult them in the manner I have stated should put the query to each other, 'What would our Christian labour market be (especially in this district) without the industry introduced by the Hebrew race? If your space will admit of giving publicity to the remarks made from a lover of fair play, it may be the means of deterring the self-imagined, pure-minded Christian, in abusing the people I have mentioned, and also teach him to endeavour 'to pick the mote from his own eye,' instead of molesting a harmless and industrious fraternity. I am, &c.,
48 and 49, Bishopsgate-street, Without, G. H. H.
September 10.[35]

The concern the Metropolitan force had for the welfare of Jews in the area was a real and valid one. The City force were solely concerned with this potential clue, but the Metropolitan force had to police the area, and there was a true fear that this writing, given its possible association with the apron piece, and therefore also with the murder in Mitre Square, could be a catalyst for disturbances or assaults against the Jewish population. H Division's superintendent, Thomas Arnold, became involved and he in turn sought the judgement of his commissioner, Sir Charles Warren. Warren had been informed of a murder in Berner Street, and had already visited Commercial Street station before arriving at Leman Street station at a little before 5.00 a.m.; here he was briefed by Superintendent Arnold as to the current situation.[36] Arnold pushed for the writing's removal, which is understandable as it was he who would have to deal with any disturbances; however, Warren decided to make the trip to Goulston Street to view the situation himself before making a decision. So pressing was the matter that Warren went to Goulston Street before attending the scene in Berner Street, and when he and Arnold arrived, Warren noted a number of both City and Metropolitan constables milling around at the scene, with one of them being City Detective Halse. Halse tried to argue the case for the writing to remain, at least until the photographer had arrived and had conducted his work. A debate then ensued, with various compromises given, such as the covering up of the writing, or the removal of certain words to make it less antagonising; however, Warren chose to remove the writing, citing the fear of assaults against the Jewish population and damage to property as his reason.

It was clear that the City Police, quite correctly, viewed the writing as a potential clue, though that is not to say they believed it to have been written by the murderer; rather, it was evidence which needed to be assessed. That they developed a policy of photographing such material is evident, and possibly born out of their close relationship with the Parisian *Le Sûreté*,[37] who utilised photography to a maximum degree during the period, as a discovery made in the archives of the City of London Police museum of a photograph of similar chalked writing testifies.[38] The photograph of the writing, made on a wooden background, possibly a door or shutter, reads,

I am going to do one on the 27th
Jac

Unfortunately the photo is cropped; however, researcher Debra Arif has located a reference to the writing in a public health document entitled *Reports of the Meetings and Discussions held in London 10–17 August 1891*, within which a visitor to the Coroners' Court museum in Golden Lane declared that a collection of photographs existed, stating, 'In the collection is a photograph of the writing found on one of the blocks of artizans' dwellings: "I am going to do one on the 27th; Jack the Ripper".'

As the infamous moniker by which the killer was soon to be known, 'Jack the Ripper', did not come into common usage until after 29 September 1888, when it appeared in the newspapers, it is logical to assume that this writing was photographed by the City of London force sometime between that date and the date of the document, August 1891. The location of 'artizans' dwellings' is confusing, as no such dwellings existed in the City of London at that time; however, artisan dwellings did exist near in Whitechapel, on the border with the city, in the form of five blocks, with one, Kings Block, being located on Stoney Lane, which lies directly between Mitre Square and Goulston Street.[39] There are newspaper reports of the discovery of writing on Kings Block; however, this seems to be a case of erroneous reporting, and an errant reference to the writing in Goulston Street; these news reports, published in the January and February 1905, were written almost twenty years after the event, and must be treated with extreme caution.[40] What should be noted is that such writing on walls did exist – examples were alleged to have been found throughout the autumn of 1888, in Hanbury Street after the Chapman murder,[41] in Cloak Lane in the City of London, in Thomas Street in Bermondsey and in Newham Street in Goodman's Fields, as well as in other locations. Most were treated for what they were – hoaxes. For the City of London force to photograph this particular piece of wall writing may be an indication that they felt it held some significance.

The body finally arrived at Golden Lane mortuary, just off Barbican within the City of London, where it was stripped, and Inspector Collard made a list of all clothing worn and items found upon the victim. This list makes interesting reading, as it not only gives us a little glimpse into the world of these transient women who merely sought to exist from day to day, but also offers an insight into a policeman's mind as Collard goes into great depth, recording the items as he fingered through them, at one point counting the spots of blood found upon the right boot:

Black straw bonnet trimmed with green & black velvet and black beads, black strings. The bonnet was loosely tied, and had partially fallen from the back of her head, no blood on front, but the back was lying in a pool of blood, which had run from the neck,

Black Cloth jacket, imitation fur edging around the collar, fur round sleeves, no blood on front outside, large quantity of Blood inside & outside back, outside back very dirty with Blood & dirt, 2 outside pockets, trimmed with black silk braid & imitation fur,

Chintz Skirt 3 flounces, brown button on waistband, Jagged cut 6½ inches long from waistband, left side of front, Edges slightly Bloodstained, also Blood on bottom, back & front of skirt.

Brown Lindsey Dress Bodice, black velvet collar, brown metal buttons down front, blood inside & outside back of neck & shoulders, clean cut bottom of left side, 5 inches long from right to left.

Grey Stuff Petticoat, white waist band, cut 1½ inch long, thereon in front, Edges blood stained, blood stains on front at bottom of Petticoat.

Very Old Green Alpaca Skirt, Jagged cut 10½ inches long in front of waist band downward, blood stained inside, front under cut.

Very Old Ragged Blue Skirt, red flounce, light twill lining, jagged cut 10½ inches long, through waist band, downward, blood stained, inside & outside back and front.

White Calico Chemise, very much blood stained all over, apparently worn thus in middle of front.

Mans White Vest, button to match down front, 2 outside pockets, torn at back, very much Blood stained at back, Blood and other stains on front.

No Drawers or Stays

Pair of Mens lace up Boots, mohair laces, right boot has been repaired with red thread, 6 Blood marks on right boot.

1 piece of red gauze Silk, various cuts thereon found on neck

1 large White Handkerchief, blood stained

2 Unbleached Calico Pockets, tape strings, cut through also top left hand corners, cut off one.

1 Blue Stripe Bed ticking Pocket, waist band, and strings cut through, (all 3 Pockets) Blood stained

1 White Cotton Pocket Handkerchief, red and white birds eye border.

1 Pr. Brown ribbed Stockings, feet mended with white.

12 pieces of white Rag, some lightly bloodstained.

1 piece of white course Linen.

1 piece of Blue & White Shirting (3 cornered).

2 Small blue Bed ticking Bags.

2 Short Clay Pipes (black).

1 Tin Box containing Tea.

1 do do do Sugar.

1 Piece of Flannel & 6 pieces of Soap.

1 Small Tooth Comb.

1 White Handle Table Knife & 1 Metal Spoon.

1 Red Leather Cigarette Case, white metal fittings.

1 Tin Match Box. empty.

1 piece of Red Flannel containing Pins & Needles.

1 Ball of Hemp

1 piece of old White Apron[42]

Also apparently on the list:

> Mustard tin containing two pawn tickets, One in the name of Emily Birrell, 52 White's Row, dated August 31, 9d for a man's flannel shirt. The other is in the name of Jane Kelly of 6 Dorset Street and dated September 28, 2s for a pair of men's boots. Both addresses are false.
>
> Printed handbill and according to a press report a printed card for 'Frank Carter, 305, Bethnal Green Road'
>
> Portion of a pair of spectacles
>
> 1 red mitten

The post-mortem of the victim was conducted on the afternoon of 30 September by City of London divisional surgeon Dr Frederick Gordon Brown, with Dr George Sequeira and Dr William Sedgwick Saunders, the City's health analyst, in attendance. Also present was H Division's surgeon, Dr George Bagster Phillips, who was to conduct the post-mortem on Stride the following day. The result was a lengthy report, which revealed that the victim had had part of her womb, and the whole of her left kidney, removed:

> I made a post mortem examination at half past two on Sunday afternoon. Rigor mortis was well marked; body not quite cold. Green discolouration over the abdomen.
>
> After washing the left hand carefully, a bruise the size of a sixpence, recent and red, was discovered on the back of the left hand between the thumb and first finger. A few small bruises on right shin of older date. The hands and arms were bronzed. No bruises on the scalp, the back of the body or the elbows.
>
> The face was very much mutilated. There was a cut about a quarter of an inch through the lower left eyelid, dividing the structures completely through. The upper eyelid on that side, there was a scratch through the skin on the left upper eyelid, near to the angle of the nose. The right eyelid was cut through to about half an inch.
>
> There was a deep cut over the bridge of the nose, extending from the left border of the nasal bone down near to the angle of the jaw on the right side of the cheek. This cut went into the bone and divided all the structures of the cheek except the mucous membrane of the mouth.

The tip of the nose was quite detached from the nose by an oblique cut from the bottom of the nasal bone to where the wings of the nose join on to the face. A cut from this divided the upper lip and extended through the substance of the gum over the right upper lateral incisor tooth. About half an inch from the top of the nose was another oblique cut. There was a cut on the right angle of the mouth as if the cut of a point of a knife. The cut extended an inch and a half, parallel with lower lip.

There was on each side of cheek a cut which peeled up the skin, forming a triangular flap about an inch and a half.

On the left cheek there were two abrasions of the epithelium. There was a little mud on the left cheek – 2 slight abrasions under the left ear.

The throat was cut across to the extent of about six or seven inches. A superficial cut commenced about an inch and a half below the lobe and about two and a half inches behind the left ear, and extended across the throat to about three inches below the lobe of right ear. The big muscle across the throat was divided through on the left side. The large vessels on the left side of the neck were severed. The larynx was severed below the vocal cords. All the deep structures were severed to the bone, the knife marking intervertebral cartilages. The sheath of the vessels on the right side was just opened. The carotid artery had a fine hole opening. The internal jugular vein was opened an inch and a half – not divided.

The blood vessels contained clot. All these injuries were performed by a sharp instrument like a knife, and pointed.

The cause of death was haemorrhage from the left common carotid artery. The death was immediate and the mutilations were inflicted after death.

We examined the abdomen. The front walls were laid open from the breast bone to the pubes. The cut commenced opposite the enciform cartilage. The incision went upwards, not penetrating the skin that was over the sternum. It then divided the enciform cartilage. The knife must have cut obliquely at the expense of the front surface of that cartilage.

Behind this, the liver was stabbed as if by the point of a sharp instrument.

Below this was another incision into the liver of about two and a half inches, and below this the left lobe of the liver was slit through by a vertical cut. Two cuts were shewn by a jagging of the skin on the left side.

The abdominal walls were divided in the middle line to within a quarter of an inch of the navel. The cut then took a horizontal course for two inches and a half towards right side. It then divided round the navel on the left side, and made a parallel incision to the former horizontal incision, leaving the navel on a tongue of skin. Attached to the navel was two and a half inches of the lower part of the rectus muscle on the left side of the abdomen. The incision then took an oblique direction to the right and was shelving. The incision went down the right side of the vagina and rectum for half an inch behind the rectum.

There was a stab of about an inch on the left groin. This was done by a pointed instrument. Below this was a cut of three inches going through all tissues making a wound of the peritoneum [sc. perineum] about the same extent.

An inch below the crease of the thigh was a cut extending from the anterior spine of the ilium obliquely down the inner side of the left thigh and separating the left labium, forming a flap of skin up to the groin. The left rectus muscle was not detached.

There was a flap of skin formed from the right thigh, attaching the right labium, and extending up to the spine of the ilium. The muscles on the right side inserted into the frontal ligaments were cut through.

The skin was retracted through the whole of the cut in the abdomen, but the vessels were not clotted. Nor had there been any appreciable bleeding from the vessels. I draw the conclusion that the cut was made after death, and there would not be much blood on the murderer. The cut was made by someone on right side of body, kneeling below the middle of the body.

I removed the content of the stomach and placed it in a jar for further examination. There seemed very little in it in the way of food or fluid, but from the cut end partly digested farinaceous food escaped.

The intestines had been detached to a large extent from the mesentery. About two feet of the colon was cut away. The sigmoid flexure was invaginated into the rectum very tightly.

Right kidney pale, bloodless, with slight congestion of the base of the pyramids.

There was a cut from the upper part of the slit on the under surface of the liver to the left side, and another cut at right angles to this, which were about an inch and a half deep and two and a half inches long. Liver itself was healthy.

The gall bladder contained bile. The pancreas was cut, but not through, on the left side of the spinal column. Three and a half inches of the lower border of the spleen by half an inch was attached only to the peritoneum. The peritoneal lining was cut through on the left side and the left kidney carefully taken out and removed. The left renal artery was cut through. I should say that someone who knew the position of the kidney must have done it.

The lining membrane over the uterus was cut through. The womb was cut through horizontally, leaving a stump of three quarters of an inch. The rest of the womb had been taken away with some of the ligaments. The vagina and cervix of the womb was uninjured.

The bladder was healthy and uninjured, and contained three or four ounces of water. There was a tongue-like cut through the anterior wall of the abdominal aorta. The other organs were healthy.

There were no indications of connexion.

I believe the wound in the throat was first inflicted. I believe she must have been lying on the ground.

The wounds on the face and abdomen prove that they were inflicted by a sharp pointed knife, and that in the abdomen by one six inches long.

I believe the perpetrator of the act must have had considerable knowledge of the positions of the organs in the abdominal cavity and the way of removing them. The parts removed would be of no use for any professional purpose. It required a great deal of medical knowledge to have removed the kidney and to know where it was placed. Such a knowledge might be possessed by some one in the habit of cutting up animals.

I think the perpetrator of this act had sufficient time, or he would not have nicked the lower eyelids. It would take at least five minutes.

I cannot assign any reason for the parts being taken away. I feel sure there was no struggle. I believe it was the act of one person.

The throat had been so instantly severed that no noise could have been emitted. I should not expect much blood to have been found on the person who had inflicted these wounds. The wounds could not have been self-inflicted.

My attention was called to the apron. It was the corner of the apron, with a string attached. The blood spots were of recent origin. I have seen the portion of an apron produced by Dr Phillips and stated to have been found in Goulston Street. It is impossible to say it is human blood. I fitted the piece of apron which had a new piece of material on it which had evidently been sewn on to the piece I have, the seams of the borders of the two actually corresponding. Some blood and, apparently, faecal matter was found on the portion found in Goulston Street. I believe the wounds on the face to have been done to disfigure the corpse.[43]

Photographs were taken by the City Police, before the post-mortem, of the deceased in an open casket. Her upper body was uncovered in these photos; by contrast, Metropolitan Police policy, and Howard Vincent's guidance, was to cover the body from the neck down, thus not exposing any of the abdominal injuries to view. Once the post-mortem was completed, further photographs were taken of the deceased hung, rather callously, naked and stitched, against the mortuary wall; other photographs, of the head, revealed the damaged face. While these photographs are obviously disturbing, they were done to record the details of her injuries, along with her height, the state of her hair, and even the tattoo of 'TC' upon her left forearm. It was an age in which photography was being explored by the police as a means of documenting and preserving evidence, and photographs were an excellent and simple way of doing this. They could be presented in court as evidence, and their factual content would be very hard to dispute.

The description of the female was circulated to all stations, and led to constables Robinson and Simmons thinking the victim could have been the drunk they had brought to Bishopsgate police station the evening before.[44] Robinson viewed the body at the mortuary and confirmed that it was; so did Gaoler Hutt; however, the name she gave at Bishopsgate of Mary Ann Kelly, and the address in Fashion Street, were shown, upon investigation, to be false leads. The two pawn tickets located by Sergeant Jones inside the empty mustard tin which lay next to the body hailed from Mr William Jones, Pawnbrokers of 31 Church Street, Spitalfields, just a few doors down from the Ten Bells public house,[45] and enquiries made there also drew a blank, as Jones could not recall the woman. The pawn ticket lead looked defunct; however, as it happened, a man recognised the name on one of the tickets, Birrell, while reading through the accounts of the dreadful double murders in the morning papers, and he came forward to Bishopsgate station with a possible name for the victim. The man, market porter John Kelly, was taken to Golden Lane Mortuary, where he confirmed that the dead woman was his partner of seven years, Catherine Eddowes.[46]

As morning broke on 30 September, City of London constables began their house-to-house enquiries in and around the area of Mitre Square. The only occupied residential property in Mitre Square was No. 3, which overlooked the murder scene. It was here that Whitechapel-born Richard Pearce lived, with his wife and his small children.[47] Pearce, who happened to be a police constable with the City of London force, was asleep at the time of the murder, and claimed to have heard nothing, stating, 'My wife and my family were in no way disturbed during the night.'[48] George Clapp, the caretaker of Copeland & Co. in Mitre Street, whose bedroom window also looked over the murder spot in Mitre Square, stated he was on the premises with his ill wife, and her nurse, all of whom heard nothing suspicious during the night. St James's Place, connected to Mitre Square via St James's Passage, held a small fire station within it, manned by three men, all of whom reported nothing unusual. A night watchman, James Blenkingsop, was watching over some roadworks in St James's Place. He recalled that a respectfully dressed man approached him at around 1.30 a.m., prior to the body being discovered at around 1.45 a.m., and asked, 'Have you seen a man and a woman go through here?' It is possible that Blenkingsop may have been mistaken about the time, and that the man was Halse, Marriott or Outram making enquiries as they pursued the killer in the aftermath of the discovery of Eddowes. St James's Place was colloquially known as Orange Market, due to the fruit stalls which set up there in the daytime; in fact, the area was known for its fruit sellers, as well as for clothes, jewellery and cigarette making, and it was a tradesman in cigarettes who became an extremely important witness in this case.

Joseph Lawende, a commercial cigarette traveller, came to the police's attention during enquiries made by the City of London force. He claimed that, during the evening of 29 September, he had been in the Imperial Club, a Jewish club in Duke Street, with two others, Harry Harris and Joseph Hyam Levy. They stayed late, and it was around 1.30 a.m. when the men decided to leave; however, they held off for a few minutes as it was still raining outside. The club was just a little north of Church Passage – a long, narrow entrance to Mitre Square, the one Constable Harvey walked down – and on the opposite side of the road. The men left the club at around 1.35 a.m., with Lawende walking a little ahead of his colleagues. He noted a man and a woman on the corner of Church Passage; her back was to Lawende, and the man was facing him. Lawende was taken to the mortuary to see if he could identify the victim as the woman he saw, but he could not, as he had not seen her face; however, he noted that the woman he had seen had been wearing dark clothing, a black jacket and bonnet, and the victim's clothing was similar. With the exception of the point that he had been wearing a cloth cap, Lawende's description of the man he had seen was subsequently held back from the inquest at the request of the City of London Police solicitor, Henry Crawford. However, Chief Inspector Swanson's overall summary report, dated 19 October 1888, reveals the man Lawende saw: around thirty years of age, five feet seven or eight inches in height, fair complexion, fair moustache, medium build, wearing a pepper-and-salt loose jacket, grey cloth cap, reddish handkerchief tied around the neck, and with the appearance of a sailor.[49] Lawende watched the woman place her hand upon the man's chest as he passed; however, he could not hear what they were discussing. Levy, walking behind Lawende with Harris, also noted the couple as they passed, stating later that the man was only three inches taller than the woman; Harris claimed that he saw only the back of the man.[50] Due to its location and timing, Lawende's observation was treated with great importance by the City of London Police, and there is a suggestion that he was even used by the Metropolitan force at future identification parades.

Mitre Square was closed off until the mid-morning of 30 September, with City inspector George Izzard issuing directions, assisted by City sergeants Amos Dudman and Phelps. This enabled Frederick Foster, a City Surveyor and the son of City of London Police Superintendent Alfred Foster[51] (who had been aiding the investigation in Mitre Square just a few hours before), to make his drawings for use at the inquest. Once this had been done, the City Police withdrew, giving Mitre Square back to the locals, and they thronged around the spot in massive crowds over the next day or so, trying to get a glimpse of the scene where poor Kate had met her end. A few days later, when the crowds had died down, the City Police returned and sent ten men down to conduct a search of the sewer systems in and around Mitre Square, but nothing of significance was found.[52] News reports also came to light that, during the weekend, while the murder was being conducted, a burglary had occurred at the post office on Aldgate High Street, just yards from Mitre Square; however, the police concluded that these matters were unrelated, and that the burglary had actually occurred on the Saturday, hours prior to the attack on Eddowes, only being discovered upon the opening of the post office on the Monday morning.

The impact of these two murders, which had occurred within an hour of each other, was to draw global scrutiny down upon London's police, and their handling of the Whitechapel Murder case was widely criticised, even by those who really should have known better. Inspector Thomas F. Byrnes, the head of the New York Police Department, displaying his ignorance about what was required to police a maze of streets such as Whitechapel, picked over Warren's performance, stating, 'With the very large force of police under his charge Sir Charles Warren, commissioner of police of London, who under the English form of government has powers autocratic, should have been able to cover the ground so thoroughly after the second crime that the third would have been impossible, or, at least, that the capture of the perpetrator would have been inevitable. It isn't as if the murders were committed in widely separated districts, which would have made the case more difficult.'[53] Byrnes, who was to find himself in a similar situation to Warren with the Carrie Brown murder of 1891, went on to describe his strategy for tackling the Whitechapel murderer. Seemingly, and unbelievably, this involved sacrificing further victims:

> With the great power of the London police I should have manufactured victims for this murder. I would have taken fifty of the female habitués of Whitechapel and covered the ground with them. Even if one fell a victim I would get the murderer. My men, un-uniformed, would be scattered over the whole district, so nothing that happened could escape them. The crimes are all of the same class, and I would have determined the class to which the murderer belonged. But pshaw! what's the use of talking; the murderer should have been caught long ago.[54]

The murderer, however, had remained uncaught, and thanks to a small letter which had allegedly been sitting on a desk at the Central News Agency since 27 September 1888, three days prior to the double murder of Stride and Eddowes, he was to be christened, infamously and notoriously.

The letter began, 'Dear Boss ... '

13

Letters, Leaflets, Lusk and a Lull

Should you know of any person to whom suspicion is attached, you are earnestly requested to communicate at once with the nearest police-station.
Metropolitan Police Public Notice, 30 September 1888

The desk upon which the letter had been sitting for those two days belonged to Tom Bulling, a journalist based at the Central News Agency in New Bridge Street, just off Blackfriars Bridge. He had, he said, received the letter on 27 September, and forwarded it on to the head of CID at Scotland Yard, Adolphus Williamson, on 29 September, with an accompanying note which read, 'The editor presents his compliments to Mr Williamson & begs to inform him that the enclosed was sent to the Central News two days ago, & was treated as a joke.'[1]

Upon the envelope, which was dated SP 27 88,[2] were the words 'The Boss Central News Office London City' in red ink, and inside, folded into four quarters, was a letter, upon which, and again in red ink, the following was written:

25 Sept 1888
Dear Boss,
I keep on hearing the police have caught me but they wont fix me just yet. I have laughed when they look so clever and talk about being on the right track. That joke about Leather Apron gave me real fits. I am down on whores and I shant quit ripping them till I do get buckled. Grand work the last job was. I gave the lady no time to squeal. How can they catch me now. I love my work and want to start again. You will soon hear of me with my funny little games. I saved some of the proper red stuff in a ginger beer bottle over the last job to write with but it went thick like glue and I cant use it. Red ink is fit enough I hope <u>ha. ha.</u> The next job I do I shall clip the ladys ears off and send to the police officers just for jolly wouldn't you. Keep this letter back till I do a bit more work, then give it out straight. My knife's so nice and sharp I want to get to work right away if I get a chance. Good Luck.
Yours truly Jack the Ripper

Dont mind me giving the trade name

Then, written at a right angle underneath:

PS Wasnt good enough to post this before I got all the red ink off my hands curse it. No luck yet. They say I'm a doctor now. ha ha[3]

The letter was received at Scotland Yard just hours before Stride and Eddowes were murdered, and it was soon followed by a second piece of communication. This was a postcard, made out in similar writing and similar ink, which was received at the Central News Agency on Monday 1 October. This time Central News did not dwell, and forwarded it straight to Scotland Yard. It read, among the red fingerprint smears,

I was not codding dear old Boss when I gave you the tip, you'll hear about Saucy Jacky s work tomorrow. double event this time number one squealed a bit couldn't finish straight off. had not got time to get ears for police thanks for keeping last letter back till I got to work again.
Jack the Ripper[4]

Within days, McCorquodale & Co. printers had produced, at the request of the Metropolitan force, a number of posters which displayed facsimiles of both the letter and postcard; these posters were placed on almost every police noticeboard in the Metropolitan jurisdiction[5] and reproduced in the newspapers, albeit with some text removed. A third letter was received by Bulling at Central News Agency on Friday 5 October; however, rather than send the original to Scotland Yard, the journalist decided to send a transcription, which read,

5 Oct 1888
Dear Friend
In the name of God hear me I swear I did not kill the female whose body was found at Whitehall. If she was an honest woman I will hunt down and destroy her murderer. If she ['was an honest woman' deleted] was a whore God will bless the hand that slew her, for the women of of [sic] Moab and Midian shall die and their blood shall mingle with the dust. I never harm any others or the Divine power that protects and helps me in my grand work would quit for ever. Do as I do and the light of glory shall shine upon you. I must get to work tomorrow treble event this time yes yes three must be ripped. will send you a bit of face by post I promise this dear old Boss. The police now reckon my work a practical joke well well Jacky's a very practical joker ha ha ha Keep this back till three are wiped out and you can show the cold meat
Yours truly
Jack the Ripper[6]

According to Evans and Skinner, in the excellent, comprehensive account of hundreds of Jack the Ripper letters published in their book *Jack the Ripper: Letters from Hell*, this third missive was held back by the Central News Agency upon the request of the Metropolitan Police. Maybe this heralded the adoption of a different tack by the police – a twofold plan to see if the author would indeed carry out his threat of three murders in one night, coupled with a desire not to propagate further panic in the East End – or maybe the police were beginning to grow a little suspicious of Mr Bulling. Certainly, many years later, it was popularly believed among police authorities that either Bulling, or his manager John Moore, did indeed write these letters to aid newspaper circulation. One contemporary policeman and former head of Special Branch in Scotland Yard, Chief Inspector John George Littlechild,[7] expanded on this in a 1913 letter which he wrote to his friend, G. R. Sims (himself a famous journalist of the day):[8]

> With regard to the term 'Jack the Ripper' it was generally believed at the Yard that Tom Bullen [*sic*, Bulling] of the Central News was the originator, but it is probable Moore, who was his chief, was the inventor. It was a smart piece of journalistic work. No journalist of my time got such privileges from Scotland Yard as Bullen. Mr James Munro when Assistant Commissioner, and afterwards Commissioner, relied on his integrity. Poor Bullen occasionally took too much to drink, and I fail to see how he could help it knocking about so many hours and seeking favours from so many people to procure copy. One night when Bullen had taken a 'few too many' he got early information of the death of Prince Bismarck and instead of going to the office to report it sent a laconic telegram 'Bloody Bismarck is dead'. On this I believe Mr Charles Moore fired him out.[9]

The newspapers were full of the details of the two latest atrocities, committed by the man who, supposedly, named himself 'Jack the Ripper'; and the police were deluged with hints, offers to assist and accusations. Communication between the City of London and the Metropolitan forces had always been fairly reliable, but now that a murder had occurred within the City of London it was imperative for the two forces to work together, and Metropolitan Commissioner Warren wrote to his City counterpart, Fraser, suggesting closer liaison. Opening with the affectionate line 'My dear Fraser', Warren wrote,

> In order to prevent our working doubly over the same ground I have to suggest that our CID should be in more constant communication with yours about the Whitechapel murders.
>   Could you send an officer to Chief Inspector Swanson here every morning to consult or may I send an officer every morning to consult with your officers. We are inundated with suggestions and names of suspects.
> Truly Yours,
> C.W.[10]

The consequence was regular liaison between Metropolitan Chief Inspector Donald Swanson and the head of the City of London's Detective Department, Inspector James McWilliam, at H Division's headquarters in Leman Street, sometimes with other detectives involved in the case, to 'confer on the subject'.[11] This resulted in the two forces sometimes merging their operations, 'cordially communicating to the other daily the nature and subject of their enquiries',[12] in the hope that efficient progress could be made. There was certainly no lack of industry. Assistant Commissioner Anderson returned from his medically advised European holiday in early October 1888, having spent part of his break in Paris so as to be close to London for ease of correspondence. Anderson was regularly updated on events in Whitechapel; however, the murders in Berner Street and Mitre Square escalated the media focus and political pressure on the investigation, and led to Home Secretary Henry Matthews recalling him to Scotland Yard, as a matter of urgency. It was hoped that Anderson could provide a differing perspective, and inject new vigour into the hunt for this murderer.[13]

As well as producing the notices regarding the letter and postcard, McCorquodale & Co. also produced 80,000 police notices, which were to be issued during intensive house-to-house enquiries. These read,

Police Notice
To the Occupier
On the mornings of Friday, 31st August, Saturday, 8th, and Sunday, 30th Sept., 1888, women were murdered in Whitechapel, it is supposed by some one residing in the immediate neighbourhood. Should you know of any person to whom suspicion is attached, you are earnestly requested to communicate at once with the nearest police-station.
Metropolitan Police Office, 30th Sept., 1888[14]

The plan was for the Metropolitan Police to saturate with these notices an area which was dominated by common lodging houses. A ring was drawn around the target region, from the 'City boundary on one hand, Lamb Street, Commercial Street, Great Eastern Railway & Buxton Street, Albert Street, Dunk Street, Chicksand Street and Great Garden Street to Whitechapel Road and back to the City boundary'.[15] In this area, the police were to conduct house-to-house enquiries and, if warranted, property searches – according to Swanson, over 2,000 lodgers were examined. Seventy-six butchers and slaughterers were also visited and questioned, and even three cowboys, who were performing in the American Exhibition, were required to account for themselves. Enquiries were made at all local asylums and infirmaries about any recently admitted or discharged persons, and the Thames River Police also aided with this mass enquiry by interviewing sailors on docked ships, or clarifying the details of Asiatics – to borrow the language of the time – known to be present in London. The result of this huge undertaking was the gathering of movement information on over

300 people of interest to the police, all of which had to be followed up, and the detention of eighty persons across London, all of whom supplied statements, all of which were investigated and verified. To highlight the vast amount of work which was conducted by both forces during this period, it is worth quoting Swanson, who, while answering questions from a departmental committee on Metropolitan Police superannuation in 1889, described his immense workload during this period of 1888: 'I had to be at the office at half-past 8 in the morning; then I had to read through all the papers that had come in, which took me till 11 pm., and sometimes 1 and 2 in the morning; then I had to go to Whitechapel and see the officers – generally getting home between 2 and 3 am.'[16]

Once the Dear Boss Letter and Saucy Jack postcard, as they were to become known, had been published in the newspapers, a flood of copycat letters began to arrive at Scotland Yard and Old Jewry alike. Rumours of more chalked scrawls claiming to be from 'Jack the Ripper' were also beginning to appear more frequently, with the handwriting compared to letter and postcard. It was not merely the police and newspapers who received such correspondence; many others, such as magistrates, businesses, hotels, and private individuals from up and down the country, and even abroad, began to receive letters signed by 'Jack the Ripper', or some other sinister sobriquet. Most were treated as hoaxes, vindictive correspondence sent by those who had a vendetta against the receiver, or by the plain disturbed, who posted such things while in an unbalanced state of mind. However, one letter, received by a builder and decorator in Mile End, had something quite unique about it: half a human kidney.

As well as working in the building and renovation trade, George Lusk was the chairman and president of the Whitechapel Vigilance Committee, and therefore was well known in the East End. He too had received some 'Ripper'-related correspondence previously; however, at 5.30 p.m., on Tuesday 16 October, a small parcel arrived at his home in Tollet Street, right on the junction with Alderney Road, in Mile End. As he opened the small package up, he came across the kidney, and with it, a letter, which read,

> From hell
> Mr Lusk,
> Sor
> I send you half the Kidne I took from one woman prasarved it for you tother piece I fried and ate it was very nise. I may send you the bloody knif that took it out if you only wate a whil longer.
> Signed
> Catch me when you can Mishter Lusk

Initially Lusk treated the letter as a joke, thinking the kidney was from a dead sheep; however, Joseph Aarons, the committee's secretary, thought that Lusk was actually quite upset upon receiving the package, and, considering that Eddowes had a kidney removed, one could understand the anxiety. Lusk festered on the matter for over a day, but, to ease minds, he, Aarons and another committee man, Charles Reeves, went the following morning to see if they could establish if the kidney piece was, in fact, human. Initially they visited the surgery of their local doctor, Frederick Wiles, but he was not in, so Dr F. S. Reed agreed to view it in his absence. Reed concluded that the kidney could be human, but he wasn't certain, and so he suggested that it should be taken to the London Hospital for review. At the hospital, the kidney was examined by the curator of the museum, Dr Thomas Openshaw, who confirmed that it had once belonged to an adult human.

The group then handed the parcel and letter over to the police at H Division headquarters in Leman Street, and Chief Inspector Swanson immediately contacted his City Police colleague in Old Jewry, Inspector McWilliam, informing him of the gruesome delivery. Arrangements were then made for the kidney piece to be sent on to the City Police for examination by their divisional surgeon, Dr Frederick Gordon Brown, while the letter was forwarded directly to Scotland Yard Central Office for their analysis. Like Dr Openshaw, Dr Brown confirmed that the kidney piece was human; however, McWilliam felt that this information ought to be kept from the public – even if it was human, the possibility remained that it could have been a hoax, maybe some kind of prank by a medical student who had removed a kidney from one of the many cadavers held in the London Hospital. The letter, once Scotland Yard had finished their initial examination of it, was sent on to Old Jewry on 20 October, where McWilliam had it photographed; he returned it to Scotland Yard four days later. Again, while the police considered this letter to be most likely a hoax, the possibility of its authenticity was not entirely dismissed – hence Williamson's decision to photograph it.

In the late Victorian period, Scotland Yard was expanding: by 1887, the Metropolitan Police had already taken over premises in and around much of Whitehall Place. It was clear to many that new premises were required, and therefore some reclaimed embankment land from the River Thames was acquired, not far from Scotland Yard itself. The Home Secretary personally selected architect Richard Norman Shaw to design what was to be known as New Scotland Yard. Construction started in 1887, but was halted in the early October of 1888, due to the discovery of a female torso in the basement of the partly built structure – this initially fed speculation that the Whitechapel murderer had moved west.[17] A left thigh was discovered at the same location just two weeks later, on 17 October, not by the police but by a journalist, Jasper Waring, who had been given permission by the Metropolitan force to search the basement vaults along with his dog, Smoker. However, the Metropolitan Police soon quashed the theory that this was another Whitechapel murder, mainly due to the fact of its location; to the fact that bloodstained newspapers dated 24 August were found near the scene; and to the fact it was a torso, not an evisceration.

The Whitehall Mystery, as it was to become known, remains unsolved to this day.

And so the hysteria persisted. *The Morning Post* of 12 October 1888 reported that 'among the many rumours that were afloat in the course of yesterday was one to the effect that some person, signing himself "Jack the Ripper", had written on a shop window in the Commercial road the words, "I am coming again", and that the writing closely resembled that of the letter and post-card which have become public property'. The murders of Smith, Tabram, Chapman and Nichols had prompted escalating media interest, and the 'double event' of Stride and Eddowes brought an explosion of interest both nationally and internationally. This media storm merely added to the tension felt around Whitechapel, where every suspicious incident was reported as if it was connected to the murders. Once incident which caused a mini-furore in the area occurred under the railway arch on Brick Lane, near to the Pedley Street junction, in early October. A cab pulled up near to the arch, two men got out, and 'deposited upon the ground a woman who was insensible'.[18] The men were being watched by three others, who raised the alarm, so they clambered swiftly back into the cab and drove off. However, possibly concerned that he may be implicated with the recent murders, one of the two men, a man named Johnson, returned to the scene, where he was promptly apprehended and taken to Commercial Street police station.[19]

Whitechapel and its surrounds, during this period, became inundated with 'privateers', members of the public who acted as solo vigilantes, and who felt that they could go one step further than the police, and hunt down Jack the Ripper. Invariably, these men were a nuisance to the police; they were sometimes mistaken for being the killer himself, and were a constant waste of police time and resources. On 4 October, during the evening, John Kinsey Joseph was seen loitering outside the entrance to Mission Hall Court, in Shoreditch, where tea was being given out to some of the streetwalking girls. This roused an H Division constable's suspicion, so he approached him, and upon inspection, it was found that he was concealing a bayonet and sheath underneath his long, white, Melton coat. Joseph was taken to Commercial Street police station, where he explained that he was 'looking for the murderer, and would run him through'.[20]

On 22 October, H Division's Superintendent Arnold produced an overview report, explaining how his division was policing the district amid the crisis caused by 'Jack the Ripper'. In it, he explained that the beats in the affected portion of Whitechapel were 'small as compared with those in the adjoining Districts of Stepney, Shadwell & St. Georges, but it is impossible to at all times to keep a constable on each beat as owing to the number of men absent from duty from sickness, leave, attending Police Court, or Sessions, or employed on special duties, which are necessary, but which no provision has been made'.[21] Arnold stated in the report that he had insufficient numbers in reserve to reduce the impact that these other duties had on patrols, explaining that 'as a consequence, some of the Beats are necessarily lengthened, thus affording an opportunity for the commission of crime'.[22] To combat this, Arnold argued for an additional twenty-five men, with ten to be based at Leman Street station, ten at Commercial Street station, and the other five to be sent to Arbour Square station. However, Arnold recognised that permanently appointed men were not easily acquirable, and recommended that the twenty-five constables should be drawn on loan from other divisions.

Although the police were under a great strain during October 1888 – conducting enquiries and searches, interviewing suspects and following up leads – there were actually no murders during this month. And as the weeks passed, the people in Whitechapel calmed a little. However, this lull was not to last long into November; in fact, it was bought to an abrupt, horrific and awful end.

14

Mary Jane Kelly
9 November 1888

You will be all right for what I have told you.
Unidentified man to Mary Kelly, witnessed by
George Hutchinson, 9 November 1888

Sir Charles Warren tendered his resignation as Commissioner of the Metropolitan Police on 8 November 1888 – not, as many assume, due to his performance during the Whitechapel murders, but rather because of a personal point of principle. Warren had taken on the commissionership in 1886, when the public's opinion of the Metropolitan Police was at a low due to it having a reputation for being lax, ineffective and inefficient; so Warren assumed that his remit was to transform the force into a more disciplined and competent organisation from top to bottom. This did not go down too well with some serving officers who had preferred the previous, more relaxed leadership of Commissioner Henderson, and even less so with a radical press who saw some of Warren's decisions, and some of his actions, as an attempt to militarise the Metropolitan force. In their eyes, this was turning the policing organisation into an oppressor of the masses; however, Warren wasn't to be put off by this negativity, and ploughed on regardless. The Home Office were not ignorant of the prevailing public opinion, and felt Warren had misunderstood why he was brought in. Yes, they wanted discipline, structure, efficiency and results – but Warren, in their view (and, it seems, his own), felt that he had carte blanche control of the Metropolitan force, and considered his superior, Home Secretary Henry Matthews, to be an equal. This led to inevitable clashes between the two, with Warren's attempts to enforce some changes in policing order and method being met by the restraining hand of the Home Office, who wanted it to be understood that the police worked for them, rather than as equals with them.

Warren was, if nothing else, loyal to his men, and would defend them to the hilt – sometimes a little farther than maybe he should have done. The Endacott and Bloy incidents, in both of which he ultimately stood by his two constables (even going as far as to criticise the magistrate in police orders when Constable Bloy was disbelieved), show a dedication to his workforce. It was only natural for Warren to respond directly to recent public criticism of the police, and this he did in an article for *Murray's Magazine* entitled 'The Police of the Metropolis'; controversy, however, erupted when Warren failed to run this article by his superior, Home Secretary Matthews, prior to its publication. Warren felt there was no need to do this; he was the commissioner, the Metropolitan force was his responsibility, and therefore he was fully entitled to defend it against unwarranted attack. Besides, this bad press may have begun to affect the recruitment of good men; Warren certainly thought so. Matthews was unimpressed, and issued a reprimand via a memorandum. Warren, insulted at being treated in such a pompous way, offered his resignation, which was accepted without debate. However, the reality was that the article was merely the final straw for Warren. He also (more privately) objected to the appointment of James Monro (who had himself resigned as Warren's assistant in August 1888 due to constant clashes with his superior); to Special Branch Section D, which did not come under Warren's authority but reported directly to the Home Secretary; and to the watching brief which Monro kept on him on behalf of the Home Secretary. Matthews's reprimand finally pushed the Metropolitan Commissioner to the point of no return. The fact that Matthews was quick to accept Warren's resignation is an indication that he, too, was feeling the strain of their relationship; however, it was agreed that Warren should remain in post until 30 November, when a successor would be ready to take over – that successor being, of all people, James Monro.

On 9 November 1888, the day after Warren handed in his resignation, Inspector Walter Beck was the duty inspector at Commercial Street police station, when, at around 11 a.m., a man burst through the main doors, quickly followed by another. The two men approached Inspector Beck and informed him of what they had just witnessed, and, upon hearing their words, the inspector grabbed his kepi, placed it upon his head, gathered a small posse of constables, and swiftly went with the pair to a small street in Spitalfields, just behind the market, named Dorset Street. Dorset Street ran west off Commercial Street from almost opposite Christ Church, and was a mixture of common lodging houses, public houses and courts.[1] Within one of these courts, Millers Court to be exact, were a series of small rented dwellings, known as McCarthy's rents, run by one of the men in the inspector's presence, John McCarthy. McCarthy and the other man (an employee of his named Thomas Bowyer) guided Inspector Beck and his men down the narrow alleyway which opened out into the court, passing a dirty door on their right, and a gas lamp on their left, before coming into the court itself. The pair swung immediately right, and motioned to Beck to look through a broken windowpane into one of the rooms. The inspector peered into the room and saw, laid upon the bed, the terribly mutilated body of a local prostitute whom McCarthy named as Mary Jane Kelly. One of the constables who claimed to be with Inspector Beck at this moment was Walter Dew, and he described how he 'tried the door. It would not yield. So I moved to the window, over which, on the inside, an old coat was hanging to act as a curtain and to block the draught from the hole in the glass'. He later stated that the sight before him was 'indescribable'.[2]

Some fifteen minutes previously, Bowyer had called upon Kelly in order to collect the rent she owed, and, upon receiving no reply to his knock upon the door, went around to the window and looked in. It must have taken Bowyer a moment or two to comprehend that what he was seeing was a terrible murder scene, but, once it registered, he left in panic for his boss, John McCarthy, whom he brought back to Millers Court to see the sight for himself. Once he had viewed the scene, McCarthy sent Bowyer off to Commercial Street police station to raise the hue and cry while he took a minute to compose himself before setting off after his employee.[3] The mutilations upon the victim's body were widespread, and very extreme, and it was plain to anyone who viewed the scene that she was beyond any aid. However, once he saw the situation, Inspector Beck moved into action. He sent for inspectors Abberline and Reid, and ordered that a telegram, allegedly containing the words 'The woman is simply cut to pieces', be issued to all stations.[4] Beck also sent for H Division surgeon Dr Bagster Phillips, from Spital Square, before instructing his constables to close off Dorset Street at each end, and to await further orders. Dr Bagster Phillips arrived at 11.15 a.m. and, having peered through the broken windowpane, was 'satisfied that the mutilated corpse lying on the bed was not in need of any immediate attention from me'.[5] Accordingly, he delayed taking any further action until the arrival, at 11.30 a.m., of Inspector Abberline. Upon entering the court, Abberline immediately liaised with both Inspector Beck and the doctor. Abberline was to later state, at the inquest, that Inspector Beck had informed him that he had already requested the presence of bloodhounds, and that Dr Bagster Phillips had suggested that they should hold back from breaking the door in to gain access, to avoid contaminating the scene with their scent, pending the arrival of these hounds. So Abberline decided that nothing more should be done until then.

On 12 September, less than a week after the murder of Annie Chapman and a little over a fortnight before the double event, a Mr L. F. S. Maberly of Dublin had sent a letter to the *Morning Advertiser*. 'Sir,' he wrote, 'Knowing by experience the sagacity and keen sense of smell of the bloodhound, I would strongly urge upon the Government the propriety of testing their powers in discovering crime.'[6] In addition, 'E.P.', from Bayswater, also wrote to the *Morning Advertiser*, claiming, 'I feel sure that, had the police been provided with a hound and a good horse, the Whitechapel murderer would have been found within six hours.'[7] However, it was a letter to *The Times* on 1 October 1888, from Mr Percy Lindley of Essex, which triggered the police's interest in the use of bloodhounds as an investigatory tool. Mr Lindley wrote,

> Sir, – With regard to the suggestion that bloodhounds might assist in tracking the East-end murderer, as a breeder of bloodhounds, and knowing their

power, I have little doubt that, had a hound been put upon the scent of the murderer while fresh, it might have done what the police have failed in. But now, when all trace of the scent has been trodden out, it would be quite useless.

Meanwhile, as no means of detection should be left untried, it would be well if a couple or so of trained bloodhounds – unless trained they would be worthless – were kept for a time at one of the police head-quarters ready for immediate use in case their services should be called for. There are, doubtless, owners of bloodhounds willing to lend them, if any of the police, which, I fear, is improbable, know how to use them.[8]

This letter was clipped and kept on Home Office files,[9] along with an exchange of correspondence between the Home Office and the Metropolitan force debating the cost and use of such hounds; however, eventually authorisation was given by the Home Office for the Metropolitan Police to spend £50 for the remainder of the financial year in the hiring and keeping of a bloodhound for police use. Commissioner Warren's idea, no doubt spurred on by the recent success of Smoker in locating human remains inside unfinished construction works at New Scotland Yard, was for a dog to be housed by a private veterinary assigned to the police, Mr A. J. Sewell, and to be turned out for duty as and when required. However, Warren wanted to see a bloodhound in action first, and so he turned to one of the best bloodhound breeders in the world.

Edwin Brough was a silk manufacturer who hailed from a small village called Scalby Mills, just outside the famous Victorian seaside town of Scarborough, and he was world renowned for breeding champion bloodhounds. Warren contacted Brough in early October 1888, proposing to trial Brough's hounds for the Metropolitan Police's use, and so Brough agreed to travel to London with two of his best, Burgho and Barnaby, for these trials. Brough doubted whether his dogs could work in a city like London. 'Personally,' he said, 'I didn't have much faith in the experiment, for the hounds had to run on a cold pavement, and there was no certainty of being able to lay them on the line of the right man. I took the dogs up as much to please the public as for any other reason.'[10] The trials were set for two days, commencing on 9 October, in Regent's Park and Hyde Park, with Warren himself acting as the 'hunted man'. Brough was dismayed at the ignorance shown by the public as to how his hounds worked, stating, 'They seemed to think that the police had only to take a bloodhound to the place where a murder had been committed, weeks or months before, and the animal would at once scent out the trail of the murderer in preference to thousands of other passers-by, and run the man down.'[11] Warren had a little more faith, to the point that he had an agreement drawn up between himself and the Metropolitan Police's vet, Sewell, setting out arrangements to keep Barnaby. It seems that he wasn't completely committed, however, as the contract remained unsigned. Warren ultimately planned to hire Barnaby, at a cost of £25, for the remainder of the financial year, while purchasing a new pup at the same time for £15. The idea was that it would be trained alongside Barnaby, eventually replacing the older hound in the March of 1889.

Matters stalled in the weeks following that October trial, because Sewell, who was acting in liaison with Commissioner Warren, had problems finding a company which would insure Barnaby against accident or death; by 2 November he had managed to find one, though certain stumbling blocks remained.[12] The Home Office had only permitted the insurance of a dog up to the sum of £100, and the cheapest Sewell could get was £150: Warren and the Home Office had to decide whether it was worth exceeding the agreed amount. Another matter compounding the situation was that, before completely committing to the idea of bloodhounds, Warren wanted to test the dogs out properly in Whitechapel; the plan was to wait for another murder. However, as October passed, no murders occurred, so Brough, frustrated at what he deemed dallying by Scotland Yard, returned to Scarborough with his dogs, Burgho and Barnaby, on 1 November. Sewell was optimistic that Brough would 'send it [Barnaby] back again when everything was arranged'.[13] Within days of Brough returning home with his dogs, however, the murder occurred in Millers Court, which later led Brough to boastfully claim that his dogs had kept Jack the Ripper away: 'This I consider some evidence of the deterrent effect which the employment of bloodhounds would have on crime, for another of the ghastly Jack the Ripper tragedies was committed shortly after it was known that the hounds had been sent back to Wyndyate.'[14]

By contrast, it would seem that Abberline and those waiting for the bloodhounds in Dorset Street were unaware that the dogs were now over 200 miles away, and had not been informed of the change of plan. While they were waiting, more medical men arrived on the scene, including Dr John Rees Gabe and City of London Police divisional surgeon Dr Frederick Gordon Brown, the latter of whom had viewed the body of the previous victim, Catherine Eddowes, in Mitre Square. Only with the arrival of H Division's Superintendent Arnold at 1.30 p.m. were the assembled parties informed that the dogs were not coming, and that access to the room should now be obtained. The locked door was promptly broken open, apparently by Kelly's landlord John McCarthy with his axe. First inside was Dr Bagster Phillips, followed by the plethora of medics and senior members of the police, stepping into a scene which most of them would recall for many years to come.[15] Bagster Phillips, at the inquest, described entering the room, and what lay before him:

> On the door being opened it knocked against a table, the table I found close to the left-hand side of the bedstead, and the bedstead was close up against the wooden partition, the mutilated remains of a female were lying two-thirds over towards the edge of the bedstead, nearest the door of entry, she had only he under linen garment on her, and from my subsequent examination I am sure the body had been removed subsequent to the injury which caused death

from that side of the bedstead which was nearest to the wooden partition. The large quantity of blood under the bedstead, the saturated condition of the palliasse, pillow, and sheet at the top corner of the bedstead nearest to the partition leads me to the conclusion that the severance of the right carotid artery, which was the immediate cause of death, was inflicted while the deceased was lying at the right side of the bedstead and her head and neck in the top right-hand corner.[16]

At 12.30 p.m., while Bagster Phillips was conducting his initial examination of Kelly in her Millers Court room, Warren, who had resigned his position but was still in post, notified the Home Office of the murder in Spitalfields, and informed them that Assistant Commissioner Anderson was assuming the commissioner's responsibility in the matter. Upon his return to London in October, one of Anderson's first contributions to the investigation into the Whitechapel murders had been to gain the assistance of Dr Thomas Bond, divisional surgeon for A Division Whitehall, giving him the special remit to attend any further murder scenes and express his opinion. So, upon hearing the news of another murder in Whitechapel, Dr Bond also made his way over to Millers Court, along with his assistant Dr Charles Hebbert, to render his assistance to Dr Bagster Phillips and the other doctors at the scene.[17] Bond's post-mortem report on Kelly's body, which was lost at an unknown date in the distant past and only rediscovered in 1987, contains some inaccuracies, such as the claim that she was naked; however, it does describe the harrowing spectacle before him at Millers Court, as well as detailing the wounds upon the body:

The body was lying naked in the middle of the bed, the shoulders flat but the axis of the body inclined to the left side of the bed. The head was turned on the left cheek. The left arm was close to the body with the forearm flexed at a right angle & lying across the abdomen, the right arm was slightly abducted from the body and rested on the mattress, the elbow was bent & the forearm supine with the fingers clenched. The legs were wide apart, the left thigh at right angles to the trunk & the right forming an obtuse angle with the pubes.

The whole of the surface of the abdomen & thighs was removed & the abdominal cavity emptied of its viscera. The breasts were cut off, the arms mutilated by several jagged wounds & the face hacked beyond recognition of the features & the tissues of the neck were severed all round down to the bone. The viscera were found in various parts viz: the uterus & kidneys with one breast under the head, the other breast by the right foot, the liver between the feet, the intestines by the right side & the spleen by the left side of the body. – The flaps removed from the abdomen and thighs were on a table.

The bed clothing at the right corner was saturated with blood, & on the floor beneath was a pool of blood covering about 2 feet square. The wall by the right side of the bed & in a line with the neck was marked by blood which had struck it in a number of separate splashes.

Bond then continues with his description of the post mortem:

The face was gashed in all directions, the nose, cheeks, eyebrows, & ears being partly removed. The lips were blanched & cut by several incisions running obliquely down to the chin. There were also numerous cuts extending irregularly across all the features.

The neck was cut through the skin & other tissues right down to the vertebrae, the 5th & 6th being deeply notched. The skin cuts in the front of the neck showed distinct ecchymosis.

The air passage was cut at the lower part of the larynx through the cricoid cartilage.

Both breasts were more or less removed by circular incisions, the muscle down to the ribs being attached to the breasts. The intercostals between the 4th, 5th & 6th ribs were cut through & the contents of the thorax visible through the openings.

The skin & tissues of the abdomen from the costal arch to the pubes were removed in three large flaps. The right thigh was denuded in front to the bone, the flap of skin, including the external organs of generation, & part of the right buttock. The left thigh was stripped of skin fascia, & muscles as far as the knee.

The left calf showed a long gash through skin & tissues to the deep muscles and reaching from the knee to 5 ins above the ankle. Both arms & forearms had extensive jagged wounds.

The right thumb showed a small superficial incision about 1 inch long, with extravasation of blood in the skin, & there were several abrasions on the back of the hand moreover showing the same condition.

On opening the thorax it was found that the right lung was minimally adherent by old firm adhesions. The lower part of the lung was broken & torn away. The left lung was intact. It was adherent at the apex & there were a few adhesions over the side. In the substances of the lung there were several nodules of consolidation.

The pericardium was open below & the heart absent.

In the abdominal cavity there was some partly digested food of fish & potatoes, & similar food was found in the remains of the stomach attached to the intestines.[18]

Dr Bond's words alone cannot completely express the destruction the killer had wrought upon Mary Kelly's body. Even her former boyfriend, Joseph Barnett, with whom she was still in contact right up until her death, could only formally identify her by her 'ear and eyes'.[19] Therefore, to preserve the scene eternally, and before any proper examination of the room took place, the police turned to a relatively new mode of evidence gathering: photography.

Earlier in the century, one of the forefathers of police forensics, Alphonse Bertillon, had recognised the impact that photographing habitual criminals could have on the investigation of future crimes. Scotland Yard initially adopted Bertillon's idea with their Habitual Criminals Register, but Bertillon was also experimenting with the idea of crime scene photography, the preservation of the crime scene on photographic plate, and its potential use as evidence during trial. Again Scotland Yard followed suit, and a photographer was called to the scene in Millers Court. An external shot of the room was taken from the court, and, going inside, probably the most recognised crime scene photograph in the world was captured – that of Kelly upon her bed.

Assistant Commissioner Anderson, with Commissioner Warren's authority, had, toward the end of October, sent Dr Bond all the medical and inquest information in relation to the previous victims, which enabled Bond to provide Anderson with a profile on the killer, one of the first of its kind ever produced. In a report he compiled for Anderson, written just a day after Kelly's murder, and after he had attended her post-mortem, Bond concluded that the killer would 'probably be solitary and eccentric in his habits' – characteristics which, in other circumstances, might have suited him for a career in writing non-fiction books – and, though it has been acutely debated over the many years since the murders, his report does make fascinating reading:

7 The Sanctuary Westminster Abbey – Nov: 10 88
Dear Sir
I beg to report that I have read the notes of the 4 Whitechapel Murders viz:
1. Buck's Row.
2. Hanbury Street.
3. Berner's Street.
4. Mitre Square.

I have also made a Post Mortem Examination of the mutilated remains of a woman found yesterday in a small room in Dorset Street

1. All five murders were no doubt committed by the same hand. In the first four the throats appear to have been cut from left to right. In the last case owing to the extensive mutilation it is impossible to say in what direction the fatal cut was made, but arterial blood was found on the wall in splashes close to where the woman's head must have been lying.

2. All the circumstances surrounding the murders lead me to form the opinion that the women must have been lying down when murdered and in every case the throat was first cut.

3. In the four murders of which I have seen the notes only, I cannot form a very definite opinion as to the time that had elapsed between the murder and the discovering of the body.

In one case, that of Berner's Street, the discovery appears to have been made immediately after the deed – In Buck's Row, Hanbury Street, and Mitre Square three or four hours only could have elapsed. In the Dorset Street case the body was lying on the bed at the time of my visit, 2 o'clock, quite naked and mutilated as in the annexed report

Rigor Mortis had set in, but increased during the progress of the examination. From this it is difficult to say with any degree of certainty the exact time that had elapsed since death as the period varies from 6 to 12 hours before rigidity sets in. The body was comparatively cold at 2 o'clock and the remains of a recently taken meal were found in the stomach and scattered about over the intestines. It is, therefore, pretty certain that the woman must have been dead about 12 hours and the partly digested food would indicate: that death took place about 3 or 4 hours after the food was taken, so one or two o'clock in the morning would be the probable time of the murder.

4. In all the cases there appears to be no evidence of struggling [*sic*] and the attacks were probably so sudden and made in such a position that the women could neither resist nor cry out. In the Dorset Street case the corner of the sheet to the right of the woman's head was much cut and saturated with blood, indicating that the face may have been covered with the sheet at the time of the attack.

5. In the four first cases the murderer must have attacked from the right side of the victim. In the Dorset Street case, he must have attacked from in front or from the left, as there would be no room for him between the wall and the part of the bed on which the woman was lying. Again, the blood had flowed down on the right side of the woman and spurted on to the wall.

6. The murderer would not necessarily be splashed or deluged with blood, but his hands' and arms must have been covered and parts of his clothing must certainly have been smeared with blood.

7. The mutilations in each case excepting the Berner's Street one were all of the same character and shewed clearly that in all the murders, the object was mutilation.

8. In each case the mutilation was inflicted by a person who had no scientific nor anatomical knowledge. In my opinion be does not even possess the technical knowledge of a butcher or horse slaughterer or any person accustomed to cut up dead animals.

9. The instrument must have been a strong knife at least six inches long, very sharp, pointed at the top and about an inch in width. It may have been a clasp knife, a butcher's knife or a surgeon's knife. I think it was no doubt a straight knife.

10. The murderer must have been a man of physical strength and of great coolness and daring. There is no evidence that he had an accomplice. He must in my opinion be a man subject to periodical attacks of Homicidal and erotic mania. The character of the mutilations indicate that the man may be in a condition sexually, that may be called satyriasis. It is of course possible that the Homicidal impulse may have developed from a revengeful or brooding condition of the mind, or that Religious Mania may have been the original disease, but I do not think either hypothesis is likely. The murderer in external appearance is quite likely to be a quiet inoffensive looking man probably middleaged and neatly and respectably dressed. I think he must be in the habit of wearing a cloak or overcoat or he could hardly have escaped notice in the streets if the blood on his hands or clothes were visible.

11. Assuming the murderer to be such a person as I have just described he would probably be solitary and eccentric in his habits, also he is most likely to be a man without regular occupation, but with some small income or pension. He is possibly living among respectable persons who have some knowledge of his character and habits and who may have grounds for suspicion that he is not quite right in his mind at times. Such persons would probably be unwilling to communicate suspicions to the Police for fear of trouble or notoriety, whereas if there were a prospect of reward it might overcome their scruples.

I am, Dear Sir,

Yours faithfully,

Thos. Bond.[20]

Having a profile on the killer was all well and good; however, it did not capture a serial killer. The basis for any investigation starts at the scene of crime; therefore, Abberline took complete charge of Millers Court with the intention of performing a meticulous evidence-gathering search, starting with the taking of a detailed inventory of all the items in the room. He noted that the kettle in the fireplace had had its spout melted off, indicating that the fire in the grate had been extremely hot at one stage. The remains of burnt clothing were found among the ashes of the fire; a candle inside a broken wine glass was also noted, along with a clay pipe, which Kelly's former boyfriend claimed was his; and many other items including furniture were listed. As well as obtaining a photographic record of Millers Court, Abberline also called in the services of a former schoolmaster from Waltham Abbey, thirty-four-year-old Inspector Charles Ledger of G Division Finsbury, and requested that he draw plans of the room for use at the inquest; both the inventory and the plans are now, unfortunately, missing from Kelly's murder file.

While Abberline and his men were working inside the room, enquiries were being made at the other rented rooms which surrounded this small court. Mrs Elizabeth Prater, who rented the room above Kelly's, stated that she was woken by two or three screams of 'Murder!' sometime between 3.00 a.m. and 4.00 a.m., but did not pay much heed to them as such screams were often heard in the neighbourhood.[21] Mary Ann Cox, a widow and self-confessed prostitute, who lived on the left-hand side of the court, at the far end, stated that she saw Kelly at around midnight, as she walked from Commercial Street, into Dorset Street and so into Millers Court, engaging with Kelly as she went into her room and saying goodnight. Cox said Kelly was 'very drunk, and could scarcely answer me',[22] and she also gave H Division CID a description of a potential suspect, because Cox revealed that Kelly was not alone. Accompanying her was a man, also drunk and carrying a quart can of beer, whom Cox described as 'about 36 years old, about 5ft 5in high, complexion fresh and I [Cox] believe he had blotches on his face, small side whiskers, and a thick carroty moustache, dressed in shabby dark clothes, dark overcoat and felt'.[23]

Throughout the day, H Division's Detective Sergeant Thick led the enquiries being made in Dorset Street itself,[24] with its wealth of lodging houses holding, according to the *Daily Telegraph*, 600 registered beds.[25] The reality was that over a thousand people were crammed into this very small street. Visits were made to the crime scene by some of the most senior constables in the Metropolitan force, with the chief constable for the Eastern District, Colonel Monsell, arriving at the court, accompanied by fellow chief constables A. C. Howard and Lieutenant-Colonel Roberts. Assistant Commissioner Anderson also visited the scene, arriving by cab at around 1.50 p.m., and he stayed in the room for quite some time.[26] At 3.50 p.m. a furniture van, covered with a tarpaulin, was allowed into Dorset Street, through the massed crowds and police cordon, pulling up outside the entrance to Millers Court. Eventually, sometime after 4.00 p.m., the doctors left the scene, and a battered coffin shell was taken off the back of the van, from under the tarpaulin, and carried through the court entrance. This caused some excitement among the crowd at the Commercial Street end of Dorset Street, because they knew that Mary Kelly was about to be taken from her room, and some successfully rushed through the blue police line to gather around the van, seeking to show their respects. Sometime later the coffin shell returned, covered in a ragged cloth, containing what remained of Mary Kelly; she was loaded onto the rear of the van before being wheeled away in silence to the Shoreditch mortuary in St Leonard's churchyard, as men doffed their caps and women stood in tears.[27]

Commercial Street, the main thoroughfare which lies at the eastern end of Dorset Street, was in the midst of some major alterations during the period of the Whitechapel murders, with the construction of the horse-drawn North Metropolitan Tramway line (running from Bloomsbury to Poplar) causing some disruption along the street.[28] This, of course, had to be policed by the men of H Division, who redirected all horse-drawn traffic away from Commercial Street so that the work could be undertaken; there had been some loss of business in and around Commercial Street, although the influx of 'navvies' brought in to undertake the laying of the rails may have kept prostitutes' profits up. All this, of course, impacted on the later investigation – so many male strangers were now milling around in the area of Dorset Street, the majority looking for a good time, and this only created more bodies for the police to interview and process. However, according to Kelly's landlord, she was in rent arrears to the fairly large amount of twenty-nine shillings, around seven weeks' worth of rent, so it is possible that this tramway construction work did actually affect Kelly's earnings. A measure of this financial desperation was also evident in the evidence given by one man, George Hutchinson.

Hutchinson, a labourer, walked into Commercial Street police station at around 6.00 p.m. on Monday 12 November 1888, stating he may have witnessed something of significance with regard to the Kelly murder. Sergeant 31H Edward Badham, in the presence of Inspector Abberline, took his statement. Hutchinson claimed that he had returned to Whitechapel from Romford, where he had been looking for work, arriving back during the early hours of 9 November. He immediately went to the Victoria Home on Commercial Street to find a bed for the night, but the home was closed, so Hutchinson took to the streets, and at around 2.00 a.m. he had just passed Thrawl Street on the east side of Commercial Street, and was heading toward Flower and Dean Street, when he came across Mary Kelly. The following is a transcription of Hutchinson's witness statement, which explains what occurred – at least, according to Hutchinson:

Commercial Street
Metropolitan Police H Division 12 November 1888
Special Report Reference to papers Re murder
At 6pm 12 George Hutchinson of the Victoria Home Commercial Street came to this station and made the following statement about 2. am I was coming by Thrawl Street, Commercial Street, and just before I got to Flower and Dean Street I met the murdered woman Kelly, and she said to me Hutchinson will you lend me sixpence. I said I cant I have spent all my money going down to Romford she said good morning I must go and find some money, she went away toward Thrawl Street, a man coming in the opposite direction to Kelly tapped her on the shoulder and said something to her they both burst out laughing. I heard her say alright to him and the man said you will be alright for what I have told you, he then placed his right hand around her shoulders. He also had a kind of a small parcel in his left hand, with a kind of a strap around it. I stood against the lamp of the ~~Ten Bells~~ Queens Head Public House, and watched him. They both then came past me and the man hid down his head, with his hat over his eyes. I stooped down and looked in the face. He looked at me stern. They both went into Dorset Street I followed them, they both stood at the corner of the court for about 3 minutes. He said something to her, she said alright my dear come along you will be comfortable. He then placed his arm on her shoulder and gave her a kiss. She said she had lost her handkerchief, he then pulled his handkerchief a red one out and gave it to her, they both then went up the Court together. I then went to the court to see if I could see them but could not. I stood there for about three quarters of an hour, to see if they came out, they did not so I went away.

Circulate to all stations Description age about 34 or 35, height 5ft 6 Complexion pale, dark eyes and eye lashes ~~dark~~ slight moustache, curled up each end, and hair dark, very surley [*sic*] looking dress, long, dark coat, collar and cuffs trimmed astracan [*sic*], and a dark jacket under, light waist coat, dark trousers dark felt hat turned down in the middle button boots and gaiters with white buttons, wore a very thick gold chain white linen collar, black tie with horse shoe pin, respectable appearance walked very sharp. Jewish appearance can be identified

George Hutchinson E Badham Sergt E Ellisdon Insp Submitted FG Abberline Insp J Arnold Sup

Witness statements were commonly taken down in writing by a policeman, either upon special report form No. 6 (the divisional form, blue in colour) or No. 7 (the Central Office form, buff in colour); or within the policeman's pocketbook, and later transcribed word for word upon the relevant form. The policeman, with the witness dictating, must include the witness's words only, and not any of his own. The taking of statements has evolved over the years, due to the huge significance of witness testimony in trials – the sanctity of the process by which information is obtained can be the deciding factor between guilt and innocence. Author and true-crime authority Stewart P. Evans, a former police constable with nigh-on thirty years' experience taking police statements, affirms that 'the taking of witness statements is one of the most important practical areas for the investigating police officer',[29] and it is imperative that the information contained on the witness statement is correctly noted down. There is a skill in obtaining the pertinent information for a statement, and that skill lies in the asking of the correct questions, with open-ended questions commonly used to gain information, and closed questions used for clarification.

The decision about when to take the statement is obviously important; the sooner the statement is taken, the fresher the witness's memory and the better his recall. Today, witness interviews are conducted, typically unbeknown to the witness, in one of two differing styles: the cognitive interview, or the management of conversation interview. The cognitive interview draws on four stages, which may or may not all be used. These are:

The reconstruction of events, which enables the witness to recount the event in general and in their own words.

The clarification that every piece of information has been passed on to the statement taker. This is an attempt to establish if any information has been held back by the witness, perhaps unwittingly, or because the witness deems it irrelevant, although it may be vital.

The recalling of the event but in a different order. This establishes which part of the event the witness feels was particularly significant to them and is often the clearest part of their recollection. The order of the event can be built around this one clear point, and is most commonly something unusual or frightening noticed by the witness.

A change of perspective. This involves the describing of the incident through the eyes of another, which gives a sense of emotion during the event, and therefore intention.

The cognitive interview also covers five areas of recall, speech characteristics, conversation, physical appearance, and names and numbers.[30] We can see that the majority of these five areas were covered in many of the witness statements taken in connection with the Whitechapel murders, including Hutchinson's. Conversation ('she said alright my dear come along you will be comfortable'), physical appearance ('respectable appearance, walked very sharp'), names (Kelly, street names, etc.) and numbers (times of sighting) are all covered in his testimony, with the only area remaining uncovered being speech characteristics. Conversation management, like the cognitive interview, allows the witness to recount the event in general. While the witness is describing what happened, the statement taker will take notes on key aspects of the event, and expands on them later during what is known as the review stage.

A good rapport between the witness and statement taker is essential, and helps to generate a concise, reliable statement. Things like appearance, relaxed body language, a show of interest, and even a little off-topic conversation about the weather, for example, can help put the witness at ease, and enable them to open up. Body language also assists the statement taker; it can give them clues as to whether the witness is nervous, angry or telling the truth, or whether they hold a particular bias against someone or something. Reviewing the statements in connection to these murders, one can see that some of these modern aspects of statement taking were covered; however, more information could still have been obtained. Stewart P. Evans, in his assessment of Hutchinson's witness statement in 'Suspect and Witness – The Police Viewpoint', points out numerous examples of 'poor practice', such as that Hutchinson never really gives us an idea of distances between himself and the couple, or himself and various locations. This information would help us to establish precise locations, and movements, as well as establishing a perspective on what Hutchinson could actually see and hear. Evans also points out, quite correctly, that the size of the parcel which Kelly's companion was carrying is not described. This could have been vital; maybe it was a weapon.[31] Even the construction of the parcel could have been significant; for example, as the reader may recall, Constable Smith, when patrolling Berner Street just prior to Elisabeth Stride's murder, saw Stride with a man who also was carrying a newspaper parcel. This was a similar scenario to the one described by Hutchinson, and CID ought to have found the connection worth noting. Clearly such matters were either deemed unimportant to the Victorian policeman, or taken as read, and it is easy to find fault from today's perspective. However, Hutchinson's statement cannot escape criticism, because these small and fairly obvious errors could have been corrected, and the missing information restored to the narrative of events.

Once the statement was written down, it was then read either by the witness or to the witness, with any errors being pointed out and rectified. Nothing was to be erased completely, or rendered illegible; a simple line would be placed through the error so that the original text could still be viewed. Again, going back to Hutchinson's statement, we see that this occurred twice, with a line running through the erroneous 'Ten Bells' before the correction 'Queens Head', and 'eye lashes dark' altered to just 'eye lashes'. Once it had been read and its contents agreed, each page of a statement was then signed by the witness. Hutchinson provided a differing signature on each of the three pages, and this may have been an indication of the level of Hutchinson's literacy, but this was still unusual in a single document. Another explanation for the discrepancy is that Hutchinson only signed one page; in this speculative variation, Sergeant Badham forgot to obtain all three signatures, and himself added the other signatures when he realised the error after Hutchinson had left. Obviously, this is not what Badham should have done; he should have recalled Hutchinson and asked him to re-read the statement and sign it, or otherwise taken a completely fresh statement, ensuring that, this time, Hutchinson added his signature to all the pages.

Despite this poor statement – which included the rather outlandish physical description of the man Hutchinson had seen with Kelly, a description which some students of the case believe shows that Hutchinson's description is a false one – Inspector Abberline still put his faith in this man's testimony. This was mainly due to the fact Abberline himself had 'interrogated' Hutchinson at Commercial Street police station, adding, 'I am of opinion his statement is true. He informed me that he had occasionally given the deceased a few shillings, and that he had known her about 3 years.'[32] Abberline also had the statement circulated to all stations, and even went as far as seconding two plain-clothes officers to accompany Hutchinson in touring through H Division with the intention of seeing if he could spot the man he described. Hutchinson and the policemen toured, but to no avail, and the man was never identified.

As with the previous murders, any incident involving an assault was pounced upon as being a murderous assault by 'Jack the Ripper' – and some incidents were classified this way by the victims themselves. At 9.00 a.m. on 21 November 1888, a few weeks after Kelly had been found, Annie Farmer's screams could be heard emanating from a lodging house in George Street, Whitechapel. Moments later, a man burst out into the street from the same building. 'What a — cow!' he was heard to exclaim, before disappearing. Farmer's throat was slightly cut, and she claimed that she had just survived a murderous attack by 'Jack the Ripper'. Investigations by H Division CID led them to conclude that Farmer had fabricated part of the story; she had brought a man back to her lodging house, but stole some money from him, bizarrely storing it in her mouth. He attempted to retrieve the money, and in the melee she lightly cut her own throat, falsely claiming that she had been attacked by the man. The man, foreseeing a potential lynching for being 'Jack the Ripper', decided to flee the scene and was, understandably, never to be seen again.

As November finished the frequency of the murders diminished, and subsequent incidents did not match those of the intense period between late August and early November 1888. However, the spectre of an uncaught murderer hung over H Division, and the reports of further murders which occurred in their jurisdiction were almost always prefixed with the words 'Another horrible murder in Whitechapel', or something to that effect. It would be a little time yet before the men of H Division could step down their search for 'Jack the Ripper'.

15

After the Canon
1888–1891

Should the words 'Whitechapel Again!' be wired from Scotland Yard it is
to be understood that a murder had been committed and the information
is to be immediately given to the police on duty that they may exercise the
greatest possible vigilance.

Memorandum issued to all
City of London police stations, 25 July 1889

As with the preceding murders, that of Mary Kelly brought a fresh explosion of negative newspaper coverage, with the radical press mainly demanding to know what action the police were taking to capture the fiend now known as 'Jack the Ripper'. The reality was that, despite the perspective of these damning news reports, H Division had a dedicated team constantly working on the Whitechapel murders, with *The Times*, reporting on the Monday after Kelly's murder, highlighting CID's ongoing enquiries since the 'double event' of 30 September:

Sergeants Thicke [*sic*], Godley, M'Carthy, and Pearce have been constantly engaged, under the direction of Inspector Abberline (Scotland-yard), in prosecuting inquiries, but, unfortunately, up to the present time without any practical result. As an instance of the magnitude of their labours, each officer has had, on average, during the last six weeks to make some 30 separate inquiries weekly, and these have had to be made in different portions of the metropolis and suburbs. Since the two above-mentioned murders no fewer than 1,400 letters relating to the tragedies have been received by the police, and although the greater portion of these gratuitous communications were found to be of a trivial or even ridiculous character, still each one was thoroughly investigated. On Saturday many more letters were received, and these are now being inquired into. The detective officers, who are now subjected to a great amount of harassing work, complain that the authorities do not allow them sufficient means with which to carry on their investigations.[1]

The Metropolitan's new commissioner, James Monro, also pointed out, in a report to the Home Office dated 7 December 1888, that 'one Inspector, 9 Sergeants and 126 Constables from the uniform branch of the Force have been employed specially in plain clothes to patrol the neighbourhood of the Murders with a view to prevent a repetition of the crime',[2] adding that many of these plain-clothes men came from other divisions within the Metropolitan force, meaning that they were working in an area they did not know, that they had the inconvenience of having to travel some distance from their homes to get to H Division, and that the labour was mainly continuous and dull night duty. He admitted that 'the work is specially irksome and unpleasant, and these men are practically doing the duty of permanent patrols'.[3] To compensate for this, Monro successfully argued that those who undertook these plain-clothes patrols within the Whitechapel area should have an increase of pay to a shilling a day for every day out of uniform;[4] despite agreeing, the Home Office also stipulated that the Metropolitan force had a limited budget of £300 for this special duty. Anything over this amount would have to be reviewed.

While Thick, Godley, McCarthy and Pearce were constantly engaged on the Whitechapel murders, the rest of H Division CID still had other matters to deal with. Just over a fortnight after Kelly's murder, on 27 November 1888, a stabbing took place near Kelly's former residence in Dorset Street. Henry Buckley, of No. 26, knifed a man named Manning in the thigh. Manning, who was with a female at the time, had just arrived at 37 Dorset Street, having taken a cab with the woman from Euston Road when Buckley assaulted him. Manning was taken to the London Hospital with a serious but not life-threatening injury, whereas Buckley was arrested and held at Commercial Street police station pending his trial. Charles Akehurst had also been arrested a week a prior to this event. He had roused suspicion when he entered a 'house of doubtful repute' in Flower and Dean Street, and made certain remarks which so offended the women there that they contacted H Division, who promptly arrived from Commercial Street and arrested him, only to release him a short time later without charge.

The final Whitechapel 'murder' of 1888 is a contentious one, as there is some doubt as to the cause of Catherine Mylett's death in mid-December 1888. Mylett, a twenty-nine-year-old Irish Cockney who was also known as Rose, was found dead some miles away from Whitechapel, in Clark's Yard, just off Poplar High Street, by Police Sergeant 26K Robert Golding, and Constable 470K Barrett, both of Bow Division. Sergeant Golding spotted her body in the long, narrow entrance to the yard, and went over with Constable Barrett to assess the situation. He initially thought that she had passed out, fallen, and died on the spot. K Division surgeon Dr Matthew Brownfield was called for; however, he was unavailable, so his assistant Dr George Harris went in his place.[5] Dr Harris noted that, apart from a little blood and mucus emanating from her nose, there were no signs of a violent assault upon the body, and later, after the body had been ordered to be taken to the mortuary, Constable Barrett stated that he took a look at the neck, and confirmed that he could find no signs of a mark. When the mortuary keeper and coroner's officer, Thomas Curtain Chivers, inspected the body, however, he claimed a mark around the neck was indeed visible. Commissioner Monro ordered his assistant, Anderson, to investigate the situation, with Metropolitan divisional surgeon-in-chief Dr Alexander MacKellar and Dr Bond's assistant Dr Charles Hebbert conducting a further examination upon Mylett's body. Both doctors concluded that Mylett had died of strangulation. H Division's surgeon, Dr Bagster Phillips, also examined the body, and agreed with MacKellar and Hebbert, even going so far as to privately declare that Mylett had been killed by the same hand as Annie Chapman. Dr Bond, who viewed the body five days later, did not agree with his colleagues, going along with Sergeant Golding's assessment of her death, and stating that Mylett, when drunk, had passed out in an awkward position, and asphyxiated on the high collar of her own dress. The inquest jury, who had the final say, officially returned a verdict of 'wilful murder by person or persons unknown'; however, the death of Catherine Mylett still attracts debate to this day.

Despite there being no Whitechapel murders for the next six months, H Division, along with the denizens of the area, were still cautious. January 1889 saw H Division exceed the agreed amount of £300 for the funding of special duty patrols, and they reported to the Home Office that they had already spent £306 13s. Commissioner Monro asked Whitehall for permission to spend a further £200 until the end of March 1889;[6] however, he was only granted a further £51, to cover the predicted overspend only. As March changed to April, then May, and as May moved on to June, the murders seemed to have ceased, and the people of Whitechapel started to feel a little easier. Then, in July, for the first time in over eight months, a woman's body was found in Castle Alley with her throat cut, and it seemed that 'Jack the Ripper' had returned.

Sergeant Badham, the man who had taken George Hutchinson's witness statement, was, at around 12.48 a.m. on 17 July, conducting his beat sergeant duties within his No. 4 section. He had just spoken to Constable 272H, Walter Andrews, who was on the No. 11 beat in Castle Alley, just off Whitechapel High Street. 'All right?' asked the sergeant. 'All right,' came Constable Andrews's response; and so Sergeant Badham left the constable to it and went to inspect the adjoining beat.[7] Badham had gone about 150 yards when he heard the shrill of a policeman's whistle being blown twice. He immediately ran back to Constable Andrews, who himself was rapidly approaching his sergeant. 'Come quick!' said the constable, and he took the sergeant to a spot in Castle Alley just outside the rear of the Goulston Street baths, where, behind two carts, lay the body of a woman. She was later identified as Alice McKenzie.

Other constables soon arrived on the scene in response to Constable Andrews's whistle blast, and Sergeant Badham put them to work, instructing Constable 101H[8] to search the immediate area, and ordering Constable 423H Joseph Allen[9] to send for divisional surgeon Dr Bagster Phillips.

CID's local inspector, Edmund Reid, was also called out to Castle Alley, along with H Division's superintendent, Thomas Arnold, who directed a more extensive search of the area.[10] Dr Bond viewed the body once it had been removed to the Whitechapel Infirmary mortuary, and he concluded that McKenzie had suffered at the same hand that despatched the other victims, even though her injuries, while similar, were by no means as extensive or as intense. McKenzie received two throat wounds – a small incision, possibly a stab wound; and a slight cut which, ultimately, caused her death. However, her throat was not cut as deeply as those of the other victims. The only other wound upon her body was a cut on her abdomen which did not open the body cavity. Her dress was 'turned up',[11] which may suggest that the killer was interrupted by Sergeant Badham and Constable Andrews, but this does not explain the 'lightness' of the throat cut when compared to the other victims. As with the Mylett death, debate has ensued on the question of whether McKenzie was a victim of 'Jack the Ripper'. The fact remains that she is included in the Whitechapel murder files.

Just over a week after the McKenzie murder, on 25 July 1889, a memorandum appeared in all the City of London police order books. This outlined some new guidance issued by the Metropolitan Police to the City force, specifying the procedure to be followed should another Whitechapel murder be discovered. It is worth reading in full, as it is yet another indication of cross-force collaboration, as well as an insight into the mechanics of conveying information at the metaphorical coalface:

Chief Office, 25 July 1889
Memorandum
The following brief outline of instructions issued to the Metropolitan Police for their guidance in the event of another Murder case arising is sent for the information of Inspectors.

The officer first arriving at the spot is to call assistance by blowing his whistle, on help arriving to search the immediate neighbourhood keeping close observation on all persons who may be found in the vicinity, send at once to the Station House and for the Surgeon.

When sufficient aid has arrived the Officers on duty will direct the constables from the adjoining beats to return at once to their beats and make careful search at all places likely to conceal the miscreant at the same to closely scrutinise all persons who may be seen about instructing their comrades on the adjacent beats to do likewise.

Should the Words 'Whitechapel Again!' be wired from Scotland Yard it is to be understood that a Murder had been committed and the information is to be immediately given to the Police on duty that they may exercise the greatest possible vigilance.
John Whatley, Chief Clerk[12]

At around 5.20 a.m. on 10 September 1889, almost two months after the discovery of Alice McKenzie's body in Castle Alley, Constable 239H

William Pennett was patrolling down Pinchin Street, just south of Berner Street, when he came across a female torso. The torso was located in the end arch which supported the London, Tilbury and Great Eastern Railway lines, on the southern side of Pinchin Street, next to its junction with Backchurch Lane. Pennett had already been involved in the Whitechapel murders investigation, conducting plain-clothes enquiries in the wake of the 'double event',[13] so he was fully aware of the potential impact his discovery would have in an area still reeling from the murder of Elisabeth Stride.

Obviously knowing there was nothing he could do to preserve life, Pennett decided to forgo the Metropolitan force's remit on discovering a dead body, and did not blow his whistle, choosing instead to instruct a passer-by to notify his brother beat constables on the adjoining beats, which resulted in constables 205H and 115H[14] being the first to render assistance to Pennett. Doctors and senior officers were also notified in what was, by now, a familiar routine. Local Inspector Edmund Reid, again, took on the case for H Division CID, instructing Sergeant Thick to lead 'inquiries at sheds, houses and places where barrows were kept',[15] ordering Sergeant White to search the 'adjoining Railway Arches and other likely places in the neighbourhood', and assigning Sergeant Godley the task of tracing missing persons, with the intention of identifying these remains.[16] Reid also commandeered the assistance of the Inspector of Dust Carts for the parish of St George in the East, requesting that his men report to him any bloodstained garments collected, information which the Inspector of Dust Carts was asked to forward on to the police.[17] One such item was found by the dustmen, in nearby Batty Street, and sent to the police, where it was enquired about by Inspector Henry Moore. In early 1889, Moore had taken over Inspector Abberline's role as lead ground detective on the Whitechapel murders case; in this instance, his enquiries led him to the satisfactory conclusion that the bloodstained clothing was due to a recent confinement at a house in the street. The Thames River Police were once again brought in to aid with enquiries, with their own Chief Inspector Moore, along with Detective Inspector Regan, directing the crafts manned by sergeants Moore, Francis, Howard, Davis and Scott, and giving the instruction to board all the vessels from the mouth of the Thames to the docks. The *City of Cork*, the *Cadiz*, the *Malaga*, the *Gallicia* and the *Lydian Monarch* were just a few of the vessels on which enquiries and searches were made. By the end of the operation, which had begun early in the day and ended late in the evening,[18] the captains of these ships and boats had all given satisfactory accounts of themselves and their men.

Medical examinations conducted upon the torso drew the conclusion that it was female, that the victim had been murdered and dismembered elsewhere, and that she may have been killed around 8 September 1889. A telegram was issued by Inspector Reid to all stations, requesting for constables to search for further body portions, but no further remains were found. While this case was temporarily linked to the Whitechapel murders, Commissioner Monro dismissed the idea, and it certainly has closer links to the Whitehall and Thames Torso mysteries of the preceding years. However, the impact that this murder, and the murder of McKenzie the previous July, had on the policing of H Division manifested itself in political argument. On 3 July,[19] after the McKenzie murder, the Home Office agreed to Commissioner Monro's request for an extra inspector, five sergeants and fifty constables[20] to be assigned in Whitechapel, and these were kept on for an extra month after the torso had been discovered in Pinchin Street; out of this augmentation, three sergeants and thirty-nine constables were put on plain-clothes duty. By November 1889, the total number had been reduced to three sergeants and thirty-nine constables, and by early January 1890, the numbers on special duty in connection to the Whitechapel murders were reduced yet again to three sergeants and twenty-six constables.[21] Further reductions, driven by lack of funds, occurred at the end of the financial year, with two sergeants and eleven constables being retained for an extra month, starting 17 March 1890.[22]

It was almost two years before another similar murder occurred in H Division, the last to be investigated as part of the Whitechapel murders case. Commissioner Monro had been replaced by Colonel Sir Edward Bradford in 1890, making Monro's tenure as commissioner the shortest in the Metropolitan Police's history. Major Henry Smith had taken up the commissionership for the City of London Police in the same year, and it was also in 1890 that Ernest Thompson, a twenty-two-year-old labourer from Wells in Norfolk, decided to join the Metropolitan Police.[23] Assigned the collar number 240H, Constable Thompson had just completed his probation on the beat; initially, he had been chaperoned by a more senior constable, but was now, on 13 February 1891, conducting his beat on his own for the first time. His patrol was a simple loop, taking between fifteen to twenty minutes to walk, and took in Chamber Street, a narrow street which ran between Leman Street to the east and Mansell Street to the west. The southern side of Chamber Street, towards the Mansell Street end, consisted of railway arches – one of which was used as a thoroughfare between Chamber Street and Royal Mint Street, mainly by railway workers – and was given the misleadingly romantic name of Swallow Gardens. Sometime after 2.15 a.m., Constable Thompson was approaching Swallow Gardens from Leman Street, and as he did he heard footsteps slowly walking away from him, into Leman Street. He could not see to whom they belonged as Chamber Street curved at that point, thus leaving the constable blind in the dark. It didn't matter, as he had his beat to conduct, so he turned left into the dank archway of Swallow Gardens. At that time, Swallow Gardens was not just a short cut; it also housed a storage yard along one half of it, which belonged to Ruben Cull, a tile maker, and Constable Thompson had to ensure that these premises were secured. As he approached the halfway point of the arch, he noticed the figure of a young woman, and immediately went over, finding that her throat was oozing blood – it had been freshly cut. Thompson recalled the footsteps that he had just heard, and wrestled with the idea of pursuing them; however, one of the girl's eyes flickered, indicating that there was still life in her, so the Constable decided to stay, and blew his whistle for assistance, which came in the form of constables 161H Frederick Hyde and 275H George Hinton. As with the previous murders, procedure kicked in, with Constable Hyde going to find the nearest doctor, Dr Frederick Oxley of Dock Street, and Constable Hinton going to Leman Street police station to inform the duty inspector there, James Flanagan.[24] Inspector Flanagan attended the location before sending for the divisional surgeon, Dr Bagster Phillips, as well as Local Inspector Reid. By some accounts, the victim was still alive when Dr Oxley arrived; however, soon the young woman sadly succumbed to her vicious injury. The victim was known to H Division as a prostitute, and formal identification came via her former boyfriend, Samuel Harris, who had read about the murder in press reports published later that day, and her elderly father, James William Coles, who confirmed that the deceased was his daughter, Frances.

Hours after the murder of Coles, the City of London force issued a directive to all its divisional inspectors for cascading:

Information for Inspectors of Divns
Re Murders
The officers making a discovery and requiring assistance will blow one prolonged blast on his whistle followed by four short distinct ones. The men in the immediate neighbourhood, on hearing this, will repeat the four short distinct blasts and hurry at once to the spot from whence the alarm proceeds carefully scrutinising and stopping, if necessary, any person they may meet. Men hearing the four short blasts will simply repeat that signal and at once keep a sharp look out but must not leave their ground.
J Whatley, Chief Clerk, Chief Office, 13 Feby 1891

It would seem that, in response to Coles's murder and Constable Thompson's dilemma as to whether he should stay with the victim or pursue a suspect, the City Police, most likely in conjunction with the Metropolitan force, came up with the whistle notification system we see described above. The new protocol enabled the discovering constable to remain with the victim, while notifying his colleagues that a murder had taken place; they, in turn, notified those further away via the four-whistle blast. This system would rapidly spread across the district, resulting in heightened vigilance, but we will never know if this idea would have worked, because, after Coles, the murders ceased.[25]

And so ended the Whitechapel murders – though, obviously, H Division did not know this at the time. Patrols were maintained, but this stretched the Secretary of State's purse, and gradually, as no further murders occurred, special duty patrols were whittled down, and policing life in Whitechapel returned to what would once have been defined as normality. That is not to say that the Whitechapel murders case was closed, as leads were still being followed and suspects investigated. Suspects such as Frederick Bailey Deeming, the infamous Rainhill murderer of the early 1890s, who was executed in Australia in 1892, has his own file within the official case file, and Melville Macnaghten, a Metropolitan Police chief constable between 1890 and 1903, wrote a memorandum in 1894, in which he named three contemporary suspects: Michael Ostrog, Montague Druitt and a Jewish man simply known as Kosminski.

Kosminski's name occurs again in a set of private annotations written down by the head of the Whitechapel murder investigations, Chief Inspector Donald S. Swanson. Swanson owned a copy of Assistant Commissioner Anderson's memoirs, *The Lighter Side of My Official Life*, published in 1910, many years after the murders, within which Anderson explains that the murderer was known, and was a poor Polish Jew from Whitechapel who had been identified by a witness; the witness, Anderson says, refused to give testimony against the man. In Swanson's copy, the former chief inspector wrote, in pencil, on page 138, that the witness would not testify because 'the suspect was also a Jew and also because his evidence would convict the suspect, and witness would be the means of murderer being hanged which he did not wish to be left on his mind'.[26] Swanson also added that 'after this identification which suspect knew, no other murder of this kind took place in London'. On one of the book's endpapers, Swanson revealed that the name of this suspect matched that of one of Macnaghten's suspects:

> Continuing from page 138. After the suspect had been identified at the Seaside Home where he had been sent by us with great difficulty in order to subject him to identification, and he knew he was identified. On suspect's return to his brother's house in Whitechapel he was watched by police (City CID) by day & night. In a very short time the suspect with his hands tied behind his back, he was sent to Stepney Workhouse and then to Colney Hatch and died shortly afterwards – Kosminski was the suspect – DSS.[27]

The debate on what is referred to as the 'Swanson Marginalia' has ebbed and flowed since it was revealed to the world in 1987, and I do not wish to tread over old ground; however, I would like to make a few observations from a policing point of view, both legal and practical. Firstly, Anderson and Swanson state that the witness refused to testify against the suspect. This simply cannot be done, as a witness, once summonsed, must testify or risk committing an offence if he fails to do so – in fact, this is an offence which carries a custodial sentence. If, as Swanson states, the suspect was taken to Colney Hatch, a well-known lunatic asylum in Middlesex, then it is reasonable to assume that the suspect was of unsound mind, and therefore ineligible for immediate prosecution, as all defendants during that period were subject to the M'Naghten rules of legal insanity, which required that 'the jurors ought to be told in all cases that every man is to be presumed to be sane, and to possess a sufficient degree of reason to be responsible for his crimes, until the contrary be proved to their satisfaction; and that to establish a defence on the ground of insanity, it must be clearly proved that, at the time of the committing of the act, the party accused was labouring under such a defect of reason, from disease of the mind, as not to know the nature and quality of the act he was doing; or, if he did know it, that he did not know he was doing what was wrong'.[28] As this suspect ended up, according to Swanson, in Colney Hatch, such an insanity defence could reasonably be assumed, leading to the suspect's incarceration in an asylum rather than death via capital punishment. In other words, the witness would not, in fact, be 'the means of [the] murderer being hanged', and could provide testimony without fearing the consequences for the defendant. My only explanation for Swanson's irreconcilable statement, as poor as it is, is that it is an either an error, which would be surprising given his experience, or a calculated choice of words designed to 'excuse' the lack of a conviction in the Whitechapel murders case, placing the onus of responsibility upon the witness. Likewise, Anderson's description of the matter, in a published book, may have been intended to reassure the public that the killer had been apprehended and secured.

Another suggested reason as to why the witness balked at providing a confirmed identification is that of *mesirah*, the act of a Jew reporting the misdemeanours of another Jew to a non-Rabbinic authority. Committing *mesirah* is forbidden under Rabbinic law, but, where acts of civic crime are concerned, the relevant non-Jewish authorities are, on most occasions, informed. Even so, this may still be done only if it is felt that the non-Jewish authority will behave in a just and fair manner. It is possible that the witness's refusal to testify could have been prompted by his desire to avoid a case of *mesirah*. Swanson's statement that the witness refused to testify because it 'would be the means of murderer being hanged which he did not wish to be left on his mind' could be a reference to the witness's concern that the suspect's hanging would be unjust given his state of mind, and may affect his (the witness's) own standing in the eyes of God. However, since we do not know whether the authorities intended to proceed with a trial, or whether the witness had assumed that a trial was pending, my presentation of *mesirah* is purely speculative. If the suspect was indeed insane, then one can understand why the police left the matter there: the man had been securely locked away in 1891, and, touch wood, no verifiable Ripper murders had taken place since 1888. Then again, this scenario would not be ideal for the victims' families' sense of justice. It is far more likely in my opinion that an indefinite period of confinement was the intention, and that this identification at the Seaside Home[29] was merely for peace of mind, rather than in pursuit of a conviction.

The setting of a 'Seaside Home' is a curious place for this identification to occur. Commonly, if we recall Edwardian East End criminal Arthur Harding, such identifications took place at police stations, with the odd one being taken at hospitals or workhouses. Initially, there was not one singular 'Seaside Home' attached to the police; since the early 1880s, the

Metropolitan and City forces had sent their ailing men to numerous private boarding homes dotted along the south coast of Great Britain, at places such as St Luke's Convalescent Home in Torquay, ran by Mr A. Barton Esq., for recuperation from illness, injury or mental stress. This was a common occurrence for the extremely fortunate Victorian working man who found himself employed by a humane company or a business with philanthropic ideals, and which could afford to look after its workforce. A joint fund was set up between the Metropolitan and City of London forces to help finance these recuperation breaks, and donations were made towards the acquisition of a permanent location. A former boarding house at 51 Clarendon Villas in Brighton was, in 1890, converted into the Convalescent Police Seaside Home, and used by the Metropolitan force, whereas the Convalescent Home for Working Men, at St Margaret's Bay, Dover, had an extension completed by October 1891, with some rooms dedicated for use by the City of London Police, and operated under the new name of Morley House. As both Anderson and Swanson, along with Macnaghten, were Metropolitan officers, it is reasonable to assume that the location for this identification was Brighton; however, Swanson also mentions that the City of London police were involved in this story, and went on to watch the suspect in Metropolitan jurisdiction *after* this identification parade. While this cooperation is not unique, as we have seen, it is a clear indicator that both the Metropolitan and City of London forces worked together on this particular suspect, the mononymous Kosminski. Even though Swanson stated that 'he had been sent [to the Seaside Home] by us', i.e., the Metropolitan force, it is just possible that the location was not the Metropolitan Police's seaside home in Brighton but the City's seaside home in Dover. The alleged identification of Kosminski is, as stated, interesting. The fact that we have two independent police officials, Macnaghten and Swanson, naming Kosminski, and two, Anderson and Swanson, detailing the events surrounding the identification, supports the conclusion that this incident did take place, but the procedural issues do leave the event open to valid questioning, and one can understand why such questions have remained.

The official Whitechapel murders case file starts with Emma Smith in April 1888, and ends with Frances Coles in the February of 1891, with the last entry, made rather aptly by Chief Inspector Donald S. Swanson, being dated 14 October 1896. This case, as with all unsolved crimes, has never been closed, and that status will remain until the perpetrator is identified beyond reasonable doubt. This will clearly never happen. Genetic fingerprinting, or DNA fingerprinting as some call it, is the only forensic tool which could – I stress *could* – identify the killer, but this relies on either the victims' or the killer's DNA being conclusively identified. As we have no ascertained samples, this outside possibility shall forever remain out of our reach; in other words, we shall never know for certain who 'Jack the Ripper' was. As with many murder cases when the killer's activities become dormant, investigations are routinely wound down. In this case, this was apparently not because – as is suggested by some – the killer was known and was either secured or deceased, but rather because all leads were investigated, no further activity worth investigating occurred, and a lack of funding meant that investigations across the Metropolitan area were necessarily restricted. Every so often, and we see it in the Whitechapel murders file, the odd tenuous lead occurs, and the last lead investigated on these unique cases was, as stated, in October 1896. It was in relation to a 'Jack the Ripper' letter: Detective Constable Payne of H Division CID referred a piece of correspondence supposedly sent by 'old Jack-the-Ripper'[30] for Central Office comparison against the Dear Boss letter, and it ended up on Chief Inspector Swanson's desk. Swanson's final words on this letter, and in the official case files, were, 'In my opinion, the handwritings are not the same. I agree as at A.[31] I beg that the letter may be put with other similar letters. Its circulation is to be regretted.'[32]

And, with those unglamorous words, official investigations into the Whitechapel murder cases, and into the identity of 'Jack the Ripper', ceased indefinitely.

Notes

1 I Beg to Report

1. Stewart P. Evans and Donald Rumbelow, *Scotland Yard Investigates* (Sutton Publishing Ltd, 2006), Preface vii.
2. It is important to note at this stage that the Whitechapel murders differ from the 'Jack the Ripper' case in as much as the Whitechapel murders occurred between April 1888 (Emma Smith) and February 1891 (Frances Coles), where as the murders attributed to 'Jack the Ripper' run from August 1888 (Mary Ann Nichols) to November 1888 (Mary Kelly).
3. Stewart P. Evans and Keith Skinner, *Jack the Ripper Sourcebook* (Robinson, 2000).
4. Philip Sugden, *The Complete History of Jack the Ripper* (Robinson, 1994).

2 The Birth of the Bobby

1. Legal Code of Alfred the Great. The book was created around AD 893 and was essentially an amalgamation of Saxon law, Mosaic law and Christian ethics. The name Doom Book is taken from the Anglo-Saxon word *dom* meaning judgement/law.
2. Shire-reeves. Shire meaning land, reeve meaning senior official. Shire-reeves evolved into the more commonly known sheriffs.
3. Later to evolve into a constable.
4. These men were part of what was known as the Travelling Assizes. Assizes were court hearings held, most commonly, every quarter, meaning cases were actually heard every four months. This ceased in 1971 with the hearing being held at local courts all year round, as most major towns and cities within the UK now have their own court buildings.
5. Also known as the Assizes to Arms of 1252.
6. The beadle covered many roles during the Victorian period, including church and parish administration. Within a policing context they were paid to assist the constable and watch when necessary with minor jobs such as crowd control, but they would also take on more demanding tasks and had the authority to arrest if required.
7. Hue and cry was the name given to the procedure of the period for calling assistance. The constable would call out, and it was expected of the public to go and assist. The old-style 'hue and cry' carried through to the mid Victorian period and can be seen in many films depicting theft in the Victorian era with the shout of 'STOP, THIEF!'.
8. Rich, Robert M., Essays on the Theory and Practice of Criminal Justice (1977).
9. Rumbelow, Donald, *I Spy Blue* (MacMillan, 1971), p. 25.
10. Small wooden construction usually with a crude seat, table and brazier (fire) outside.
11. Hitchens, Chris, *The Metropolitan Police Force: Its Creation and Records of Service* (The National Archives Podcast Series No. 18).
12. Aldermen, one per ward, were senior officials elected to the Court of Aldermen and responsible for the administration of the City. It is from this court that future lord mayors of London were elected.
13. Later increased to ten men.
14. Jonathan Wild (*c.* 1683–1725).
15. Charles Hitchen (*c.* 1675–1727). Hitchen bought the office of under-marshal for £700 from an almost bankrupt City of London Corporation in 1712.

16. Subdivisions of wards.
17. Henry Fielding (1707–54). A satirist and novelist famous for writing *Tom Jones*, Fielding also held an interest in the judicial and penal systems which resulted in him being appointed as chief magistrate.
18. The Bow Street Court was established in 1740 under Magistrate Colonel Sir Thomas de Veil.
19. John Fielding, later Sir, (1721–80). Appointed by Henry in 1750, John Fielding was blinded while serving in the Navy at the age of nineteen. He was also pivotal in the setting up of the Lambeth Orphanage for Girls and became one of its original guardians in 1758.
20. To aid with funding, the Bow Street constables hired out their services and even policed private parties (Private correspondence, Mervyn Mitton).
21. By 1805 the Bow Street Patrol had altered its name to Bow Street Horse Patrol and the red waistcoat was introduced (Private correspondence, Mervyn Mitton).
22. The Popery Act 1689 basically banned the practice of the Catholic religion.
23. Known as the Bill for the Further Prevention of Crimes and for the Speedier Detection and Punishments of Offenders Against the Peace in the Cities of London and Westminster, the Borough of Southwark and Certain Parts Adjacent to Them; see Rumbelow, Donald, *I Spy Blue* (MacMillan, 1971), p. 97.
24. Rumbelow, Donald, *I Spy Blue* (MacMillan, 1971), p. 20.
25. Justices of the peace as were.
26. Extract from the 1798 Official Government Report on Finance and Police.
27. Also known as the Thames River Police.
28. The Pool of London is actually formed by the Upper Pool (between London Bridge and the Tower) and the Lower Pool (from the Tower to Rotherhithe). It is part of the Port of London, which runs along the Thames from London to the estuary at the North Sea.
29. Thames Police: History, Thames Magistrates' Court, Thames Police Museum
30. Patrick Colquhoun (1745–1820). Initially a very successful linen trader in the US, Scots-born Colquhoun was a businessman and later magistrate. A true police reformist, his impact on the creation of the Metropolitan Police force must not be underestimated.
31. *Treatise on the Police of the Metropolis* (1796) by Patrick Colquhoun is an insight into the causes and effects of crime in that period of history. There were seven editions by 1806.
32. Henry Dundas, 1st Viscount Melville, Baron Dunira (1742–1811).
33. William Pitt the Younger (1759–1806). Pitt the Younger was both prime minister and Chancellor of the Exchequer during his tenure from 1783 to 1801.
34. A parochial institution created under the various Poor Law Acts, where the destitute could stay and be fed for a short period in exchange for hard labour. It was the last resort of many, as it was a very harsh environment. This was intentional, as the overseers wished to actively discourage people from staying.
35. Sir Robert Peel (1788–1850). Prime minster 1834 to 1835 and 1841 to 1846. Home Secretary 1822 to 1827 and 1828 to 1830.
36. More acts were to come into effect for Ireland and in later years for Great Britain.
37. Sir John Cam Hobhouse (1786–1869). 1st Baron Broughton, Member of Parliament for Westminster.
38. Correspondence from Sir Robert Peel to John Hobhouse dated 12 December 1828.
39. Mayne and Rowan initially had the title justices of the peace. This was changed to commissioner in 1839. However, their role as justice of the peace remained. In fact, all commissioners were justices of the peace until 1974, when the role changed to one of constable.
40. Sir William Alexander (1754–1832). Chief Baron of the Exchequer of Pleas 1824–31. At the time, this office was responsible for common law and equity, with the chief baron holding its most senior position outside the treasurer and the Chancellor of the Exchequer.
41. Supposedly named because the blueness of the uniform reminded some of the colour of live lobsters, it is most likely a jibe out of fear of a militarised police force, as the red-coated British Army were called 'Red Lobsters'.
42. *Imperial Parliament*, 2 June 1829.
43. *Westmorland Gazette*, 18 July 1829.
44. Eugène François Vidocq (1775–1857).
45. This uniform had to be worn both on and off duty. During the summer months, constables were permitted to wear lighter summer trousers which were white in colour. Constables paid for their own uniform, with the government reimbursing them upon their departure from the force.
46. Hitchens, Chris, *The Metropolitan Police Force: Its Creation and Records of Service* (The National Archives Podcast Series No. 18).

47. A guinea was a coin in use between 1663 and 1814. However, the term remained in use and was associated with shillings. This because a guinea was worth twenty-one shillings.
48. Watch houses were buildings used by the watchmen as places of refuge.
49. *Quarterly Review*, 129(257) (1870).
50. Begg, Paul and Keith Skinner, *The Scotland Yard Files* (Headline Publishing, 1992), p. 37.
51. Rumbelow, Donald, *I Spy Blue* (MacMillan, 1971), p. 114.
52. The merge was due to a Bill passed by the Court of Common Council.
53. Rumbelow, Donald, *I Spy Blue* (MacMillan, 1971), p. 133.
54. Numbers of men.

3 Recruitment

1. Adolphus Williamson (1830–1889). Known affectionately as 'Dolly', he was superintendent in the Metropolitan Force at the time of the Turf Fraud Scandal, becoming chief constable of CID in 1886. A well-respected policeman who had worked his way up through the ranks from constable throughout thirty-nine years of dedicated service, he died in office in 1889.
2. Druscovich had learnt Moldovan from his father, and was employed by his uncle on a trading vessel across the Mediterranean Sea as a youth. He also worked for the British Consulate in Wallachia, Romania for a period, thus enabling him to pick up many languages.
3. Haia Shpayer-Makov, *The Ascent of the Victorian Detective: Police Sleuths in the Victorian and Edwardian Era* (2011).
4. The latter two, Littlechild and Roots, were to be connected to the Jack the Ripper case in later years.
5. For an excellent account of this case read *The Chieftain* (History Press, 2011) by Chris Payne, Detective Chief Inspector George Clarkes' great-great-grandson.
6. Lieutenant Colonel (later Sir) Edmund Henderson (1821–1896) succeeded Acting Commissioner Douglas Labalmondière in 1869.
7. The Habitual Criminals Register: a comprehensive record of habitual criminals, giving height, weight, identifying features and so on. In later years it featured photographs of these repeat offenders.
8. James Monro (1838–1920). He entered straight into the Metropolitan Force in 1884 in the dual role of assistant commissioner and head of CID, taking over the latter position from Charles Howard Vincent. Monro resigned in 1888 due to clashes of personality with Commissioner Warren. However, Monro did return to the Met as commissioner upon Warren's resignation, holding the position for only eighteen months, the shortest commissionership in the Met's history.
9. Sir Charles Edward Howard Vincent (1849–1908). Knighted in 1896, Howard Vincent joined the Met when he became the head of the newly created Criminal Investigation Department in 1878. Highly thought of by his seniors, peers and men who served under him, Howard Vincent set many of the standards to which CID and policing as a whole adhere to today. His setting of the police code laid out the procedures and protocols adhered to not only during the Victorian period but for many years after.
10. Dr (Sir) Robert Anderson (1841–1918). Anderson was working for the Home Office at the time of the Fenian attacks in 1883. Predominantly a barrister, he became a Home Office advisor on political crime in 1868, resigning the position in 1884. He was asked to assist the then Met CID head (and assistant commissioner), James Monro, in the field of political crime in 1887; however, due to Monro's resignation in 1888, Anderson replaced him in all roles, holding the positions until his resignation in 1901. Anderson was to become a controversial character during the period of the Whitechapel murders of 1888 and beyond. To this day his actions and words connected to the case have been hotly debated and mulled over, as they will be for years to come.
11. This was Warren's second visit as a military man to South Africa; the previous began in 1876 when Warren was sent to survey the boundary between Griqualand and Orange Free State. He fought in the Transeki War of 1877–78 and ended up as the Administrator for Griqualand, having the town of Warrenton named after him in his honour.
12. For an excellent comprehensive overview of Warren's career, read Stewart P. Evans & Donald Rumbelow, *Jack the Ripper: Scotland Yard Investigates*, Chapter 1 – 'A Gentleman of Angularities' (Sutton Publishing, 2006).
13. MEPO 4/10.
14. Or to The Old Jewry if you were applying to join the City of London Force.
15. Though by 1888 the age range ran from twenty-one to thirty-five years old.
16. Initially the height stipulation was 5 ft 10 in, however this was relaxed due to the fact not

many of that height were applying. By the time Warren had taken the commissionership the height restriction was 5 ft 8 ½ in, but Warren soon returned it to 5 ft 9 in.

17. MEPO 4/36. *Instruction Booklet for Candidates and New Constables* (1871).
18. The following is taken from *The City of London Forces Application*, hence the slightly differing wording. The context remained the same for both forces.
19. The requisite to reside in the City of London was relaxed during the 1890s, however residence was strictly monitored and a close location to the City was preferred. The Met force did not have such a restriction, although they also chose where their men did reside. See Policeman chapter.
20. If joining the City of London Police Force.
21. While the City of London police differed slightly, the basic processes of recruitment remained for both forces. I have decided to concentrate on the Metropolitan Force for the moment to avoid confusion. Also, candidates' day fluctuated throughout the period; in some records it is noted as a Monday.
22. *The Daily Graphic*, 19 August 1907.
23. Dr Alexander Oberlin MacKellar (1845–1904), Metropolitan Police Surgeon in Chief from 1885 until his death. He was to play a prominent part in the Whitechapel Murder series.
24. Kennington Lane section house was created in 1885 and attached to the police station there, at the junction of Kennington Lane and Renfrew Road. The site is now the Gilmour section house, and still accommodates policemen who require lodgings.
25. The Old Jewry was the predominant location for the City of London Police Force's preparatory class, along with residency and training at Bishopsgate Police Station.
26. Seventy was the base number, however up to 100 could be retained depending on numbers of men required to fill vacancies. MEPO 2/442, Internal Home Office Memorandum A46887/7, 23 April 1887.
27. Police Orders, 6 January 1868, also Mike Waldren QPM, *Early Police Firearms* (Police History Series, 2007).
28. 'Training the Metropolitan Policeman – An historical survey from 1829 to 1910'. Metropolitan Police Historical Centre.
29. Edwin Woodhall, *Detective and Secret Service Days* (1929).
30. In 1904 a report was published in relation to Rose and the adequacy of police training at the time. The report was highly critical of the methods used, stating that too much time was spent on the parade ground and not enough time was spent on theoretical and methodical work. It also criticised the standard of education the recruits showed, with ex-CID Chief Howard-Vincent stating that 'the many mistakes of recruits today are due to the ignorance and lack of theoretical knowledge. The beat Police recruits come from farms and, at worse, domestic service.' Unsurprisingly, Rose retired three years after this report was published, just as the Metropolitan Force moved to a new training centre in Peel House.
31. A contemporary report into training showed that some of the candidates at Kennington Lane were actually sending communications of 'an unsavoury nature' to each other.
32. MEPO 4/352.
33. A reserve constable supplemented a division as and when required.
34. Metropolitan Police Orders – Wednesday 1 June 1870.
35. A sub-division is a force of men located within a police station. All police stations are, officially, sub-divisions.
36. George W. Cornish, *Cornish of the Yard: His Reminiscences and Cases* (New York: MacMillan Co., 1935).
37. 'Training the Metropolitan Policeman – An historical survey from 1829 to 1910'. Metropolitan Police Archives.
38. Within the City of London force, men were not permitted to live outside the City, however this was relaxed in the early 1890s due to the fact that lodgings within the City limits were increasingly difficult to find. In fact, City Detective Baxter Hunt, who worked on the Eddowes case in 1888, lived in Cartwright Street, Whitechapel, in 1891, a stone's throw away from the Pinchin Street torso discoverer, Met Constable Pennett, who lived in the Peabody Buildings a street away.
39. City PC 922 Richard Pearce was living at No. 3 Mitre Square, opposite the site of Ripper victim Catherine Eddowes' murder. As No. 4 Mitre Square was empty premises, and as Pearce was later to find lodgings in White Lion Street Spitalfields in 1891, it is reasonable to assume that Pearce was one of these 'Caretaker' PCs.
40. The recital of the rules and regulations was a common thread throughout training and consolidation period. It was heavily installed into the men.
41. A slang term for a policeman's informer.

4 Police Stations and Section Houses

1. Peter Kennison & David Swinden, *Behind the Blue Lamp Policing North and East London* (Coppermill Press, 2003), p. 315.
2. *Ibid.*
3. Now Crowder Street.
4. Charles Tempest Clarkson & J. Hall Richardson, *Police!* (Field & Tuer, The Leadenhall Press, 1889). The shops were converted into a station in 1847.
5. Superintendent Thomas Arnold (1835–1906), a former grocer who joined the Metropolitan Force in 1855 before resigning to fight in the Crimean War some months later. Returned to the Met in 1856 and worked his way through the ranks. Arnold spent the majority of his policing life in the East End before retiring in February 1893. Arnold's residence was in Arbour Square, near to the police station which also sat within his division.
6. Chief Inspector John West (b. 1842) joined the Met in 1865 and worked in N Division, V Division and K Division before moving to H Division in 1884.
7. Local Inspector Edmund Reid (1846–1917) was Local Inspector (CID) H Division from 1888 till 1896. Like Arnold, a former grocer's boy, waiter, pastry cook, and steward, to name but four of his sixteen jobs prior to joining the Metropolitan Police in 1872, Reid can be described as an infectious character. Upon his retirement after a lengthy and respected police career, the *Weekly Despatch* newspaper stated that Reid reached professional standards as a singer and actor, and was also a world-record balloonist to boot. The inspiration for writer Charles Gibbons' fictional Detective Dier, Reid has found a new popularity in recent years as the main character in the recent BBC drama *Ripper Street*, and is played by Matthew MacFadyen.
8. The 1891 census shows Local Inspector Reid and family actually residing at Commercial Street station. As such privileges were permitted to his rank, one suspects this was his residence in 1888.
9. Robert Clack, *Scenes of Crime, Casebook Examiner*, Issue 5, December 2010.
10. *Ibid.*
11. MEPO 2/898, 'Report on the Conditions of Metropolitan Police Stations' (1881), p. 3. While declared unfit as an operational police building, Denmark Street watch house was still in use as an independent section house.
12. A Class 2 building was an already-built property converted for police use, and the final class, 3, was an ordinary building which had not been altered specifically for police use but which was still utilised by them. MEPO 2/898, 'Report on the Conditions of Metropolitan Police Stations' (1881).
13. Chief Architect and Surveyor to the Metropolitan Police; S.C.L.L.C, Norton Folgate Trustees' Minutes, 22 March 1876.
14. MEPO 2/898, 'Report on the Conditions of Metropolitan Police Stations' (1881), p. 3.
15. The introduction of the blue lamp is unknown, however in Fido & Skinner's *The Official Encyclopaedia of Scotland Yard* (Virgin Publishing Ltd, 1999), the authors mention a police order of 1861, within which it was decreed that three out of four sides of the lamp be paned with blue glass. Incidentally, Queen Victoria so disliked the blue lamp at Bow Street station, a station she passed regularly on her way to the opera, that she had it changed. This was due to the fact that it reminded her of her dear departed Albert, who had died in the Blue Room at Windsor Castle, so Bow Street had a regular lamp outside their building.
16. As a rule, one person would be confined to one regular cell; however, due to sheer numbers, the reality was somewhat different, with multiple strangers being confined to one cell on busy weekend nights. That said, the station sergeant did have the authorisation to arrange and transfer prisoners to stations that could accommodate more prisoners.
17. Stoves were lit from 4 p.m. until 10 p.m. only between 1 October and 31 March. Police Orders, 20 December 1887.
18. MEPO 2/898, 'Report on the Conditions of Metropolitan Police Stations' (1881), 7. And Police Orders, 20 December 1887.
19. *City of London Police Orders, Regulations and Acts of Parliament 1839–1894*, Sec 27, p. 9.
20. C. E. Howard-Vincent, *The Police Code* 1889, p. 165.
21. Interestingly, unlike today's procedure, money not connected to an offence was allowed to remain with the prisoner, as stated in the Howard-Vincent's police code of 1889.
22. If a charge was made against the prisoner, and therefore court proceedings were in progress, the prisoner's property book would be handed over to the courts along with the items and charge sheet, and would be the court's responsibility from then on.
23. *City of London Police Orders, Regulations and Acts of Parliament 1839–1894*, Sec 26, p. 9.
24. MEPO 2/338, Executive Branch memorandum on used of Police Matrons collated throughout June 1894.

25. MEPO 2/338, Metropolitan Police memorandum dated 13 June 1894.
26. City of London Police Station No. 6 (Bishopsgate) Order Book, 1891. City of London Police Museum.
27. Louisa Twining (1820–1912). Artist, historian, authoress and member of the tea-making Twining family, Louisa was a dedicated champion of the Poor Law and relief, becoming a guardian for Kensington and Tonbridge Poor Law Unions.
28. *Pall Mall Gazette*, 20 July 1888.
29. *Ibid.*
30. Incidentally, a special searching room was situated inside the City of London police station in Bishopsgate.
31. C. E. Howard-Vincent, *The Police Code* (1889), p. 139.
32. City of London Police Station No. 6 (Bishopsgate) Order Book, 1863–1893.
33. A telephone system was in place for both forces in 1888, but it was in its infancy. The first police telephone posts, or alarm posts as they had initially been called, had arrived in London from the United States of America, via Glasgow, in 1888 and were being trialled in N Division's Islington area.
34. Who would telegram Shadwell.
35. Police Orders, 5 June 1888.
36. Drill: the marching of a group of men in various formations, either with or without arms, predominantly a military activity.
37. Charles Tempest Clarkson & J. Hall Richardson, *Police!* (Field & Tuer, The Leadenhall Press, 1889).
38. MEPO 2/170. Draft police orders entitled 'Drill – Emendations & Corrections', 6 November 1886.
39. Legend has it that these horse-drawn vans were named after no-nonsense US lodging-house-keeper Maria Lee, of Boston, in 1830. Lee had a reputation for assisting Boston Police Department in escorting drunks from her lodging house to the station cells. So feared was her reputation that Boston officers threatened drunks with the prospect of Lee, who was African-American, by stating that if they didn't behave 'we shall send for Black Maria' to aid with transportation. The Metropolitan Force had eight Black Maria vans in 1888 – small vans pulled by two dray horses, with small cells within each van, each cell being big enough to accommodate one person.
40. *London City Press*, 30 December 1865.
41. Mr George Borlais-Childs (1814–1888), F.R.C.S., succeeded by Dr Frederick Gordon Brown as City of London Police Divisional Surgeon in 1885.
42. *The London City Press*, in its 22 December 1864 edition, highlighted issues the City Police had had in constructing the station and hospital by reporting a complaint made by a neighbour of the City Police, Mr Chadwick, who pointed out that tenants on the site of the proposed new build had been 'evicted from their dwellings without any notice' and that 'for four months work had been at a standstill'.
43. *Lost Hospitals of London*. Author unstated.
44. Approximately ten kilograms.
45. Pets were fairly common in police stations. Cats, as stated, were often used to help eliminate vermin; however some dogs also undertook the role, which lead to terriers becoming a common choice of station dog. Early group photos taken at H Division's HQ, Leman Street, show the presence of a dog, and a series of group photos taken at the City Force's Snow Hill station, just a few years apart, show the same dog grown from pup to maturity.
46. Martin Fido & Keith Skinner, *The Official Encyclopaedia of Scotland Yard* (Virgin Publishing Ltd, 1999), p. 18.
47. City of London Police Medical Department report on DC Edward Marriott (Warrant No. 5830), by Dr F. G. Brown, dated 1 April 1909.
48. Neil Bell & Robert Clack, 'Detective Constable Edward Marriott', *Ripperologist*, issue 115, July 2010.
49. Martin Fido & Keith Skinner, *The Official Encyclopaedia of Scotland Yard* (Virgin Publishing Ltd, 1999). p. 238.
50. As the men residing there covered a section within the division.
51. Another section house, referred to as Aldgate Section House, was situated at 21a Commercial Street, between Wentworth Street and Whitechapel High Street, and was used from the Edwardian period until at least 1939. However this section house, oddly enough, belonged to G Division Finsbury. MEPO 2/2615.
52. Board: payment in exchange for a room/bed and meals.
53. It is worth noting that each section house had its own crockery, specially stamped with the divisional letter and sub-divisional station house name.

54. MEPO 2/395. Report into the duties of Section House Sergeants, 20 March 1895.
55. The provisions shop was usually based in the mess and had set opening hours. Small provisions could be bought here, along with pipe tobacco and woodbines.
56. MEPO 2/898. Report on the Conditions of Metropolitan Police Stations (1881), p. 11.
57. Martin Fido & Keith Skinner, *The Official Encyclopaedia of Scotland Yard* (Virgin Publishing Ltd, 1999), p. 33.
58. *The Reading Mercury*, 17 June 1899.
59. Fifty-six to sixty-five kilograms.
60. MEPO 2/898. Report on the Conditions of Metropolitan Police Stations (1881), p. 11.
61. Relief: the word used in reference to a beat constable's shift, the period he is on the beat, or a group of constables undertaking that shift.

5 Blue Bottles

1. Charles Booth (1840–1916). Ship owner, merchant and social researcher who is best known for his stand-out work regarding poverty within the working classes of London between 1889 and 1903, including his poverty maps, which are a valued resource.
2. Charles Booth, *Life and Labour, Vol 1: Poverty*, p. 233.
3. George Duckworth, later Sir (1868–1934). Charles Booth's secretary and half-brother to writer Virginia Woolf.
4. Victor Bailey, *Charles Booth's Policemen: Crime, Police and Community in Jack the Ripper's London*. (Breviary Stuff Publications, 2014), p. 13. The Booth Collection is held at the British Library of Political and Economic Science, London School of Economics.
5. Police Orders, 1 September 1888. Strength of force numbers, usually issued in police orders at the beginning of every month. The number of men for H Division was to rise to 587 by 29 December 1888; such was the impact of the murders upon the police strength.
6. *The Daily Mail*, 16 July 1901.
7. Not to be confused with H Division's head of CID in 1888, Inspector Edmund Reid.
8. *Police Walks* B351, ff. 15, 23. Victor Bailey, *Charles Booth's Policemen, Crime, Police and Community in Jack the Ripper's London*. (Breviary Stuff Publications, 2014), p. 33.
9. *Police Walks* B346, f. 32–33, 57–59. Victor Bailey, *Charles Booth's Policemen, Crime, Police and Community in Jack the Ripper's London*. (Breviary Stuff Publications, 2014), p. 33.
10. Charles Booth, *Life and Labour, vol 2, Religious Influences*, p. 98.
11. *Police Walks* B356, f. 125. Bailey, Victor *Charles Booth's Policemen, Crime, Police and Community in Jack the Ripper's London*. (Breviary Stuff Publications, 2014), p. 35.
12. Revd Samuel Augustus Barnett (1844–1913), and his wife, Henrietta (1851–1936), later Dame, were social reformers who established a university settlement in Toynbee Hall, yards away from St Judes, in 1884. This was a place where social reform volunteers, mainly students from Oxford and Cambridge universities, would come to provide aid to the poor of the community as well as gain valuable insight into the issues concerned, and therefore come up with possible solutions to the problems endured by those suffering poverty in the East End and the nation as a whole.
13. *The Times*, 19 September 1888.
14. Victorian slang for a physical beating.
15. Charles Tempest Clarkson & J. Hall Richardson, *Police!* (Field & Tuer, The Leadenhall Press, 1889), pp. 100–102.
16. Each force ran its own pension scheme during 1888.
17. Charles Tempest Clarkson & J Hall Richardson, *Police!* (Field & Tuer, The Leadenhall Press, 1889), pp. 100–102. It must be noted that specialist duty sergeants, inspectors, station sergeants and so on would have a little extra in their pay packet compared to others of the same rank who undertook regular duties.
18. *Ibid.*
19. *Ibid.*
20. Charles Tempest Clarkson & J. Hall Richardson, *Police!* (Field & Tuer, The Leadenhall Press, 1889), pp. 100–102.
21. MEPO 2/476, Civil Service examination on Police on promotion. Executive Office memorandum 277464 dated March 1899.
22. MEPO 2/476, and Police Orders. 26 August 1899.
23. The total number of policemen in operation, within a division, at that moment in time.
24. MEPO 2/476. Metropolitan Police Executive branch memorandum. 12 October 1899.
25. *Ibid.*
26. *Ibid.*
27. *Ibid.*

28. C. E. Howard-Vincent, *The Police Code* 1889, pp. 115–16.
29. Long was also suspended in the autumn of 1888, for reasons unknown, however he was reinstated in December. Police Orders, 14 December 1888.
30. City of London Police Constable 881/944 Edward Watkins' Record of Service.
31. Neil Bell & Robert Clack, 'City Beat PC 881 Edward Watkins', *Ripperologist*, Issue 105, August 2009.
32. *Police Walks* B151, f. 25. Victor Bailey, *Charles Booth's Policemen, Crime, Police and Community in Jack the Ripper's London.* (Breviary Stuff Publications, 2014), p. 18.
33. *Ibid.*
34. The minstrels, who performed in a minstrelsy fashion, were white men who blacked their faces to mimic negros and performed song, dance and comical routines. They were bought over to Great Britain from the United States just after the civil war there. The Metropolitan Police Minstrels followed suit, as was the style of that era, until they disbanded in 1933 due to the instruction of the then Commissioner Trenchard, who disliked the fact the minstrels were touting, door to door, tickets for their shows, putting pressure, so he felt, on the public to purchase these tickets. Trenchard set up a commissioners' fund in place of the minstrels, ensuring that the Widows' and Orphans' fund maintained a steady charitable income.
35. For further information of the Police Widows' and Orphans' Fund see: www.met-cityorphans. org.uk/history.php.
36. *Lloyds Weekly Newspaper*, 6 January 1889.
37. Mervyn Mitton, *The Policeman's Lot* (Quiller Press Ltd, 1985), p. 122.
38. Mervyn Mitton, *The Policeman's Lot* (Quiller Press Ltd, 1985), p. 123.
39. There are many variations of the police uniform, such as ceremonial and mess dress for example. To describe all would be a thankless task, therefore only the regular duty uniform shall be described unless otherwise stated.
40. The final crown design most commonly used in the British Police force was the 'spike and ball' design, which was phased out during the early part of the twentieth century due to injuries it caused.
41. Due to the fact the City Force had a far smaller force of men, there was no need to include a divisional number upon the helmet.
42. Police Orders, 7 March 1864.
43. In 1897 two styles of uniform were used, a summer and winter one, with worsted blue Serge material used for the lighter summer uniform, and the heavier blue Melton cloth retained for the winter uniform.
44. Mervyn Mitton, *The Policeman's Lot* (Quiller Press Ltd, 1985), p. 117.
45. Police Orders, 31 December 1887.
46. The practice of issuing new boots was dropped in 1897, with a granting of a boot allowance taking its place.
47. Martin Fido & Keith Skinner, *The Official Encyclopaedia of Scotland Yard* (Virgin Publishing Ltd, 1999), p. 271.
48. Police Orders, 11 January 1887. Incidentally, Tipsaves, a hollowed-out wooden or brass tube within which documents, such as warrants, carried by constables, and seen as a symbol of authority to arrest, were phased out in this police order. From here on, constables were required to carry their authority to arrest, known as a policeman's warrant card, in a pocket upon their person.
49. C. E. Howard-Vincent, *The Police Code* (1889), p. 184.
50. Some truncheons had a lead core, however the author is unable to establish when this was introduced.
51. Private correspondence, Simon Topman (Acme Whistles, formerly J. Hudson & Co). Incidentally, the Metropolitan whistle could also be purchased by the public, with warehouse companies putting in mass orders for their night watchmen. Those used by the Metropolitan Force were stamped with the words 'Metropolitan Police', and would also have an issue and test stamp number stamped upon them. When the City of London Force began to use whistles, they ensured 'City Police' was stamped on their batches of whistles.
52. City of London Police Station No. 6 (Bishopsgate) Order Book entry, 21st May 1889.
53. *Ibid.*
54. City of London Police Station No. 6 (Bishopsgate) Order Book entry, 9 January 1890.
55. *The City of London Police Orders and Regulations book 1839–1894*, Constables section 8, p. 25.
56. The dominant supplier of restraints to the Metropolitan and City Forces was Hiatt & Co., of Birmingham, who also provided them with other ironmongery such as travelling irons, police staves, sabres, pistols, rattles and even helmet plates.
57. C. E. Howard-Vincent, *The Police Code* (1889), p. 91.

58. *Ibid.*
59. Police Order, 6 January 1872.
60. Spare reservoirs of oil were provided to those on longer beats, and commonly stored at fixed point posts.
61. Chief Inspector John West, acting superintendent when the murders begin, due to Superintendent Thomas Arnold being on leave. Arnold returned to post at end of October 1888.
62. *Daily News*, 5 October 1888.
63. Police Orders, 1 August 1887, stating the lamp contract for the trimming, cleaning and repairing of lanterns and lamps, had been awarded to J & C Christie of 3 and 5 Mansell Street, Aldgate, London.
64. Police Orders, 21 April 1888.
65. Mervyn Mitton, *The Policeman's Lot* (Quiller Press Ltd, 1985), p. 101.
66. C. E. Howard-Vincent, *The Police Code* (1889), p. 127.
67. Until the introduction of chevrons upon their sleeves in 1864, sergeants used horizontal stripes on their armlets to indicate their rank.
68. Police Orders, 31 December 1887.
69. Police Orders, 31 December 1887.
70. C. E. Howard-Vincent, *The Police Code* (1889), p. 68.
71. Charles Tempest Clarkson & J. Hall Richardson, *Police!* (Field & Tuer, The Leadenhall Press, 1889), p. 299.
72. *Ibid.*
73. Sir Henry Hawkins (1817–1907), later Lord Brampton. Sat as judge on notable cases such as Dr Thomas Neill Cream (1892) and the Muswell Hill murder (1896).
74. The City of London Force used a similar book, *The City of London Police Orders and Regulations*.
75. Publication was switched from Bow Street to Scotland Yard in 1883.
76. Martin Fido & Keith Skinner, *The Official Encyclopaedia of Scotland Yard* (Virgin Publishing Ltd, 1999). p. 40.
77. Charles Dickens (Jr), *Dickens Dictionary of London 1888* (Old House Books, 1993).
78. MEPO 2/489, Special Service Charges. National Debt Office Report, 19 November 1891.
79. MEPO 4/36 *Instruction Booklet for Candidates and Constables* (1871), p. 16.
80. Worship Street Police Court also covered the Whitechapel area.
81. C. E. Howard-Vincent, *The Police Code* 1889, p. 76.
82. *Police Walks* B350, f. 37.
83. Victor Bailey, *Charles Booth's Policemen, Crime, Police and Community in Jack the Ripper's London* (Breviary Stuff Publications, 2014), p. 21.
84. It is worth noting that, on average, the City of London beats were of a shorter distance than their Metropolitan counterparts.
85. There was the odd unique beat where the relief times were altered, for special locations such as the Royal Mint.
86. City of London PC 881 Edward Watkins, who found the body of Catherine Eddowes in Mitre Square, notified jurors at her inquest that he had been working his beat 'left handed', i.e. his beats had more left turns than right, meaning that he had reversed his beat when he found her.
87. The period during the Whitechapel murder series, between the double event of 30 September 1888 and Mary Kelly's murder on 9 November 1888, where no murders occurred, is referred to by most students of the case as the 'October lull'.
88. *The Daily News*, 19 October 1888.
89. During the night of 29 October 1888, at the height of the Jack the Ripper scare, City of London policemen were instructed to keep an eye out for suspicious couples, i.e. prostitutes and their clients. This would have been the kind of directive stated at muster, just prior to the commencement of the beats.
90. This is what City PC 881 Edward Watkins is referring to when he states he was on duty at 9.45 p.m. (he was at muster) and on his beat by 10 p.m., which was the night relief start time. In the fifteen-minute interval he was being marched to his beat starting point.
91. The constable who was due to be relieved would finish his last patrol at the beat's starting point, and should be in position by the changeover time of 6 a.m. early relief, 2 p.m. late relief and 10 p.m. night relief.
92. Constables were required to note any broken lamps on their beats in their notebooks and report them to the beat sergeant upon return to the station. The sergeant or inspector would notify the Board of Works, under whose jurisdiction street lighting came, via the issuing of

a Morning Report, and it was then the responsibility of the Board of Works to ensure the lamp was fixed as swiftly as possible.

93. Occurrence book, where all matters are recorded. This could include incidents on a beat, various crimes reported, visitors such as doctors, MPs etc., and any other matter worthy of note.

94. Victor Bailey, *Charles Booth's Policemen, Crime, Police and Community in Jack the Ripper's London*. (Breviary Stuff Publications, 2014), p. 20.

95. As reported in the *Daily News*, 19 October 1888, and MEPO 4/36 *Instruction Booklet for Candidates and Constables*, first published in 1871.

96. MEPO 4/36, *Instruction Booklet for Candidates and Constables* (1871).

97. MEPO 2/209. Home Office Act of Parliament 23 April 1887.

98. This was altered due to the amendment of the Licensing Act in 1902.

99. It wasn't unheard of for the superintendent to conduct the odd inspection, if he so wished.

100. *The City of London Police Orders and Regulations book 1839–1894*, Constables section 4, p. 24. A similarly worded passage can also be found in C. E. Howard-Vincent, *The Police Code* (1889), p. 71 and *Police* by Charles Tempest Clarkson and J. Hall Richardson, Leadenhall Press 1889.

101. It must be noted that PC Mizen denied this, and that the murder occurred upon J Division's jurisdiction (Bethnal Green).

102. *Police Walks* B350. f. 49. Superintendent John Mulvaney had, in 1895, taken on Thomas Arnold's role as H Division's superintendent two years after Arnold had retired, and remained in that position until 1911. He spent the majority of his police career in Whitechapel, having originally been assigned there as a constable in 1871.

103. Victor Bailey, *Charles Booth's Policemen, Crime, Police and Community in Jack the Ripper's London* (Breviary Stuff Publications, 2014), p. 24, n. 51.

104. MEPO 2/203. List of shelters open for the night for unfortunate women 1892.

105. Martin Fido & Keith Skinner, *The Official Encyclopaedia of Scotland Yard* (Virgin Publishing Ltd, 1999). p. 257.

106. *The City of London Police Orders and Regulations book 1839–1894*, p. 36.

107. *The Daily News*, 19 October 1888.

6 Tecs

1. Sir James Graham (1792–1861), Home Secretary 1841–1846.

2. Paul Begg & Keith Skinner, *The Scotland Yard Files* (Headline Publishing, 1992), p. 37.

3. Haia Shpayer-Makov, *The Ascent of the Victorian Detective: Police Sleuths in the Victorian and Edwardian Era* (2011).

4. *Ibid.*

5. Sir Charles Warren, 'The police of the Metropolis', *Murray's Magazine*, 1888.

6. Charles Tempest Clarkson & J. Hall Richardson, *Police!* (Field & Tuer, The Leadenhall Press, 1889), pp. 262–263. When Howard Vincent first took on the role as head of CID in 1878, he initially used those considered the dimmest in uniformed branch as plain-clothed men, and gave them duties which were akin to those of a glorified messenger boy; however, his opinions soon changed.

7. *Ibid*, p. 264.

8. The Metropolitan Police Museum, based at Scotland Yard and established around 1869, is better known as the Black Museum or, today, as the Crime Museum. The museum is not open to the public.

9. Police Orders, 1 September 1888.

10. Plain-clothes work was actually undertaken during the early years of the Metropolitan Force; however, this was a case of uniformed constables donning civilian clothes for a month when walking their beats, in order to catch out any wrong-doers. It resulted in failure as the local public instantly recognised the constable anyway.

11. C. E. Howard-Vincent, *The Police Code*, 1889, p. 53.

12. Arthur Harding, *My Apprenticeship to Crime*, chapter 8, 'Gibraltar Gardens 1904'. (1969), p. 125. Arthur Harding, born in 1886 in the Old Nichol slums around Shoreditch, became a well-known East End criminal in the area from the Edwardian period onwards. He wrote his autobiography, *My Apprenticeship to Crime*, in 1969. Raphael Samuels used Harding's work in his biography of him in 1981. It was entitled *East End Underworld: Chapters in the Life of Arthur Harding*. See Bishopsgate Institute's online archives.

13. *Ibid*. p. 52. On rare occasions, such as sickness or bereavement, ticket-of-leave men could send a letter explaining the situation, rather than appear in person.

14. Victor Bailey, *Charles Booth's Policemen, Crime, Police and Community in Jack the Ripper's London*. (Breviary Stuff Publications, 2014), p. 42.

15. *Ibid.*

16. Victor Bailey, *Charles Booth's Policemen, Crime, Police and Community in Jack the Ripper's London*. (Breviary Stuff Publications, 2014), pp. 42–43.

17. *Police Walks* B353. f. 225.

18. Detective Constable Robert Sagar (1852–1924). Part of the City of London Force from 1880 to 1905, alleged to have conducted observations on a Jack the Ripper suspect in Butcher's Row, Aldgate, with some authors speculating it was Aaron Kosminski or David Cohen.

19. City of London Police Detective Division. Statements, Reports, Correspondence on cases under investigation. CLA/048/AD/11/008.

20. Haia Shpayer-Makov, *The Ascent of the Victorian Detective: Police Sleuths in the Victorian and Edwardian Era* (2011).

21. Commission Report, 1878, p. 180.

22. By 1889, Great Britain had extradition treaties with France, Germany, Austria-Hungary, Brazil, Spain, Italy, Belgium, The Netherlands, Denmark, Sweden and Norway, Switzerland, Hayti (Haiti), USA, Grand Duchy of Luxemburg, Salvador, Guatemala, Russia and Mexico.

23. George Dilnot, *Scotland Yard: The Methods and Organisation of the Metropolitan Police* (Percival Marshall & Co., 1915).

24. *Ibid.*

25. Charles Tempest Clarkson & J. Hall Richardson, *Police!* (Field & Tuer, The Leadenhall Press, 1889), p. 298. Observation is to watch a suspect, surveillance is both to watch and follow a suspect.

26. The chief inspector is a senior uniformed officer; however, a requirement for this role was that he had extensive experience as a plain-clothed officer, with the reasoning being that he would have a unique understanding of both uniformed and detective requirements. Detectives never made the transition into uniform unless during special circumstances or via demotion.

27. Despatch carts were used, and based at a pre-selected sub-divisional station (Arbour Square for H Division). Despatch bags for each individual sub-divisional station were used. The despatch drivers were required to abide to a strict timetable, with the arrival times for Leman Street, H Division HQ being 8.12 a.m., 11.42 a.m., 5.42 p.m. and 9.42 p.m., each with a three-minute turnaround. Police Orders, 20 March 1888.

28. Victor Bailey, *Charles Booth's Policemen, Crime, Police and Community in Jack the Ripper's London*. (Breviary Stuff Publications, 2014), p. 62. *Police Walks* B349, f.43.

29. *Ibid.* p. 66.

30. *The Belfast Newsletter*, 21 September 1888.

31. C. E. Howard-Vincent, *The Police Code 1889*, p. 24.

32. George Dilnot, *Scotland Yard: The Methods and Organisation of the Metropolitan Police* (Percival Marshall & Co. 1915).

33. *Ibid.*

34. *Police Walks* B353, ff. 227, 229. Victor Bailey, *Charles Booth's Policemen, Crime, Police and Community in Jack the Ripper's London* (Breviary Stuff Publications, 2014), p. 40.

35. C. E. Howard-Vincent, *The Police Code* (1889), p. 64. The tap-room comment is in reference to a public house, or a bar in a hotel.

36. Informer.

37. Victor Bailey, *Charles Booth's Policemen, Crime, Police and Community in Jack the Ripper's London*. (Breviary Stuff Publications, 2014), pp. 40–41.

38. Frederick George Abberline (1843–1929), probably the most well-known policeman connected to the Whitechapel murders. A Dorset man by birth, Abberline joined the Metropolitan Force in 1863, serving in uniform firstly at N Division Islington, then Y Division Highgate, before being moved in to plain clothes in 1867. Promoted to inspector in H Division in 1873, he served many years there before moving to A Division Whitehall in 1887, and then on to Scotland Yard to join the prestigious Central Office CID. He was moved back in to Whitechapel in 1888 to work with Local Inspector Edmund Reid during the murder scare. Abberline held valuable knowledge regarding the villains and people of Whitechapel, with H Division's acting superintendant John West specifically, and officially, requesting Abberline's assistance from Central Office on 8 September 1888.

39. Nicholas Connell & Stewart P. Evans, *The Man who Hunted Jack the Ripper: Edmund Reid and the Police Perspective* (Rupert Books, 2000), p. 9. Also, 2nd edition (Amberley, 2009), p. 27.

40. Frogg, Moody, *Sergeant William Thick, Journal of the Whitechapel Society* (2006).

41. Nicholas Connell, *Walter Dew: The Man Who Caught Crippen* (Sutton Publishing, 2006), p. 6. Dew was a young detective constable in Whitechapel at the time of the murders in 1888.
42. Jack London, *The People of the Abyss* (Echo library, 2007), p. 11. First published in 1903.
43. Victor Bailey, *Charles Booth's Policemen: Crime, Police and Community in Jack the Ripper's London.* (Breviary Stuff Publications, 2014), p. 41.

7 Emma Smith, 4 April 1888

1.   Emma Smith's case is currently missing from the Whitechapel murders files, lost while in transition to the National Archives. However, notes taken by Ian Sharp (for the 1973 BBC programme *Jack the Ripper*) and Don Rumbelow enable us to review part of the records which were available until recently.
2.   Nicholas Connell, *Walter Dew: The Man who Caught Crippen* (Sutton Publishing, 2005), p. 7.
3.   Paul Begg, Martin Fido & Keith Skinner, *The Complete Jack the Ripper A–Z* (John Blake Publishing Ltd, 2010), p. 473. As Smith also stated she had left her husband, it is reasonable to assume either the widow's story was a cover to gain sympathy, or that she had left her husband and that he had died sometime after that.
4.   Charles Tempest Clarkson & J. Hall Richardson, *Police!* (Field & Tuer, The Leadenhall Press, 1889).
5.   Charles Dickens (Jnr), *Dickens Dictionary of London 1888* (Old House Books, 1993). The pattern for these inspections was an irregular one, for obvious reasons.
6.   A mention must be made of the 'rents'. These rents were rooms rented out by the landlord to individuals or families, and sometimes these tenants rented the rooms to sub-tenants, such was the demand for space.
7.   Jack London (1876–1916). His best-known novels include *The Call of the Wild* and *White Fang*.
8.   Jack London, *The People of the Abyss* (1903).
9.   The witness who saw this was Margaret Hames (or Hayes), a fellow lodger at 18 George Street who herself had been attacked a few months prior to Smith.
10. Stewart Evans & Keith Skinner, *The Ultimate Jack the Ripper Sourcebook* (Robinson, 2001), p. 4. This report was transcribed by the authors from notes made by Donald Rumbelow during the 1970s. The original report is unfortunately now missing. (Private correspondence with Stewart Evans.)
11. Chief Inspector John West was acting superintendent at the time, covering Superintendent Thomas Arnold's role as the latter was on leave during this period.
12. Deputy lodging-house keeper.
13. Cited as 'Hayes' in some reports. Hames claimed to have seen Smith in Poplar, a few miles away from the lodging house, only hours before her attack, talking to a man dressed in a dark suit and wearing a white silk handkerchief round his neck. Hames herself had been assaulted by two men the day before Smith's attack, being hit in the mouth by one of them.
14. Better known as Whitechapel church, from which the area takes its name.
15. The exact location is unknown. Smith had pointed out the scene as she was escorted to the London Hospital. Numerous news reports state it was at the junction, others state opposite 10 Brick Lane. Paul Begg, John Bennett & Jaakko Luukanen, *Jack the Ripper CSI: Whitechapel* (Andre Deutsch, 2012), p. 29.
16. Smith's reluctance to go to hospital was understandable, as the common East End mantra at the time was that if you went in, you rarely came out.
17. *The Times*, 9 April 1888.
18. Franchised coroners would operate within smaller areas, such as Samuel Langham in the City of London. The county coroners in the London area of that period, such as Wynne Baxter, Dr Roderick Macdonald, Dr Thomas Diplock and George Danford Thomas, had large districts covering many parishes, which they would continually move across almost every day except Sunday, travelling from inquest to inquest. (Private correspondence David O'Flaherty.)
19. Wynne Edwin Baxter (1844–1920). Prominent coroner of the period, Baxter presided over seven inquests in connection to the Whitechapel murders (Smith, Nichols, Chapman, Stride, Mylett, McKenzie and Coles) as well as the famous Lipski/Angel case the previous year. Baxter also presided at the inquest into the death of Joseph Merrick (The Elephant Man) and, towards the end of his career, at the inquests into the deaths of the combatants at the Siege of Sidney Street. He was also Mayor of his home town, Lewes, in 1881. For an excellent biography on Baxter read *Inquest, London* by Adam Wood, in *Ripperologist* magazine, issue 61, September 2005.

20. A letter would be issued to the witness's home address, requesting that they collect the summons from a named police station.
21. It must be noted that once an inquest is under way, the parish officer acts as the clerk, swearing in jurors and witnesses as well as taking jurors to view the body.
22. *Lloyds Weekly*, 8 April 1888.

8 Martha Tabram, 7 August 1888

1.   Today's Gunthorpe Street.
2.   Metropolitan PC 226 H Thomas Barrett (Warrant number 67481).
3.   MEPO 3/140, f. 34.
4.   Paul Begg, Martin Fido & Keith Skinner, *The Complete Jack the Ripper A–Z* (John Blake Publishing Ltd), 2010, p. 506.
5.   Another resident of George Yard Buildings, Alfred George Crow, had actually come across a body on the same spot at 3.30 a.m., upon his return from work. Assuming it was a drunk asleep, he left and proceeded to his rooms.
6.   Little is known about Dr Timothy Robert Killeen's life. Author M. W. Oldridge, in his Murder & Crime series book, *Whitechapel & District* (The History Press, 2011), notes that Killeen was probably an Irishman by birth, probably from a quiet and rural area, and very likely Catholic. He also notes that Killeen's name drops from the Medical Directory in 1907 and that he was living in Ennis, Co. Clare, Ireland, at this time. M. W. Oldridge has found, in the Irish Civil Registration Deaths index (1864–1958), that Killeen died in the first quarter (Jan, Feb, Mar) of 1912. (Private correspondence M. W. Oldridge, January 2014.)
7.   The instruction to obtain medical assistance can be found in MEPO 4/36 *Instruction Booklet for Candidates and Constables* (1871) and the City of London Police Orders, Regulations and Acts of Parliament 1839–1894.
8.   *East London Advertiser*, 11 August 1888.
9.   Located next to the Whitechapel Underground station. The inquest was adjourned by Collier pending identification of the body, and police enquiries. It resumed a fortnight later on 23 August 1888.
10. Statement of Dr Timothy Killeen given at the inquest into Martha Tabram's death. *The Times*, 10 August 1888.
11. *East London Advertiser*, 11 August 1888.
12. Why PC Barrett did not investigate this obvious reference to a prostitute and client is unknown, however it wasn't uncommon for a constable to be lax in their judgement of such matters, for the want of an 'easy life'.
13. Inspector Edmund Reid's summary report, 16 August 1888. MEPO 3/140, ff. 44–8.
14. The previous day, 6 August 1888, was a summer bank holiday, a traditional time for people to enjoy themselves by attending fairs and events, meeting family, and so on. However, it was more traditional in the East End to spend this holiday drinking and enjoying the events of the music hall. Some soldiers were granted leave during these days and those who had committed minor offences, such as the drunk and disorderly, were handed over to the Army's superior officers to be dealt with. According to Booth's Police Walks, the police were more lenient with drunks during bank holidays.
15. Inspector Edmund Reid's summary report, 24 September 1888. MEPO 3/140, ff. 52–9.
16. *East London Observer*, 18 August 1888.
17. Inspector Edmund Reid's summary report, 24 September 1888. MEPO 3/140, ff. 52–9.
18. In Chief Inspector Donald Swanson's overall summary report into Tabram's death, dated September 1888, he states that the regimental log book actually records Skipper's precise time of returning to barracks as 10.05 p.m. MEPO 3/140, ff. 36–42.
19. Alias Luckhurst. Often spelt Bousefield, this spelling of her name is taken from the St George in the East Baptism register of 23 April 1876 in connection to her daughter Mary Ann. Coincidentally, the next child on the list, and therefore baptised on the same day, is William Charles Thick, son of H Division's Detective Sergeant in 1888, William Thick. (M. W. Oldridge, private correspondence, Jan 2014.)
20. *The Echo*, 10 August 1888.

9 Mary Ann 'Polly' Nichols, 31 August 1888

1.   C. E. Howard-Vincent, *The Police Code*, 1889, p. 143.
2.   Professor David Taylor, *The Metropolitan Police and Working-Class Women in the Late 1880s*. *The Whitechapel Society Magazine*, Issue No. 54.

3. *Gloucester Citizen*, 1 February 1888; *Sheffield Evening Telegraph*, 1 February 1888; and the *Pall Mall Gazette*, 15 & 21 February 1888.

4. *Pall Mall Gazette*, 15 February 1888.

5. *Pall Mall Gazette*, 21 February 1888.

6. *Funny Folks*, 18 February 1888.

7. *The Star*, 3 September 1888, inquest testimony of Charles Bretton (Britton).

8. *The Times*, 3 September 1888, inquest testimony of PC 97 J John Neil. News report on the inquest held into the death of Mary Ann Nichols. Located in Home Office File, Ref HO 144/221/A49301C, ff. 6–7. No known official transcript of the inquest has survived.

9. Known as Durward Street since 1892, after a campaign was launched by the locals to change the name due to the connotations it had with the Nichols murder.

10. Paul Begg & John Bennett, *Jack the Ripper CSI: Whitechapel* (Andre Deutsch, 2012), p. 56.

11. Dr Rees Ralph Llewellyn (1849–1921), Matriculation University of London 1869, Licentiate Society of Apothecaries 1873, Member of the Royal College of Surgeons England 1874, Licensed Royal College of Physicians London 1876, Medical Officer to East and East Central Districts of London, and City Missions.

12. C. E. Howard-Vincent, *The Police Code* (1889), p. 106.

13. Cross is the name used at inquest, and the surname of his stepfather, ex-police constable Thomas Cross. However, census returns, and other material, shows that he predominantly used the family name of Lechmere. For the sake of continuity, I shall use the name of Cross.

14. *The Times*, 4 September 1888, inquest testimony of Charles Cross. News report on the inquest held into the death of Mary Ann Nichols. Home Office File Ref HO 144/221/A49301C, f. 8.

15. *Ibid.*, inquest testimony of Robert Paul. Home Office File Ref HO 144/221/A49301C, ff. 9–10.

16. *Ibid.*, inquest testimony of Charles Cross. Home Office File Ref HO 144/221/A49301C, f. 8.

17. *Ibid.*, inquest testimony of PC 56H Jonas Mizen. Home Office File Ref HO 144/221/A49301C, f. 8.

18. Martin Fido & Keith Skinner, *The Official Encyclopaedia of Scotland Yard* (Virgin Publishing Ltd, 1999), p. 8.

19. Police Orders, 8 September 1888.

20. Also known as Brittain or Britten in various newspaper accounts.

21. Thain did admit that his cape was at the slaughterers', claiming that a 'Brother Officer', most likely Constable Neil, had taken it there on his behalf. However, Thain claimed he went straight to Dr Llewellyn's and did not stop to speak to anyone.

22. *The Times*, 4 September 1888, inquest testimony of Walter Purkiss. News report on the inquest held into the death of Mary Ann Nichols. Home Office File Ref. HO 144/221/A49301C, ff. 9–10.

23. *Ibid.*, Inquest testimony of Emma Green. Home Office File Ref. HO 144/221/A49301C, ff. 9–10.

24. *Ibid.*, Inquest testimony of Patrick Mulshaw. Home Office File Ref. HO 144/221/A49301C, ff. 9–10.

25. *The Times*, 3 September 1888, inquest testimony of PC 97 J John Neil. Home Office File Ref. HO 144/221/A49301C, ff. 6–7.

26. *Ibid.*, inquest testimony of Dr Rees Ralph Llewellyn. Located in Home Office File Ref. HO 144/221/A49301C, ff. 6–7.

27. *Evening News*, 3 September 1888.

28. Special Report by Inspector John Spratling, 31 August 1888, countersigned by J Division Superintendent James Keating. MEPO 3/140, ff. 239–41.

29. *Evening News*, 3 September 1888.

30. Special Report by Inspector John Spratling, 31 August 1888, countersigned by J Division Superintendent James Keating. MEPO 3/140, ff. 239–41. S.S. refers to side spring.

31. *The Times*, 4 September 1888, Inquest testimony of Inspector John Spratling. News report on the inquest held into the death of Mary Ann Nichols. Home Office File Ref. HO 144/221/A49301C, f. 8.

32. Local Inspector Joseph Henry Helson (1845–1920). Metropolitan Force 1869–1895, officially replaced Inspector Edmund Reid as Local Inspector of J Division Bethnal Green's CID in October 1887.

33. There is some confusion about the undressing of the victim. Mann and Hatfield, the mortuary attendants, claimed that they were not instructed to leave the body alone, and so continued to undress the cadaver as they had done on previous occasions. However, at

the inquest, Detective Sergeant Patrick Enright of J Division CID was adamant that he had clearly instructed the attendants not to touch the body.

34. *The Illustrated Police News*, 8 September 1888.
35. Prince's Road.
36. *The Illustrated Police News*, 8 September 1888.
37. C. E. Howard-Vincent, *The Police Code* (1889), p. 59.
38. *The Echo*, 1 September 1888. Samuel Hubert Seccombe, born in Devonshire in 1865, emigrated to Australia in 1891. See also the website JTRForums.com, 'Dr Llewellyn's Assistant'.
39. The City Force regularly, though not exclusively, used the Metropolitan Force's photographic unit, with perhaps the most famous example being the photographs taken by the Metropolitan Police at the crime scene in the City of London's Cutler Street, better known as the Houndsditch Murders, in 1910. The Metropolitan Force's photographic log book, held at the Metropolitan Police Heritage Centre, contains this entry, and states the photos were used as evidence against one of the accused conspirators, Nina Vassilleva.
40. The mortuary photographs of Martha Tabram and Frances Coles, at either end of the Whitechapel Murder series, have the stamp of photographer Louis Grumprecht on the rear. However, as Robert McLaughlin points out in his excellent work on the photographs concerning the murders, *The First Jack the Ripper Victim Photographs* (Zwerghaus Books, 2005), Gumprecht's studio was taken over by Joseph Martin in 1887. It seems as if Martin continued to use Gumprecht's stamp throughout 1888 and 1889, as the address remained the same.
41. Robert McLaughlin, *The First Jack the Ripper Victim Photographs* (Zwerghaus Books, 2005). p. 66.
42. Further Report by Local Inspector Joseph Helson dated 7 September 1888, in reference to Special Report dated 31 August 1888. MEPO 3/140, ff. 235–238.
43. *The Evening Standard*, 1 September 1888.
44. Many civilian staff were employed by the police to cover administration. The clerk of works was one of these positions, with responsibility for paperwork concerning the maintenance of police-owned buildings.
45. Paul Begg & John Bennett, *Jack the Ripper CSI: Whitechapel* (Andre Deutsch, 2012), p. 71.
46. Also referred to as Emily Holland, Nelly Holland and, possibly due to a mishearing by the press at inquest, Jane Oram.
47. *The Times*, 4 September 1888, inquest testimony of Ellen Holland (erroneously reported as Jane Oram). News report on the inquest held into the death of Mary Ann Nichols. Home Office File Ref. HO 144/221/A49301C, f. 8.
48. Further Report by Local Inspector Joseph Helson dated 7 September 1888, in reference to Special Report dated 31 August 1888. MEPO 3/140, ff. 235–238.
49. Philip Sugden, *The Complete History of Jack the Ripper* (Robinson Publishing Ltd, 1995), p. 42. Author M. W. Oldridge has located another child, William Edward Walker, who was Nichols' first-born child, born on 17 December 1864, sadly dying six months later, on 17 June 1865. St Brides, Fleet Street, Baptism Register, 8 January 1865 & West Kensington St Mary Burial Register, 1865.
50. Neal Shelden, *The Victims of Jack the Ripper* (Inkling Press, 2007), p. 6–7.
51. *Daily News*, 3 September 1888.
52. Philip Sugden, *The Complete History of Jack the Ripper* (Robinson Publishing Ltd, 1995), p. 46.
53. Paul Begg, Martin Fido & Keith Skinner, *The Complete Jack the Ripper A–Z* (John Blake Publishing Ltd, 2010), p. 376.
54. *Daily News*, 3 September 1888.
55. Melville Macnaghten (1853–1921). Knighted in 1907, Macnaghten became the Metropolitan Police's assistant chief constable of CID in 1889, before moving into the senior chief constable role in 1890. He served as assistant commissioner from 1902 until his retirement in 1913.
56. *The Evening Standard*, 7 September 1888.

10 Annie Chapman, 8 September 1888

1. Inspector Joseph Linuss Chandler (1850–1923), Metropolitan Police 1873–1898. Demoted to sergeant in 1892 for drunkenness while on duty.
2. *The Times*, 14 September 1888, inquest testimony of Divisional Inspector Joseph Chandler. News report on the inquest held into the death of Annie Chapman. Home Office file HO 144/221/A49301C, ff. 16–17.

3. One Special Report compiled by H Divisional Inspector Joseph Chandler dated 8 September 1888, MEPO 3/140, ff. 9–11.

4. Dr George Bagster Phillips (1837–1897). MBBS, MRCS Eng, LM, LSA. Divisional surgeon for H Division Whitechapel from 1865 until his death in 1897.

5. Another witness, John Davis, stated at inquest that the fence was five feet in height.

6. *The Times*, 13 September 1888, inquest testimony of Amelia Richardson and Harriet (Annie) Hardiman. News report on the inquest held into the death of Annie Chapman. Home Office file HO 144/221/A49301C, ff. 14–15.

7. *Ibid.* Inquest testimony of Amelia Richardson.

8. Inquest reports by *The Times* names them as Mr and Mrs Copsey; however, Paul Begg, in *The Facts* (Robson Books, 2004), refers to the Copseys as actually being two sisters called Cooksley, citing the *Eastern Post* newspaper report of 15 September 1888. He also cites the *Manchester Guardian* dated 10 September 1888, where a similar name – Cooksly – was used, along with a first name of Eliza.

9. *The Times*, 13 September 1888, inquest testimony of Amelia Richardson and Harriet (Annie) Hardiman. News report on the inquest held into the death of Annie Chapman. Home Office file HO 144/221/A49301C, ff. 14–15.

10. *Daily Telegraph*, 14 September 1888. Inquest testimony of Dr George Bagster Phillips. News report on the inquest held into the death of Annie Chapman.

11. *The Times*, 14 September 1888, inquest testimony of Divisional Surgeon Dr George Bagster Phillips. News report on the inquest held into the death of Annie Chapman. Home Office file HO 144/221/A49301C, ff. 16–17.

12. *Ibid.* Bagster Phillips had an exchange with the coroner, Wynne Baxter, regarding the inclusion of the full post-mortem results, with the doctor stating that any further depth of information could 'only be painful to the feelings of the jury and the public'; however, the coroner, quite rightly, decided that Bagster Phillips should give a full account of the injuries.

13. *The Times*, 20 September 1888, inquest testimony of Edward 'Ted' Stanley. News report on the inquest held into the death of Annie Chapman. Home Office file HO 144/221/A49301C, ff. 18–19. Stanley, aka 'The Pensioner', admitted that his claim to be an ex-military man, hence his use of the nickname Pensioner, was false.

14. Divisional inspectors were uniformed officers. Police Orders of 20 September 1888 stated that Chandler is 'authorised to be employed in plain clothes with the usual allowance from 8 inst' (this month), and therefore Chandler undertook Reid's detective role, and continued to assist H Division CID after Reid returned.

15. *The Times*, 13 September 1888, inquest testimony of John Richardson. News report on the inquest held into the death of Annie Chapman. Home Office file HO 144/221/A49301C, ff. 14–15.

16. Various spellings also include Cadosche and Cadosh. Cadosch was christened Charles Albert, but seemingly chose to be known by the name Albert.

17. Colin MacDonald, 'What became of Albert Cadosch?' *Ripperologist* 126, June 2012.

18. Colin MacDonald, 'Charles Albert Cadosch and his family' *Ripperologist* 132, June 2013.

19. *The Times*, 15 September 1888.

20. Elizabeth Long also used the name Durrell on police records, noted down as 'Long Mrs. Alias Durrell'. Home Office File HO 144/221/A49301C, f. 136.

21. *The Times*, 20 September 1888, inquest testimony of Elizabeth Long. News report on the inquest held into the death of Annie Chapman. Home Office file HO 144/221/A49301C, ff. 18–19.

22. *Ibid.*

23. Police Orders, 8 September 1888.

24. *The Times*, 11 September 1888, inquest testimony of Timothy Donovan. News report on the inquest held into the death of Annie Chapman. Home Office file HO 144/221/A49301C, ff. 13.

25. The official identification of the body as Annie Chapman was made by the deceased's brother, Fountain Smith.

26. John Sivvey, also referred to as Jack Sivvey or Siffey. It is not known whether his surname was real or a mere take on his occupation as a sieve maker.

27. *The Times*, 11 September 1888, inquest testimony of Amelia Palmer (referred to erroneously as Farmer). News report on the inquest held into the death of Annie Chapman. Home Office file HO 144/221/A49301C, ff. 13.

28. Located on the corner of Dorset Street and Commercial Street, known locally as Ringer's, after the landlady, Matilda Ringer.

29. *The Times*, 20 September 1888, inquest testimony of Eliza Cooper. News report on the inquest held into the death of Annie Chapman. Home Office file HO 144/221/A49301C,

ff. 18–19. This is Cooper's tale, but one account has Chapman spotting Cooper exchanging Stanley's 2s piece for a penny in the pub, and the fight escalating from there. See, Paul Begg & John Bennett, *Jack the Ripper CSI: Whitechapel* (Andre Deutsch, 2012), p. 91.

30.   Further report compiled by Detective Inspector Joseph Chandler, dated 15 September 1888, MEPO 3/140, ff. 17–20.

31.   Via Chief Inspector Donald S. Swanson.

32.   File cover regarding request for authority to act on behalf of Inspector Joseph Chandler by Inspector Frederick Abberline, countersigned by Chief Inspector Donald S. Swanson and Senior Assistant Commissioner Alexander Carmichael Bruce on behalf of the Assistant Commissioner Sir Robert Anderson. Divisional Ref H915/4, MEPO 3/140, f. 20. Sir Alexander Carmichael Bruce (1850–1926), knighted in 1903, undertook the role of assistant commissioner (CID) in the place of Sir Robert Anderson while the latter was on sick leave.

33.   Paul Begg & John Bennett, *Jack the Ripper CSI: Whitechapel* (Andre Deutsch, 2012), p. 104.

34.   *The Times*, 12 September 1888.

35.   Whitechapel Infirmary, Porters' Admission and Discharge Register 19 February 1888–1 March 1889. Ref.: STBG/WH/123/020.

36.   Further Report by Local Inspector Joseph Helson (J Division) dated 7 September 1888, in reference to Special Report dated 31 August 1888. MEPO 3/140, ff. 235–238.

37.   *The Sheffield and Rotherham Independent*, 1 September 1888.

38.   Report compiled by Divisional Inspector Jonathon Styles (Y Division Highgate) dated 11 September 1888, Divisional Ref Y 5574. MEPO 3/140, ff. 12–13.

39.   Inspector Styles refers to the suspect as Joseph Isenschmid; however, his actual name was Jacob Isenschmidt. To avoid confusion, Styles's version is used.

40.   Stewart P. Evans & Donald Rumbelow, *Jack the Ripper: Scotland Yard Investigates* (Sutton Publishing, 2006), p. 88.

41.   Isenschmid was initially sent to Islington Workhouse by Y Division police, and the workhouse in turn placed him in the care of Fairfield Road Infirmary Asylum as they had the facilities to deal with such patients.

42.   Further Report compiled by Detective Sergeant William Thick dated 17 September 1888, MEPO 3/140, ff. 26–28.

43.   Report compiled by Local Inspector Joseph Helson (J Division) dated 19 September 1888, MEPO 3/140, ff. 29–31.

44.   Report compiled by Detective Inspector Frederick Abberline dated 18 September 1888, MEPO 3/140, ff. 24–25.

45.   Report compiled by Local Inspector Joseph Helson (J Division) dated 19 September 1888, MEPO 3/140, ff. 29–31.

46.   John Sweeney, *At Scotland Yard* (Grant Richards, 1904). Sweeney worked for the Irish Bureau, an organisation within the Metropolitan Police specifically created, in 1883, to tackle the growing issue of Fenian terrorist attacks, but funded by imperial funds, not Metropolitan Police funds. Sweeney moved to Special Branch when the Irish Bureau was completely encompassed by Special Branch (aka the Secret Department, internally known as Section D) in 1888.

47.   Commissioner Warren's instruction for cascading to all relevant ranks. Stewart P. Evans & Donald Rumbelow, *Jack the Ripper: Scotland Yard Investigates* (Sutton Publishing), 2006, p. 86.

11   Elisabeth Stride, 30 September 1888

1.   *The Star*, 8 September 1888.

2.   *The Echo*, 8 September 1888.

3.   *The Star*, 10 September 1888.

4.   *The Irish Times*, 17 September 1888.

5.   *The East London Observer*, 22 September 1888.

6.   Charles Reeves, born Samuel Isaacs (died 22 November 1906). Stephen Ryder, 'Charles Reeves' *Ripper Notes*, Issue 27.

7.   From the memoirs of Ada Reeve (1874–1966), actress and daughter of Charles Reeves, famous for her music hall, pantomime and comedies during the Edwardian era, as well as appearing in numerous films, including *They Came to a City* (1944) and, at the age of eighty-five, *A Passionate Stranger* (1957).

8.   Cyril Russell & Harry Samuel Lewis, *The Jew in London* (New York: Thomas Y. Crowell & Co. Publishers, 1901).

9.   The club was actually two buildings in one.

10. The 1881 and 1911 censuses state Marylebone, however the 1901 census and H Division register states Paddington.

11. Lamb's marriage banns, from his 1876 wedding to Sarah Dent at St John's church in Bethnal Green, state his occupation as servant. One assumes he gave this occupation in reference to his role as a civil servant, not wishing for his exact occupation to be known.

12. The 1881 and 1891 census returns. Incidentally, Lamb's youngest son, Edwin, was found to be deaf and dumb, and grew up to be a baker. Another daughter, Louisa, was four months old in the 1891 census, but she died in 1898. Finally, the youngest of the Lamb children, William, was born in 1896, and was a machinist in the 1911 census.

13. H Division Register. William E. Ayliffe (Warrant No. 73338). Aged twenty-two at the time, five feet nine inches in height, he was a former butcher who joined the Metropolitan Force on 6 February 1888, and was transferred to P Division (Camberwell) on 21 December 1888.

14. *The Times*, 2 October 1888, inquest testimony of Morris Eagle. News report on the inquest held into the death of Elisabeth Stride.

15. *The Times*, 3 October 1888, inquest testimony of Constable Henry Lamb 252H. News report on the inquest held into the death of Elisabeth Stride.

16. *Ibid*.

17. *Ibid*.

18. *The Times*, 4 October 1888, inquest testimony of Edward Johnson. News report on the inquest held into the death of Elisabeth Stride.

19. Cachous were small breath-freshening sweets, often used by prostitutes of the time.

20. *The Daily Telegraph*, 3 October 1888, inquest testimony of Dr Frederick William Blackwell. News report on the inquest held into the death of Elisabeth Stride.

21. *Ibid*.

22. Inspector Charles Pinhorn (1849–1920) was in the Metropolitan Force from 1868 to 1893.

23. *The Times*, 6 October 1888, inquest testimony of Local Inspector Edmund Reid. News report on the inquest held into the death of Elisabeth Stride.

24. *Ibid*.

25. Diemshitz is the name used in the police file on Stride, however he is most commonly referred to as Diemschutz in news reports and most books upon the subject.

26. *The Times*, 2 October 1888, inquest testimony of Louis Diemshitz. News report on the inquest held into the death of Elisabeth Stride.

27. *The Times*, 6 October 1888, inquest testimony of Philip Krantz. News report on the inquest held into the death of Elisabeth Stride.

28. *The Times*, 6 October 1888, inquest testimony of Local Inspector Edmund Reid. News report on the inquest held into the death of Elisabeth Stride.

29. *Ibid*.

30. *Née* Gustafsdotter.

31. Daniel Olsen, 'Elisabeth's story: A documentary narrative of Long Liz Stride's early life in Sweden', *Ripperologist*, issue 52, March 2004.

32. Paul Begg, Martin Fido & Keith Skinner, *The Complete Jack the Ripper A–Z* (John Blake Publishing Ltd, 2010), p. 493. The removal, according to Begg, Fido and Skinner, may have been down to the fact Stride had gained suitable employment, which was a valid reason to be struck off the prostitute register.

33. Sarah Harris, surname could also be Harrison. It seems she and Douglas were lodgers at the Packers' home. All stated they saw and heard nothing unusual.

34. Report by Detective Sergeant Stephen White dated 4 October 1888. MEPO 3/140/221/A49301C, ff.212–14.

35. *Ibid*.

36. *Ibid*.

37. Le Grand was actually a significant criminal, a thief with numerous aliases, such as Charles Grant and Christian Nielson, who was also imprisoned for blackmail and making threats.

38. Summarisation of a statement made by Matthew Packer by Assistant Commissioner Alexander Carmichael Bruce dated 4 October 1888. MEPO 3/140/221/A49301C, ff.215–216.

39. *The Times*, 4 October 1888, inquest testimony of Elizabeth Tanner, Charles Preston and Catherine Lane. News report on the inquest held into the death of Elisabeth Stride.

40. *The Daily Telegraph*, 6 October 1888, inquest testimony of William Marshall. News report on the inquest held into the death of Elisabeth Stride.

41. Incorrectly noted as Boyd and Christian Streets in some newspaper accounts.

42. Evidence provided by Superintendent John Mulvaney (H Division Whitechapel) Royal Commission on Alien Immigration, Vol. IX, 8469 1903. Victor Bailey, *Charles Booth's Policemen, Crime, Police and Community in Jack the Ripper's London* (Breviary Stuff Publications, 2014). p. 102.

43. Overall summary report compiled by Chief Inspector Donald S. Swanson on 19 October 1888. HO 144/221/A49301C, ff. 148–159.

44. *Ibid.*

45. C. E. Howard Vincent, *The Police Code 1889*, pp. 119–120. It must be noted that, despite this guidance, Howard Vincent was fully aware that the press could serve as a valuable tool in investigations. The police's relationship with the newspapers was contradictory: it was extremely complex and fraught, yet also co-operative.

46. Charles H. Cutbush was the executive branch superintendent at the time of the murders.

47. Police Orders, 2 February 1888.

48. Israel Lipski (1865–1887), convicted in 1887 for the murder of Miriam Angel in Batty Street, one street away from Berner Street. 'Lipski' was, according to Anderson and Abberline, an often-used anti-Semitic insult during this period of late 1880s.

49. Overall summary report compiled by Chief Inspector Donald S. Swanson on 19 October 1888. HO 144/221/A49301C, ff. 148–159.

50. It was, eventually, released to *The Police Gazette* on 19 October, though by that time the matter was already in the press.

51, *The Star*, 1 October 1888.

52. *Ibid.*

53. A handful of multilingual detectives were employed by Scotland Yard, however, these men were constantly assigned to cases, thus restricting their availability.

54. Edward Henry (1850–1931), Metropolitan Police Commissioner from 1903 to 1918, knighted in 1906. An innovative commissioner who was responsible, while assistant commissioner in 1901, for the introduction of the Fingerprint Bureau, and later as commissioner for typewriters to Scotland Yard and all stations, and a full telephone system across the Metropolitan Force. Henry survived an assassination attempt in 1912.

55. Victor Bailey, *Charles Booth's Policemen, Crime, Police and Community in Jack the Ripper's London* (Breviary Stuff Publications, 2014), p. 107.

56. Report by Superintendent John Mulvaney, dated 18 April 1900, upon the use of interpreters in H Division Whitechapel. MEPO 2/376.

57. Letter of complaint to Metropolitan Police Commissioner Warren by Mr James Steiner, dated 30 May 1895. MEPO 2/376.

58. MEPO 2/376.

59. *The Times*, 4 October 1888.

60. *Ibid.*

12 Catherine Eddowes, 30 September 1888

1. Neil Bell & Robert Clack, 'City Beat: City PC 931 Louis Robinson', *Ripperologist*, issue 102, May 2008. Modern research has failed to show that number 29 existed, and this may have been an error on Robinson's part.

2. Inquest testimony of City Constable 931 Louis Robinson, Coroner's Inquest (L), 1888, No. 135, Catherine Eddowes' inquest 1888 (London Metropolitan Archives).

3. City Constable George Simmons (*c.* 1845–1905), City of London Police from 1861 to 1890. Robert Clack's research has found that Simmons died in 1905 from injuries sustained in an accident; he fell off a cart while collecting hedge clippings. The horse was still attached to the cart and suddenly moved, throwing Simmons head first off the cart. He was partially paralysed from the shoulders down, and succumbed to injuries to his spine some days later. *Police Review*, 27 October 1905.

4. City Sergeant 44 James George Byfield (1848–1927), City of London Police from 1868 until 1895.

5. City Constable 968 George H. Hutt stated that drunks were not searched, however, anything with which they could injure themselves was removed.

6. City Constable 968 George Henry Hutt (1854–1918), City of London Police from 1879 until his resignation in 1889 due to his suspension for assaulting a prisoner who was in the dock at Moor Lane. He was taken on as a constable at Smithfield Market very soon after, leaving there in 1906. See also Neil Bell & Robert Clack, *City Beat: City PC 968 George Hutt*, *Ripperologist*, issue 103, June 2009.

7. Inquest testimony of City Constable 968 George H. Hutt, Coroner's Inquest (L), 1888, No. 135, Catherine Eddowes' inquest 1888 (London Metropolitan Archives).

8. *Ibid.*

9. Inquest testimony City Station Sergeant James Byfield, Coroner's Inquest (L), 1888, No. 135, Catherine Eddowes' inquest 1888 (London Metropolitan Archives).

10. The City of London Force had a policy of releasing their drunks when they were deemed

capable of looking after themselves, whereas the Metropolitan Force released them at dawn, around 6 a.m.

11. Inquest testimony of City Constable 968 George H. Hutt, Coroner's Inquest (L), 1888, No. 135, Catherine Eddowes' inquest 1888 (London Metropolitan Archives).

12. City of London Police Order Books for 6 Division (Bishopsgate), 1889–1891.

13. City Constable 881 Edward Watkins (1844–1913), Metropolitan Constable from 1870 until 1871, then City of London Police from 1871 until 1896. See also Neil Bell & Robert Clack, 'City Beat: City PC 881 Edward Watkins', *Ripperologist*, issue 105, August 2009.

14. Neil Bell & Jake Luukanen, 'As far as Mitre Square' *Ripperologist*, issue 71, September 2006.

15. Often named as Taylor in many reports, articles and books; however, the discovery by Philip Hutchinson in 2007 of an 1892 quote for frames shows that he signed his own name as Charles Tayler.

16. Inquest testimony of City Constable 881 Edward Watkins, Coroner's Inquest (L), 1888, No. 135, Catherine Eddowes' inquest 1888 (London Metropolitan Archives).

17. George Morris (1834–1907) was in the Metropolitan Force from 1856 until 1863; he rejoined in 1864 before resigning again in 1882.

18. City Constable 964 James Harvey (1855–1903), City of London Police from 1876 until 1889.

19. Inquest testimony of City Constable 946 James Harvey, Coroner's Inquest (L), 1888, No. 135, Catherine Eddowes' inquest 1888 (London Metropolitan Archives).

20. City Constable Frederick Holland (b. 1863), in the City of London Force from 1885 until he was forced to resign in 1898 for an accumulation of misdemeanours, the final one being his absence from his beat for fifty minutes. He was a carman in later life and was still alive in 1911. For a full account see Neil Bell & Robert Clack, 'City Beat: City PC 814 Frederick Holland', *Ripperologist*, issue 109, December 2009.

21. Dr George William Sequeira (1858–1926), MRCS, LSA (London Hospital).

22. City of London Inspector Edward Collard (1846–1892), City of London Police from 1868 until his death, while a chief inspector, in 1892.

23. Station inspector is akin to the Metropolitan's duty inspector.

24. Dr Frederick Gordon Brown (1843–1928) LSA, MRCS, LM, City of London Police divisional durgeon from 1886 until 1914. Freemason, Grand Officer of the Grand Lodge of England, as well as Senior Past Master of the Society of Apothecaries, and former President of the Hunterian Society.

25. Inquest testimony of City Inspector Edward Collard, Coroner's Inquest (L), 1888, No. 135, Catherine Eddowes' inquest 1888 (London Metropolitan Archives).

26. Inquest testimony of Dr George William Sequeira, Coroner's Inquest (L), 1888, No. 135, Catherine Eddowes' inquest 1888 (London Metropolitan Archives).

27. Report compiled by City Inspector James McWilliam, 27 October 1888, ref. HO 144/221/ A49301C, ff. 162–70.

28. Inquest testimony of City Detective Constable 607 Daniel Halse, coroner's inquest (L), 1888, No. 135, Catherine Eddowes' inquest 1888 (London Metropolitan Archives).

29. Prostitutes would wear thimbles and tap upon the windows and sills of local late-night businesses to entice the workers inside to come out.

30. Major Henry Smith (1835–1921), Chief Superintendent of the City of London Police from 1885 to 1890, and commissioner from 1890 until 1901. Smith acted as commissioner during Commissioner Colonel Sir James Fraser's leave, which coincided with the Mitre Square murder, and seemingly remained in charge of the investigation of this crime upon Fraser's return.

31. Report compiled by City Inspector James McWilliam, 27 October 1888, ref. HO 144/221/ A49301C, ff. 162–70.

32. Inquest testimony of Metropolitan Constable 254A Alfred Long, coroner's inquest (L), 1888, No. 135, Catherine Eddowes' inquest 1888 (London Metropolitan Archives). The text is disputed, with differing variations and spelling, but this version of the writing was the one read out in court and noted.

33. Report compiled by Metropolitan Constable Alfred Long 254A, 6 November 1888, ref. HO 144/221/A49301C, ff. 195–6.

34. As the matter was in relation to a murder occurring within the City of London Police's jurisdiction, and the dwellings were located in Metropolitan territory, the onus fell upon the City of London Police to lead the investigation into this particular case.

35. *The Evening News*, 11 September 1888. The author of the letter, as claimed the *Jewish World* of 15 September 1888, was George Henry Hutt, a City of London constable who, as

gaoler for Bishopsgate police station, dealt with the victim found in Mitre Square only hours before she was murdered.

36. Report on the Whitechapel murders, Mitre Square murder, compiled by Metropolitan Police Commissioner Sir Charles Warren, 6 November 1888, ref. HO 144/221/A49301C, ff. 173–81.

37. The Parisian equivalent of CID.

38. The writing photo was discovered during a research visit to the City of London Police Museum Archives by John Bennett, Robert Clack, Catherine Coulthard (Curator), Laura Prieto and myself, on 18 February 2011.

39. The Artizan Labourers & General Dwellings Company was a philanthropic organisation which built dwellings for the working classes, in a similar vein to the Peabody Trust.

40. Neil Bell & Robert Clack, 'The victim photographs and some wall writing', *Ripperologist*, issue 127, August 2012.

41. This was later to be dismissed as a hoax.

42. Official list of clothing and possessions found upon Catherine Eddowes, attached to the inquest papers, coroner's inquest (L), 1888, No. 135, Catherine Eddowes' inquest, 1888 (London Metropolitan Archives).

43. Notes taken by Coroner Samuel Langham during the inquest testimony of Dr Frederick Gordon Brown, coroner's inquest (L), 1888, No. 135, Catherine Eddowes' inquest 1888 (London Metropolitan Archives), punctuation added.

44. *The Daily Telegraph*, 3 October 1888.

45. *The Times*, 2 October 1888.

46. Eddowes and Kelly had just returned from hop-picking in the Kent countryside, where they made the acquaintance of another couple, the female of which was named as Emily Birrell. Birrell gave Eddowes the pawn ticket, which was for a man's shirt, as she had no need for it, and felt it would fit Eddowes' partner, John Kelly.

47. City Constable 922 Richard William Pearce (*c*. 1850 – death unknown), City of London Police from 1873 until 1898. He became a licensed victualler porter by 1901, and possibly died in West Ham in 1907. See also Neil Bell & Robert Clack, 'City Beat: City PC 922 Richard Pearce', *Ripperologist* issue 107, October 2009.

48. Inquest testimony of City Constable 922 Richard Pearce, coroner's inquest (L), 1888, No. 135, Catherine Eddowes' inquest, 1888 (London Metropolitan Archives).

49. Overall summary report compiled by Chief Inspector Donald S. Swanson on 19 October 1888. HO 144/221/A49301C, ff. 148–159.

50. *The Evening News*, 9 October 1888.

51. Paul Begg, Martin Fido & Keith Skinner, *The Complete Jack the Ripper A–Z* (John Blake Publishing Ltd), 2010, p. 175.

52. *The Morning Advertiser*, 2 October 1888.

53. *Daily Northwestern*, Oshkosh, Wisconsin, USA, 3 October 1888.

54. *Ibid.*

13 Letters, Leaflets, Lusk and a Lull

1. MEPO 3/3153, f. 1.

2. 27 September, 1888.

3. MEPO 3/3153, ff. 2–4.

4. MEPO 3/142, ff. 2–3.

5. Stewart P. Evans & Keith Skinner, *Jack the Ripper: Letters from Hell* (Sutton Publishing, 2001), p. 32.

6. *Ibid.*, p. 35.

7. Chief Inspector John George Littlechild (1847–1923), was in the Metropolitan Police from 1867 until 1893. He was in CID at Scotland Yard from 1871, working his way through the ranks to Chief Inspector in 1882. He became Head of Section D, Special Branch in 1883, where he remained until his retirement in 1893. Due to his position as Head of Section D, Littlechild would have had an insight into the majority of unique cases involving the Metropolitan Police, including the Whitechapel murders.

8. George Robert Sims (1847–1922), journalist, dramatist, novelist, poet and celebrity of his day.

9. Private correspondence from John George Littlechild to G. R. Sims, dated 23 September 1913, quoted with the kind permission of Stewart P. Evans.

10. MEPO 1/48.

11. Report compiled by City Inspector James McWilliam dated 27 October 1888, ref HO 144/221/A49301C, ff. 162–70.

12. Report compiled by Chief Inspector Donald S. Swanson dated 6 November 1888. Ref. HO 144/221/A49301C, ff. 184–194.

13. Sir Robert Anderson, *The Lighter Side of My Official Life* (Hodder and Stoughton, 1910), p. 135.

14. Police Notice, 30 September 1888, MEPO 3/141. f. 184.

15. Overall summary report compiled by Chief Inspector Donald S. Swanson on 19 October 1888. HO 144/221/A49301C, ff. 148–159.

16. House of Commons Parliamentary Papers, Departmental Committee upon Metropolitan Police Superannuation, 29 November 1889.

17. A part of the same torso, a right arm, had been found on the Thames foreshore at Pimlico on 11 September 1888.

18. *Dundee & Argus Courier*, 6 October 1888.

19. *Ibid.*

20. *Dundee & Argus Courier*, 5 October 1888.

21. Report by H Division Superintendent Thomas Arnold, compiled 22 October 1888. MEPO 3/141, ff. 164–166.

22. *Ibid.*

14 Mary Jane Kelly, 9 November 1888

1. Dorset Street was also where a previous victim, Annie Chapman, had had lodgings, at Crossingham's.

2. Nicholas Connell, *Walter Dew, The Man Who Caught Crippen* (Sutton Publishing, 2006), pp. 35–7.

3. One suspects that the scene turned McCarthy's stomach somewhat.

4. *The Manchester Guardian*, 10 November 1888.

5. Inquest testimony of Dr George Bagster Phillips, inquest into the death of Mary Jane Kelly, held at Shoreditch Town Hall on 12 November 1888. MJ/SPC, NE1888, Box 3, Case Paper 19, London Metropolitan Archives.

6. *The Morning Advertiser*, 14 September 1888.

7. *Ibid.* 15 September 1888.

8. *The Times*, 2 October 1888.

9. HO 144/221/A49301E.

10. *Some Scarborough faces, past and present; being a series of interviews reprinted from Scarborough Magazine 1894–1898* (Scarborough Gazette Print, 1901).

11. *Ibid.*

12. Correspondence from Mr A. J. Sewell, veterinary surgeon to Metropolitan Police Commissioner Sir Charles Warren, 2, 5 & 7 November 1888. Ref. MEPO 2/188.

13. Correspondence from Mr A. J. Sewell, veterinary surgeon to Metropolitan Police Commissioner Sir Charles Warren, 2 November 1888. Ref. MEPO 2/188.

14. *Some Scarborough faces, past and present; being a series of interviews reprinted from Scarborough Magazine 1894–1898* (Scarborough Gazette Print, 1901). Wyndyate was the name of the Brough family home.

15. The first meeting of the Metropolitan Police Surgeons Association was held the Wednesday before Kelly's death, on 7 November 1888. The Metropolitan chief surgeon, McKellar, was in attendance, as were Drs Bond and Bagster Phillips, along with City of London surgeon, Dr Frederick Gordon Brown and, in practically his final act before tendering his resignation, Metropolitan Police Commissioner Sir Charles Warren. It is highly likely that the Whitechapel murders were discussed during this meeting, and perhaps plans to deal with future murders were discussed. If so, this may go some way towards explaining why so many doctors were in attendance at Millers Court on the day of Kelly's murder. See *British Medical Journal*, 10 November 1888.

16. Inquest testimony of Dr George Bagster Phillips, Inquest into the death of Mary Jane Kelly, held at Shoreditch Town Hall on 12 November 1888. MJ/SPC, NE1888, Box 3, Case Paper 19, London Metropolitan Archives.

17. Dr Thomas Bond (1841–1901), FRCS, MB, BS. Consultant to Westminster Hospital, Bond was the Metropolitan Police surgeon to A Division, Whitehall, from 1867 until his death in 1901. He worked on many of the Whitechapel murder cases, the Thames torso case and the Whitehall mystery case, as well as the Percy Lefroy Mapleton case in 1881 (alongside Chief Inspector Donald S. Swanson). He committed suicide on 6 June 1901, most likely due to chronic insomnia brought on by a bout of extreme painful illness.

18. Medical report by Dr Thomas Bond, 'Notes of examination of body of woman found murdered and mutilated in Dorset Street', MEPO 3/3153, ff. 12–14.

19. Inquest testimony of Joseph Barnett, inquest into the death of Mary Jane Kelly, held at Shoreditch Town Hall on 12 November 1888. MJ/SPC, NE1888, Box 3, Case Paper 19, London Metropolitan Archives.
20. Report into the Whitechapel murders compiled by Dr Thomas Bond on 10 November 1888. Ref. HO 144/221/A49301C, ff. 220–223.
21. Witness statement of Elizabeth Prater, given on 9 September 1888. MJ/SPC, NE1888, Box 3, Case Paper 19, London Metropolitan Archives.
22. Witness statement of Mary Ann Cox, given on 9 September 1888. MJ/SPC, NE1888, Box 3, Case Paper 19, London Metropolitan Archives.
23. *Ibid*. Cox stated she had had a good view of the man due to the position of a gas lamp just opposite Kelly's door.
24. Stewart P. Evans & Donald Rumbelow, *Scotland Yard Investigates* (Sutton Publishing, 2006), p. 186.
25. *The Daily Telegraph*, 10 November 1888.
26. Stewart P. Evans & Donald Rumbelow, *Scotland Yard Investigates* (Sutton Publishing, 2006), p. 186.
27. *The Irish Times*, 10 November 1888.
28. Bernard Brown, 'Inspector Spratling's pass' *Ripperologist*, Issue 29, June 2000. Incidentally, construction work was completed just after the death of Mary Kelly, with the line opening on 15 November 1888.
29. Stewart P. Evans, *Ripper Notes: Suspect and Witness – The Police Viewpoint* (Inklings Press, 2005).
30. This goes by the acronym SCANN.
31. Stewart P. Evans, *Ripper Notes: Suspect and Witness – The Police Viewpoint* (Inklings Press, 2005).
32. Special Report by Inspector Frederick G. Abberline complied on 12 November 1888. MEPO 3/140, ff. 230–232.

15 After the Canon, 1888–91

1. *The Times*, 12 November 1888.
2. Report to the Home Office on use of plain-clothes patrols in Whitechapel, compiled by Metropolitan Police Commissioner James Monro, dated 7 December 1888. Ref. HO144/221/A49301G, ff. 4–7.
3. *Ibid*.
4. A daily total costing H Division £5 per day.
5. Debra Arif & Robert Clack, 'A Rose by Any Other Name: The Death of Catherine Mylett, 20 December 1888', *Ripperologist*, issue 108, November 2009.
6. Report to the Home Office on use of plain-clothes patrols in Whitechapel, compiled by Metropolitan Police Commissioner James Monro, dated 26 January 1889. Ref. HO144/221/A49301G, ff. 14–16.
7. Initial report regarding the murder of Alice McKenzie compiled by Sergeant Edward Badham 31H, on 17 July 1889. Ref. MEPO 3/140, ff. 272–273.
8. According to H Division register, this was either Robert Spicer or George Neve.
9. Constable Allen's beat also took him into Castle Alley. He stopped at the murder scene at 12.35 a.m., some fifteen minutes before Constable Andrews' arrival, to have a small snack (which was permitted), before continuing on with his beat. He noted nothing suspicious then.
10. Summary Report regarding the murder of Alice McKenzie, compiled by H Division Superintendent Thomas Arnold on 17 July 1889. Ref. HO144/221/A493011 Ref. ff. 7–10.
11. Report and post mortem report on Alice McKenzie by Dr George Bagster Phillips, dated 17 July 1889. Ref. MEPO 3/140, ff. 259–262.
12. City of London Police Order Book No. 6 (Bishopsgate) 1889–1891.
13. Police Orders, 10 October 1888.
14. H Division Register. Possibly Richard Hart (Warrant No. 58917), a musician from Canterbury in Kent who joined the Metropolitan Force on 26 April 1875, and later transferred to the Reserves.
15. Summary Report compiled by Inspector Edmund Reid, dated 11 September 1889. Ref. MEPO 3/140, ff. 148–150.
16. *Ibid*.
17. *Ibid*.
18. *New York Herald*, 11 September 1889. Ref. MEPO 3/140, ff. 134–135.

19. Report on augmentation compiled by Metropolitan Commission James Monro, on 18 September 1889. Ref. HO 144/221/A49301G, ff. 30–32.

20. This is a combined number consisting of one inspector, three sergeants and thirty constables taken from duty in Trafalgar Square, and two inspectors, two sergeants and twenty constables from other divisions. Ref. MEPO 3/141, f. 21.

21. Report on augmentation compiled by Metropolitan Commission James Monro, on 18 January 1890. Ref. HO 144/220/A49301G, f. 36.

22. Approval Report compiled by Assistant Commissioner Alexander Carmichael Bruce on 17 March 1890. Ref. HO 144/221/A49301G, f. 40.

23. Thompson joined on 29 December 1890.

24. Report compiled by H Division Superintendent Thomas Arnold, on 13 February 1891. Ref. MEPO 3/140, ff. 112–114. It is worth noting that, at some stage during the Coles investigation, samples of her blood were taken for testing.

25. A seaman known as Tom Sadler was suspected of the murder of Frances Coles, but was subsequently released.

26. Chief Inspector Donald S. Swanson's handwritten notes in his personal copy of *The Lighter Side of My Official Life* by Sir Robert Anderson, p. 138. Also see Adam Wood & Keith Skinner, 'Red Lines and Purple Pencil: A History of the Swanson Marginalia', *Ripperologist*, Issue 128, October 2012.

27. *Ibid.*

28. United Kingdom House of Lords' decision announcement on the Daniel M'Naghten Case, 26 May 1843. M'Naghten shot and killed Edward Drummond that year; Drummond was the personal secretary to Sir Robert Peel, the Prime Minister (and the former Head of the Metropolitan Police). It was an error, as M'Naghten's intended target was Peel himself. A question rose over M'Naghten's sanity during the trial, which led to his acquittal. In response to this, guidelines were set up to protect those suffering from mental illness from trial, as it was considered they were in no position to defend themselves. These guidelines were known as the M'Naghten Rules, and once they were reviewed in relation to a specific case, and agreed upon, they resulted in the offender being placed in a secure asylum for an indefinite period.

29. Seaside homes were places where constables were sent to recuperate from illness, injury or mental stresses. Many private homes were used along the coast and in the countryside, and these were hired by both the City and the Metropolitan forces, however in 1890 the Convalescent Police Seaside Home opened in Brighton.

30. Letter received by H Division CID on 14 October 1888. Ref. MEPO 3/142, ff. 234–235.

31. 'A' was a marginal note by Abberline's replacement, Chief Inspector Moore, who stated, 'In conclusion I beg to observe that I do not attach any importance to this communication.'

32. Report compiled by Chief Inspector Donald S. Swanson, on 16 October 1896. Ref. MEPO 3/142, ff. 157–159.

Acknowledgements

I would thank the many people who have shared their own research with me, and aided in mine. If I have forgotten to mention anyone who has helped in this work, forgive me, it is unintentional. Please contact my publishers, and we shall ensure that correct accreditation appears in any subsequent editions.

It gives me immense pleasure to thank the following:

Robert Anderson, Greg Baldock, Stuart Bates (for providing information on Metropolitan Police helmets), John G. Bennett, Howard Brown, Nina Brown, Martin Fido, Cameron Hampton, Michele Heemskerk (for the kind permission to publish the photograph of Albert Cadosch), Robert House, Philip Hutchinson and Margaret Whitby-Green (for the kind permission to publish the John Gordon Whitby photographs), the late and much-missed Paul Kearney, Peter Kennison, Robert J. McLaughlin, Colin MacDonald, Cris Marlow, Frogg Moody, Jackie Murphy, David O'Flaherty (for sharing his information on Victorian coroner's courts), Chris Payne, Chris Phillips, Laura Prieto, Camille Ponchant, Ally Ryder, Stephen Ryder, the late and much-missed Chris Scott, Sue Shore, Jennifer Shelden, Neal Shelden, J. G. Simons, Don Souden, Nevil Swanson (for kind permission to publish artefacts belonging to Chief Inspector Donald S. Swanson), James Treversh (Police Memorabilia Collectors Club), Nicholas Wood and Janet Payne (from the Apothecaries Hall Society, for kind permission to publish the photograph of Dr Frederick Gordon Brown), members of Casebook Jack the Ripper and JTR Forums.com websites, the Leicestershire & Rutland Family History Society, London Metropolitan Archives, the National Archives, the Bishopsgate Institute, the Whitechapel Society 1888, the *Ripperologist* magazine, the Friends of the Metropolitan Police Historical Collection, *The Peeler Magazine, On a 728* magazine, members of the Gentlemen's Military History Club website, and, of course, the City of London Police and the Metropolitan Police forces, who have been extremely accommodating with their help and advice over these past few years.

I would also like to extend a specific note of gratitude to the following, all of whom I've never met; I respect their work immensely, and they are a constant reliable source. The late Bernard Brown, Nicholas Connell, Professor Clive Emsley, Professor William Fishman, Professor Haia Shpayer-Makov, the late Phillip Sugden and Richard Whittington-Egan.

A special mention must be given to the following, without whom this book simply would not exist. Firstly, I'd like to thank Christian Duck of Amberley Publishing, who took a chance with me and guided this fledgling author through the perils of his first book with consideration and support; I could not ask for better. Catherine Coulthard, record archivist and curator at the City of London Police Museum, who supplied copious amounts of tea and biscuits, and gave free reign to explore the City of London Archives, which led to the discovery of new information pertaining to the Jack the Ripper case; Catherine was the catalyst for this work. Neil Paterson and Alan Moss, from the Metropolitan Police Heritage Centre, who answered my endless emails, aided during my research trips, and gave permission to use Metropolitan Police images. Phillip Barnes-Warden, also of the Metropolitan Police Heritage Centre, who patiently guided me through records and ledgers during my numerous visits, who took time to explain certain aspects of policing, as well as berating me for my disappointing choice of cheap biscuits. Donald Rumbelow, whose work I've admired for many years, for taking a little time out during the making of the *Jack the Ripper: The Definitive Story* documentary to speak with me and give his insight into life as a City of London Police constable. Photographer, graphic artist and author Andrew Firth, for his assistance in this work, and our endless walks around the East End. Former police constable and author Mervyn Mitton, who guided me through all things related to police equipment and its history; he was always ready with a response to my emails, and I thank him for his kind permission to use extracts from his book. Author and historian Neil R. Storey, a kindred spirit who generously shared his extensive knowledge on all matters police over a drink or two in the White Hart. Huge thanks must go to highly respected researcher and writer Debra Arif, for her generosity in sharing her outstanding research and permitting me to use it, and for her belief in my work. A note of thanks goes to Sean Crundall, a tenacious and excellent researcher who tracked down the only known photograph of Dr Frederick Gordon Brown, and who also endured long telephone conversations with me on the case; I hope his work shall be published one day, as it should be. Paul Begg, who guided me through the initial stages of this project, and was there with steady advice and encouragement. I am very much indebted to Keith Skinner, who provided a wealth of information regarding the Metropolitan Police, was always ready to respond to my questions, invited me to conduct some of my research at the Metropolitan Police Heritage Centre, and also let me view some rare historical documents; a true gent. A heartfelt thanks goes to Stewart P. Evans and his wife, Rosie, for the warm hospitality shown during visits to their lovely home, the advice, the education, the generosity in permitting me to use images and information, and for patience shown, thank you both. Adam Wood has also shown me great hospitality and generosity during the completion of this book, has been there to help solve so many problems, and listen to my constant moans and groans; a true rock of a friend who is always there to rely on. Thanks Woody. A specific note of thanks must go to author M. W. Oldridge, known to his friends as Mark Ripper, for taking months out of his own time to proofread this work, and for providing invaluable nuggets of advice. I cannot express just how large a task this was. Mark's attention to detail is outstanding, and is only surpassed by his knowledge of the case and history in general, and I am eternally grateful to Mark for undertaking this vital work. I now wish to extend a particular mention to one of the most respected and authoritative researchers and authors in the field, Robert Clack. I have worked many times with Rob, and I'm constantly amazed of his knowledge not just on the Whitechapel murders and the Jack the Ripper case but on many other infamous crimes. His geographical expertise has been a constant source for me, and his honest appraisal has stood me in good stead. We have conducted many a walk around the East End together, and embarked on many a research trip too, with the majority of the information we have found while working together being in this book. Words cannot express the gratitude I have for Rob, and as he isn't one for such fawning, I shall just state a simple, 'Cheers, mate.'

Finally, I would like to express my deepest expression of thanks to my family, for the unfaltering support and love they have provided, and their unshakeable belief in me, which helped enable this vision to become a reality. My mum and dad, Sheena and Mick, my brothers Stephen and Simon, and especially Michelle, Kirby and Millie, thank you, I love you all, this book is dedicated to you.

Index

Abbreviations

PC	Police Constable
DC	Detective Constable
PS	Police Sergeant
DS	Detective Sergeant
Insp	Inspector
DI	Detective Inspector
Ch Insp	Chief Inspector
DCI	Detective Chief Inspector
Supt	Superintendent
Ch Con	Chief Constable

Aarons, Joseph 157, 192–193
Abberline, DI Frederick 106, 138, 146, 148, 149, 150, 151, 152, 153, 163, 198, 200, 205
Aldgate 172, 173–174,
Aldgate High Street 171, 174, 186
Alexander, Lord Chief William 22
Allen, PC 423H Joseph 213
ambulance (Bischoffshiem) 132–133
Anderson, Dr (later Sir) Robert 25, 32, 50, 139, 153, 163, 191, 201, 203, 206, 213, 218, 219, 220, 224 n.10
Andrews, PC 272H Walter 213, 214
appointments 73, 75, 79, 86, 87, 101 *see also* Bullseye lamps, handcuffs, pocket notebooks & truncheons
Arbour Square police station 43, 47, 50, 79, 83, 91, 195
Arif, Debra 150, 179
Arnold, H Div Supt Thomas 26, 43, 85, 119, 146, 161, 167, 178, 194–195, 200, 207, 214, 226 n.5
Atherley Jones, MP Llewellyn 129
Ayliffe, PC 426H William 158, 159, 161–162

Badham, PS Edward 144, 206, 207, 210, 213, 214
Baggallay, Magistrate 129, 130
Bagster Phillips, Dr George 133, 141, 143, 144, 147, 148, 161, 181, 198, 200–201, 213, 217
Barber & Co. 133
Barnett, Henrietta 62
Barnett, Joseph 202
Barnett, Rev Samuel 62–63

Barrett, PC 226H Thomas 119, 120, 122–123, 125, 126
Barrett, PC 470K 212
Batchelor, J. H. 163
Baxter, Coroner Wynne 115, 117, 121, 138, 162, 177
beadles 12, 15
beat book 85
beats 37, 61, 86, 87–88, 91, 117, 118, 170, 194, 214, 215 *see also* Police Code (1889), The
length 75, 85–86, 195
'marking' 90
night beats 76,
reliefs & shifts 86
beat wheel 85
Beck, Insp Walter 197, 198
Beichteller, Mrs 150
belts 80
Benjamin, Corp 123–124
Berner Street 157, 158, 159, 161, 163, 164, 166, 170, 172, 178, 191, 203, 204, 209, 215 *see also* Dutfield's Yard
Berry, Supt 150
Bertillon, Alphonse 202–203
Bethnal Green 42, 106, 113, 130, 131, 134, 146
Bethnal Green Road 42, 181,
Bethnal Green Road police station (J Div) 26, 50, 132
Bettles, PC 190H Willie 176
Birrell, Emily 181, 185
Bishopsgate 79, 149, 178
Bishopsgate police station (City) 45, 47, 51, 52, 79, 136, 171, 173, 174, 176, 184, 185
infirmary 51
'black Monday' 32
Blackwell, Dr Frederick 159, 160
bloodhounds 198–200
Bloy, PC 79K 129–130, 196–197
Board of Works 76, 77–78, 133, 168
Bond, Dr Thomas 201–202, 203–205, 213, 214
boots 52, 58, 70, 73
Wellington 23
Borlais-Childs, Dr George 51
Bousfield, Mary 125

Bow Street Police Office 15, 16, 17, 18, 20, 22, 24, 37, 70, 71, 93
Bowyer, Thomas 197–198
Bradford, Col Sir Edward 216
Bretton, Charles 133
Brick Lane 61, 112, 113, 115, 116, 119, 120, 143, 147, 150, 194
Britannia public house 148
Brough, Edwin 199–200
Brown's Yard 134 *see also* Buck's Row
Brushfield Street 113, 147, 149
Buck's Row 90, 131, 132, 133, 134, 135, 139, 140, 141, 157, 203 *see also* Brown's Yard
Bulling, Thomas 188–190
bullseye lamps 73, 75–76, 79, 80, 87, 90, 131, 158, 159, 160, 172, 176 *see also* appointments *and* Christie, Messers J & C
Buswell, Harriett 94
Byfield, City PS 44 James 171–172
Byrnes, NYPD Insp Thomas F. 186–187

Cadosch, Albert 146, 147
Candidates' Day 35
capes 58, 80, 87
Carmichael Bruce, Sir Alexander 70, 149, 153, 163
Carter, Insp 62
Cass, Elizabeth 128–129, 164
Castle Alley 174–175, 213, 214
'caterers' 54
Caunter, DS Eli 123, 124
cells 40, 44, 45–47, 48, 49, 51, 58, 89, 126, 171, 172
Chandler, Insp Joseph 141, 142, 144, 146, 147, 148–149
Chapman, Annie 84, 104, 147–148, 149, 150, 153, 154, 162, 177, 179, 198, 213
 inquest 151
 press coverage 194
Chapman, John 148
Christ Church (Spitalfields) 61, 113, 197
Christie, Messers J & C (Lamp contractors) 79 *see also* Bullseye lamps
Church Passage 173, 185
City of London Police Act (1839) 11, 24
City of London Police museum 179
City of London Police orders and regulations book, The 85,
City Marshal 14
'*city-wide patrole*' 17
Clapp, George 185
Clarke, DCI George 31
Coles, Francis 217, 220
Coles, James William 217
Collar number (Flash) 40, 70, 71, 72, 80, 83, 103
Collard, City Insp Edward 173, 174, 176, 179
Collier, Deputy Coroner George 121
Collins, 12HR Albert 159, 162
Colquhoun, Patrick 18–19
Commercial Road 43, 113, 120, 136, 157, 158, 159, 162, 164, 165, 166, 194

Commercial Street 5, 76, 104, 112, 147, 157, 191, 197, 205, 206, 207
Commercial Street police station (H Div) 42, 43–49, 50, 51, 57–59, 61, 79, 84, 85, 97, 104, 124, 141, 142, 149, 161, 167, 176, 178, 194, 195, 197, 198, 206, 210, 212
Complete Jack the Ripper A–Z, The (Begg, Fido & Skinner) 111
Conditions of Metropolitan Police Stations (1881), Report on the 58
Connelly, Mary Ann (Pearly Poll) 124–125, 126
constables
 accommodation 40, 53–54, 58, 69
 allocation of a division 64
 appointment and period of duty 12
 argumentation increase 212, 216, 228 n.5
 armlets 79
 beats 61, 75, 85–90
 class & pay 64, 65, 66
 clerk 45
 conduct 34
 debt 103 *see also* Police Code (1889), The
 drink 69, 87 *see also* Misconduct & punishment, and Police Code (1889), The
 early years 12–20
 fixed-point duty 84
 height 33, 34, 36, 80
 jurisdiction 131
 'knocking up' 90
 misconduct & punishment *see* Police Code (1889), The
 parish 12
 physical ailments & requirements 36, 58, 94–95
 recruitment 33–34
 reserves 44, 49, 50, 51, 65, 153, 169
 secondment 170, 174
 sick 52, 53, 85
 specials 45
 training 37
Convict License Holders 97 *also see* Supervisees *and* Ticket of leave men
Convict Supervision Office 96, 97
Cooney's lodging house 137
Cooper, Eliza 147, 148
Copsey 143
Cornish, Supt George 39
Coverdale, Annie 129–130
Cowdry, Samuel 136, 138
Cox, Mary Ann 205
Cracknell, PC 376Y 152
crime reports 102
Criminal Investigation Dept (CID) 25, 30, 31, 66, 82, 92, 94, 95, 96–97, 100, 101–103, 121, 136, 138, 139, 142, 146, 149, 188, 190, 211 *see also* Detective Department (City)
 H Div 43, 106, 107, 121, 122–123, 124, 127, 137, 148, 150, 152, 163, 164, 165, 166, 205, 209, 210, 212, 214, 215, 221
 J Div 135, 136, 138, 152
 Y Div 151

Criminal Statutes Repeal Act (1827), The 20
Cross, Arthur 136
Cross, Charles 90, 132, 140
Cross, Richard Assheton 94
Crossingham's lodging house 147, 148, 149
cutlasses 36–37, 45, 80

Daily News 76, 86, 88, 138
Daily Telegraph 206,
Darling, DI 99
Davidson, City DC 98, 99
Davis, John 85, 142–143
Deeming, Frederick Bailey 218
Denmark Street 42, *see also* Section Houses
Der Arbeter Fraint (The Worker's Friend) 162
detectives 93, 94
class & pay 65, 94
  division/local 94
  informers 105 *see also* Police Code (1889),
    The
  liaison 98, 190–191
  misconduct & punishment 95–96 *see also*
    Police Code (1889), The
  observations & surveillance 104
  recruitment 96
  standards of education 94–95, 100
  training 95
  undercover work 104,
Detective Branch 24, 30, 31, 93, 94
Detective Department (City) 100, 173–174,
  191, 218
Dew, DC Walter 106, 111, 197–198
Digby, Supt 99
Dirty Dick's public house 149
divisional register 40
Dolden, DC Charles 163
Donovan, Timothy 147, 148
Doom Book 11
dormitories 58
Dorset Street 61, 91, 113, 147, 148, 181, 197,
  198, 200, 203, 204, 205, 206, 207, 212
Downes, City DS 176
drunk & disorderly 88
Druscovich, Ch Insp Nathan 30–31
Druitt, Montague J 218
Dudman, City PS Amos 186
Duke Street 173, 185
Dunlap, A Div Supt Joseph 25, 59
Dutfield's Yard 158, 161, 170 *see also* Berner
  Street
divisions, list of Met & City in 1888 25–29

Eagle, Morris 158, 159, 161
Eagle Place (Whitechapel Mortuary) 134
Eddowes, Catherine 48, 52, 57, 69, 89, 171,
  185, 186, 187, 189, 193, 194, 200 *see also*
  Jane Kelly & Mary Anne Kelly
Ellen Street 157
Ellisdon, Insp Ernest 119, 120, 121
Endacott, PC 42DR Bowden 128–129, 164,
  196
Enright, DS Patrick 135, 138
Evans, John 147, 148
Evans, Stewart P. 9, 106, 190, 208–209

Evening News 134, 163, 177
Evening Standard 139, 140
Extradition Act (1870), The 30

Fairfield Road Infirmary Asylum 152
Farmer, Annie 210
'*Fenian Barracks*' 62
Fiddymont, Mrs 149, 150
Fielding, Henry 15, 16, 82, 223 n.17
Fielding, John 15, 16, 223 n.19
Fingerprint Bureau 136
Flanagan, Insp James 217
Flowerdew & Co. Interpreters 168
Flower & Dean Street 61, 112, 113, 137, 164,
  207, 212
Foster, City Supt Alfred 70, 176, 186
Foster, Surveyor Frederick 186
Fraser, Col Sir James 28, 70, 99, 174, 190
Froggatt, Edward 31
Frying Pan public house 137
further reports 103
Funny Folks 130

George, Private 125
George Street 61, 112, 113, 114–115, 117,
  120, 210
George Yard 119, 122, 123, 155
  buildings 120
Gilpin & Co. (helmet providers) 71
Godley, DS George 135, 138, 211, 212, 215
Golden Lane Mortuary 172, 175, 176, 179,
  185
Golding, PS 26K Robert 212, 213
Gordon Brown, Dr Frederick 52, 173, 175,
  181, 193, 200
Gordon Riots, The 16–17, 19
Goulston Street 174–175, 176, 177, 178, 179,
  184,
  baths 213
  wall writing 176
greatcoats 58, 80, 87
Great Marlborough Street police court 18
Green, Emma 133, 135
Green, James 134
Green James (Hanbury Street) 142, 143

Habitual Criminals Act (1869), The 96
Habitual Criminals Register 31, 96, 202–203,
  224 n.7
Hall-Richardson, J 53, 59, 95
Halse, City DC Daniel 174, 175, 177–178,
  185
Hames, Margaret 115, 116
Hanbury Street 78, 91, 113, 132, 140, 141,
  142, 146, 148, 149, 157, 179, 203
handcuffs 23, 73, 75 *also see* appointments &
  Police Code (1889), The
  Hiatt 104 (Darby) 75
  Figure of Eight (Come along or Nippers) 75
Hardiman, Harriett 143
Harding, Arthur 97, 98, 106, 219
Harriott, Capt John 18–19
Harris, Dr George 212,
Harris, Harry 185, 186

Harris, Samuel 217
Harris, Sarah 163
Harvey, Daniel Whittle 24
Harvey, City PC 964 James 173, 185
Haslip, Dr George 115, 116, 118
Hatfield, James 135
Haynes, Insp John 24, 93
H Division (Whitechapel)
  jurisdiction boundary in 1888 42
  lodging houses locations within 113
  section houses *see* section houses
  subdivisions 42–43
  telegram codes 50
Hebbert, Dr Charles 201, 213
Henderson, Col Sir Edmund 31–32, 33, 37, 70, 94, 139, 155, 196
helmets 58, 71–72
Helson, Local Insp Joseph 135–136, 138, 150–151, 152
Hiatt & Co. 75, 79
Hinton, PC 275H George 217
Hitchen, Charles 14
HM Customs 43
Hobhouse, Sir John Cam 20, 22
Holland, Ellen 137
Holland, City PC 814 Frederick 173
Holland, Henry 84–85, 142, 143
Howard, Ch Con A.C. 206
Howard Vincent, Sir Charles Edward 32, 82, 94, 95, 139, 184, 224 n.9
Hudson & Co, J. 74
Hutchinson, George 196, 206–208, 209–210, 213
Hunt, City DC Baxter 57, 177
Hyde, PC 161H Frederick 217

Imperial Club 185,
'information' 81
inspectors
  accommodation 59, 161
  class & pay 65
  drill 51
  duty 44, 45, 48, 83, 133, 158, 197, 217
  examinations 65, 66–67
  office 45, 45, 52
  procedure at crime scene 101–102
  reliefs 83
  special reports 102
  store room 45
Inspector of Dust Carts 215
Instruction Book for Candidates and Constables 38, 88
International Working Men's Educational Club 157, 158
interpreters 100, 167–168
Isenschmid, Joseph 151–152
Islington Workhouse 152
Izzard, City Insp George 57, 176, 186

Jack the Ripper 84, 89, 93, 111, 126, 194, 200, 210, 211, 213, 214, 220, 221
  Dear Boss letter 188
  Dear Friend letter 189
  Saucy Jacky postcard 189

letters 188–190, 192
  wall writing 179, 192, 194
Jack the Ripper: Letters from Hell (Evans & Skinner) 190
Jack the Ripper or When London walked in terror (Woodhall) 38
Jones, City PS 92 Herbert 175, 184
Jones & Co, William (Military outfitter) 71
Jones, William (Pawnbroker) 184
Justices of the Peace Act (1361), The 12

Kearley & Tonge Wholesale Grocers 173
K Division Bow (formally Stepney) 42, 43, 50, 57, 93, 212
'Kelly, Jane' 181 *see also* Eddowes, Catherine
Kelly, John 185
'Kelly, Mary Anne' 184 *see also* Eddowes, Catherine
Kelly, Mary Jane 91, 172, 196, 197, 198, 200, 201, 202, 203, 205, 206, 207, 209, 210, 211, 212
Kennington Lane police station 36, 38, 53
Kent, James 142, 143
Killeen, Dr Timothy 119, 120, 121, 122, 123, 124, 234 n.6
Kirby, PS 10J Henry 133–134
Krantz, Philip 162
Kosminski 218, 220

Lamb, PC 252H Henry 154, 158, 159, 161
Lane, Catherine 164
Langham, Coroner Samuel 175
Larceny Act (1827), The 20
La Sûreté *Nationale* 22, 179
Lawende, Joseph 185–186
Ledger, Insp Charles 205
Lee, Annie 115
Leman Street 216
Leman Street police station, H Div HQ 26, 42–43, 46, 47, 50, 79, 83, 133, 151, 157, 158, 159, 161, 165, 166, 167, 177, 178, 191, 193, 195, 217
Leach, DS Stephen 146, 150
'Leather Apron' 150–152, 177, 188
Le Grand, Charles 163
Levy, Joseph Hyam 185, 186
Littlechild, Ch Insp George 31, 190, 243 n.7
Llewellyn, Dr Rees Ralph 131, 133, 134, 135, 136
lodging houses 61, 76, 78, 112–113, 145, 146, 147, 176, 191, 206
  keepers 105–106
London Docks 43
London Hospital 114, 115, 116, 117, 130, 157, 193, 212
London, Jack 106, 111, 113 *see also People of the Abyss, The*
London and Westminster Police Bill (1875), The 17
Long, PC Alfred 69, 170, 174–175, 176, 177
Long, Elizabeth 147
Lusk, George 157, 192–193
'*Lusk*' Letter 192

M'Carthy, DS 211
M'Naghten Rules 218
McCarthy, John 197, 198, 200
McKellar, Dr Alexander O 25, 36, 38, 52, 213
McKenzie, Alice 213, 214, 216
McWilliam, Insp James 174, 176, 177, 191, 193
MacDonald, Archibald 17
Macnaghten, Sir Melville 139, 218, 220, 236 n.56
Malicious Injuries to Property Act (1827), The 20
Man who Hunted Jack the Ripper, The (Connell & Evans) 106
Mann, Robert 134, 135
Mantle, DS 99
Marriott, City DC Edward 52–53, 174, 185
Martin, Joseph 136
Matthews, MP Henry 48, 139, 191, 196, 197
Mayne, Sir Richard 22, 31, 37, 93
Meiklejohn, Insp John 31,
mess (Canteen) 54–58, 81
Metropolitan & City Relief Fund 53
Metropolitan Police Act
  (1829) 11, 17, 21–22, 128
  (1839) 24
Mickle, Dr William 152
Mitre Square 52, 57, 69, 89, 170, 172–179, 185, 186, 191, 200, 203
Mizen, PC 56H Jonas 90, 131–132, 133, 134, 140
Monk, Mary Ann 136
Monro, James 25, 32, 50, 70, 101, 139, 197, 212, 213, 216, 224 n.10
Monsell, Ch Con Lt-Col Bolton James 25, 33, 67, 206
Moore, Insp Henry 163, 215
Moore, John 190
Morgan, Insp 98
Morning state reports 67, 81, 100, 102, 103
Morris, George 173
Mulvaney, Supt John 91, 167, 231 n.104
Mulshaw, Patrick 133
Mumford, James 133
Museum of Fire Arms (Peckham) 37
Mylett, Catherine (Rose) 212, 213, 214

Neil, PC 97J John 130–132, 133, 134, 137, 141, 157
Nichols, Edward 137, 138
Nichols, Mary Anne (Polly) 90, 128, 136–138, 139, 144, 146, 150, 154, 157, 162, 194
  children 137
Nichols, William 137, 138
night refuges 91

oath 38–39
occurrence book 87, 231 n.95
Offences against the Person Act (1828), The 20
Old Jewry 25, 28, 35, 49, 81, 98, 173, 176, 192, 193
Old Montague Street 121, 134, 140, 157

Olympic games 57
Openshaw, Dr Thomas H 193,
Ordinance
  of 1233 13
  of 1252 12
Osborn Street 116, 137, 139
Ostrog, Michael 218
Outram, City DS Robert 174, 185
Oxley, Dr Frederick 217

Packer, Matthew 157, 163–164
Paitt, PC 51H 57
Pall Mall Gazette 48, 130
Palmer, Amelia 147–148
Palmer, Prof Edward Henry 32
Palmer, Ch Insp William 31
Paul, Robert 132,
Pawnbrokers Lists 81, 100, 145
Payne, DC 221
Pearce, DS 211
Pearce, Insp Nicholas 24, 93
Pearce, City PC 922 Richard 69, 185, 242 n.48
Peel House 36, 23, 24, 30, 31, 37, 42, 70, 71
  Acts 20
Peel, Sir Robert 11, 20–21, 22
  Nine Points of Policing 23
People of the Abyss, The 106, 111, 113–114, see also London, Jack
Pennett, PC 239H William 214–215
Phelps, City PS 13 William 186
photography 136, 184
  habitual criminals 202
  use at crime scene 203
  use in evidence gathering 179, 202
Pigott, William 150, 152
Pinchin Street 158, 215, 216
  torso 215
Pinhorn, Insp Charles 161
Pitt, William (The younger) 19
pistols 37, 45
Pizer, John 150–151, 152
Pocket notebook 73, 79, 101, 103 see also Appointments
Police! (Tempest Clarkson & Hall Richardson) 42, 51, 59, 95
Police Code (1889), The 60, 64, 82, 126
  arrest 105
  beat alterations 86–87
  constables in debt 103
  handcuffs use 75 see also appointments & handcuffs
  identification parades 125–126
  informers 105
  jurisdiction 131
  misconduct 67–68
  Police Gazette, The 16, 82, 88
  prisoners' refreshment 49
  prostitutes, arrest of 128–130 also see Vagrancy Act (1824), The
  punishment 68
  rabid dogs 81
  release of information 165

truncheon use 74 *see also* truncheons
unidentified bodies 136
police courts 40, 43, 48, 83, 155, 168, 194
Police Fire Brigade 33
police matrons 47–48, 49, 54
police notice 191
police orders 50, 53, 67, 81, 86, 100
'police walks' 60
Pope's Head public house 150
Poplar High Street 212
Prater, Elizabeth 205
preparatory class/school 33, 35–38, 40, 51
Preston, Charles 164,
Preventions of Crimes Act (1871), The 96, 97
Prince Albert public house 149, 152
public houses opening & closing times 88
Purkiss, Walter 131, 133, 135

Queen's Head public house 207

Reed, Dr F. S. 193
Reeves, Ada 157
Reeves, Charles 157, 193
Reeves, John 119, 120, 122
Regan, DI 215
Reid, H Div Local Insp Edmund 43, 100, 106,
    114–115, 116, 117, 121, 122–126, 127,
    146, 161, 162, 198, 214, 215, 217
Reid, Insp Joseph 61
remand parades 96
*Reports of the Meetings and Discussions held
    in London 10–17 August 1891* 179
Richardson, Amelia 143, 146
Richardson, John 146
Roberts, Ch Con Lt-Col 206
Robinson, City PC 931 Louis 171, 184
Rose, Ch Insp George 35–36, 38
Rowan, Col Sir Charles 22, 31, 53, 93
Royal Mint 43, 50, 83
Royal Mint Street 216
Rumbelow, Donald 9, 89
Russell, Mary 115–116

Sagar, City DC Robert 98–99
Schwartz, Israel 165–167
Scotland Yard 30, 36, 38, 45, 49–50, 52, 64,
    66, 74, 81, 93, 94, 96–98, 100, 102–106,
    136, 138, 146, 149, 153, 163, 164, 176,
    188–189, 190, 191–193, 199, 200–203, 211,
    214,
  Crime museum 95
  Great 23, 35
  New 193–194, 199
*Scotland Yard Investigates (Evans &
    Rumbelow)* 9
*Scotland Yard: The methods and organisation
    of the Metropolitan Police (Dilnot)* 105
Seccombe, Samuel 136
section houses 40, 53
  Denmark Street 53
  Mile End Road 53
Sequeira, Dr George 173, 175, 181
sergeants 24, 40, 65, 73, 78, 83
  armlet 80

class & pay 65
clerk 45
custody 47
drill 36
duty 44, 45, 48, 83
examinations 66
misconduct & punishment *also see* Police
    Code (1889), The
schoolmaster 31
section (beat) 41, 73, 75, 84–87, 89–90, 133
section house 36, 54–57
special duty 83
station 47
widows of 70
Shadwell police station 43, 47, 50, 79, 81
Shaw, DI 98–99
Shaw, Richard Norman 193
Sheffield and Rotherham Independent, The
    150
shire-reeves 11
Siege of Sidney Street 37
'Siffey, Anne' 141, 147, 148 *see also*
    Chapman, Annie
Simmons, City PC 959 George 171, 184
Sivvey, John 148, 237 n.26
Skinner, Keith 190
Skipper, Private 125
Smith, Emma 111–112, 114, 115, 116,
    117–118, 119, 120, 121, 127, 130, 154,
    194, 220
Smith, Major Henry 28, 74, 104, 176, 216,
    241 n.30
Smith, PC 425H William 159, 164–165, 166,
    209
Special Branch (Sec D) 104, 139, 190, 197
special duties 30, 75, 81, 82–83, 194
special reports 103, 146
Spitalfields Market 146, 147
Spooner, Edward 161
Spratling, Insp John 134, 135
St George in the East church mortuary 162
St James Passage 173, 185
St James Place 185
St Marys Church (Whitechapel) 43, 116,
Stanley, Edward (Ted) 145, 148
Staples, John 18
Stevens, William 149
stop & search 91
Stride, Elisabeth 162, 164–165, 166, 168,
    170, 172, 181, 187, 189, 194, 209, 215
Stride, John 162
Stride, PC 158T Walter 162
Styles, Insp John 151–152
superintendents 24, 51, 35, 40, 51, 67, 70,
    82, 98, 165
  examinations 67
  office 30
  pay 65
  special duties 82–83
  special report 102
supervisees 97 *also see* Convict License
    Holders *and* Ticket of leave men
'Sus Laws' *see* Vagrancy Act (1824), The

suspicious deaths procedure 101–102
Swallow Gardens 216
Swanson, Ch Insp Donald S 153, 165, 168, 186, 190–191, 192, 193, 218–219, 220, 221
 marginalia 218

Tabram, Henry 119, 125
Tabram, Martha 119, 120, 121, 122, 124, 125, 127, 136, 154, 155, 194,
 inquest 126
Tanner, Elizabeth 164
Tayler, Charles 172
Taylor Bros Mustard & Cocoa Mill 116
telegraph system and codes 38, 49–50
Tempest-Clarkson, Charles 53, 59, 95
Ten Bells public house, The 184, 207
Thain, PC 96J John 131- 135, 173
Thames Division (River Police) 24, 50, 73, 191, 215
 Wapping 28, 50
Thames Torso Mystery 216
Thick, DS William 106, 146, 151–152, 206, 211, 212, 215
Thompson, PC 240H Ernest 216–217
Thompson, Robert 146
Thomson, Supt James J 94
Thrawl Street 61, 112, 113, 137, 207,
Ticket of leave men 97–98 *see also* Convict License Holders *and* supervisees
Tompkins, Henry 133
Tottenham Outrage, The 37
Tower of London Barracks 42, 122,
translation 100, 167–168
Trial of the Detectives (Turf Fraud Scandal) 30–31, 94
trousers 70, 71, 72–73
truncheons 13, 23, 71, 73–74, 81, 101, 105, 153 *see also Appointments & Police Code, The*
 pocket 23, 72
tunic 23, 71–73, 75, 80, 87, 89
Turner, Alfred 168
Turner, Henry 120, 125
Twining, Louisa 48, 227 n.27
tythingmen 11, 12

Vaccination Act (1873), The 38
Vagrancy Act (1824), The 90–91, 128
 (Prostitutes)
Vedy, PC 62

Vedy, Supt 104
Vidocq, Eugène François 22–23
vigilance & patrol committees 154–156, 163, 192

Walker, Edward 137, 138, 139
Walker, Mr 143
Warren, Sir Charles 25, 32–33, 37, 46, 50, 51, 52, 70, 76, 78, 95, 101, 129, 130, 139, 141, 153, 163, 165, 168, 170, 178, 186, 187, 190, 196–197, 199–200, 201, 203
watch houses 24, 42, 44,
watchmen ('*Charlies*') 13–14, 15, 16, 20, 21
Watchmen & Beadles Regulation Act (1737), The 15
Watkins, City PC 881 Edward 69, 172–173
Webb, City DS Harry 98–99
Wellington Barracks 35, 36, 37, 38, 50, 64, 154
Wellington, Duke of 20, 22
Wensley, Frederick Porter 40, 106
West India Merchant Co. 18, 19
West, Ch Insp (acting Supt) John 43, 76, 115, 116, 117, 146, 151, 161
Westmoreland Gazette, The 22
Whicher, Insp Jonathan 24, 93–94
whistles 72, 73, 74, 75, 84, 156, 157, 158, 159, 172, 173, 213, 215, 229 n.53 *see also* appointments
 City of London Police first use 74
 four blasts instructions 217
 guidance for use 75, 214
 how to wear 214
 Metropolitan Police first use 74
White, DS Stephen 163, 164, 215
Whitechapel High Street 157, 174, 175, 213,
Whitechapel Infirmary Workhouse 150
 mortuary 134, 214
Whitehall Mystery 193–194
widows & orphans fund 64–65, 70
Wilcox, Sarah 143
Wild, Jonathan 14
Williamson, Ch Con Adolphus 25, 30, 146, 188
Willmott's lodging house 137
Wilson, MP H. J. 129
witness statements 208–210
Woodhall, DI Edwin 38
workhouses 19, 91, 113, 114
Working Lads Institute 121, 138
Wormwood Scrubs prison 37